# ENVIRONMENT & ECOLOGY COMPENDIUM

## For IAS Prelims General Studies (Paper1) & State PSC EXAM

• **Corporate Office :** 45, 2nd Floor, Maharishi Dayanand Marg, Corner Market, Malviya Nagar, New Delhi-110017

Tel. : 011-49842349 / 49842350

**Typeset by Disha DTP Team**

Printed at Repro Knowledgecast Limited, Thane

# DISHA PUBLICATION

## ALL RIGHTS RESERVED

### © Copyright Publisher

*No part of this publication may be reproduced in any form without prior permission of the publisher. The author and the publisher do not take any legal responsibility for any errors or misrepresentations that might have crept in. We have tried and made our best efforts to provide accurate up-to-date information in this book.*

**For further information about the books from DISHA,**

Log on to **www.dishapublication.com** or email to **info@dishapublication.com**

# CONTENTS

# ECOLOGY AND ENVIRONMENT

## Introduction

In this chapter we will study about ecology and environment in general; and ecosystem, food chain, food-web, ecological pyramids, succession, nutrition cycling, biomes, population interactions, ecological indicators, importance of ecosystems in particulars.

## ECOSYSTEM

- The term 'ecosystem' was proposed by a British ecologist **A.G. Tansley (1935)**. It represents the basic fundamental, functional unit of ecology which comprises of the biotic community together with its abiotic (non-living) environment.
- Ecosystem is the functional unit of nature where living organisms interact with each other and with their environment.
- Ecosystems can be recognized as self regulating and self sustaining units of landscapes that may be **terrestrial** or **aquatic**. Forests, grasslands and deserts are **examples of terrestrial ecosystems**. The **aquatic ecosystems** can be either fresh water (ponds, lakes, streams) or salt water (marine estuaries) type.

- Ecosystem may be **natural** (forest, sea), if developed under natural conditions or **artificial** (garden, aquarium, agriculture) if created by man.
- Ecosystem is normally an **open system** because there is a continuous and variable entry and loss of energy and materials. Ecosystem is known by different terms *i.e.*, biogeocoenosis or geobiocoenosis or microcosm or ecosom or biosystem, etc. the whole earth can be called biosphere or ecosphere.
- Ecosystem is composed of a variety of abiotic (non-living) and biotic (living organisms) components that function in an interrelated fashion.

## Kinds of Ecosystem

Ecosystem can be classified as :

**Natural ecosystem:** The ecosystem which are completely dependent on solar radiation e.g. forests, oceans, grasslands, lakes, rivers and deserts. This type of ecosystem is a source of food, fuel, fodder and medicines.

**Man-made ecosystem:** The ecosystem which are dependent on solar energy, e.g. agricultural fields and aquaculture ponds. Such ecosystems are also dependent on fossil fuels, e.g. urban and industrial ecosystem.

**Ecosystem Composition**

Formed of two components

**Abiotic Component**

- Physical or climatic components Like, temperature, water, soil, light, humidity, pressure, etc.
- Inorganic compounds Like, water, minerals (sulphur, nitrogen, phosphorus etc) and atmospheric gases ($O_2$, $N_2$, $CO_2$, etc).
- Organic Compounds Includes organic substances present in dead bodies of plants and animals.

**Biotic Component**

Classified into 3 main groups on the basis of mode of nutrition

**Producers**
- Organisms which carry out photosynthesis.
- E.g. plants, algae and bacteria.
- Also called autotrophs.

**Consumers**
- Organisms which derive their food directly or indirectly from the producers.
- Also called heterotrophs.

Further divided into 4 categories

**Primary consumers**
- Also called herbivores.
- Directly feed on producers (green plants).
- E. g. Protozoans, grasshoppers, caterpillar, cattle etc.

**Secondary consumers**
- Also called carnivores, or primary carnivores.
- They prey upon herbivores, like.
- water insects, Hydra, deer, rabbit, cattle, goat etc.
- Egs. lion, tiger, etc.

**Tertiary consumers**
- They feed on primary carnivores, like snakes eats frogs, a bird eats all types of fishes.
- Also called secondary carnivores.

**Omnivores**
- They feed on botk plants & animals. egs. Rat, human, etc.

**Decomposers**
- Also called reducers or micro consumers or saprobes.
- They obtain their nutrition from organic remains.
- E.g. Fungi and certain bacteria.

Components of Ecosystem

# Components of Environment

|   |   |
|---|---|
| **Abiotic** | **Biotic** |
| Water | Man |
| Energy | Animals |
| Radiation | Green Plants |
| Fire | Non-Green Plants |
| Temperature & heat Flow | Parasites |
| Gravity | Symbionts |
| Atmospheric gases and wind | |
| Soil | |
| Geologic substratum | |
| Topography | |

# Structure and Function of Ecosystem

- Ecosystem is self sustained functional units.
- The structure of an ecosystem can be expressed by the following terms –

  **Species compositor:** Plant and animal species found in an ecosystem.

  **Stratification:** Vertical layers of plants.

  **Standing crop:** Amount of biomass.

  **Standing state:** Amount of inorganic substances.

## Species composition

- It differs from one ecosystem to another depending upon geography, topography and climate.
- Each ecosystem has a biotic community composed of particular grouping of species.
- Maximum species composition occurs in tropical rainforests and coral reefs. Minimum occurs in deserts and arctic regions.

## Stratifications

- Stratification is the occurrence of vertical zonation in the ecosystem & indicates the presence of favorable environmental conditions, for *e.g.*, trees occupy top vertical strata or layer of a forest, shrubs and herbs & grasses occupy the bottom layers.
- Stratification helps in accommodation of large number & types of plants in the same area. It also provide a number of microhabitat & niches for various types of animals.
- It is absent or poor where environmental conditions are unfavorable, *e.g.* desert ecosystems have very few trees & shrubs.

## Standing crop

- Standing crop is the amount of living biomass in an ecosystem. It indicates the productivity & luxuriance of growth.
- It is expressed in the form of number or biomass of organisms per unit area.
- A terrestrial ecosystem with high standing crop possesses a forest while the one with low standing crop occurs in grassland followed by arid ecosystem.

## Standing state

- The amount of nutrients, *e.g.* nitrogen, phosphorus & calcium present in the soil at any given time is known as **standing state**.
- The proper functioning of an ecosystem takes place through the following processes:
  - Productivity
  - Decomposition
  - Relationship of producers and consumers
  - Flow of energy through different trophic levels, and
  - Cycling of nutrients.

# Productivity

- **Productivity** refers to the rate of biomass production *i.e* the rate at which sunlight is captured by producers for the synthesis of energy rich organic compounds.
- It is of **two types** – primary productivity and secondary productivity.
- **Primary productivity** is the amount of biomass produced per unit area over a time period by plants during photosynthesis.
- It is expressed in terms of weight ($g^{-2}$) or energy (kcal $m^{-2}$). It is of **two types: GPP and NPP.**
- **Gross primary productivity (GPP)** – It is the rate of production of biomass or accumulation of energy by green plants per unit area per unit time. GPP depends on the chlorophyll content.
- **Net primary productivity (NPP)** – It is the amount of biomass which has been stored by green plants.
- The net primary productivity results in the accumulation of plant biomass, which serves as the food of herbivores & decomposers.
- NPP is equal to the rate of organic matter created by photosynthesis minus the rate of respiration and other losses.

  **Net primary productivity = Gross primary productivity – Respiration losses. (or GPP–R = NPP)**
- **Secondary Productivity** is the amount of biomass synthesized by consumers per unit area per unit time.
- Consumers tend to utilize already produced food materials in their respiration and also convert the food matter to different tissues by an overall process. So secondary productivity is not divided into 'gross' and 'net' amounts.
- The annual net primary productivity of the whole biosphere is approximately 170 billion tons of organic matter.

# Decomposition

- **Decomposition** is the breakdown of complex organic compounds of dead bodies of plants and animals into simpler inorganic compounds like $CO_2$, water & various nutrients.
- The organisms carrying out decomposition are called **decomposers**.
- Decomposers include **micro-organisms** (bacteria and fungi), **detritivores** (earthworm) and some **parasites**.

## Process of Decomposition

- Decomposition is physical as well as chemical in nature and consists of the following processes:
  - **Fragmentation:** It is the formation of smaller pieces of dead organic matter or detritus by detritivores. Due to fragmentation, the surface area of detritus particles is greatly increased.
  - **Catabolism:** Chemical conversion of detritus into simpler inorganic substances with the help of bacterial and fungal enzymes is called catabolism.
  - **Leaching:** Water soluble substances (formed as a result of decomposition) are leached to deeper layers of soil.
  - **Humification:** If decomposition leads to the formation of colloidal organic matter (humus), the process is called **humification**. Humus is highly resistant to microbial action and undergoes extremely slow decomposition. It serves as a reservoir of nutrients.
  - **Mineralisation:** Formation of simpler inorganic substances (like $CO_2$, water and minerals) is termed **mineralisation**.

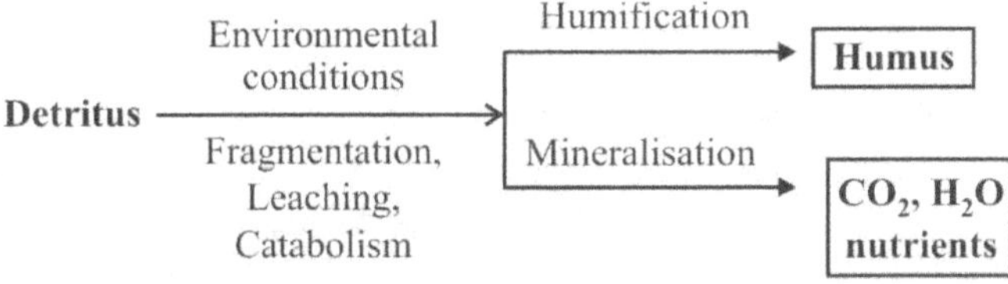


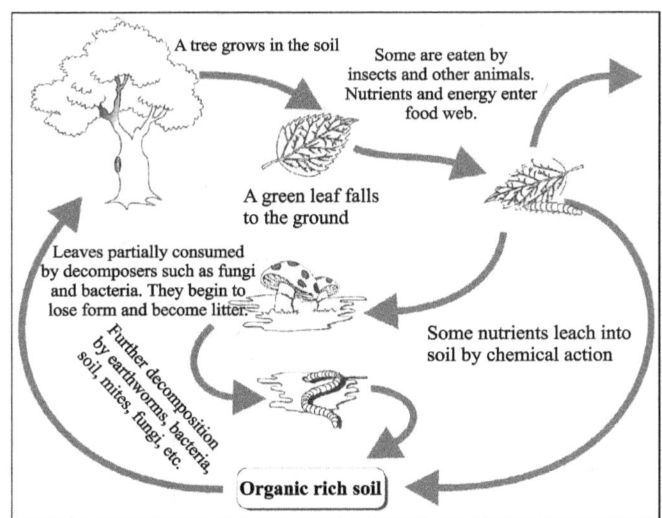


Diagrammatic representation of decomposition cycle in a terrestrial ecosystem

## Factors Affecting Decomposition

- The rate of decomposition is dependent on many factors like chemical nature, temperature, availability of oxygen, moisture, etc.

- **Chemical nature of detritus:** Decomposition of detritus is slow if contains chitin, tannins and cellulose. It is rapid if detritus possesses more of nitrogenous compounds like proteins, nucleic acids and reserve carbohydrates.

- **Temperature:** At a temperature more than 25°C, decomposers are very active in soils having good moisture and aeration. In humid tropical regions, it does not take more than 3-4 months for complete decomposition of detritus. However, under low temperature conditions (> 10°C) of soils, the rate of decomposition is very slow even if moisture and aeration are optimum. Because of it, complete decomposition of detritus may take several years or even decades.

- **Moisture:** An optimum moisture helps in quicker decomposition. Reduction in moisture reduces the rate of decomposition as in areas of prolonged dryness like tropical deserts where otherwise the temperature is quite high. Excessive moisture also impedes decomposition. It may promote pearl formation.

- **Aeration:** It is required for the activity of decomposers and detrivores. A reduced aeration will slow down the process of decomposition.

- **Soil pH:** Detrivores are fewer in acidic soils. Microbial activity is also low in such soils. Detrivores are abundant in neutral and slightly alkaline soils while decomposers microbes are rich in neutral and slightly acidic soil.

# Energy flow

- Energy is the ability to do work. The main source of energy for an ecosystem is the radiant energy or light energy derived from the sun. 50% of the total solar radiation that falls on earth is **photosynthetically active radiation (PAR)**. The amount of solar radiation reaching the surface of the earth is 2 cals/sq.cm/min. It is more or less constant and is called **solar constant or solar flux**. About 95 to 99% of the energy is lost by reflection. The light energy is converted into chemical energy in the form of sugar by photosynthesis.

$$6H_2O + 6CO_2 + Light \rightarrow 6C_6H_{12}O_6 + 6O_2$$

- The rate of energy transfer between elements of an ecological system is called **energy flow**. The **flow of energy is unidirectional** in the ecosystem.

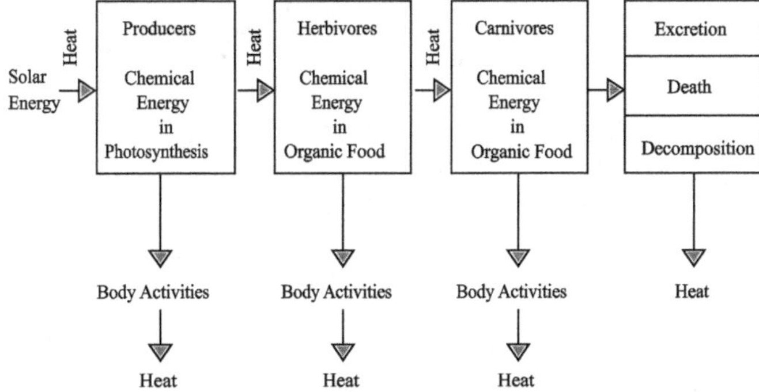


Energy Flow in an Ecosystem

- Plants utilize 2-10% of PAR in photosynthesis.

- The energy formed by the green plants (producers) then flows through different trophic levels of ecosystem *i.e.*, primary, secondary and tertiary consumers.

- **Producers** include green plants which are capable of manufacturing their own food. These are able to fix the energy obtained from the sun. Producers are autotrophic, generally chlorophyll bearing organisms.

- **Consumers (phagotrophs)** cannot make their own food but are directly or indirectly dependent on producers for obtaining food. Consumers may be:
  - Primary consumers or **herbivores**.
  - Secondary consumers or **primary carnivores**.
  - Tertiary consumers or **secondary carnivores**.

- **Primary consumers** obtain their food by directly feeding on producers (plants), **secondary consumers** from primary consumers (herbivores) and **tertiary consumers** from secondary consumers.

- The conversion of radiant energy of sun into chemical energy and its subsequent transfer to other organisms occurs in accordance with the laws of thermodynamics.

- **First law of thermodynamics** states that energy is neither created nor destroyed but can be transferred from one component to another. *E.g.* sunlight energy can be transformed into energy of food & heat.

- **Second law of thermodynamics:** At each step of energy transformation, there occurs dissipation of energy and increase in disorderliness.

- **Trophic structures** of ecosystem is a type of producer-consumer arrangements in which each food level is called **trophic levels**.

- All trophic levels in an ecosystem are connected by transfer of food or energy.

- Two aspects with respect to energy flow in ecosystem are important. *First*, the energy flows unidirectional *i.e.* from producers through herbivores to carnivores; it cannot be transferred in the reverse direction. *Second*, the amount of energy flow decreases with successive trophic levels. Producers capture only a small fraction of solar energy (1 – 5 percent to total solar radiation), and the bulk of initialized energy is dissipated mostly as heat. Part of the energy captured in gross production of producers is used for the maintenance of their standing crop (respiration) and for providing food to herbivores. The unutilized net primary production is ultimately converted to detritus, which serve as energy source to decomposers. Thus, energy actually used by the herbivore trophic level is only a small fraction of energy captured at the producers levels.

- A large amount of energy is lost at each trophic level. It is estimated that 90% of the energy is lost when it is transferred from one trophic level to another. Hence, the amount of energy available decreases from step to step. Only about 10% of the biomass is transferred from one trophic level to the next one in a food chain. And only about 10% chemical energy is retained at each trophic level. When the food chain is short, the final consumers may get a large amount of energy. But when the food chain is long, the final consumer may get a lesser amount of energy.

## Food chain

- The ecosystems is characterized by the energy flow and the circulation of material through its members. The different

**Detritus food chains is**

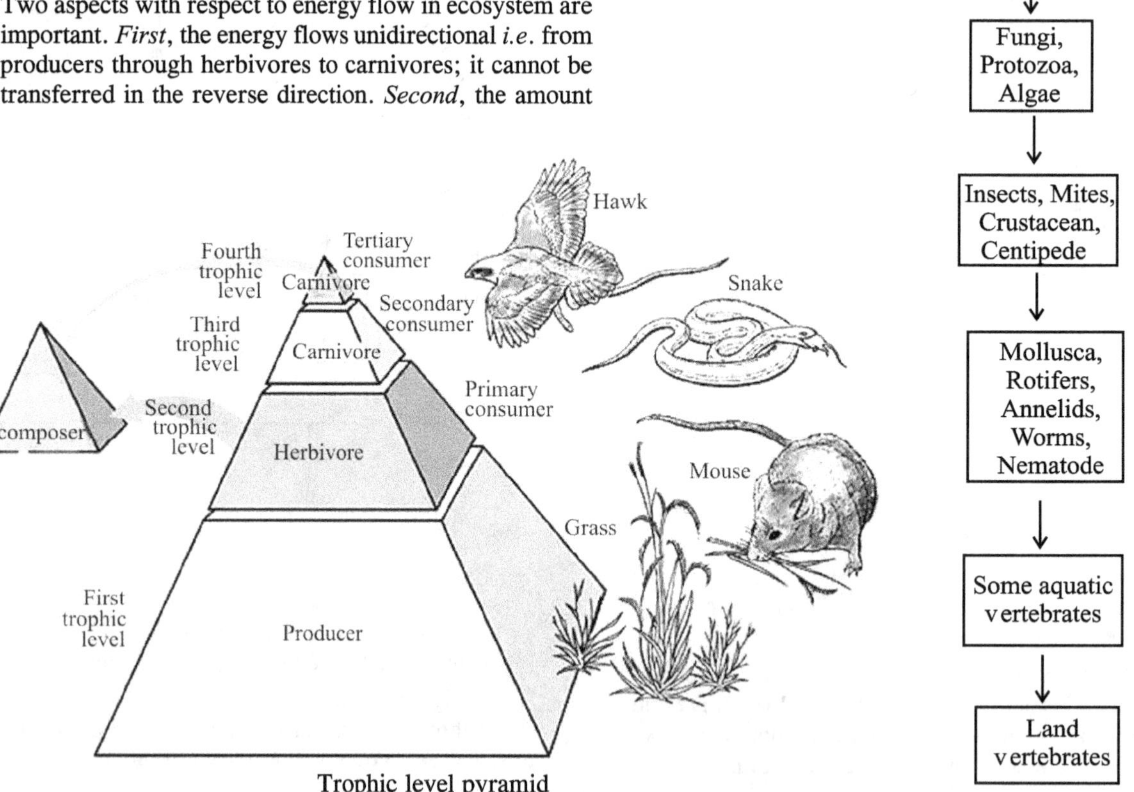


Trophic level pyramid

organisms of an ecosystem are linked together by their nutritional requirements. Individual related in this manner constitute a food chain.

- **Food chain** is an order or sequence of different organisms which are arranged in a way that the food is passed from one type of organism to other organisms such that the organisms of one order or trophic level are the food of the organisms of next order.

- **Types of food chains:** The food chains are of two types, namely:

  **(i) Grazing food chain:** This food chain starts from plants, goes throu gh herbivores and ends in carnivores.

  Plant → Herbivores → Primary Carnivores → Sec. Carnivores.

  This type of food chain depends on the autotrophs which capture the energy from solar radiation.

  A few chains are given below:

  Grass → Grasshopper → Lizard → Hawk

  Grass → Mouse → Snake → Hawk

  Phytoplankton → Zooplankton → Fish → Snake.

  The grazing food chain is further divided into two types, namely: (a) Predator (b) Parasitic.

  **(ii) Detritus food chain:** It starts from dead organic matter and ends in inorganic compounds. There are certain groups of organisms which feed exclusively on the dead bodies of animals and plants. These organisms are called **detritivores**. The detritivores include algae, bacteria, fungi, protozoans, insects, millipedes, centipedes, crustaceans, mussels, clams, annelid worms, nematodes, ducks, etc.

## Difference between Grazing and Detritus food chains

|   | Grazing food chain | Detritus food chain |
|---|---|---|
| 1. | The chain begins with producers as the first trophic level. | The chain begins with detritivores and decomposers as the first trophic level. |
| 2. | Energy for the food comes from sun. | Energy for the food comes from organic remains or detritus. |
| 3. | Food chain adds energy into the ecosystem. | It retrieves food energy from detritus and prevents its wastage. |
| 4. | The food chain binds up inorganic nutrients. | The food chain helps in releasing inorganic nutrients to the cycling pool. |
| 5. | It account for less energy flow because most organisms die without having been eaten. | Detritus food chain can account for more energy flow. |
| 6. | Cattle grazing in grassland, deer browsing in forest and insects feeding on crops and trees are most common biotic constituents of grazing food chain | In the forest, an example of detritus food chain is : detritus ⟶ Soil Bacteria ⟶ Earthworms. |

# Food web

- **Food web** refers to a group of inter- related food chains in a particular community. Under natural conditions, the linear arrangement of food chain hardly occurs & these remain indeed inter-connected with each other through different types of organisms at different trophic level.

- Simple food chains are very rare in nature. This is because each organism may obtain food from more than one tropic level. In other words, one organism forms food for more than one organisms of the higher trophic level.

- Food webs are very important in maintaining equilibrium (homeostasis) of ecosystem.

  **Example:** In a grassland ecosystem

  - Grass → Grasshopper → Hawk
  - Grass → Grasshopper → Lizard → Hawk
  - Grass → Rabbit → Hawk
  - Grass → Mouse → Hawk
  - Grass → Mouse → Snake → Hawk

- **Significance of food web:** Food webs are very important in maintaining the stability of an ecosystem. *For example*, the deleterious growth of grasses is controlled by the herbivores, when one type of herbivores increase in number and control the vegetation.

Similarly, when one type of herbivorous animal becomes extinct, the carnivore predating on this type may eat another type of herbivore.

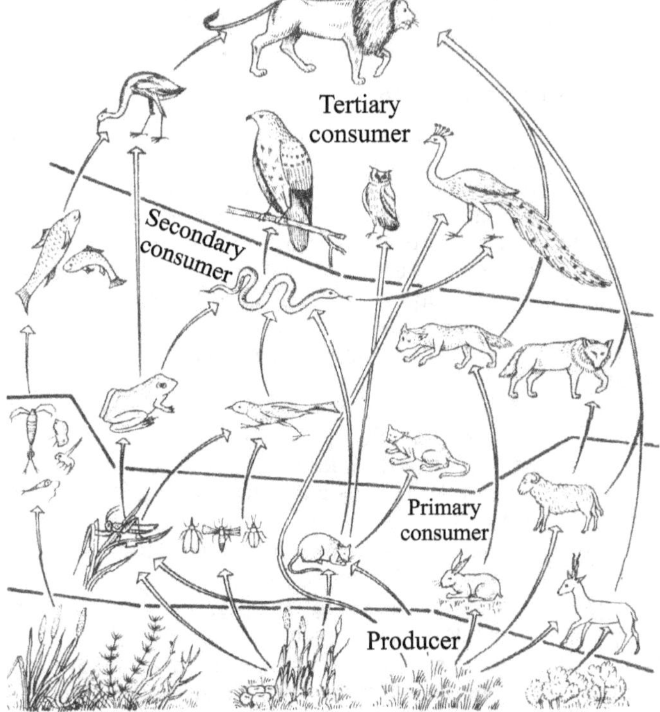


Food web in a grassland ecosystem

## Difference between Food chain and Food web

|  | **Food chain** | **Food web** |
|---|---|---|
| 1. | It is a straight single pathway through, which food energy travels in an ecosystem. | It consists of a number of food chain through which food energy passes in the ecosystem. |
| 2. | Members of higher trophic level fed upon a single type of organisms of lower trophic level. | Members of higher trophic level can feed as a number of alternative organisms of the lower trophic level. |
| 3. | Presence of separate and isolated food chains adds to the instability of the ecosystem. | Presence of food web increases the stability of the ecosystem. |
| 4. | It does not add to the adaptability and competitiveness of the organisms. | Food web increases adaptability and competitiveness of the organisms. |

# TYPES OF ECOSYSTEMS

Ecosystems are of various types including the following:

## Terrestrial Ecosystem

**Tundra:** Tundra is the world coldest and driest biome. This type of biome is totally snow covered vegetation at mountain tops.

- Soils are rich in organic matter due to slow decomposition rate and it is also one among the earth's three major carbon dioxide sink. There are three types of tundra- 1. Arctic Tundra 2. Antarctic Tundra 3. The Alpine Tundra

## Grassland Ecosystem

A grassland ecosystem is the collection of plants, animals and micro-organisms that live within  an environment where grasses are the primary form of vegetation. Grasslands cover around 40 percent of the earth's surface, and they exist in both temperate and tropical regions, generally within the dry interior areas of land masses. Such grassland experience wide range of temperature from about –20 to 30°C in extrem winter and warm summer. The amount of rainfall in grassland ecosystems is too little to support many large plants, though some trees do occur.

- In tropical grassland ecosystems, the heavy precipitation of the rainy season follows months of dry heat.
- Temperate grasslands alternate periods of abundance with periods of dormancy when the temperatures are too cold for growth.
- Some grassland ecosystems, such as the savanna or the prairie, produce tall grasses.
- Others, such as the windy steppes, grow very short grasses often less than an inch high.

Grassland ecosystems can support high densities of grazing animals. They are home to many familiar and fascinating species that live in herds, including zebras and antelopes, and the predators that prey on them, like lions and cheetahs.

- **Temperate grassland:** Such types of grassland have cold winters and warm summers. Summer temperature ranges to 38˚C in summer and as low as -40˚C in winter. Various species of grassland which include purple needle grass, blue grass, and buffalo grass are found here. Located between temperate forest at high latitude and desert at subtropical latitude and nown by different names in different parts of the world as:
  - The Prairies of the great plains of North America
  - The Pampas of South America
  - The Veldt of South Africa
  - The Steppes of Central Euraisa
  - The Savanna in Africa

## Forest Ecosystems

Forest ecosystem is the scientific study of the interrelated patterns, processes, flora, fauna and ecosystems in forests. The management of forests is known as forestry, silviculture, and forest management. A forest ecosystem is a natural woodland unit consisting of all plants, animals and micro-organisms (Biotic components) in that area functioning together with all of the non-living physical (abiotic) factors of the environment. Forests accumulate large amounts of standing biomass, and many are capable of accumulating it at high rates, i.e. they are highly productive. Since trees can grow larger than other plant life-forms, there is the potential for a wide variety of forest structures (or physiognomies). The infinite number of possible spatial arrangements of trees of varying size and species makes for a highly intricate and diverse micro-environment in which environmental variables such as solar radiation, temperature, relative humidity, and wind speed can vary considerably over large and small distances.

## Indian Forest Types

There are sixteen types of Indian forest. These are:

### (i) Tropical Wet evergreen forest

Wet evergreen forests are found along the Western Ghats, the Nicobar and Andaman Islands and all along the northeastern region. It is characterized by tall, straight evergreen trees. The more common trees that are found here are the jackfruit. betel nut palm, jamun, mango, and hol- lock. The trees in this forest form a tier pattern: shrubs cover the layer closer to the ground, followed by the short structured trees and then the tall variety. Beautiful fern of various colours and different varieties of orchids grow on the trunks of the trees.

### (ii) Tropical Semi-evergreen forests

Semi-evergreen forests are found in the Western Ghats, Andaman and Nicobar Islands, and the Eastern Himalayas. Such forests have a mixture of the wet evergreen trees and the moist deciduous trees. The forest is dense and is filled with a large variety of trees of both types.

### (iii) Tropical Moist deciduous forests

Moist deciduous forests are found throughout India except in the western and the north-western regions, The trees are tall, have broad trunks, branching trunks and roots to hold them firmly to the ground. Some of the taller trees shed their leaves in the dry season. There is a layer of shorter trees and evergreen shrubs in the undergrowth. These forests are dominated by sal and teak, along with mango, bamboo, and rosewood.

## (iv) Littoral and swamp

Littoral and swamp forests are found along the Andaman and Nicobar Islands and the delta area of the Ganga and the Brahmaputra. They have roots that consist of soft tissue so that the plant can breathe in the water.

## (v) Tropical Dry deciduous forest

Dry deciduous forests are found throughout the northern part of the country except in the North-East. It is also found in Madhya Pradesh, Gujarat, Andhra Pradesh, Karnataka, and Tamil Nadu. The canopy of the trees does not normally exceed 25 metres. The common trees are the sal, a variety of acacia, and bamboo.

## (vi) Tropical Thorn forests

This type is found in areas with black soil: North, West, Central, and South India. The trees do not grow beyond 10 metres. Spurge, caper, and cactus are typical of this region.

## (vii) Tropical Dry evergreen forest

Dry evergreens are found along Tamil Nadu, Andhra Pradesh and Karnataka coast. It is mainly hard-leaved evergreen trees with fragrant flowers, along with a few deciduous trees.

## (viii) Sub tropical Broad-leaved forests

Broad-leaved forests are found in the Eastern Himalayas and the Western Ghats, along the Silent Valley. There is a marked difference in the form of vegetation in the two areas. In the Silent Valley, the poonspar, cinnamon, rhododendron, and fragrant grass are predominant. In the Eastern Himalayas, the flora has been badly affected by the shifting cultivation and forest fires. These wet forests consist mainly of evergreen trees with a sprinkling of deciduous here and there. There are oak, alder, chestnut, birch, and cherry trees. There are a large variety of orchids, bamboo and creepers.

## (ix) Sub tropical Pine forests

Pine forests are found in the steep dry slopes of the Shiva lik Hills, Western and Central Himalayas, Khasi, Naga, and Manipur Hills. The trees predominantly found in these areas are the chir, oak, rhododendron, and pine as well as sal, am la, and laburnum are found in the lower regions.

## (x) Sub tropical Dry evergreen forests

Dry evergreen forests normally have a prolonged hot and dry season and a cold winter. It generally has evergreen trees with shining leaves that have a varnished look. These forests are found in the Shivalik Hills and foothills of the Himalayas up to a height of 1000 metres.

## (xi) Montane Wet temperate forests

In the North, Montane wet temperate forests are found in the region to the east of Nepal into Arunachal Pradesh, receiving a minimum rainfall of 2000 mm. In the North, there are three layers of forests: the higher layer has mainly coniferous, the middle layer has deciduous trees such as the oak and the lowest layer is covered by rhododendron and champa.

In the South, it is found in parts of the Niligiri Hills, the higher reaches of Kerala. The forests in the northern region are denser than in the South. Rhododendrons and a variety of ground flora can be found here.

## (xii) Himalayan Moist temperate Forest

This type spreads from the Western Himalayas to the Eastern Himalayas. The trees found in the western section are broad-leaved oak, brown oak, walnut, rhododendron, etc. In the Eastern Himalayas, the rainfall is much heavier and therefore the vegetation is also more lush and dense. There are a large variety of broad-leaved trees, ferns, and bamboo. Coniferous trees are also found here, some of the varieties being different from the ones found in the South.

## (xiii) Himalayan Dry temperate Forest

This type is found in Lahul, Kinnaur, Sikkim, and other parts of the Himalayas. There are predominantly coniferous trees, along with broad-leaved trees such as the oak, maple, and ash. At higher elevation, fir, juniper, deodar, and chilgoza are found.

## (xiv) Sub alpine forest

Sub alpine forests extend from Kashmir to Arunachal Pradesh between 2900 to 3500 metres. In the Western Himalayas, the vegetation consists mainly of juniper, rhododendron, willow, and black currant. In the eastern parts, red fir, black juniper, birch, and larch are the common trees. Due to heavy rainfall and high humidity the timber line in this part is higher than that in the West. Rhododendron of many species covers the hills in these parts.

## (xv) Moist alpine scrub

Moist alpines are found all along the Himalayas and on the higher hills near the Myanmar border. It has a low scrub, dense evergreen forest, consisting mainly of rhododendron and birch. Mosses and ferns cover the ground in patches. This region receives heavy snowfall.

## (xvi) Dry alpine scrub

Dry alpines are found from about 3000 metres to about 4900 metres. Dwarf plants predominate, mainly the black juniper, the drooping juniper, honeysuckle, and willow.

**Desert:** Desert biome is the driest of all the biome and is located at 30° North & South and cover about one fifth of the earth's surface.

- Most of the desert receive about 250 mm of rain . Due to poor canopy and sparse distribution of plants. The leaf area index is less than one and productivity is also less.

- Most of the desert receive about 250 mm of rain per year as compared to rainforest which receive over 2,000 mm. The largest desert on Earth is Antarctica. They are classified into:
- **Arid deserts:** These types of deserts are found in North-America, South-America, Africa, and Southern Asia where there is low latitudes. Here generally the temperature is hot and dry with few occurrence of rainfall in winters. In daytime it is very hot as there are no clouds to cover the earth. The soil here is mostly sand or coarse and rocky. Here, vegetation is mostly shrubs and small trees and leaves are adapted to retain water. The animals are generally active during night.
- **Semi-arid deserts:** These deserts are found in North-America, Europe, Russia and Northern Asia. Here also there is low rainfall during winters. Here animals can be found in daytime but under the tress or shades.
- **Coastal deserts:** These deserts are found in areas which are warmer to cooler such as in Neotropic and Nearctic area. Here, the summers are long and warmer while the winters are short and cold. The sand consists of alkaline and the soil is porous so that rain water can enter the ground. Mostly the vegetation here is thick foliage with good water retention quality. The roots of these plants re near to the surface so that they can get water before water drains to the soil. Animals of these deserts comprise rough skinned amphibians, birds of prey, scavenger mammal's reptiles and insects. Animals here are largely nocturnal during the warmer months.
- **Cold deserts:** They are the deserts which occur mainly in the cold regions. Here the temperature during the warmest month is $10°C$. they are mostly covered with snow and ice and due to this they do not support life. Animals in the cold desert are burrowers, even the carnivores and reptiles, which even though cold-blooded, have made their homes in the cold desert. Antarctica is the largest cold desert.

# Aquatic Ecosystem

An aquatic ecosystem is an ecosystem in a body of water. Communities of organisms that are dependent on each other and on their environment live in aquatic ecosystems. The two main types of aquatic ecosystems are marine ecosystems and freshwater ecosystems.

- **Marine Ecosystem:** Marine ecosystems cover approximately $71\%$ of the Earth's surface and contain approximately $97\%$ of the planet's water. They generate $32\%$ of the world's net primary production. They are distinguished from freshwater ecosystems by the presence of dissolved compounds, especially salts, in the water. Approximately $85\%$ of the dissolved materials in seawater are sodium and chlorine. Seawater has an average salinity of 35 parts per thousand (ppt) of water. Actual salinity varies among different marine ecosystems. Marine ecosystems can be divided into many zones depending upon water depth and shoreline features:

(1) The oceanic zone is the vast open part of the ocean where animals such as whales, sharks, and tuna live.

(2) The benthic zone consists of substrates below water where many invertebrates live. The intertidal zone is the area between high and low tides; in this figure it is termed the littoral zone.

(3) Neritic zones can include estuaries, salt marshes, coral reefs, lagoons and mangrove swamps.

(4) Abyssal Zone, hydrothermal vents may occur where chemosynthetic sulfur bacteria form the base of the food web.

Classes of organisms found in marine ecosystems include brown algae, dino-flagellates, corals, cephalopods, echinoderms, and sharks.

### Sea Life

Sea regions are broadly divided into coral reefs, estuaries and oceans.

- **Oceans:** They are the biggest and the most varied of the ecosystem. Most of the oxygen in the atmosphere is generated by the algae. Here salt water evaporates and turns to rain which in turn falls on land. Large amount of carbon dioxide is absorbed by the algae in the atmosphere. Inter - tidal zone is the zone which connect ocean to the land. Only few species exist in rocky coastal areas as very few tides reach there.
- **Other oceanic zones:** Deep sea which is also called benthic zone is the host to slit, sand and slowly decomposing organisms. Sunlight does not reach these areas so these areas are very cold. There are only few plants here and animals include starfish, anemones, sponges, amongst others, as well as several micro-organisms. Abyssal zone is the deepest part of the ocean. Fishes such as oddities and many species of invertebrates are found here.
- **Coral Reefs:** They are the marine ridges and mounds which are formed due to the decomposition of calcium carbonate of living organisms. Coral consist of animal and algae tissues. It is a living organism. Corals use tentacles to catch microorganisms like animals do and feed by the process of photosynthesis like plants. The coral reef is also host to other species such as starfish, octopi and other mollusks. Coral animals cannot live in water cooler than $65°F$ $(18°C)$, therefore coral reefs are found mostly in warm, shallow, and tropical seas.
- **Estuaries:** Transition area between river and sea is called estuary. They are highly productive and rich in nutrients. There are many different names of estuaries like bays, sounds, inlets, harbors, and sloughs.
- **Freshwater Ecosystem:** Freshwater ecosystems cover $0.78\%$ of the Earth's surface and inhabit $0.009\%$ of its total water. They generate nearly $3\%$ of its net primary production. Freshwater ecosystems contain $41\%$ of the world's known fish species.

There are two basic types of freshwater ecosystems:

(a) **Lentic:** slow moving water, including pools, ponds, and lakes.

(b) **Lotic:** faster moving water, for example streams and rivers

(a) **Lentic Zone:**

(1) **Lake ecosystems:** It can be divided into zones. The first, the littoral zone, is the shallow zone near the shore. This is where rooted wetland plants occur. The off shore areas

may be called the pelagic zone, the photic zone may be called the limnetic zone and the aphotic zone may be called the profundal zone.

(2) **Pond Ecosystem:** Ponds are small bodies of freshwater with shallow and still water, marsh, and aquatic plants. They can be further divided into four zones: vegetation zone, open water, bottom mud and surface film. The size and depth of ponds often varies greatly with the time of year; many ponds are produced by spring flooding from rivers. Food webs are based both on free-floating algae and upon aquatic plants.

(b) **Lotic Zone:** The major zones in river ecosystems are determined by the river bed's gradient or by the velocity of the current. Faster moving turbulent water typically contains greater concentrations of dissolved oxygen, which supports greater biodiversity than the slow moving water of pools. These distinctions form the basis for the division of rivers into upland and lowland rivers.

## Fresh water Life

The name freshwater is due to the less salt content in them. They exist in various forms such as lakes, rivers, ponds, swamps or wetland and are host to wide variety of plants and animals.

- **Lakes:** Lakes are the water bodies which can exists for centuries other than others like ponds which dry up frequently. The littoral zone, which is close to the shore, is host to a extensive range of species due to its warm and shallow environment. Several species of invertebrates, crustaceans, plants and amphibians bloom in this environment and in turn offer food for predators such as birds, reptiles and other creatures inhabiting the shoreline.

## Wetlands/Ramsar sites

large variety of flora and fauna grows in other still water bodies or wetlands like swamps, glades and marshes. Trees such as Cypress which are highly adaptable to high humidity of this region also grow in wetland. Other plants such as pond lilies and sedges also grow here. Animals found here are different types of reptiles, mammals, amphibians and birds and hundreds of insects. Starting point of rivers and streams are mostly snow and ice melting and spring. At the end, they end up in ocean or in other water body. Flora and fauna are different here from the lakes and ponds as the water is continuously flowing. Depending upon water temperature and the exposure of riverbanks to the sunlight small fishes such as river trout and crayfish can be found in several areas. Salmon and other vigorous fishes can be found in cold areas while fishes like catfish, carp, and other bottom feeders can be found in warm areas which are rich in sediments and decaying matter. River plants comprise floating weeds and algae, mostly found forming around rocks and submerged tree roots.

The area where freshwater meets saltwater, is called an estuary; this area generally features distinctive features, trees and algae, seaweed, wetland flora, and several species of invertebrates, birds, reptiles and crustaceans congregate into a composite ecosystem, serving as a trade center to the world's aquatic biomes.

## Mangroves

- Mangrove trees are an indigenous species to tropical as-well-as subtropical regions with approximately 70 identified species worldwide. They are a major contributor to the littoral and marine environments & Mangrove trees are halophytes, plants that thrives in salty condition & Mangroves have the ability to grow where no other tree can, thereby making significant contributions that benefit the coastal ecology. Their coverage of shorelines and wetlands provides many diverse species of birds, mammals, crustacea, and fish a unique, irreplaceable habitat Mangroves preserve water quality and reduce pollution by filtering suspended material and assimilating dissolved nutrients.

- The tree is the foundation in a complex marine food chain and the detrital food cycle. The detrital food cycle was discovered by two biologists from the University of Miami, Eric Heald & William alum, in 1969. As mangrove leaves drop into tidal waters they are colonized within a few hours by marine fimgi and bacteria that convert difficult to digest carbon compounds into nitrogen rich detritus material. The resulting pieces covered with microorganisms become food for the smallest animals such as worms, wailq, shrimp, mollusks, mussels, barnacles, clams, oysters, and the larger commercially important striped mullet These detritus eaters are food for carnivores including crabs and fish, subsequently birds and game fish follow the food chain, culminating with man. Many of these species, whose continued existence depends on thriving mangroves, are endangered or threatened. It has been estimated that 75% of the game fish and 90% of the commercial species in south Florida rely on the mangrove system. The value of red mangrove prop root habitat for a variety of fishes and invertebrates has been quantitatively documented. Data suggest that the prop root environment may be equally or more important to juveniles than are sea grass beds, on a comparable area basis. Discovery of the importance of mangroves in the marine food chain dramatically changed the respective governmental regulation of coastal land use and development.

### Role of mangroves

- Mangrove plants have (additional) special roots such as prop roots, pneumatophores which help to impede water flow and thereby enhance the deposition of sediment in areas (where it is already occurring), stabilize the coastal shores, provide breeding ground for fishes.

- Mangroves moderate monsoonal tidal floods and reduce inundation of coastal lowlands.

- It prevents coastal soil erosion.

- It protects coastal lands from tsunami, hurricanes and floods.

- Mangroves enhance natural recycling of nutrients.

- Mangrove supports numerous flora, avifauna and wild life.

- Provide a safe and favorable environment for breeding, spawning, rearing of several fishes.

- It protects coastal Inland from adverse climatic elements.

- It supplies woods, fire wood, medicinal plants and edible plants to local people.

- It provides numerous employment opportunities to local communities and augments their livelihood.

# ECOLOGICAL PYRAMIDS

- The number, biomass and energy of organisms gradually decrease from the producer level to the consumer level. The number of individuals present or amount of biomass synthesized or amount of energy stored at successive trophic levels in an ecosystem can be graphically represented in the form of pyramids. These are called **ecological or Eltonian pyramids.** The use of ecological pyramid was first described by **Charles Elton in 1927.**

- In the ecological pyramid, the producer forms the base and the final consumer occupies the apex.

- Three ecological pyramids which are studied are – **pyramid of number, pyramid of biomass and pyramid of energy.**

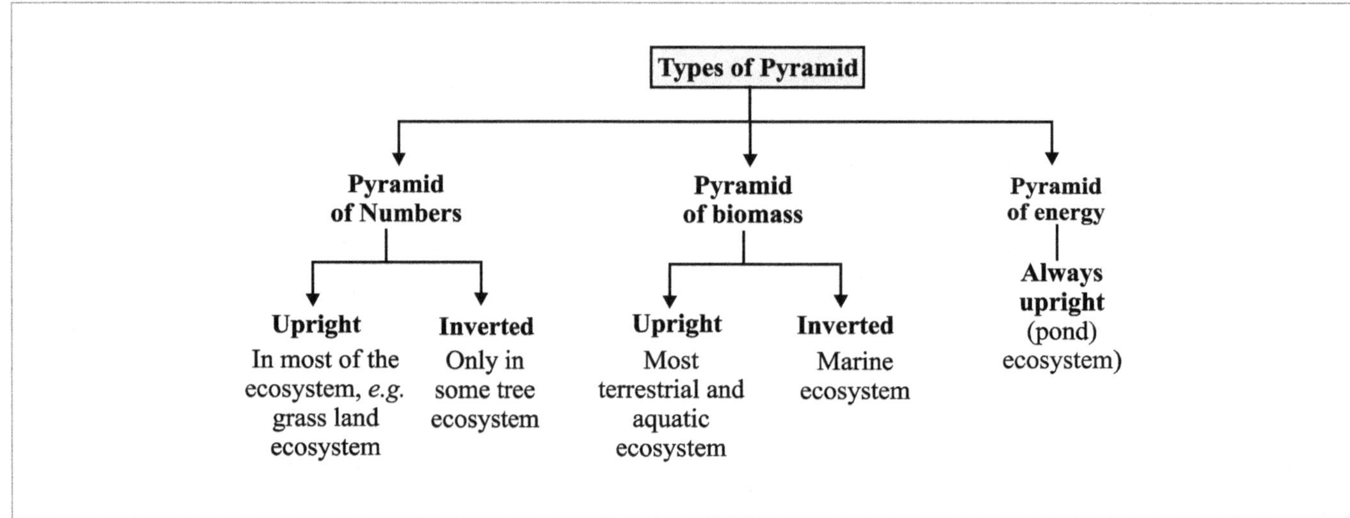


## Pyramid of Number

- Pyramid of number is **usually upright.**
- It is a graphical representation of numerical strength of various populations in different trophic levels per unit area of an ecosystem with producer forming base, intermediate levels forming intermediate tiers & apex formed by top carnivores.
- In an ecosystem, number of individuals is generally maximum at the producer level. The number of herbivores is lesser than the producers. Similarly, the number of carnivores is lesser than the herbivores. Number of producers per unit area is more in pond ecosystem than grassland ecosystem. In forest ecosystem the pyramid of number is intermediate. Here the number of primary consumers is more than producers as well as top consumers.
- **In a cropland ecosystem:** In croplands the crops are more in numbers. The grasshoppers feeding on crop plants are lesser in number. The frogs feeding on grasshopper are still lesser in number. The snakes feeding on frogs are fewer in number.
  Crop → Grasshopper → Frogs → Snakes → Hawks
- **In a grassland ecosystem:** In a grassland the grasses are there in large numbers. The consumers decrease in the following order.
  Grass → Grasshopper → Lizard → Hawk
  Grass → Rabbit → Fox → Lion
- **In a pond ecosystem:** The number in a pond ecosystem decreases in the following order.
  Phytoplankton → Zooplankton → Fishes → Snakes

- The pyramid of number of a single tree is **spindle-shaped.**
- Sometimes the pyramid of number is **inverted** in parasitic food chain.

## Pyramid of Biomass

- Biomass refers to the total weight of living matter per unit area. In an ecosystem the biomass decreases from the producer level to the consumer level.
- Pyramid of biomass of terrestial ecosystem is **upright** because at each successive trophic level the biomass tends to decrease, starting from primary producers and ending in top consumers.
- Pyramid of biomass of **aquatic ecosystem is inverted.**
- **In a grassland:** In a grassland the biomass of grasses is the maximum, and it gradually decreases towards the consumer level in the following order.
  Grass → Mouse → Snake → Hawk
  Grass → Grasshopper → Lizard → Hawk
- **In a forest:** In a forest the biomass of trees is the maximum and the biomass of the top consumer is the minimum. The decrease in weight occurs in the following order :
  Plants → Deer → Fox → Tiger
  Plants → Rabbit → Fox → Lion

## Pyramid of Energy

- The energy flow in an ecosystem is from the producer level to the consumer level. At each trophic level 80 to 90% of energy is lost. *Hence*, the amount of energy decreases from the producer level to the consumer level.
- Pyramid of energy is always **upright** because during the flow of energy from one trophic level to the next one, there always occurs a loss of energy.

- **10 per cent Law:** Only 10% of the total energy stored in a trophic level is transferred to the next trophic level of a food chain. This law was given by Lindemann (1942).

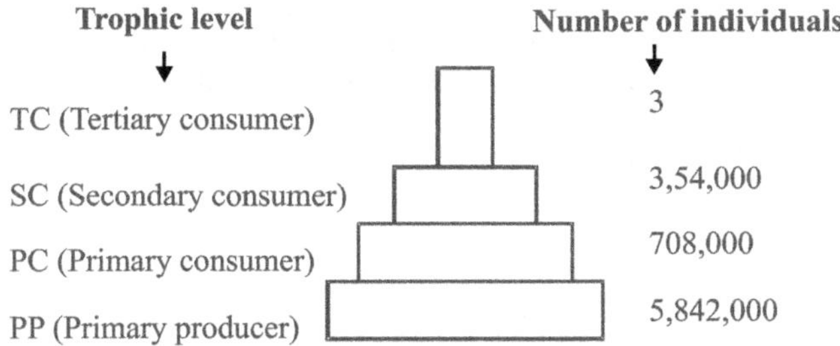

**Trophic level** → | **Number of individuals** →
TC (Tertiary consumer) — 3
SC (Secondary consumer) — 3,54,000
PC (Primary consumer) — 708,000
PP (Primary producer) — 5,842,000

*Pyramid of numbers in a grassland ecosystem.*
Only three top-carnivores are supported in an ecosystem based on production of nearly 6 millions plants.

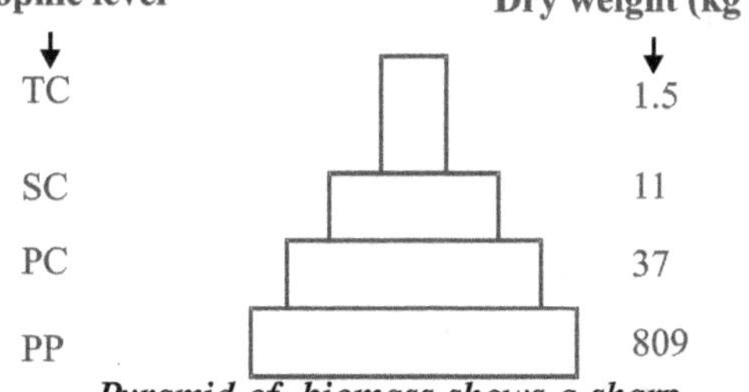

**Trophic level** → | **Dry weight (kg m)$^{-2}$** →
TC — 1.5
SC — 11
PC — 37
PP — 809

*Pyramid of biomass shows a sharp decrease in biomass at higher trophic levels*

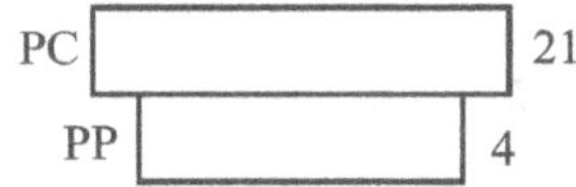

PC — 21
PP — 4

*Inverted pyramid of biomass-small standing crop of phytoplankton supports large standing crop of zooplankton.*

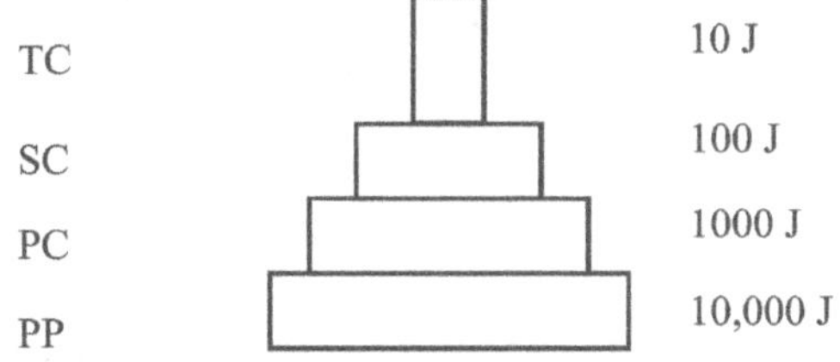

TC — 10 J
SC — 100 J
PC — 1000 J
PP — 10,000 J

**1,000,000 J of Sunlight**

*An ideal pyramid of energy. Observe that primary producers convert only*

- **In a grassland:** In a grassland green plants trap the maximum light energy. The energy gradually decreases towards the top consumer level.

Grass → Grasshopper → Lizard → Hawk

Grass → Rabbit → Fox → Lion

Grass → Mouse → Snake → Hawk

- **In a pond:** In a pond maximum energy is trapped by the phytoplankton. Then the amount of energy decreases towards the top-consumer level.

Phytoplankton → Zooplankton → Fish → Snake

Phytoplankton → Zooplankton → Small fish → Large fish

# ECOLOGICAL SUCCESSION

- Ecological succession is the successive development of different biotic communities at the same site. The communities develop one after another till the development of a community which is near equilibrium with the environmental conditions. This is called **climax community**.

- Climax community is the stable perpetuating and final biotic community that develops at the end of biotic succession. It has maximum diversity & niche specialization.

- The first biotic community which invades a base area is called **pioneer community**. It is characterized by high growth rate and short life span.

- The transitional communities which develop during the ecological succession or in between the pioneer and climax community are called **seral communities**.

**Pioneer community**
(First biotic community at the base area)
↓
**Seral community**
(Various biotic communities that develops during succession)
↓
**Climax community**
(The stable, self perpetuating & final biotic community)

- The entire series of communities that is characteristic of given site is called a **sere**.

**Difference between Pioneer community and Climax community**

| | **Pioneer community** | **Climax community** |
|---|---|---|
| 1. | It is the first biotic community which develops in bare area. | It is the final biotic community that develops in an area. |
| 2. | It is established over a previously bare area. | It occurs over an area previously occupied by several communities. |
| 3. | It consists of a fewer small sized organisms. | It consists of numerous large and small sized organisms. |
| 4. | The area is hostile for pioneer community. | The area is favorable for the climax community. |
| 5. | Life span is short. | Life span is long. |
| 6. | Growth is fast. | Growth is slow. |
| 7. | It is soon replaced by the next seral community. | It is stable. It is not replaced by any other community. |

- A sequence of seres is characterized not only by the changes in the set of population present, but also by a progressive increase in the diversity of species and the total quantity of living mass. The sequence of seres for a given region is often fully predictable, both with respect to the general types of population expected at each sere and to seral duration.

## Characteristics of Ecological Succession

- Formation of soil, increase in thickness and differentiation of soil.
- Increase in humus content of soil.
- Increase in biomass.
- From small lived plants to long lived plants.
- From unstable biotic community to stable biotic community.
- From lesser species diversity to higher species diversity.
- Increased niche specialization.
- Development of stratification.
- Succession occurs in both animals and plants communities side by side.
- From simple food chains to complex food chains and formation of food webs.
- From aquatic or arid environment to mesic environment.

## Types of Succession

- Succession is of **two types:** Primary and Secondary
- **Primary succession:** It is the ecological succession occurring in an area where no organisms are found, like bare rocks.
- **Secondary succession:** This type of succession takes place in those areas where all the previous biotic communities have been destroyed, *e.g.*- burned forests, flooded fields.

**Difference between primary succession and secondary succession**

|  | **Primary succession** | **Secondary succession** |
|---|---|---|
| 1. | It occurs in an area which has been bare from the beginning. | Secondary succession occurs in an area which has been denuded recently. |
| 2. | Soil is absent at the time of beginning of this succession. | Soil is present. |
| 3. | No humus in the beginning. | Humus is present before the very beginning. |
| 4. | Reproductive structure of any previous community are absent. | Reproductive structures of the previous occupants are present in the area. |
| 5. | Pioneer community comes from the outsides. | Pioneer community develops partly from the previous occupants and partly from the migrants. |
| 6. | Many seral community. | Few seral community. |
| 7. | Long time for completion. | Less time for completion. |

## Succession in plants

- Ecological succession may be of the following types depending upon the climatic conditions of the area where it starts.
- Successions are variously designated as **xerosere/lithosere** (succession **on bare rock**), **hydrosere** (succession in **water**), **psammosere** (succession **on sand**).

### Hydrach/Hydrosere Succession

- Hydrosere is a sequence of communities that reflects the developmental stages in a plant succession, which commences on soil, submerged by fresh water.
- **Hydrach succession** takes place in wetter areas like ponds, lakes etc. and the successional series progress from hydric to the mesic conditions.

**Climax forest community** (Mesophytic)
(*e.g., Tropical rain etc*)
↑
**Woodland stage**
(*e.g., Salix, Almus etc*)
↑
**Sedge meadow stage**
(*e.g., Juncus, Cyperus*)
↑
**Read swamp stage**
(*e.g., Typha, Sagittaria, etc*)
↑
**Floating stage**
(*e.g., Nymphaea, Pistia, Wolffia, Azolla*)
↑
**Submerged stage**
(*e.g., Hydrilla, Elodea, Najas, Chara, etc*)
↑
**Pioneer stage**
(*e.g., Diatoms, bacteria, dinoflagellates euglenoids, etc*).

Structure of hydrosere

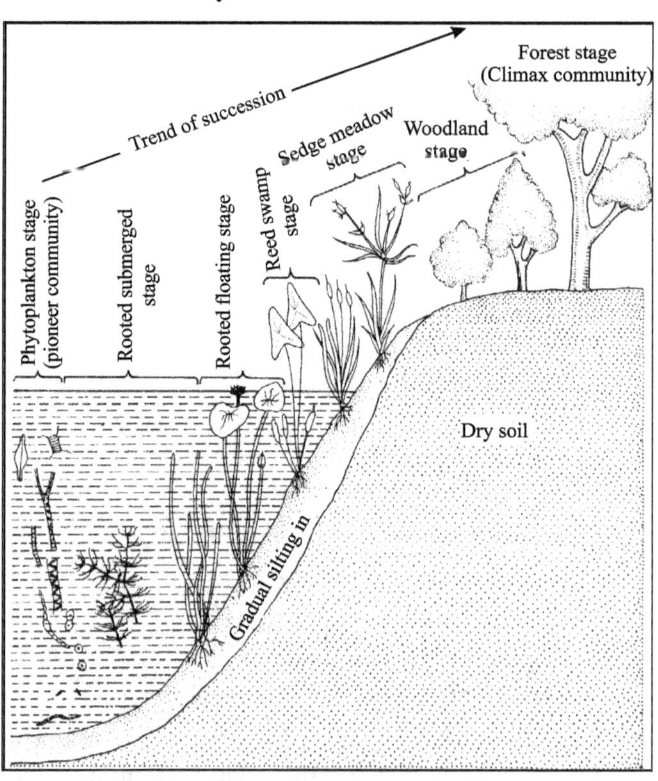


Diagram showing different plant communities appearing at different stages of a hydrosphere originating in a pond.

## Xerarch Succession

- Xerarch succession starts in dry areas & the series progress from xeric to mesic conditions.
- Stages in xerarch occurring on bare rock is called **lithosere.**
- Pioneer of this succession depends on climate. In tropical areas the pioneers are cyanobacteria or blue green algae. In temperate areas, they are crustose lichens.

**Climax forest community**
(mesophytic)
↑
**Shrub stage**
(*e.g., Rhus, Phytocarpus*)
↑
**Herbaceous stage**
(*e.g., Eleusine etc*)
↑
**Moss stage**
(*e.g., Polytrichum, Toxila*)
↑
**Foliose lichen stage**
(*e.g., Parmellia, Dermatocarpon, etc*)
↑
**Crustose lichen stage** (pioneer stage)
(*e.g., Rhizocarpous, Rinodina etc*)

**Flow chart 14.4 :** The
Structure of lithosere/xerosere

- The ecological succession on bare rocks includes the development of following communities –

Crustose lichens → foliose lichens → mosses → grasses → shrubs → trees.

## NUTRIENT CYCLING

- These are the cyclic events by which various nutrients which are essential for the living organisms are transferred from one form to other. During these cycles, the nutrients pass from the biotic components to the abiotic components and *vice-versa,*; hence these are also called **biogeochemical cycles.**
- **Two types** of nutrient cycles are –
  - (i) **Gaseous cycles** (nitrogen, oxygen, carbon cycles)
  - (ii) **Sedimentary cycles** (phosphorus, sulphur cycles)
- In gaseous cycle, the main reservoirs of chemicals are the atmosphere and ocean.
- In sedimentary cycles, the main reservoirs are soils and rocks.

## Nitrogen & ($N_2$) Cycle

Nitrogen cycle is a process by which nitrogen is converted between its various chemical forms. 78% of earth atmosphere is nitrogen. Nitrogen cycle is necessary because plants cannot absorb nitrogen directly; they can only absorb in the form of *nitrate*. Nitrogen cycle have 5 important processes, i.e., fixation, ammonification, nitrification, assimilation and denitrification.

1. **Nitrogen fixation:** It is the process of conversion of nitrogen ($N_2$) to ammonia ($NH_3$) because it is the only method by which organisms can attain nitrogen through atmosphere. Bacteria called *Rhizobium* fix nitrogen, be residing in the roots of plants making root nodules.
2. **Nitrification:** It is the process of conversion of ammonia ($NH_3$) to nitrate ($NO_{-3}$)
$$NH_3 \rightarrow NO_2 \rightarrow NO_{-3}$$
3. **Assimilation:** It is done by plants roots. Since nitrogen is present in nitrate form it is absorbed along with water from the soil and then converted into organic matter by plants.
4. **Ammonification:** It is the process of conversion of organic nitrogen compounds to $NH_3$. Urea and uric acid are excreted by animals in soil along with nitrogen components, these components are converted into ammonia by bacteria, like-Bacteria → nitrification → assimilation
5. **Denitrification:** It is the reduction of $NO_{-3}$ to gaseous nitrogen $N_2$. It is done by denitrifying bacteria (*Pseudomonas*) which convert nitrates/nitrites into elemental nitrogen, which escapes to atmosphere completing the cycle.

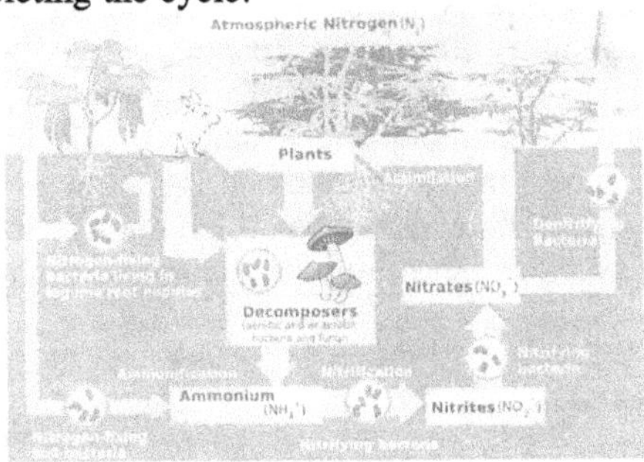

## Oxygen & ($O_2$) Cycle

- Oxygen is a very important element for the existence of all flora and fauna. Atmosphere contains 21% of oxygen.
- The main source of oxygen is atmosphere. Plants and animals absorb oxygen through respiration either from water or air and leaves through photosynthesis.
- In respiration process some of the oxygen returns to the atmosphere in the form of carbon dioxide and water vapour. During the process of photosynthesis gaseous oxygen is released completing the oxygen cycle.
- The source of ozone is the oxygen in the atmosphere. Ozone layer protects the living being from the UV radiation which reaches the earth.
- By burning fossil fuels man decreases the amount of oxygen in the atmosphere and increases the carbon dioxide content.

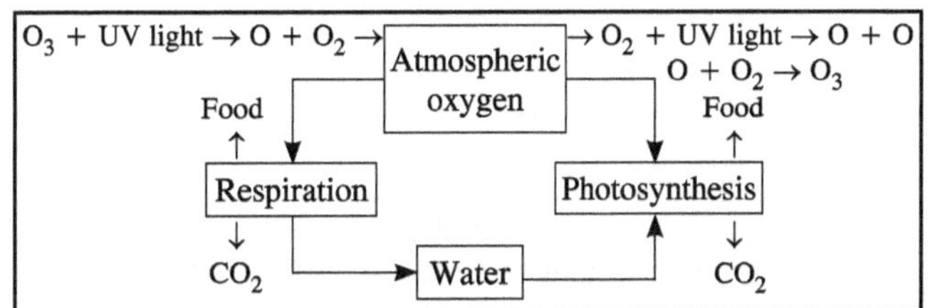

Oxygen Cycle

As the oxygen concentration in the atmosphere remains constant at 21%, it is likely that natural degradation of ozone must occur to maintain the ozone : oxygen equilibrium. The oxygen cycle is affected most by human activities such as running of automobiles and consumption of fossil fuels, thus releasing more carbon dioxide in the atmosphere.

## Carbon Cycle

- Carbon is present in carbohydrates, proteins and fats.
- Carbon is taken up by green plants as $CO_2$ for photosynthesis.
- Carbon is present as $CO_2$ in atmosphere, as graphite and carbonates in rocks and also in fossil fuels (coal, petroleum).
- Ocean are big reservoirs of carbon.
- Carbon is released as $CO_2$ in atmosphere during –
  - respiration of plants and animals
  - burning of fossil fuels
- Carbon is also released in atmosphere as methane by rice fields and marshes.
- **Carbon cycle** is **cyclic representation of carbon** assimilation by green plants (photosynthesis) which then passes into bodies of animals (plants are eaten) and finally during respiration of plants & animals & decompositions by microbes, the carbon dioxide is returned back to the atmosphere. *Thus,* carbon is cycled through transfer and transformation between biotic and abiotic components.

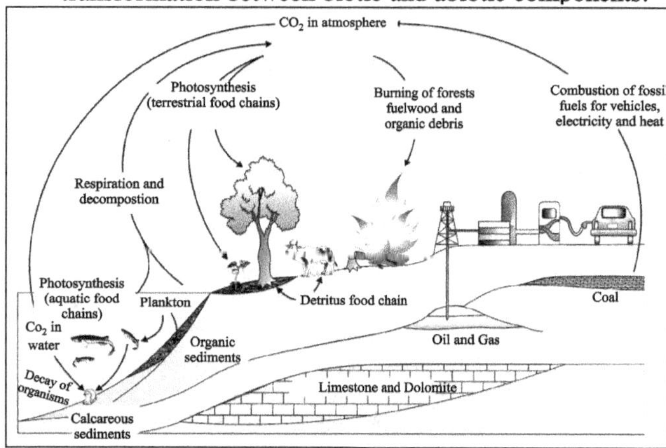


Simplified model of carbon cycle in the biosphere

## Phosphorus Cycle

- Phosphorus is an important element for living beings.
- The cycling of phosphorus between biotic & abiotic components of the environment represent phosphorus cycle.
- Phosphorus is present in
  - biomembranes (as phospholipids).
  - nucleic acids (as phosphoric acid).
  - nucleotides (as AMP, ADP, ATP etc).
  - bones and teeth (as hydroxyapetite).
- Consumers obtain phosphorus directly or indirectly from plants.
- Phosphorus is also present in phosphatic rocks.

- Phosphorus is released during the decomposition of plant and animal remains.
- The released phosphorus may reach the deeper layers of soil and gets deposited as phosphate rocks.
- Phosphorus containing rocks are mined for manufacture of fertilizers, which provide an additional supply of an organic phosphates to the abiotic environment.

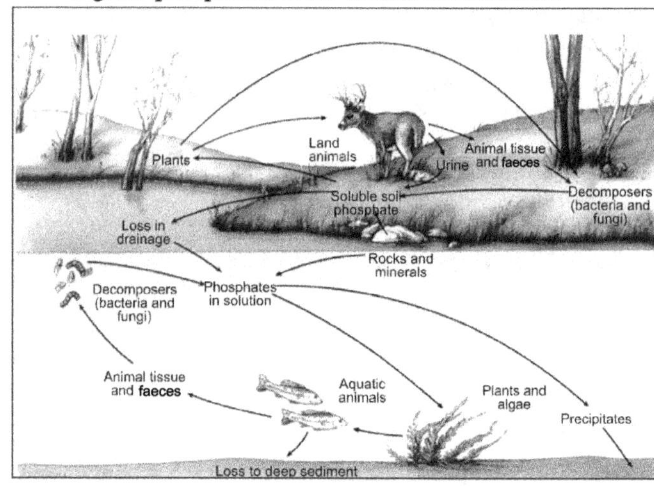


Phosphorus cycle

- All plants and animals eventually die and in due time, their organic remains or debris decay through the action of micro-organism and the phosphates are release into the water for recycling.

# BIOMES

**Community Ecology or Synecology:** Community ecology is a study of pattern and processes involving at least two species on many spatial and temporal scale which include the distribution, structure, abundance, demography, and interactions between coexisting populations.

**Biomes:** Biome is a part of large ecosystem that have common characteristic due to similar climates and can be found over a range of continent. In other words biomes are largely natural eco-system wherein we study the total assemblage of plant and animal communities. Though a biome includes both plant and animal communities but a biome is usually identified and named on the basis of its dominant vegetation. Most of the ecologists have recognized at least nine different biomes.

Land biome include tropical rain forest coniferous forest, temperate broad leaf deciduous forest, mediterranean forest, tropical deciduous forest, tropical scrub, grassland, tundra and desert.

| **Biomes of India** |
|---|
| There are five biomes in India. They are: |
| (i)  Tropical Humid Forest |
| (ii)  Tropical Dry of Deciduous Forest (including monsoon forest) |
| (iii)  Warm deserts and semi-deserts |
| (iv)  Coniferous Forest |
| (v)  Alpine meadows |

## Populations or Attribution of Population

The population is a group of individuals of a particular species, which potentially interbreed and live in a well defined geographical area, and also share or compete for similar resources.

For ecological point of view a group of asexual individuals is also known as population.

Examples of populations are

1. Tigers in a national park
2. Rats in an abandoned building
3. Lotus plants in a pond
4. Teak-wood trees in a forest
5. Bacteria in a petri-dish

The natural selection also operates at population level.

The population has certain attributes or peculiar features which are not represented by the individuals. The important attributes are *Life expectancy, sex ratio, birth rate, death rate, age distribution* etc.

**Birth or Natality rate** – It is the number of births per thousand of a population per year. It can also be represented in percentage, or per capita, i.e., per individual.

If there were 50 lotus plants in a pond last year. This year the population has increased to 58 due to reproduction, then birth rate per capita can be calculated as

$$58 - 50 = 8$$
$$8/50 = 0.16 \text{ offspring per lotus per year}$$

Or per capita birth rate per year = 0.16

**Death or Mortality rate** – It is the number of deaths occurring in a population of one thousand per year.

This can also be represented in percentage or per capita.

If in a population of 50 house flies, 5 died in a week, then the per capita death rate per week can be calculated as $5/50 = 0.1$

**Life Expectancy** – It is the length of time for which an individual of a given species can expect to live.

*It is the characteristic of a population*, but not of a species. It is defined as the age at which half the population still survives $(M_{50})$. The life expectancy differs with sex and time period.

- **(Life Span** – It is the maximum number of years a member of a species has been known to survive. The life span of human is estimated to be 121 years. *The* (maximum) *life span is the characteristics of a species.* In *Drosophila,* Domestic dog and Tortoise the life spans are 3 months, 20 years and more than 150 years respectively.)

- **Population growth** – The gross value of population growth is calculated as the difference of birth rate and death rate.

- **Dispersal** – The movement of the individuals in or out of the population affects the size of population. The movement of individuals into a population is called **Immigration**, and movement, out of the population is called **Emigration**.

- A set of local populations connected by dispersing individuals is called a **Metapopulation**.

- The *accurate population growth* involves migrant individuals also, which means the -

- **Population growth = (Birth rate + Immigrants) – (Death rate + Emigrants)**

- **Zero Population Growth** – When birth rate equals death rate, and the growth of the population is Zero, i.e. the size of the population remains constant, it is called Zero Population Growth or **Demographic Transition**. Considering migration, at zero population growth:

- **Birth rate + immigrants = Death rate + emigrants**

- Bio-Index number – It is the ratio of birth rate to the death rate. In case of Zero population growth the bio-index number is one

$$\text{Bio-index number} = \frac{\text{Birth rate}}{\text{Death rate}}$$

- **Population size:** The population size may range from few individuals to millions depending upon species, geographical area, impact of predators, outcome of competition and effect of pesticides etc. Sometimes the population size is either too big to measure or meaningless, then the size is more technically called as population density.

- The **population density** can be defined as the number of individuals per square unit area (in terrestrial organisms) or per cubic unit area (in aquatic or aerial organisms). Sometimes the population density is not required and only Relative density serves the purpose. For example, the fish caught per trap in a lake can be used as population density.

- If we compare about 200 *Parthenium* plants with one huge Banyan tree, the population density too becomes less useful. In such cases the **Biomass** or percent cover is used for the measure of population size. In some cases the organisms cannot be seen or counted directly, then the population size is measured indirectly from faecal pellets or pug marks etc.

- **Sex ratio** - It is the number of females per thousand of males.

- **Age and Sex structure** – It is the proportion of individuals of different age and sex. It is depicted in pyramidal form plotting percentage of population of each sex in each age-class.

- In developing countries, like India, it is less steep as it has a larger number of younger people. In developed countries it is steeper which represents nearly stable population.

**Age distribution Pyramids** – For constructing age pyramids, 3-age groups are taken into consideration.

1. Pre-reproductive age (0-14 years)
2. Reproductive age (15-60 years).
3. Post reproductive age ( > 60 years).

There are 3-types of pyramids, i.e. 1. Triangular, 2. Bell shaped and 3. Urn-shaped

1. **Triangular Pyramid** - It indicates **expanding population** with high growth rate.
2. **Bell shaped Pyramid** – It indicates **stable population** with Zero growth rate
3. **Urn-Shaped Pyramid** – It indicates **declining population** with growth rate in minus.

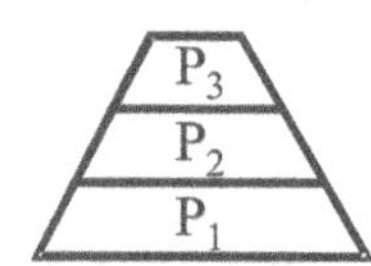
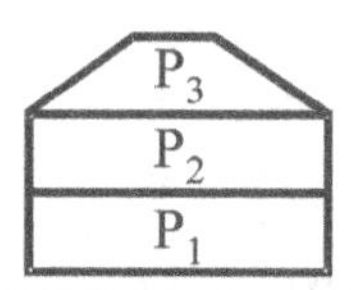
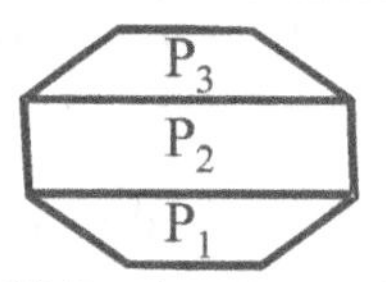

(A) Triangular pyramid  (B) Bell-shaped pyramid  (C) Urn shaped pyramid

$P_1$ = Pre-reproductive age,  $P_2$ = Reproductive age,
$P_3$ = Post reproductive age

## Population interactions

In nature no species can survive in isolation. Even the plant species, which can synthesize their own food, cannot survive alone. They need soil microbes to break down the organic matter in the soil and return the inorganic nutrients for absorption. Besides, plants also need animals (insects) for pollination. Thus in nature, plants, animals and microbes do not and cannot live in isolation but interact in various ways to form biological community. The interspecific associations arise from the interaction of populations of different species. Such associations can be beneficial, harmful (detrimental) or neutral (neither beneficial nor harmful).

Following are different interspecific associations/ interactions. The '+' indicates beneficial interaction, '--' detrimental and '0' neutral interaction.

**Population Interactions**

| S.N. | Name of interaction | Species A | Species B |
| --- | --- | --- | --- |
| 1 | Parasitism | + | − |
| 2 | Commensalism | + | 0 |
| 3 | Mutualism | + | + |
| 4 | Predation | + | − |
| 5 | Competition | − | − |
| 6 | Amensalism | − | 0 |

## Parasitism

In this interaction one species (Parasite) is benefitted and the other (Host) is harmed  (+, −). The parasitism ensures free **lodging** and free **meals**. Many parasites are host specific while others can parasitize on various species of host.

The hosts evolve special mechanisms to reject or resist the parasite. The parasite on the other hand evolves the mechanisms to counteract and neutralize their effects. The parasites have following types of special adaptations for their survival

1. Loss of unnecessary sense organs
2. Presence of suckers or adhesive organs to attach to the host body
3. Loss of digestive system
4. High reproductive capacity
5. Complex life cycle with one or two hosts

Majority of the parasites harm the hosts by reducing their growth, reproduction, survival and population density. They may also make the host physically weak and vulnerable to predation. The parasites can be of 3-types

1. Ectoparasite           2.   Endoparasite
3. Brood parasite

## Ecoparasites

The **ectoparasites** live or feed on the external surface of the host. The most familiar examples are lice and bed bug on human, tick on dogs and leech on cattle. The mosquitoes cannot be considered as true ectoparasites, since they take only meal from the host-body, and do not make lodging. Amongst plants the common example is **Cuscuta,** which has lost both chlorophyll and leaves during evolution and parasitizes hedge plants. The other parasites are copepods, *Petromyzon* and hagfishes, for which the hosts are marine fishes.

Bed bug          Petromyzon on fish          Tick-Dog

## Endoparasites

The **endoparasites** live inside the body of the host. Their morphological and anatomical features are greatly simplified, but their life cycles are more complex because of their extreme specialization. Their reproductive potential is very high. They can be **monogenetic** (involving single host) or **digenetic** (involving two hosts). The common monogenetic endoparasites are *Ascaris* (round worm) and *Entamoeba* in small and large intestine respectively. The familiar digenetic endoparasites are *Taenia* (tape worm) and *Fasciola* (liver fluke) in intestine and liver respectively. The *Plasmodium* is also a digenetic endoparasite in human and female *Anopheles* mosquito. The filarial worm is similarly a lymph parasite.

## Brood Parasites

The koel or cockoo is a **brood parasite** and lays the eggs in the nest of the host, crow, who incubates them. The eggs of the parasitic bird has evolved resemblances with the host's eggs in colour and shape and size.

## Commensalism

In this interaction one species is benefitted and other is neutral i.e., neither benefitted nor harmed (+ , 0). The association of *'egret and the cattle'* is the classical example of commensalism. As the cattle move during grazing, they stir up and flush out the insects from the vegetation which otherwise be difficult for the egret to find and catch. Here the cattle gets no benefit from egret. The other examples of commensalisms are 'clown fish hiding in the colony of sea anemone', 'orchid growing as an epiphyte on mango tree' and the 'barnacle growing on the back of whale'. Here, sea anemone, mango tree and whale derive no benefit from the association.

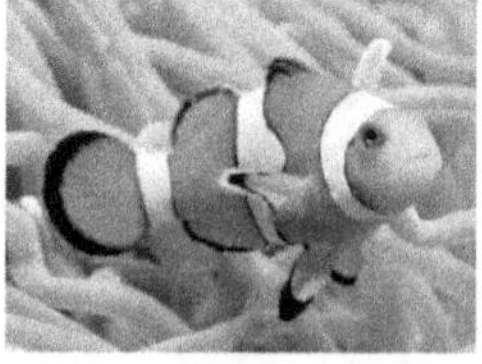
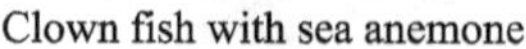

Clown fish with sea anemone

Egret and Buffalo

## Mutualism

In this interaction both the species are benefitted (+, +). **Lichens** is such relationship between fungus and photosynthetic algae/ cyanobacteria. The **Mycorrhizae** is also a similar association between fungus and the roots of higher plants. The fungi here, helps the plant in absorption of essential nutrients from the soil, while plant provides the food to the fungus. In plant-animal association there has occurred co-evolution of mutualism. In many species of fig trees there is a close one-to-one relationship with the species of wasp, for pollination. The female wasp pollinates the fig inflorescence while searching for suitable site for egg laying (oviposition). She lays the eggs inside the fruit and the seeds of the fruit are also consumed by the developing larvae of the wasp. Thus, both are mutually benefitted. Some plants have evolved special structures for pollination by insects like bees, butterflies and bumble bees. To ensure guaranteed pollination the Mediterranean orchid **(Ophrys)** employs *sexual deceit*, in which one petal of the flower resembles very closely with the female of the bee in shape, colour and markings. The male bee perceives that petal as female bee and attempts *pseudocopulation* with the flower and during the process, the pollen grains are dusted over the body of male bee. When the same bee pseudocopulates with other flowers, the pollen grains are transferred to them. Thus pollination occurs. This is a fascinating example of co-evolution in orchid and the bee maintaining the close relationship in colour pattern, shape, size and marking.

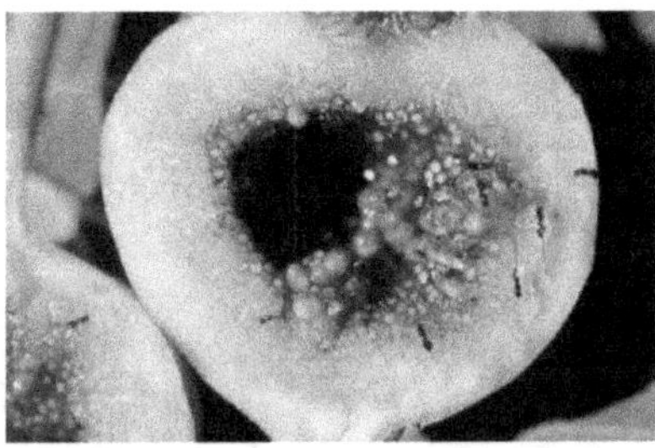

## Predation

Like parasitism, in this interspecific interaction also one species is benefitted and the other is harmed (+, –). The common examples of predator and prey are, Tiger and deer, cat and mouse, and lion and zebra. In a broader ecological sense the sparrow feeding on seed, or the herbivorous animals eating plants, are also predators. The predators have following important roles in the community.

1.  They (herbivores) act as a conduit for transferring energy, fixed by plants, to higher trophic levels.
2.  They keep prey population under check. Otherwise, the prey may achieve high population density to make the ecosystem unstable.

    (When ever an exotic species is introduced into a new geographical area, the species grow exponentially in the absence of natural predators. The following examples of exotic or alien species will support the above statement. Introduction of prickly pear (cactus) into Australia; Nile perch into lake Victoria (East Africa) and *Eicchornia* into water bodies in India. The other examples of exotic species that spreaded rapidly due to absence of predators are *Parthenium, Lantana* and *Clarias* etc.)

3.  Predation also reduces competition amongst preys species and maintains species diversity. (When *Pisaster* (star fish), a predator, was removed from American pacific coast, about 10 species of invertebrates got extincted because of interspecific competition).

If a predator however, overexploits the prey, the prey might become extinct, following which the predator may also become extinct due to lack of food. In nature this is a rare event.

The prey species have evolved various defence mechanisms to lessen the impact of predation. They either run away or have poison secretion/ stings, warming colouration and distasteful nature in various insects or show camouflage (insects, frogs).

The herbivores are plant predators. Amongst insects about 25% are phytophagous. But unlike animals the plants cannot run away from predators and therefore, have evolved varieties of morphological and chemical defenses against herbivores. The common examples of morphological defense are thorns in *Acacia* and Cactus, while chemical defenses against herbivores, grazers or browsers, are secretion of nicotine, caffeine and quinine in Tobacco, coffee and *Cinchona* respectively, and cardiac glycosides in *Calotropis*.

## Competition

It is defined as an interspecific process in which the fitness of one species (measured in terms of 'r') is significantly lower in the presence of another species. It is (–, –) relationship. Charles Darwin also considered the interspecific competition a potent force in organic evolution. The competition generally occurs when closely related species compete for the same but limiting or depleting resources.

However, competition may also occur between totally unrelated species for the same resource. For example, the Flamingos (birds), visiting S. American lakes, compete with the resident fishes for the common food, zooplanktons.

The competition may ever occur when resources like food and space etc. are abundant, since the feeding efficiency of one species may be reduced due to interfering presence of other species. This competition is called **interference Competition.**

Gause's 'competition exclusion principle' states that two closely related species competing for the same resource cannot co-exist indefinitely and the competitively inferior will be eventually eliminated. This is, however, true only when resources are limited.

The species facing competition may sometimes evolve such mechanisms that promote co-existence rather than exclusion. One such mechanism is **'Resource partitioning'**, i.e., avoiding competition by either choosing different timings of feeding or behavioural differences in feeding pattern. In nature the tortoise of Galapagos islands became extinct within decade after goats, competitively superior, were introduced on the island, due to greater browsing efficiency of the goat.

It has also been found in nature that when a competitively superior species is experimentally removed, a species whose distribution is restricted to small geographical area expands its distributional range dramatically and expands into a larger area (**Competitive release**)

## Amensalism

In this association one species is harmed but the other remains neutral (–, 0). For example the fungus, *Penicillium notatum* growing close to bacteria, like Staphlococcus, kills the bacteria due to the secretion of penicillin, whereas the fungus remains unaffected. Similarly the leaves falling from the tree either kill or adversely affect the growth of the seedling population underneath the tree.

## Ecological Indicators

Ecological indicators are used to communicate information about ecosystems and the impact human activity has on ecosystems to groups such as the public or government policy makers. Ecosystems are complex and ecological indicators can help describe them in simpler terms that can be understood and used by non-scientists to make management decisions.

There are different types of ecological indicators:

(a) **Keystone Species:** A keystone species is a species that has a disproportionately large effect on its environment relative to its abundance. Such species are described as playing a critical role in maintaining the structure of an ecological community, affecting many other organisms in an ecosystem and helping to determine the types and numbers of various other species in the community.

(b) **Umbrella Species:** Umbrella species are species selected for making conservation-related decisions, typically because protecting these species indirectly protects the many other species that make up the ecological community of its habitat. Species conservation can be subjective because it is hard to determine the status of many species.

(c) **Flagship Species:** The concept of flagship species has its genesis in the field of conservation biology. The flagship species concept holds that by raising the profile of a particular species

## Ecosystem Services

- Human beings benefit from a multitude of resources and processes that are supplied by natural ecosystem. Collectively, these benefits are known as **ecosystem services,** *for example*, healthy forest ecosystems purify air and water, migrate droughts and floods, cycle nutrients, generate fertile soils, provide wildlife habitat, maintain biodiversity, pollinate crops, provide storage site for carbon and also provide aesthetic, cultural and spiritual values.

- Services can be subdivided into **5 categories -**

  (i) **Provisioning:** Such as the production of food and water.

  (ii) **Regulating:** Such as the control of climate and disease.

  (iii) **Supporting:** Such as nutrients cycle and crop pollination.

  (iv) **Cultural:** Such as spiritual and recreational benefits, and

  (v) **Preserving:** Which includes guarding against uncertainty through the maintenance of diversity.

## Importance of ecosystem

**Ecosystem play very important role for the survival of different species and their surroundings altogether.**

- **Energy:** Study of ecosystems provides information about amount of energy flowing into them, its harvesting ability and availability at various levels.

- **Biogeochemical cycling:** Density of ecosystem is governed by degree of biogeochemical cycling and the amount of inorganic nutrients entering the ecosystem from outside.

- **Food webs:** Each ecosystem has a number of food webs. The knowledge of food webs is helpful to restore a degraded ecosystem and prevent unscientific exploitation of different ecosystems.

- **Protection:** Each ecosystem whether natural or man made requires protection from pollutants and pests.

- **Inter-relationships:** Study of ecosystems gives information about inter-relationships amongst various types of organisms as well as between organisms and their abiotic environment.

- **Carrying capacity:** By knowing the carrying capacity of ecosystem, it can be known as to what is the number of producers and consumers which can be supported by that ecosystem.

- **Inputs:** The shortage on inputs can be known and corrected.

# Exercise -1

1. The highest rate at which individuals can be harvested without reducing the population size is called maximum sustainable yield of a
   (a) Population    (b) Community
   (c) Ecosystem    (d) Landscape

2. Ecological restoration is the process of rebuilding a degraded ecosystem till
   (a) it becomes pollution free and provides solace to the people.
   (b) it becomes free of disturbance.
   (c) its structure and functions are restored.
   (d) it starts providing some ecosystem services.

3. A species the population of which is low enough for it to be at risk of becoming extinct, but not low enough that it is in imminent danger of extinction is called
   (a) Endangered species
   (b) Threatened species
   (c) Vulnerable species
   (d) Rare species

4. The technique, which is fastest for measuring organic carbon is.
   (a) COD        (b) $BOD_5$
   (c) $BOD_7$       (d) TOC

5. As the number of species in a food web increases
   (a) Food chain length tends to increase.
   (b) System tends to be unstable.
   (c) Energy flow decreases.
   (d) System tends to collapse completely.

6. In an aquatic system, the presence of noxious gases such as $H_2S$ and $CH_4$ is associated with
   (a) abundant algal growth
   (b) oxygen depletion
   (c) absence of macrophytic vegetation
   (d) excess of dissolved oxygen

7. A structure with hundreds of species non-linearly interlinked for their livelyhood is called :
   (a) Guild        (b) Food chain
   (c) Food web     (d) Pyramid

8. Ecosystem restoration deals with restoring :
   (a) Ecosystem integrity
   (b) Biodiversity
   (c) Physical environment
   (d) Ecosystem resistance

9. At which stage of ecological succession, an ecosystem exhibits, photosynthesis (P) = Respiration (R) :
   (a) Pioneer stage    (b) Mid seral stage
   (c) Climax stage     (d) Early seral stage

10. Arctic Tundra is situated around :
    (a) 66.58 N      (b) 55.58 N
    (c) 458 N        (d) 66.58 S

11. The nature of food web at the developmental stage of a succession is :
    (a) linear, predominantly grazing
    (b) linear, predominantly detritus
    (c) weblike, predominantly detritus
    (d) weblike, predominantly grazing

12. Which of the following is correct regarding the ecosystem?
    (a) primary consumers are least dependent upon producers
    (b) primary consumers out-number producers
    (c) producers are more than primary consumers
    (d) secondary consumers are the largest and most powerful.

13. Homeostasis is
    (a) tendency of biological systems to change with change in environment
    (b) tendency of biological systems to resist change
    (c) disturbance of self regulatory system and natural controls
    (d) biotic materials used in homeopathic medicines.

14. Food chain in which microorganisms breakdown the food formed by primary producers is
    (a) parasitic food chain    (b) detritus food chain
    (c) consumer food chain     (d) predator food chain.

15. If we completely remove the decomposers from an ecosystem, its functioning will be adversely affected because of:
    (a) mineral movement will be blocked
    (b) the rate of decomposition will be very high
    (c) energy flow will be blocked
    (d) herbivores will not receive solar energy.

16. The abundance of a species population, within its habitat, is called:
    (a) relative density     (b) regional density
    (c) absolute density     (d) niche density.

17. The primary succession refers to the development of communities on a:
    (a) forest clearing after devastating fire
    (b) newly-exposed habitat with no record of earlier vegetation
    (c) freshly cleared crop field
    (d) pond, freshly filled with water after a dry phase.

18. Which of the following pairs is correctly matched?
    (a) parasitism – intra-specific relationship
    (b) uricotelism – aquatic habitat
    (c) excessive perspiration – xeric adaptation
    (d) stream lined body – aquatic adaptation.

19. The 'niche' of a species is meant for
    (a) habitat and specific functions of a species
    (b) specific place where an organism lives
    (c) specific species function and its competitive power
    (d) none of these.

20. What is a keystone species?
    (a) a species which makes up only a small proportion of the total biomass of a community, yet has a huge impact community's organization and s
    (b) a common species that has plenty of biomass yet has a fairly low impact on the community organization
    (c) a rare species that has minimal impact on the biomass and on other species in the community
    (d) a dominant species that constitutes a large proportion of the biomass and which affects many other species.

21. The population of an insect species shows an explosive increase in numbers during rainy season followed by its disappearance at the end of the season. What does this show?
    (a) the food plants mature and die at the end of the rainy season
    (b) its population growth curve is of J-type
    (c) the population of its predators increases enormously
    (d) S-shaped or sigmoid growth of this insect.

22. Which one of the following statements is correct?
    (a) Both Azotobacter and Rhizobium fix atmospheric nitrogen in root nodules of plants.
    (b) Cyanobacteria such as Anabaena and Nostoc are important mobilizers of phosphates and for plant nutrition in soil
    (c) At present it is not possible to grow maize without chemical fertilizers
    (d) Extensive use of chemical fertilizers may lead to eutrophication of nearby water bodies.

23. Atmospheric nitrogen is converted to nitrogen oxides
    (a) when fossil fuels are burned at high combustion temperatures.
    (b) if the sun is shining brightly and there is a temperature inversion.
    (c) on cloudy days when carbon and soot levels are unusually high.
    (d) if radon gas is present when gasoline is burned in automobiles.

24. Having covered millions of acres of grasslands, the toxic weed leafy spurge has caused serious damage to the lower regions of Himachal. Being toxic in nature it is avoid by both cattle and horses alike. Leafy spurge has spread completely across many neighboring states of Uttaranchal. If left uncontrolled in these states, leafy spurge populations will:
    (a) keep growing indefinitely.
    (b) reach their carrying capacity.
    (c) shift from a S-curve to a constant rate of growth.
    (d) shift from an S-shaped curve to a *J-shaped* growth curve.

25. Some beetles escape from a ship and fly to a small island covered with grass but with no trees or beetle predators. As the beetles feed, they destroy all the grasses. But with abundant food, the beetle population soars, doubling in size every month. After about a year, the population crashes as thousands of beetles have destroyed almost all of the plants and there is little left to feed the large population. This scenario best illustrates
    (a) constant growth followed by equilibrium.
    (b) a population that has stabilized near its carrying capacity.
    (c) exponential growth followed by a population crash.
    (d) logistic growth ending at its carrying capacity.

26. Which one of the following statements about the carbon, phosphorus, and nitrogen cycles is true ?
    (a) The major source of carbon used by plants is the soil
    (b) The major source of nitrogen used by plants is the air.
    (c) Phosphorus has no atmospheric component.
    (d) Bacteria drive the phosphorus cycle.

27. Synecology deals with
    (a) Ecology of many species
    (b) Ecology of many populations
    (c) Ecology of community
    (d) None of these

28. Ecotype includes a type of species in which are environmentally induce variations are:
    (a) Temporary (b) Genetically not related
    (c) Genetically fixed (d) None of the Above

29. Primary productivity of the open oceans is very limited because of:
    (a) the shortage of water.
    (b) the shortage of light.
    (c) the shortage of nutrients.
    (d) low temperature.

30. The economic gap between developing and industrialized countries may best be narrowed by
    (a) the adoption of democratic forms of government in developing countries.
    (b) industrialized countries increasing shipments of food supplies to developing countries.
    (c) industrialized countries harvesting more natural resources in developing countries.
    (d) stabilizing population growth in developing countries.

31. The term Biocoenosis was proposed by
    (a) A G Tansley (b) Karl Mobius
    (c) R H Whittaker (d) Robert Hooke

32. Biomes with permafrost are most likely:
    (a) covered in coniferous forests at high latitudes.
    (b) in temperate zones with deciduous trees.
    (c) located near the poles and without any trees.
    (d) located at high altitudes nearest the equator.

33. Consumers that eat plants rely upon:
    (a) chemical energy stored in organic molecules produced by photosythesis.
    (b) kinetic energy stored in organic molecules produced by photosynthesis.
    (c) photosynthesis to convert potential energy to kinetic energy.
    (d) entropy to generate heat to drive kinetic processes in their bodies.

34. Species that occur in different geographical regions separated by special barrier are:
    (a) Allopatric (b) Sympatric
    (c) Sibling (d) None of the Above

35. Deciding to use a natural enemies approach to control the mites that infect her crops, a farmer purchases 10,000 ladybugs in the spring and spreads them over her 100 acre fields. This represents the use of natural:
    (a) predators (b) parasitoids
    (c) pathogens (d) plant-eaters

36. Density-independent factors such as earthquakes and hurricanes are:
    (a) abiotic factors that maintain a population near equilibrium.
    (b) biotic factors that maintain a population near equilibrium.
    (c) abiotic factors that are not involved in maintaining a population near its equilibrium.
    (d) biotic factors that are not involved in maintaining a population near its equilibrium.

37. Developing a new form of ecological pest control, researchers engineer crops to produce the pheromones of the pest. The crops now produce the pest pheromone, overwhelming the fields and causing the male pests to fail to find a mate. This new form of ecological pest control combines:
    (a) natural enemies and cultural control.
    (b) cultural and natural enemies control.
    (c) genetic and cultural control.
    (d) genetic and natural chemical control.

38. Dung beetles feeding on the waste of cattle, grazing on hay in a field, represent:
    (a) a decomposer feeding on the wastes of a consumer eating a producer.
    (b) a producer feeding on the wastes of a producer eating a consumer.
    (c) a producer feeding on the wastes of a consumer eating a producer.
    (d) a consumer feeding on the wastes of a decomposer eating a producer.
39. Ecosystem sustainability primarily results from the:
    (a) relationships between the organisms in an ecosystem.
    (b) number of predators found in the ecosystem.
    (c) frequency of fires or other natural disasters in an ecosystem.
    (d) total amount of biomass that exists in an ecosystem.
40. Ecotones:
    (a) contain only species found in the bordering ecosystems.
    (b) have the same abiotic characteristics as the bordering ecosystems.
    (c) consist of two or more landscapes.
    (d) are transitional regions between ecosystems.
41. Energy transfer between trophic levels in aquatic systems is generally:
    (a) less efficient than terrestrial food pyramids.
    (b) less efficient than a detritus food web because aquatic systems lack fungi.
    (c) inverted, in which more energy is transferred from one trophic level up to the next.
    (d) more efficient than terrestrial food pyramids.
42. In a forest, deer, raccoons, squirrels, and other animals eat and find shelter. A detritus food web occurs as their wastes accumulate on the forest floor. In this detritus web
    (a) deer and raccoons function as the producers.
    (b) fungi and earthworms function as producers.
    (c) decomposers function as consumers.
    (d) the deer and raccoons represent decomposers.
43. In an ecosystem with many similar species, we typically find:
    (a) intense interspecific competition for food.
    (b) competitors using different resources.
    (c) intense interspecific competition for nesting sites.
    (d) adaptations for battles and interspecific competition.
44. In an ecosystem, the replacement of one new species for another because of direct competition for the same resources defines:
    (a) intraspecific competition.
    (b) the competitive exclusion principle.
    (c) character displacement.
    (d) resource partitioning.
45. Maintaining sustainable human exploitation of ecosystem capital will be increasingly difficult because of:
    (a) the over reliance on grains and other plants as a significant portion of the human diet.
    (b) the expanding number of viral and bacterial human diseases.
    (c) the growing human population on Earth.
    (d) decreases in worldwide ocean levels.
46. Persistent organic pollutants (POPs) reach toxic levels in organisms in natural ecosystems in large part because of biomagnification, in which the highest concentrations of POPs are found in:
    (a) primary producers (b) secondary producers
    (c) primary consumers (d) secondary consumers

47. Some birds have been seen to consume certain soils in what is called geophagy. In some cases, the soils help the birds digest toxins that occur in their diets. These birds eating soil represent a member of the:
    (a) biosphere consuming a component of the lithosphere.
    (b) hydrosphere consuming a component of the atmosphere.
    (c) lithosphere consuming a component of the biosphere.
    (d) atmosphere consuming a component of the hydrosphere.
48. In a food chain of a grassland ecosystem the top consumers are:
    (a) Herbivores
    (b) Carnivores
    (c) Bacteria
    (d) Either Carnivores or Herbivores
49. Biotic Potential is counteracted by:
    (a) Competition with other organism
    (b) Producer is the largest
    (c) Limitation of food supply
    (d) None of the above.
50. Which of the following represents a type of mutualism?
    (a) A red-tailed hawk pounces on a field mouse for dinner.
    (b) A large herd of zebra graze lazily across the broad savannah
    (c) A mosquito draws a blood meal from the back of an elk.
    (d) A nectar-feeding bat swoops in to drink nectar from some flowers.
51. Which one of the following illustrates interspecific competition?
    (a) The largest wolves in a pack are the first to feed on a freshly killed deer.
    (b) Two honeybees from the same colony converge on a flower to collect pollen & nectar.
    (c) Advertising its nectar with red colors, a columbine flower attracts a hummingbird for a meal.
    (d) Standing near the dead antelope, vultures wait for the lions to finish their meal.
52. Why are there so few ecosystems with more than four levels of consumers?
    (a) because biomass decreases by about 90% at each level moving up.
    (b) because top consumers compete with and kill each other with increasing population size.
    (c) because consumers at these highest levels typically form social groups that stop reproducing at high densities.
    (d) because predators at the highest levels simply are not intelligent enough to hunt other top predators.
53. Regulating and cultural services provided by natural ecosystems:
    (a) are typically the most economically valued components of ecosystems.
    (b) are public goods usually provided by markets.
    (c) include goods such as fresh water, wild foods, and livestock.
    (d) are essential but difficult to value in monetary terms.
54. The phrase "ecosystem capital" is better than the phrase "natural resources" because ecosystem capital:
    (a) includes the ecological value of natural ecosystems.
    (b) includes the economic value of an ecosystem's goods and services.
    (c) does not include the value of natural ecosystems.
    (d) does not include the economic value of an ecosystem's goods and services.

55. A sandy and saline area is the natural habitat of an Indian animal species. The animal has no predators in that area but its existence is threatened due to the destruction of its habitat. Which one of the following could be that animal?
    (a) Indian wild buffalo    (b) Indian wild ass
    (c) Indian wild boar       (d) Indian gazelle

56. In addition to global climate change, humans are negatively impacting coral reefs by:
    (a) destructive harvesting of fish for food or pets.
    (b) using large amounts of coral rock to pave roads.
    (c) destroying large regions of coral reefs for commercial aquaculture.
    (d) introducing alien species that are thought to be more productive.

57. The concept of sustainable development relates to:
    (a) consumption levels
    (b) exhaustible resources
    (c) social equity
    (d) Intergenerational equity

58. The variability among living organisms from all sources including terrestrial, marine and other ecosystems and the ecological complexes of which they are part which includes diversity within species, between species of ecosystems refers to:
    (a) geographical diversity
    (b) zoological diversity
    (c) ecological diversity
    (d) biological diversity

59. 'Population dividend' refers to:
    (a) total number of population
    (b) youthful age structure of a population
    (c) relatively high proportion of experienced aged people
    (d) migration from richer region to poorer region

60. Inclusion strategy does not focus on:
    (a) reduction of inequality
    (b) reduction of poverty
    (c) diversifying livelihood for tribal population
    (d) getting poorer countries close

61. Which one of the following is the best description of the term 'ecosystem'?                    **(IAS Prelims 2016)**
    (a) A community of organisms interacting with one another.
    (b) That part of the Earth which is inhabited by living organisms.
    (c) A community of organisms together with the environment in which they live
    (d) The flora and fauna of a geographical area

62. Which one of the following is the best description of the term 'ecosystem'?                    **(IAS Prelims 2015)**
    (a) A community of organisms interacting with one another.
    (b) That part of the Earth which is inhabited by living organisms.
    (c) A community of organisms together with the environment in which they live
    (d) The flora and fauna of a geographical area

63. Which one of the following is the national aquatic animal of India?                    **(IAS Prelims 2015)**
    (a) Saltwater crocodile    (b) Olive ridley turtle
    (c) Gangetic dolphin       (d) Gharial

64. In India, in which one of the following types of forests is teak a dominant tree species?          **(IAS Prelims 2015)**
    (a) Tropical moist deciduous forest
    (b) Tropical rain forest
    (c) Tropical thorn scrub forest
    (d) Temperate forest with grasslands

# Exercise -2

## Statement Based MCQ

1. Leslie matrix population model is generally used to determine.
    1. The growth of population.
    2. The age distribution within population over time
    3. The prey-predator interactions.
    Choose the correct answer :
    (a) 1 only              (b) 1 and 3 only
    (c) 2 and 3 only        (d) 1 and 2 only

2. Which of the following groups contains only easily biodegradable items?
    1. Grass, flower and leather
    2. Grass, wood and plastic
    3. Fruits, peel cake and lime juice
    4. Cake, wood and grass.
    Which of the above is/are correct?
    (a) 1 and 2             (b) 2 and 3
    (c) 1, 3 and 4          (d) All of these

3. Food chains differ from food webs in that:
    1. food chains are single sequence of who eats whom in a community.
    2. food chains better represent the entire community.
    3. food webs represent the complex interaction among food chains.
    4. food chain is the flow of energy in a population.
    Which of the following statement(s) is/are correct?
    (a) 1 and 2             (b) 1 and 3
    (c) 1, 2 and 3          (d) 1, 2, 3 and 4

4. Which of following is/are tend (s) in ecological succession ?
    1. An increase in complexity of species
    2. An increase in productivity
    3. An increase in community stability and species diversity
    4. A decrease in nonliving organic materials.
    Which of the above is/are correct?
    (a) 1 and 2             (b) 1 and 4
    (c) 1, 3 and 3          (d) 1, 2, 3 and 4

5. Which of the following include(s) ecosystem services ?
    1. Purification of air and water by forests
    2. Forests mitigate droughts and flood
    3. Forests act as store house of carbon
    4. Forests influence hydrological cycle
    Which of the above is/are correct?
    (a) 1 and 3             (b) 1 and 4
    (c) 1, 2 and 3          (d) 1, 2, 3 and 4

6. Which one is not the dynamic aspect of an ecosystem?
    1. Producers and mineral cycles
    2. Consumers and mineral cycles
    3. Producers and energy flow
    4. Energy flow and mineral cycles

Which of the above is/are correct?
(a)　1 and 2　　　　　　　(b)　2 and 4
(c)　1, 2 and 3　　　　　　(d)　All of these

7.　Which of the following statements are true about ecosystem? Select the correct answer from the codes:
1.　Ecosystem comprises both biotic and abiotic components.
2.　Solar radiation is the main driving force of the ecosystem.
3.　Ecosystem is a closed system.
4.　Ecosystem does not have its own productivity
**Codes:**
(a)　1 and 2　　　　　　　(b)　2 and 3
(c)　1 and 3　　　　　　　(d)　3 and 4

8.　Which of the following are the incorrect statements about 'Keystone species'.
1.　Keystone species are the small-sized plants and organisms which have large effect on the environment.
2.　Keystone species play critical role in maintaining the structure of an ecological community.
3.　Keystone species do not generally affect other organisms.
(a)　1 and 2　　　　　　　(b)　2 and 3
(c)　1 and 3　　　　　　　(d)　All are correct

9.　Which of the following are correct statements about light in aquatic environments?
1.　Water selectively reflects and absorbs certain wavelengths of light.
2.　Photosynthetic organisms that live in deep water probably utilize red light.
3.　Light intensity is an important abiotic factor in limiting the distribution of photosynthetic organisms.
(a)　1 only　　　　　　　　(b)　2 only
(c)　1 and 3 only　　　　　(d)　2 and 3 only

10.　The producers in ecosystems include which of the following?
1.　prokaryotes　　　　　2.　algae
3.　plants
(a)　1 only　　　　　　　　(b)　2 only
(c)　3 only　　　　　　　　(d)　1, 2, and 3

11.　Aquatic primary productivity is often limited by which of the following?
1.　light　　　　　　　　　2.　nutrients
3.　pressure
(a)　2 only　　　　　　　　(b)　3 only
(c)　1 and 2 only　　　　　(d)　1, 2, and 3

12.　Consider the following statements:
1.　Interactions between the two organism in which one organism kills sand feed on the second organisms, is called Parasitism.
2.　Mutualism is the way two organisms of different species biologically interact in a relationship in which each individual derives a fitness benefit.
Which of the statements given above is/are true?
(a)　1 only　　　　　　　　(b)　2 only
(c)　1 and 2 both　　　　　(d)　None

13.　Consider the following statements:
1.　In ecology, an ecosystem is a naturally occurring assemblage of organism (plant, animal and other living organism - also referred to as a biotic community of biocoenosis) living together with their environment (or biotope), function as a unit of sorts.
2.　The term "ecosystem" first coined by Arthur Tansely.
Which of the statements given above is/are correct?
(a)　1 only　　　　　　　　(b)　2 only
(c)　1 and 2 both　　　　　(d)　None

14.　Which of the following statements is true?
1.　Circulation of energy in the biosphere ecosystem is cyclical.
2.　Circulation of matter in the biosphere ecosystem is unidirectional.
Select the correct answer using the codes given below:
(a)　1 only　　　　　　　　(b)　2 only
(c)　1 and 2 only　　　　　(d)　None

15.　Consider the following statements:
1.　Waste are of two types, biodegradable and non-biodegradable.
2.　Blue-green algae are producers.
3.　Biodegradable wastes should be separated and kept in blue colour bins for garbage collectors.
Which of these statement(s) is/are correct ?
(a)　1 and 2　　　　　　　(b)　2 and 3
(c)　1, 2 and 3　　　　　　(d)　None

16.　Not all parasitism involves feeding on the body of the host. The exception is:
1.　Ectoparasitism　　　　2.　Endopasitism
3.　Parasitoids　　　　　　4.　Brood Parasitism
Choose the option from the codes given below:
(a)　1 only　　　　　　　　(b)　2 only
(c)　3 only　　　　　　　　(d)　4 only

17.　When two organisms attempt to utilize the same resource, the result is:
1.　A fundamental niche
2.　Competition
3.　Commensalism
4.　Mutualism
Choose the correct option from the codes given below:
(a)　1 and 2　　　　　　　(b)　2 only
(c)　3 and 4　　　　　　　(d)　1, 2, 3 and 4

18.　With reference to food chains in ecosystems, consider the following statements:
1.　A food chain illustrates the order in which a chain of organisms feed upon each other.
2.　Food chains are found within the populations of a species.
3.　A food chain illustrates the numbers of each organism which are eaten by others.
Which of the statements given above is/are correct?
(a)　1 only　　　　　　　　(b)　1 and 2 only
(c)　1, 2 and 3　　　　　　(d)　None

19.　With reference to the food chains in ecosystems, which of the following kinds of organism is/are known as decomposer organism/organisms?
1.　Virus　　　　　　　　　2.　Fungi
3.　Bacteria
Select the correct answer using the codes given below.
(a)　1 only　　　　　　　　(b)　2 and 3 only
(c)　1 and 3 only　　　　　(d)　1, 2 and 3

20.　Consider the following :
1.　Bats　　　　　　　　　　2.　Bears
3.　Rodents
　　The phenomenon of hibernation can be observed in which of the above kinds of animals?
(a)　1 and 2 only
(b)　2 only
(c)　1, 2 and 3
(d)　Hibernation cannot be observed in any of the above

21.　Which of the following adds/add carbon dioxide to the carbon cycle on the planet Earth?
1.　Volcanic action
2.　Respiration
3.　Photosynthesis
4.　Decay of organic matter

Select the correct answer using the code given below.
(a) 1 and 3 only        (b) 2 only
(c) 1, 2 and 4 only     (d) 1, 2, 3 and 4

22. With reference to two non-conventional energy sources called 'coalbed methane' and 'shale gas', consider the following statements :
    1. Coalbed methane is the pure methane gas extracted from coal seams, while shale gas is a mixture of propane and butane only that can be extracted from fine-grained sedimentary rocks.
    2. In India, abundant coalbed methane sources exist, but so far no shale gas sources have been found.
    Which of the statements given above is/are correct?
    (a) 1 only           (b) 2 only
    (c) Both 1 and 2    (d) Neither 1 nor 2

23. The study of relationship of living organism with each other and with their environment is called ____.
    1. Economy
    2. Ecology
    3. Geography
    4. Environment
    Which among the following defines the statement
    (a) 1 only        (b) 2 only
    (c) 3 only        (d) 4 only

24. Consider the following statement related to Abiotic
    1. Abiotic components of ecosystem are the living features of ecosystem on which the living organism depends.
    2. Abiotic component is referred to the physical environment and its numerous interacting variables.
    Which among the following statement is correct
    (a) 1 only        (b) 2 only
    (c) Both 1 and 2    (d) None of the Above

25. What is the name of processes of Nitrogen cycle?
    1. Nitrogen Fixation    2. Nitrification
    3. Assimilation         4. Denitrification
    Choose the correct option
    (a) 1 and 2       (b) 3 and 4
    (c) 1, 2, 3        (d) 1, 2, 3, 4

26. Which equation explains Nitrification?
    1. $NH_3 \boxtimes NO_2 \boxtimes NO{-}_3$
    2. $NH_3 \boxtimes NO_3 \boxtimes NO{-}_2$
    3. $NH_3 \boxtimes NO_4 \boxtimes NO{-}_2$
    Select the correct answer from the following codes
    (a) 1 only        (b) 2 only
    (c) 3 only        (d) All of the Above

27. What is the purpose of Ozone layer?
    1. Protects UV rays to reach on earth
    2. Helps UV rays to reach earth
    3. The source of ozone is the oxygen in the atmosphere
    Choose the correct code
    (a) 1 and 2       (b) 2 and 3
    (c) 1 and 3       (d) 1, 2, 3

28. Consider the following statements:
    1. Burning fossil fuel decreases oxygen in atmosphere
    2. Burning fossil fuel increases carbon dioxide
    3. The main source of oxygen is atmosphere
    Which among the following code is incorrect?
    (a) 1 only        (b) 2 only
    (c) 3 only        (d) None of the Above

29. How is the oxygen cycle effected?
    1. Human activities
    2. Running of automobiles
    3. Consumption of fossil fuels
    Choose the correct code
    (a) 1 and 2       (b) 2 and 3
    (c) 1 and 3       (d) 1, 2, 3

30. With reference to the process of photosynthesis for carbon dioxide, which of the following statement is correct?
    1. Through the process of photosynthesis carbon enters into non-living world in the form of carbon dioxide.
    2. Recycling of carbon is done by the burning of fossil fuels.
    Select the correct answer from the following codes
    (a) 1 Only        (b) 2 only
    (c) 1 and 2       (d) Neither of the Above

31. Which of the following is not involved in the continuous water exchange?
    1. Stones          2. Air
    3. Land           4. Sea
    Choose the correct code
    (a) 1 only        (b) 2 only
    (c) 1 and 2       (d) 3 and 4

32. Name the elements that help in creating phosphorous cycle?
    1. Rocks         2. Earth crust
    3. Air            4. Water
    Choose the correct code
    (a) 1 and 2       (b) 3 and 4
    (c) 1 and 3       (d) 1 and 4

33. Why phosphorous is not found in atmosphere?
    1. It doesn't combine well with other elements
    2. It just cannot be found
    3. The sun evaporates it
    4. At normal temperatures and pressure, phosphorous is at a liquid state
    Choose the correct code from the following statement regarding phosphorous
    (a) 1 only        (b) 2 only
    (c) 3 only        (d) 4 only

34. How does phosphorous enter plants in the soil?
    1. Photosynthesis    2. Water in the soil
    3. Rocks on the sand
    Choose the correct answer
    (a) 1 only        (b) 2 only
    (c) 3 only        (d) 1, 2, 3

35. Megatherms is defines as
    1. Organisms living in tropical regions
    2. Organisms living in subtropical regions
    3. Organisms living in temperate regions
    Choose the correct definition of Megatherms
    (a) 1 only        (b) 2 only
    (c) 3 only        (d) None of the Above

36. Consider the following related to humidity
    1. Humidity is the water vapor present in the atmosphere.
    2. Humidity is measured by barometer
    3. Humidity is defined as molecules of water/unit volume
    Choose the correct code
    (a) 1 and 2       (b) 2 and 3
    (c) 1 and 3       (d) 1, 2, 3

37. Consider the following statement in regards to ecosystem
    1. Components of an ecosystem include Biotic
    2. Components of an ecosystem include Abiotic
    Which of the following statement is correct?
    (a) 1 only
    (b) 2 only
    (c) 1 and 2
    (d) None of the Above
38. The process of cycling of minerals and components through the ecosystem is called_____
    1. Biological cycle
    2. Biogeochemical cycle
    3. Biochemical cycle
    Choose the correct code
    (a) 1 only
    (b) 2 only
    (c) 3 only
    (d) None of the Above
39. Name the forest that is found in Asia, Europe.
    1. Boreal Forest
    2. Temperate Deciduous Forests
    3. Tropical or Rainforests
    Choose the correct name
    (a) 1 only
    (b) 2 only
    (c) 3 only
    (d) All of the Above
40. Consider the following statement
    1. The soil of Temperate Deciduous forests is richer than boreal forests.
    2. Temperate Deciduous forests are mostly found in the equatorial belt of the plant.
    Which statement is incorrect?
    (a) 1 only
    (b) 2 only
    (c) 1 and 2
    (d) None of the Above
41. Which forest does not see winter season?
    1. Boreal Forest
    2. Temperate Deciduous Forests
    3. Tropical Forest
    Choose the correct code
    (a) 1 only
    (b) 1 and 2
    (c) 1, 2, 3
    (d) 3 only
42. How much desert area exists on the planet?
    (a) One third
    (b) Half
    (c) One fifth
    (d) One fourth
43. Marine lives are found in which place?
    1. Ocean
    2. Lake
    3. Ponds
    4. Sand
    Choose the correct code
    (a) 1, 2
    (b) 3, 4
    (c) 1, 2, 3
    (d) 1, 2, 3, 4
44. The water that has less content of salt is called ________.
    1. Sea
    2. Fresh water
    3. Oil
    Choose the correct code
    (a) 1 only
    (b) 2 only
    (c) 3 only
    (d) All of the Above
45. Consider the following statement
    1. Atmospheric temperature of the place depends upon the slope, altitude, latitude, topography.
    2. Temperature increases as we go from equator to poles.
    3. Temperature lowers as we go from equator to poles
    Choose the incorrect statement
    (a) 1 only
    (b) 2 only
    (c) 3 only
    (d) None of the Above
46. Consider the following statements
    1. Three-fourth of the earth surface is covered by water but less than 3% is fresh water used for human consumption.
    2. Of the total fresh water available, Ice-cap has highest share of 2% followed by ground water 0.68%.
    Select the correct answer using the code given below.
    (a) 1 only
    (b) 2 only
    (c) 1 and 2
    (d) Neither of the Above
47. With reference to phosphorus cycling, consider the following statements
    1. The natural reservoir of phosphorus is atmosphere, which contains phosphorus in the form of phosphates.
    2. Herbivores and other animals obtain phosphorus from plants.
    3. Unlike carbon cycle, there is no respiratory release of phosphorus into atmosphere.
    Which of the statements given above is/are correct?
    (a) 1 and 2
    (b) 2 and 3
    (c) 1 and 3
    (d) 1, 2, 3
48. What is the name of the cycle where the continuous and balanced process of evaporation, precipitation, transpiration and runoff of water takes place.
    1. Hydrological
    2. Tropological
    3. Hyper logical
    Choose the correct option
    (a) 1 only
    (b) 2 only
    (c) 3 only
    (d) None of the Above
49. Water in a wetland can be
    1. Fresh
    2. Brackish
    3. Static
    Select the correct answer using the codes given below.
    (a) 1 and 2
    (b) 1 and 3
    (c) 2 and 3
    (d) 1, 2 and 3
50. Consider the following statement related to humidity
    1. Specific humidity
    2. Absolute humidity
    3. Relative humidity
    4. Non relative humidity
    Which among the following is not the type of humidity?
    (a) 1 only
    (b) 2 only
    (c) 3 only
    (d) 4 only
51. Consider the following statement
    1. Steppe is found in low latitudes and middle latitudes.
    2. Prairies are humid and densely covered tall grasslands
    3. Savanna are the areas of thick high grasses
    Choose the correct code
    (a) 1 only
    (b) 2 only
    (c) 3 only
    (d) 1, 2, 3
52. On which of the following can you find the Bureau of Energy Efficiency Star Label? **(IAS Prelims 2016)**
    1. Ceiling fans
    2. Electric geysers
    3. Tubular fluorescent lamps
    Select the correct answer using the code given below.
    (a) 1 and 2 only
    (b) 3 only
    (c) 2 and 3 only
    (d) 1, 2 and 3
53. Consider the following statements **(IAS Prelims 2016)**
    1. Most of the world's coral reefs are in tropical waters.
    2. More than one-third of the world's coral reefs are located in the territories of Australia, Indonesia and Philippines.
    3. Coral reefs host **far more number** of animal phyla than those hosted by tropical rainforests.
    Which of the statements given above is/are correct ?
    (a) 1 and 2 only
    (b) 3 only
    (c) 1 and 3 only
    (d) 1, 2 and 3

# Hints and Explanations

## EXERCISE-1

1. (a) 2. (c) 3. (a) 4. (d) 5. (a) 6. (b)
7. (c) 8. (a) 9. (c) 10. (a) 11. (a)
12. (c) An ecosystem may be defined as a structural and functional unit of the biosphere comprising living organisms and their non-living environment that interact by means of food chains and chemical cycles resulting in energy flow, biotic diversity and material cycling to form a stable, self supporting system.
The organisms in an ecosystem are classified into 3 main categories-producers, consumers and decomposers. The consumers utilize materials and energy stored by the producers. Decomposers obtain their food molecules from the organic materials of dead producers and consumers. In a true ecosystem, producers are more than consumers (herbivores and carnivores).
13. (b) The ability to maintain a steady state within constantly changing environment is essential for the survival of living systems. The maintenance of a constant internal environment is called homeostasis.
14. (b) The dead organic matter of plant or animal is called as detritus. While a part of it remains on the soil surface as litter, the other part enters the soil. Many animals such as protozoan's, nematodes, insects etc. depend on detritus and hence they are called as detrivores. Even the human beings are detrivores when they eat cooked food. From detritus, the chain proceeds to detrivores, then to carnivores and finally to top carnivores.
15. (a) Decomposers are aprotrophs which decompose the organic remains by secreting extracellular digestive enzymes. They are also known as mineralisers as they release minerals trapped in organic remains. So in the absence of microorganisms the flow of mineral will stop.
16. (d) Niche is specific part of habitat occupied by individuals of a species which is circumsribed by its range of tolerance, range of movement, microclimate, type of food and its availability, shelter, type of predator, and timing of activity. A habitat has several ecological niches and supports a number of species. An ecological niche is used by a single species. Two or more species cannot use the same niche despite having a mutualistic association. The abundances of a species population within its habitat is called niche density.
17. (b) When succession begins on an area which has not been previously being occupied by a community e.g. a new exposed rock area, sand dunes, new islands, deltas, shore or recent lava flow, it is known as primary succession. The first group of organisms (plants or animals) which become established in such an area is termed the pioneer community.
18. (d) Streaming body is a secondary aquatic adaption. It is found in animals that live permanently in water but most of them are amphibious in nature. The stream lined body consists of compression of head, body and tail into a curved stream lined form.

There is no protruberance over the body so that the animal can move easily through water. Parasitism is a relationship between two organisms of different species in which one organism called parasite obtains its food directly from another living organism called host.
In xeric adaptation perspiration is reduced to conserve water. Uricotelism is characteristic of terrestrial animals which excrete uric acid.
19. (a) Niche is specific part of habitat occupied by individuals of a species which is circumscribed by its range of tolerance, range of movement, microclimate, type of food and its availability, shelter, type of predator, and timing of activity.
A habitat has several ecological niches and supports a number of species. An ecological niche is used by a single species. Two or more species cannot use the same niche despite having a mutualistic association.
20. (a) Keystone species are those species which has significant and disproportionately large influence on the community structure and characteristics. It has often considerably low abundance and biomass as compared to dominant species. Removal of such species causes serious disruption in structure and function of community.
21. (b) 22. (d) 23. (a) 24. (b) 25. (c)
26. (c)
27. (c) Synecology is the branch of ecology that deals with the ecological interrelationships among communities of organisms.
28. (b) Ecotype includes species which are genetically not related. Sometimes it's also known as ecospecies, which describes a genetically distinct geographic variety, population or race within a species, which is adapted to specific environmental conditions.
29. (c) 30. (d)
31. (b) Biocoenosis, is an association of different organisms forming a closely integrated community. The term was proposed by Karl Mobius.
32. (c) 33. (a)
34. (a) Allopatric species are those which occur in different geographical area. While, sympatric species are those which occur within the same geographical areas.
35. (a) 36. (c) 37. (d) 38. (a) 39. (a)
40. (d) 41. (c) 42. (a) 43. (b) 44. (b)
45. (c) 46. (d) 47. (a)
48. (b) in a food chain the top consumers are carnivores while the organism which occupy the lowest level are the producers which produces their own food and are further utilized by other species known as consumers.
49. (d) Biotic potential is the ability of a population of living species to increase under ideal environmental conditions – sufficient food supply, no predators, and a lack of disease. An organism's rate of reproduction and the size of each litter are the primary determining factors for biotic potential.
50. (d) 51. (d)
52. (a) 53. (d) 54. (a) 55. (b) 56. (a)

57. (d) Intergenerational equity is a concept that says that humans 'hold the natural and cultural environment of the Earth in common both with other members of the present generation and with other generations, past and future. It means that we inherit the Earth from previous generations and have an obligation to pass it on in reasonable condition to future generations. The goal of sustainable development is Intergenerational equity.

58. (d) Biological diversity is used to refer to the total number of different species on Earth. A collection of this biodiversity would include human beings, Bengal tigers, sugar maples, oyster mushrooms, bacteria, and the millions of other living organisms found on Earth.

59. (b) Population dividend or Demographic dividend refers to a period - usually 20 to 30 years - when fertility rates fall due to significant reductions in child and infant mortality rates. It occurs when the proportion of working people in the total population is high because this indicates that more people have the potential to be productive and contribute to growth of the economy.

60. (d)

61. (a) An ecosystem includes all of the living things (plants, animals and organisms) in a given area, interacting with each other, and also with their non-living environments (weather, earth, sun, soil, climate, atmosphere).

62. (c) An ecosystem includes all of the living things (plants, animals and organisms) in a given area, interacting with each other, and also with their non-living environments (weather, earth, sun, soil, climate, atmosphere).

53. (c) The Gangetic dolphins have been declared as the National Aquatic Animal of India .River Dolphin is the National Aquatic Animal of India. The Ministry of Environment and Forests notified  the Ganges River Dolphin as the National Aquatic Animal on 18th May 2010. This mammal is also said to represent the purity of the holy Ganga as it can only survive in pure and fresh water.

64. (a) The tropical moist deciduous forests are found in Sahyadris, the north-eastern parts of the peninsula and along the foothills of the Himalayas. Teak and sal are found in these forests.

### EXERCISE-2

1. (c)
2. (c)  3. (a)  4. (c)  5. (d)  6. (c)
7. (a) Ecosystem is the dynamic community of living organism with physical environment. Thus, it comprises of both biotic and abiotic components. Solar energy is the ultimate source of energy in it, so is the main driving force. Dynamic energy transfers occur making it an open system. The autotrophs make the ecosystem's biotic components self-sufficient.

8. (c) Keystone species are not necessarily small sized though they put great effect on the environment. They play very critical role in maintaining the structure of an ecological community by affecting many other organisms. An ecosystem may experience a dramatic shift if a keystone species is removed, even though that species may be small part of the ecosystem by measures of biomass or productivity.

9. (c)  10. (d)  11. (c)

12. (b) In Parasitism, the parasite does not kill the host rather it derives its nutrition from the host in which the later is not affected. The interaction in which an organism kills the other for food is called Predation.

13. (c) Sir Arthur Tansley first used the term ecosystem in 1935.

14. (d) Circulation of energy in the biosphere ecosystem is unidirectional, it is derived from the sun and goes through one trophic level to another. The matter however circulated in cyclic manner.

15. (a) Biodegradable wastes should be separated and kept in green colour bins for garbage collectors.

16. (d) Brood parasites are organisms that use the strategy of brood parasitism, a kind of kleptoparasitism found among birds, fish or insects, involving the manipulation and use of host individuals either of the same (intraspecific brood-parasitism) or different species (interspecific brood-parasitism) to raise the young of the brood-parasite.

17. (b) Since a community comprises all the species that occur at a particular location, one of the most important things about communities is how the species interact with one another.
    Four different types of interactions between different species (inter specific interactions) have been identified:
    Competition -Two organisms mutually harm one another
    Predator–prey or parasite–host- One organism benefits, the other is harmed
    Mutualism- Both organisms benefit
    Commensalism- One organism benefits, the other is not affected

18. (a) A food chain illustrates the order in which a chain of organisms feed upon each other.
    A food chain is the sequence of who eats whom in a biological community to obtain nutrition.
    Sample:- Grassland Biome
    GRASS > GRASS HOPPER > RAT> SNAKE > HAWK

19. (b)  20. (c)       21. (c)       22.   (d)

23. (b) The branch of science which deals with the study of relation between plants and animals to each other along with their environments is called ecology.

24. (b) Abiotic components of ecosystem are the nonliving features of ecosystem on which the living organism depends. It is basically referred to the physical environment and its numerous interacting variables.

25. (d) Nitrogen cycle is necessary because Plants cannot absorb nitrogen directly instead it is absorbed in the form of nitrate. Nitrogen cycle have 5 important processes i.e. fixation, ammonification, nitrification, assimilation and denitrification.

26. **(a)** Nitrification is the process of conversion of ammonia.

27. **(c)** The source of ozone is the oxygen in the atmosphere. Ozone layer protects the living being from the UV radiation which reaches the earth.

28. **(d)** Oxygen is a very important element for the existence of all flora and fauna. Atmosphere contains 21% of oxygen. The main source of oxygen is atmosphere. Plants and animals absorb oxygen through respiration either from water or air and leaves through photosynthesis. In respiration process some of the oxygen returns to the atmosphere in the form of carbon dioxide and water vapour. During the process of photosynthesis gaseous oxygen is released completing the oxygen cycle. The source of ozone is the oxygen in the atmosphere. Ozone layer protects the living being from the UV radiation which reaches the earth. By burning fossil fuels man decreases the amount of oxygen in the atmosphere and increases the carbon dioxide content.

29. **(d)** The oxygen concentration in atmosphere is 21%. The oxygen cycle is effected by human activities such as running automobiles and consumption of fossil fuels which release more carbon dioxide in the atmosphere.

30. **(b)** Process of photosynthesis of carbon dioxide is explained in following steps:
- Through the process of photosynthesis carbon enters into living world in the form of carbon dioxide.
- This organic compound (food) is then passed from the producers to the consumers (herbivores & carnivores).
- By the process of respiration or decomposition of dead bodies of plant and animals by decomposers this carbon returns back to the surrounding medium.
- Recycling of carbon is also done by the burning of fossil fuels.

31. **(a)** There is a continuous exchange of water between living organisms, air, land and sea.

32. **(a)** Phosphorus cycle is also called as sedimentary cycle because the main reservoir is rocks and the earth crust.

33. **(d)** Phosphorous is not found in atmosphere because at normal temperature and pressure phosphorous is at a liquid state.

34. **(b)** Phosphorous enters into the soil through water.

35. **(a)** Organisms living in tropical regions are called regions are called mesotherms, in temperate regions are called regions are called hekisthotherms.

36. **(c)** Humidity is the water vapor or water in gaseous form present in the atmosphere. It can also be defined as molecules of water/unit volume. It is measured by Hygrometer.

37. **(c)** Components of an ecosystem include Biotic and Abiotic.

38. **(b)** The cycles (carbon and nitrogen cycle) involves phases of weathering of rocks, uptake and storage by organisms and return to the pool of soil, the atmosphere or ocean sediments.

39. **(a)** Boreal or taiga forests forests are found in Asia, Europe, Siberia and North America where there are shorter and warmer summers with longer winters.

40. **(a)** Tropical or Rainforests are mostly found in the equatorial belt of the plant.

41. **(d)** Tropical or Rainforests are found in the equatorial belt of the plant. There is no winter season in these forests, sunlight fall for 12 hours and seasons is mostly rainy or dry with small change in the temperature.

42. **(c)** Desert covers one fifth of the planet.

43. **(c)** Marine lives are the plants, animals and living organisms which are found oceans, lakes, ponds etc.

44. **(b)** The water that has less content of salt is called fresh water.

45. **(b)** Atmospheric temperature of the place depends upon the slope, altitude, latitude, topography, etc. temperature lowers as we go from equator to poles – tropical, subtropical, temperate and arctic.

46. **(c)** Three-fourth of the earth surface is covered by water but less than 3% is fresh water used for human consumption. Of the total fresh water available, Ice-cap has highest share of 2% followed by ground water 0.68%.

47. **(b)** Herbivores and other animals obtain phosphorus from plants. There is no respiratory release of phosphorus into atmosphere.

48. **(a)** Hydrological cycle is the continuous and balanced process of evaporation, precipitation, transpiration and runoff of water.

49. **(d)** The Ramsar definition of wetlands is fairly wide, including "areas of marine water the depth of which at low tide does not exceed six meters" as well as fish ponds, rice paddies and salt pans. wetlands can be freshwater as well. Freshwater wetlands are not connected to the ocean. They can be found along the boundaries of streams, lakes, ponds or even in large shallow holes that fill up with rainwater. Freshwater wetlands may stay wet all year long, or the water may evaporate during the dry season.

50. **(d)** Humidity is of 3 types: Specific, Absolute, Relative

51. **(d)** Steppe is found in low latitudes and middle latitudes. Prairies are humid and densely covered tall grasslands. Savanna are the areas of thick high grasses.

52. **(d)** (i) The Bureau of Energy Efficiency is an agency of the Government of India, under the Ministry of Power created in March 2002 under the provisions of the nation's 2001 Energy Conservation Act. The agency's function is to develop programs which will increase the conservation and efficient use of energy in India. The government has proposed to make it mandatory for all appliances in India to have ratings by the BEE starting in January 2010.
(ii) According to centre for science and environment (CSE), both 1 and 3 are correct. There is only option (d) whether such combination is possible.
Ref:*http://cseindia.org/content/energy-efficient-appliances*

53. **(c)**
- Coral reefs are found in tropical and subtropical regions. Most of them are located between Tropics of Capricorn and Cancer, so yes #1 is indeed right.
- According to UNEP, % of world area covered by each region: Indonesia 18%, Australia: 17% and Philippines: 9% so collectively that'll be more than 33%. Hence #2 is right.
- Coral reefs include a wide range of diversity with 32 of the 34 animal phyla present, in contrast to only 9 phyla represented in tropical rainforest. So, #3 is also right. Thus, answer is D: 1, 2 and 3

Environmental issues are harmful effects of human activity on the biophysical environment. Environmentalism, a social and environmental movement, addresses environmental issues through advocacy, education and activism.

Our environment is constantly changing, which no one can deny. With these great environment changes, it becomes highly important for us to become increasingly aware of the environmental problems as well. With a monumental inundation of natural disasters, warming and cooling periods, different types of weather forms and much more, people should be aware of what types of environmental problems our earth is facing.

Our planet is on the verge of a severe environmental crisis. Current environmental problems make us susceptible to disasters and tragedies, now as well as in the future. We are in a phase of planetary emergency, with environmental problems blooming around us. Unless we address the various issues proactively and sincerely we are surely going to be wrecked with these disasters. All the current environmental problems need an urgent attention.

## DIFFERENT ENVIRONMENTAL ISSUES AND ITS EFFECT ON CLIMATE

Environmental issues are increasing day by day and it has an adverse effect on climate. Some of the Environmental issues are discussed below:

### Global Warming

Atmoshpheric gases like carbondioxide ($CO_2$), nitrogen oxide ($NO_2$) methane ($CH_4$), chlorofluro carbons (CFCs) and water vapour have the ability of trapping the outgoing radiation (infrared) from the surface of earth. Such trapped infrared radiation by the earth's surface cannot pass through these gases present in the atmosphere and exhibits the thermal energy or heat in the atmosphere. As a result the temperature of atmosphere is on rise globally. The phenomenon of increase in temperature i.e. heating in green houses are known as green house effect. The increase in the temperature of earth's surface is known as global warming. Global warming leads to rising temperatures of the oceans and the earth's surface causing melting of polar ice caps, rise in sea levels and also unnatural patterns of precipitation such as flash *floods*, excessive snow or desertification.

### Effects of Global Warming/Climate Change

The Intergovernmental Panel on Climate Change (IPCC) was established in 1988 by the World Meteorological Organization (WMO) and the United Nations Environment Programme (UNEP) in recognition of the problem of global warming. IPCC has estimated the following effects of global warming:

- Earth's temperature will rise by 1-30°C in next few decades, leading to extreme weather changes (heat waves, hurricanes and severe winters), changes in ocean currents and marine life. The largest glacier chain in the tropics is melting fast because of rising temperatures and peaks are turning brown. This trend is endangering future water supplies. Glaciers serve agriculture, hydel plants and feed rivers that supply water to the sprawling cities and shanty towns on Peru's bone-dry Pacific coast. **Quelccaya**, in southern Peru, the world's largest tropical ice-cap, is retreating at about 200 feet per year, up from 20 feet per year in the 1960s. **Lonnie Thompson,** a leading glacier expert of Ohio State University, monitoring glacier retreat on the Andes, Himalayas and Kilimanjaro, said that the rate of ice loss in glaciers all over the world is actually accelerating.

- If $CO_2$ concentration doubles, Earth's temperature may rise by 50°C. Coastal areas will see a rise in water levels by 0.5-5.0 feet due to melting of mountain glaciers, polar ice-caps, etc.

- Islands like **Maldives** would get submerged. In 1999, two uninhabited islands in the South Pacific (**Tebua Tarawa and Abanuea**) were submerged by rising sea levels, and two neighboring inhabited islands (**Kiribati** *and* **Tuvalu**) are on the brink of submersion as well.
- The biggest glacier in the **Peruvian Andes** was retreating by 5 meters per year some 20 years ago; today it is shrinking by 33 meters per year. The second largest glacier on Earth, the Greenland ice sheet, is thinning at an unprecedented rate of one meter each year.
- The Arctic Sea ice has thinned by 40% in the last two decades, while Mount Everest is losing height at the rate of 1.5 meters per year.

As global warming's, terrifying threat increases, our planet's nations come together at the Paris Climate Conference (2015) to fight for our future.

In the wake of the Paris conference America must lead the fight against global warming. We need to embrace clean energy and leave our dirty fossil fuels in the ground.

Here are five key steps the U.S. leaders should take to protect our planet.

**(i) Suppost a just, ambitions and binding international climate treaty:**

Under the paris framework and beyond, the U.S. should back efforts to end fossil fuel use in developed nations by 2050.

**(ii) Strengthen the clean power plan:**

The U.S. needs to move rapidly away from all fossil fuels and toward wildlife-friendly sources of clean energy.

**(iii) Cut pollution from airoplanes and other unregulated sources:**

The Environmental protection Agency acknowledges that airoplane pollution endangers our climate.

**(iv) Halt new fossil fuel development in America's oceans and on our public lands:**

Ending new fossil fuel leasing on public lands and offshore areas controlled by the U.S. would keep upto 450 billion tons of green house gases from polluting the atmosphere, according, to a recent analysis prepared for the centre by scientists at *Ecoshift*.

**(v) Crack down on fossil fuel exports and transport**

We must halt the dangerous push to send America's dirty fossil fuels abroad.

## Global Warming -Impacts

- Rise in Sea level
- Changes in rainfall patterns.
- Increased likelihood of extreme events such as heat wave, flooding, hurricanes, etc.
- Melting of the ice caps.
- Melting of glaciers.
- Widespread vanishing of animal populations due to habitat loss.
- Spread of disease (like malaria, etc).
- Bleaching of Coral Reefs.
- Loss of Plankton due to warming of seas.

## Control of Global Warming

- Cutting down the use of fossil fuel
- Improving efficiency of energy fuel
- Reducing deforestation
- Planting the trees
- Slowing down the growth of human population
- Reduction in the emission of green- house – gases into the atmosphere.

# Green House Effect

The earth gets energy from the sun in the form of sunlight. The earth's surface absorbs some of this energy and heats up. That's why the surface of a road can feel hot even after the sun has gone down because it has absorbed a lot of energy from the sun. The earth cools down by giving off a different form of energy, called infrared radiation. But before all this radiation can escape to outer space, greenhouse gases in the atmosphere absorb some of it, which makes the atmosphere warmer. As the atmosphere gets warmer, it makes the earth's surface warmer, too. Without this Greenhouse effect the earth would be at least 30 degrees cooler, in which life would not exist.

## Greenhouse Gases

A greenhouse gas (GHG) is a gas in an atmosphere that absorbs and emits radiation within the thermal infrared range. This process is the fundamental cause of the greenhouse effect. The primary greenhouse gases in Earth's atmosphere are *water vapour, carbon dioxide, methane, nitrous oxide, ozone,* and *chlorofluorocarbons*.

- **Water vapour** contributes to 36-72% of Greenhouse effect.
- **Carbon Dioxide** ($CO_2$) arises from burning fossil fuels and as a result of deforestation. It contributes to 9-26% of Greenhouse effect. It is the primary greenhouse gas emitted through human activities.
- **Methane** ($CH_4$), also called *"Marsh gas"*, arises from rice paddies, wetlands, enteric fermentation in cattle, burning of wood, and landfills. It is responsible for about 4-9% of Greenhouse effect.
- **Nitrous Oxide** ($NO_2$) contributes (5%) which arises from coal burning, biomass burning, and breakdown of chemical fertilizers.
- **Chlorofluorocarbons** (*CFCs*) and their replacements (15%) are 1000 times more heat absorbent than carbon dioxide. They reach the atmosphere from *refrigeration* and *air conditioning, aerosol sprays*, and *foam packaging industry*.
- **Ozone contributes** to 3-7% of Greenhouse effect. The largest net source of tropospheric ozone is influx from the stratosphere. Large amounts of ozone are also produced in the troposphere by photochemical reactions, the amounts increasing with high levels of air pollution.

Unfortunately, recent human activities such as burning fossil fuels to run automobiles, heat homes and businesses, and power factories are causing increased concentrations of greenhouse gases, thereby resulting in more heat being trapped. The planet is losing less heat and, as a result we are beginning to experience Global Warming.

Estimates indicate there has been a 25% increase in $CO_2$, concentration in the last 100 years and this is expected to double in the next 50 years, e.g. **Brazil** alone contributes billions of tons of $CO_2$, every year due to *deforestation*.

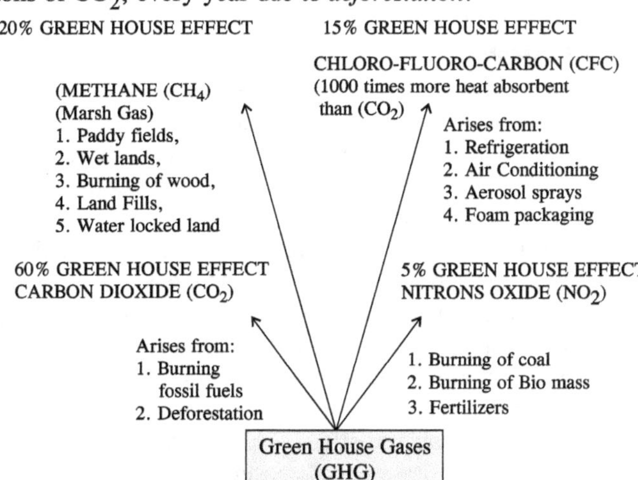


## Ozone Depletion

**Ozone** $(O_3)$ is a gas found throughout the atmosphere, but most highly concentrated in the stratosphere, between *10 and 50 km* above the sea level, where it is known as the *"Ozone layer"*.

- This Ozone layer forms a *protective shield* for the earth from the harmful *ultra-violet radiation* from outer space, particularly *UV-B* rays which affects *DNA molecules*, causing damage to the outer surface of plants and animals and also marine life. In humans it causes skin cancer, eye cataracts and is a general immuno-suppressant.

- *"Ozone Holes"* were first discovered over *Antarctica* by the British Antarctica Survey in *1983*. Levels of ozone are dropping very fast, resulting in parts of the layer becoming thin and 'holes' developing because only a small percentage of O, gets naturally replenished every year.

- In **1974, Mario Molina** and Sherwood Roland of the **University of California** discovered that a group of synthetic chemical substances known as *CFCs* and *HCFCs* destroy ozone in the stratosphere. These chemicals are inert, non-flammable, non-toxic, and lighter than air and can remain intact for years. They contain Chlorine and Fluorine, common being CFC-ll, CFC-12, CFC-22 and CFC- 13.

- **'Halons'** containing **'Bromine'** and used in the fire-fighting industry, are 100 times more potent than CFCs.CFCs are commonly used in Air-conditioners and the Refrigeration industry (Freon gas), aerosol propellants (in perfumes and deodorants), in the foam packaging industry (Styropor, Thermocol) and as solvents for greases and glues.

- The ozone (O3) found in upper part of the atmosphere, i.e. Stratosphere, is Good ozone, since, it acts as a shield for absorbing UV-radiations from sun. The UV rays are highly injurious to living organisms. The DNA and Proteins of living organisms preferentially absorb UV rays. These high energy rays break the chemical bonds of these polymers. The ozone that is formed in lower atmosphere, i.e., Troposphere, is Bad ozone, since, it harms plants and animals.

- Compounds like Carbon Tetrachloride and Methyl Chloroform are also found to release Chlorine (Halogens) which ultimately destroy the stratospheric Ozone.

- Du Pont (USA) and ICI (UK) have developed certain substitutes like HFC (Hydrofluorocarbon) and HCFC (Hydro-Chloro-Fluoro Carbon), e.g. HCFC-123 which contain less Chlorine than CFC, but these are not effective, permanent solutions.

- Cheaper alternatives for refrigeration being developed are Propane and Ammonia as coolants, which are completely environment friendly.

## Unit for Ozone Thickness

The thickness of ozone in a column of air, from the ground to the top of the atmosphere, is measured in Dobson units. (1- Dobson unit = 10 μm thickness of ozone under standard temperature and pressure.) The term Dobson is after the name of Gordon Dobson of Oxford University. When the ozone thickness becomes less than 220 DU it is considered as thinning of ozone or the ozone hole.

## Deforestation

The process of clearance of forest by burning or logging is called deforestation. The main reasons for deforestation are trees or derived charcoal are used as, or sold, for fuel or as a commodity, while cleared land is used as grassland for livestock, plantations of commodities, and settlements. Deforested areas usually sustain extensive adverse soil erosion and regularly damage into wasteland.

**Causes of deforestation**

There are numerous causes of deforestation such as
(i) Expansion of farming land
(ii) Logging and fuel wood
(iii) Overgrazing
(iv) Fires
(v) Mining
(vi) urbanization/Industrialization and Infra-structure.
(vii) Air Pollution
(viii) Wars and role of military
(ix) Tourism
(x) Over population and poverty
(xi) land rights, land tenure and inequitable land distribution resources
(xii) Economic, i.e. development/land conversion value, fiscal policies, etc.
(xiii) Under valuing the forest
(xiv) Corruption and political cause

---

### Jhum Cultivation (Slash and Burn Agriculture)

In North- East states of India Jhum cultivation has been responsible for deforestation. The farmers cut-down the trees of forest and burn the plant – remains. The 'land' so developed is use for farming or cattle grazing , and 'ash' is used as fertilizer. After cultivation, the area is left for several years so as to allow its recovery. The farmers then move on to other forest areas and repeat the process.

During earlier days of Jhum cultivation enough time-gap was given for land – recovery from the effect of cultivation. Later, with increasing population , and repeated cultivation, the recovery phase was done away, and this resulted with deforestation.

---

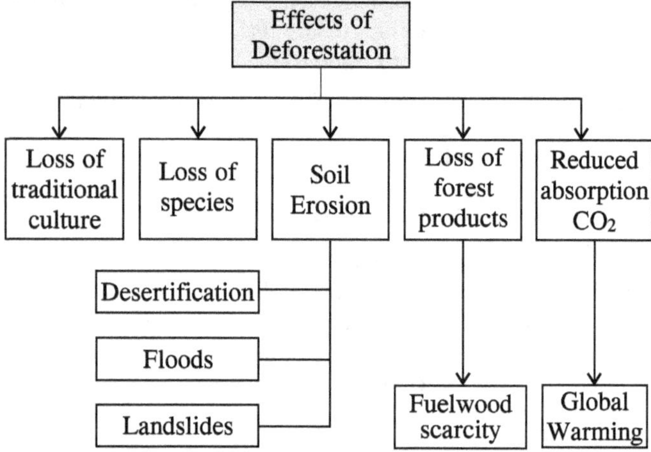


## Strategies to reduce deforestation

Strategies to reduce deforestation should be a combination of pro-active role of national, state, municipalities, civil societies and private sector in the following ways-

(i) Reducing Population growth

(ii) Reducing emissions from deforestation and forest degradation

(iii) Increase the area and standard of management of protected areas

(iv) Increase the area of forest reserved for timber production

(v) launch the mass awareness programme regarding value of forest.

(vi) Encouraging substitutes

(vii) Increase area of forest plantation

(viii) Government initiatives through policies and action-plan

(ix) Participatory forest management and rights

(x) Increase investment in research, education and extension

(xi) Improve the information base and monitoring

## Reforestation

It is the process of restoring a forest. Though the reforestation may occur naturally in a deforested area , but it is speeded up by planting the forest trees.

(*Please remember that* the management of forests for the benefit of the entire ecosystem is called **Silviculture**. The **Forestry**, on the other hand, is the practice of growing and managing forest trees for the production of commercial timber).

# POLLUTION

Pollution is an undesirable change in physical, chemical or biological characteristics of air, land, water or soil. The agents that bring about such an undesirable change are called Pollutants.

To improve the quality of environment (air, water and soil), and control pollution, the Government of India passed Environment (Protection) Act in 1986.

## Air Pollution

Air pollution is defined as the presence of any liquid, gaseous or solid substance which includes noise and radi active radiation in the atmosphere in such concentration that may be directly and indirectly injurious to human or other living organisms, plant, property or interferes with the normal environmental process.

The main issue among environmentalists and researchers especially in developed countries is *air pollution*.

- The main pollutants of air pollution are *particulate matter*, *PAHs*, *lead*, ground-level *ozone, heavy metals, Sulphur dioxide, benzene, carbon monoxide* and *nitrogen dioxide*.

- Air pollution is also responsible for climate change due to the higher greenhouse effect, acid rain, and the depletion of the ozone layer that constitute important global environmental problems.

- Air pollution is the main reason of ill health and death by natural and man-made sources.

- Tobacco smoke, house cleaning items, insecticides industries, automobiles, power generation, combustion of solid fuels for cooking, poor maintenance of cars and other automobile, etc. are the main cause of air pollution.

- Air pollution can be of two types: *indoor* and *outdoor*.

- *Indoor air pollution* is restricted to buildings only. It is the amount of chemical, biological and physical contaminants in the air inside a building. Building materials, central heating and cooling devices, painting colours, stoves, gas heater, and tobacco smoke, etc. are the examples of indoor air pollution.

- Release of several air pollutants into the atmosphere which causes severe threat to living organisms or upsetting the functioning of environment is called outdoor air pollution.

## Outdoor air pollution

- Out door air pollution constitutes of the air pollution which is caused out side one buildings for example, burning of garbage, vehicles, etc.

## Contributors of Pollutants

- There are natural pollutants of air like animal decay.

- Volcanic eruptions release more sulphur fumes than all power plants and all industries in the world.

- Lightning bolts create nitrogen oxides just as automobiles and industrial furnaces do.

- Trees emit hydrocarbons called **terpenes** causing bluish haze.

- The major cause of air pollution, at least in the metro cities, is the increasing number of automobiles.

## Effects

- There is mounting evidence that our whole planet is affected by pollution. The South Pole seems fairly clean because 90 % of earth's population lives in northern hemisphere. Yet in 1985 scientists detected a major hole in protective ozone screen over Antarctica.
- The North Pole, on the other hand, resembles a cool town.

In winter when the Arctic is tilted into long nights and the sun cannot generate cleansing winds and precipitation, the largest single mass of pollution sits atop the globe like a dirty cap composed of mixture of gases and particles, sulphates and soot.

- Tracing pollutants has become a vital necessity as air currents do not follow political boundaries.

## Pollutants and their Effects

| Sr. No. | Pollutant | Origin | Effect |
|---|---|---|---|
| 1. | Arsenic (As) | Coal, oil furnaces, glass factories | Lung and skin cancer |
| 2. | Benzene ($C_6H_6$) | Refineries, motor vehicles | Leukemia |
| 3. | Cadmium (Cd) | Smelters, coals, oil furnaces | Damage to lung, kidney, bones |
| 4. | Chlorine (Cl) | Chemical Industries, volcanic activities | Causes irritation |
| 5. | Carbon monoxide (CO) | Motor vehicles, smelters, coal steel plants | Starves body of oxygen, damages heart |
| 6. | Fluoride (F) | Smelters, steel plants | Mottles teeth in children |
| 7. | Hydrocarbons | Unburnt gasolene fumes, motor vehicles | Combines with nitrogen oxides in sunlight to form smog, causes irritation in eyes and nose |
| 8. | Formaldehyde (HCHO) | Chemical plants | Allergenic, carcinogenic, headaches, burning sensation in the throat, and can aggravate *asthma symptoms* |
| 9. | HCl (Hydrogen chloride) | Incinerators | Irritates eyes and lungs |
| 10. | Hydrogen fluoride (HF) | Fertilizer plants Smelters | Irritates skin, eyes, mucous membrane |
| 11. | Mercury (Hg) | Coal, smelters oil furnaces | Tremors, nerve troubles |
| 12. | Nitric acid ($HNO_3$) | Formed from $NO_2$ causes acid rain | Respiratory diseases |
| 13. | Nitrous acid ($HNO_3$) | Formed from $NO_2$ and water vapour | Respiratory disease |
| 14. | Hydrogen sulphide ($H_2S$) | Refineries, Pulp mills | Nausea, irritates eyes |
| 15. | Sulphuric acid ($H_2SO_4$) | Formed from $SO_2$ in sunlight with | Respiratory diseases hydroxyl ions |
| 16. | Manganese (Mn) | Steel and sulphur dioxide power plants | Parkinson's diseases |
| 17. | Nickel (Ni) | Smelters, coal, oil | Lung Cancer furnaces |
| 18. | Nitric Oxide (NO) | Motor Vehicles, coal, oil furnaces | Oxidizes to $NO_2$ |
| 19. | Nitrogen dioxide ($NO_2$) | Formed in Sunlight from NO | Bronchitis Loss of resistance to influenza forms Ozone |
| 20. | Ozone ($O_3$) | Ground level ozone formed from nitrogen oxides ($NO_x$) and volatile organic compounds (VOCs) | Asthma, irritates eyes sunlight from nitrogen oxides and hydrocarbons |
| 21. | Lead (Pb) | Motor vehicles, high smelters | Brain damage |
| 22. | Silicon Tetra fluoride ($SiF_4$) | Chemical plants | Lung diseases |
| 23. | Sulfur dioxide ($SO_2$) | Smelters Coal, Oil furnaces | Irritates eyes, breathing problems |

## Prevention of air pollution

Air pollution can be reduced with the help of-

(i) using smokeless sources of energy like smokeless stoves, biogas, solar and wind energy.

(ii) using devices for filtering smoke in chimneys of factories and power houses.

(iii) Planting more trees.

(iv) Locating industries away from residential areas.

(v) Strictly checking pollution levels in automobiles exhaust emission by using catalytic converter.

(vi) Using CNG.

### Auto Fuel policy

The vehicular emission norms were introduced in India in year 2000 and in the same year **Bharat Stage norms** were adapted. The **Bharat stage II**, equivalent to **Euro II** norms, was made applicable in 11- cities, i.e. Agra, Ahmadabad, Bengaluru, Chennai, Delhi, Hyderabad, Kanpur, Kolkata, Mumbai, Pune and Surat. It had to be applicable to all automobiles throughout the country from April 1st 2005.

From 1st April 2005, all automobiles had to meet **Euro III** emission specifications in the above 11- cities.

By 1st April 2010, they had to meet **Euro IV** norms.

The rest of the country, by 2010, had to meet **Euro III** emission norms for automobiles and the fuel.

According to the norms of **Euro III** the sulphur was to be controlled at 150 ppm (parts per million) in petrol, and 350 ppm in diesel. The aromatic hydrocarbon were to be regulated at 42 % of the fuel. The goal was to reduce sulphur to 50 ppm and hydrocarbon to 35 % of the fuel.

According to the corresponding fuel the vehicular engines were also needed to be upgraded.\ **Bharat Stage- IV (BS-IV)** in certain States and Union Territories is to be introduced on **1st April, 2016,** and in the rest of country on **1st April, 2017.**

In March 2017, supreme court of India banned the registration of BS-III vehicles in New Delhi.

**BS-V** emission norms for vehicles across the entire country will be implemented from 2019.

**BS-VI** for four wheelers will be enforced in India from year **2023.**

## National Air Quality Index

National Air Quality Index was launched by the Prime Minister in April, 2015 starting with 14 cities to dis-seminate air quality information. The AQI has six categories of air quality, viz Good, Satisfactory, Moderately Polluted, Poor, Very Poor and Severe with distinct colour scheme. Each of these categories is associated with likely health impacts. AQI considers eight pollutants (PM10, PM 2.5, $NO_2$, $SO_2$, CO, $O_3$, $NH_3$ and Pb) for which (up to 24-hourly averaging period) National Ambient Air Quality Standards are prescribed.

### AQI Category, Pollutants and Health Breakpoints

| AQI Category (Range) | $PM_{10}$ 24-hr | $PM_{2.5}$ 24-hr | $NO_2$ 24-hr | $O_3$ 24-hr | CO 8-hr ($mg/m^3$) | $SO_2$ 24-hr | $NH_3$ 24-hr | Pb 24-hr |
|---|---|---|---|---|---|---|---|---|
| **Good (0-50)** | 0-50 | 0-30 | 0-40 | 0-50 | 0-1.0 | 0-40 | 0-200 | 0-0.5 |
| **Satisfactory (51-100)** | 51-100 | 31-60 | 41-80 | 51-100 | 1.1-2.0 | 41-80 | 201-400 | 0.5-1.0 |
| **Moderately polluted (101-200)** | 101-250 | 61-90 | 81-180 | 101-168 | 2.1-10 | 81-380 | 401-800 | 1.1-2.0 |
| **Poor (201-300)** | 251-350 | 91-120 | 181-280 | 169-208 | 10-17 | 381-800 | 801-1200 | 2.1-3.0 |
| **Very poor (301-400)** | 351-430 | 121-250 | 281-400 | 209-748* | 17-34 | 801-1600 | 1200-1800 | 3.1-3.5 |
| **Severe (401-500)** | 430+ | 250+ | 400+ | 748+* | 34+ | 1600+ | 1800+ | 3.5+ |

*One hourly monitoring (for mathematical calculations only)*

# Water Pollution

- Water pollution is a kind of pollution which involves the contamination of water sources or bodies on which several aquatic animals depends on for their life support.
- Polluted water comprises of Industrial discharged wastes, sewage water, and rain water pollution.
- Quality of soil and vegetation is affected by the polluted water. Pollutants in water comprise a extensive kind of chemicals, pathogens, and physical chemistry or sensory changes. Many of the chemical substances are toxic or even dangerous.
- Pathogens can produce water borne disease in humans and animals.
- Polluted water is discharged in water polluting the aquatic flora and fauna.
- Washing clothes near lakes and rivers is one of the reason of water pollution since, detergents cause a condition called **"Eutrophication"** which blocks sunlight from entering inside that water body thus reducing oxygen standards in the water and causing an inhabitable environment.

## Types of Water Pollutants

- **Physical pollutants** – e.g. Hot water, Oil spill
- **Chemical pollutants** – e.g. Inorganic compounds (Nitrates, phosphates and fluorides, etc.) Biocides and Heavy metals (Hg, As, Pb, Cd etc.)
- **Biological pollutants** – e.g. Bacteria, protozoans, viruses, helminthes and other pathogens.

All domestic sewage and industrial effluents, without being treated, are dumped into nearby river.

## Types of Water Pollution based on causes & pollutants

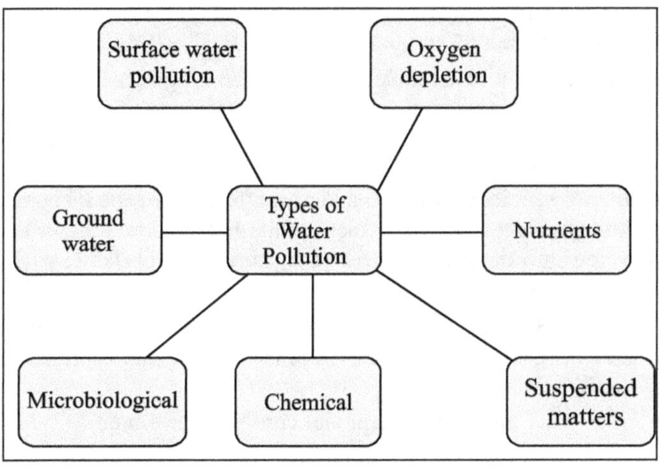


## (I) Sewage

Even 0.1 % of impurities by sewage, makes the water unfit for human use. These impurities of domestic sewage may include

- Suspended solids – e.g., Sand, silt and clay
- Colloidal materials – e.g., Faecal matter, bacteria and fibres of cloth and paper
- Dissolved materials – e.g. Nutrients like Nitrates, phosphates, sodium, calcium and ammonia etc.

The solids from such sewage are easy to remove by physical treatment but the removal of nutrients, toxic metal ions and organic compounds is difficult. (In municipal waste, the detergent residues have excess phosphates, and the organic remains have excess nitrates.)

The presence of a large amount of nutrients in water also causes excessive growth of planktons or free floating algae to produce **Algal bloom**. Such algal blooms

- Deteriorate the quality of water
- Cause the mortality of fishes
- Imparts distinct colour to water bodies
- May be extremely toxic to human beings and aquatic animals

## (II) Industrial Wastes

Unlike domestic sewage, the waste water from the industries, like chemical industry, paper industry, petroleum industry and metal extraction and process industry, often contain toxic substances like, heavy metals and variety of Organic compounds (e.g., DDT).

Some toxic substances of industrial waste- water may undergo **biological magnification (Biomagnification)** in the aquatic food chain. Since such toxic substances cannot be metabolized or excreted. They get accumulated in the organisms and from there they pass on to  the next higher trophic level.

The increase in the concentration of the toxicant at successive trophic levels is called **Biomagnification**. This phenomenon is well known for DDT and Mercury.

The high concentration of DDT in fish – eating birds due to biomagnifications of DDT in aquatic food chain has resulted in

- Disturbance in the Calcium metabolism
- Thinning of egg –shell, causing premature hatching of chickens
- Decline in birds- population

## (III) Agricultural Sources

- Fertilizers contain major plant nutrients such as nitrogen, phosphorus and potassium.
- Excess fertilizers may reach the ground water by leaching or may be mixed with surface water of rivers, lakes and ponds by runoff and drainage.
- Pesticides include insecticides, fungicides, herbicides, nematicides, rodenticides and soil fumigants.
- They contain a wide range of chemicals such as chlorinated hydrocarbons, organophosphates, metallic salts, carbonates, thiocarbonates, derivatives of acetic acid etc.' Many of the pesticides are non-degradable and their residues have long life.
- The animal excreta such as dung, wastes from poultry farms, piggeries and slaughter houses etc. reach the water though run off and surface leaching during rainy season.

## (IV) Global Warming

- An increase in earth's temperature due to greenhouse effect results in global warming. It increases the water temperature and result in death of aquatic animals and marine species which later results in water pollution.

## (V) Radioactive Waste

- Nuclear energy is produced using nuclear fission or fusion. The element that is used in production of nuclear energy is Uranium which is highly toxic chemical. The nuclear waste that is produced by radioactive material needs to be disposed off to prevent any nuclear accident. Nuclear waste can have serious environmental hazards if not disposed off properly. Few major accidents have already taken place in Russia and Japan.

## (VI) Urban Development

- As population has grown, so has the demand for housing, food and cloth. As more cities and towns are developed, they have resulted in increase use of fertilizers to produce more food, soil erosion due to deforestation, increase in construction activities, inadequate sewer collection and treatment, landfills as more garbage is produced, increase in chemicals from industries to produce more materials.

## (VII) Leakage from the Landfills

- Landfills are nothing but huge pile of garbage that produces awful smell and can be seen across the city. When it rains, the landfills may leak and the leaking landfills can pollute the underground water with large variety of contaminants.

## (VIII) Animal Waste

- The waste produce produce by animals is washed away into the rivers when it rains. It gets mixed up with other harmful chemicals and causes various water borne diseases like cholera, diarrhea, jaundice, dysentery and typhoid.

## (IX) Underground Storage Leakage

- Transportation of coal and other petroleum products through underground pipes is well known. Accidentals leakage may happen anytime and may cause damage to environment and result in soil erosion.

## (X) Burning of Fossil Fuels

- Fossil fuels like coal and oil when burnt produce substantial amount of ash in the atmosphere. The particles which contain toxic chemicals when mixed with water vapor result in acid rain. Also, carbon dioxide is released from burning of fossil fuels which result in global warming.

## (XI) Mining Activities

- Mining is the process of crushing the rock and extracting coal and other minerals from underground. These elements when extracted in the raw form contains harmful chemicals and can increase the amount of toxic elements when mixed up with water which may result in health problems. Mining activities emit several metal waste and sulphides from the rocks and is harmful for the water.

## (XII) Marine Dumping

- The garbage produce by each household in the form of paper, aluminum, rubber, glass, plastic, food if collected and deposited into the sea in some countries. These items take from 2 weeks to 200 years to decompose. When such items enters the sea, they not only cause water pollution but also harm animals in the sea.

## (XIII) Hot Water

Another important category of pollutant is heated waste water, released from electricity generating units, like thermal power plants. Such thermal water damages aquatic fauna and flora **(Thermal Pollution)**. It also reduces the number of temperature sensitive organisms. Besides, the thermal waste water also reduces the amount of dissolved gases. However, in extremely cold area, such water may enhance the growth of plants and fishes.

There is ageing of water bodies in nature which affect the aquatic ecosystem. Such natural ageing of a water body due to biological enrichment of its water, leading to depletion of species diversity, is called **Eutrophication**.

## (XIV) Oil Spills / Pollution

The oil spill is an accidental discharge of petroleum in ocean or estuaries causing *oil pollution* of marine ecosystem.

The oil exploration, oil refineries and offshore oil mining contribute to oil pollution affecting planktons, fish and marine birds. The oil, being lighter than water, spreads as a thin film which is called an **'Oil slick'**. The oil slick is also harmful to coral reefs.

# Ecological Sanitation (Eco San)

Generally a lot of water is required for the removal of wastes. We use tremendous amount of water to flush the toilet.

The EcoSan is a sustainable system for handling human excreta or faecal matter by using dry 'Composting Toilets'. Such toilets are very useful for the rural areas where sewer systems are not possible and water supplies are very limited. These toilets are hygienic, efficient, practical and cost effective for the disposal of human waste. With this method the human excreta can be recycled into natural fertilizer (a resource) which lessens the load of chemical fertilizers.

These EcoSan recycle water and organic nutrients of human wastes back into the local environment. Thus such sanitation systems

- Protect the environment and conserve the water
- Prevent diseases by minimizing the entry of pathogens in to water cycle, and thus promote health.
- Recycle the nutrients and organic matter

## Diseases caused by Water Pollution

The most common water pollution diseases involve digestive system and infections diseases, it may cause many others like-

(a) *Infections diseases caused by pathogens* from animal fecal origins involving:- Typhoid, Giardiasis, Amoebiasis, Ascariasis, Hookworm

(b) *Diseases caused by polluted beach water* :- Gastroenteritis, Diarrhea, Encephalitis stomach craps and aches, vomiting, Hepatites, Respiratory infections

(c) Liver damage and cancer caused by chlorinated solvents, MTBE.

(d) Kidney damage caused by a series of chemicals found in contaminated water.

(e) Neurological problems due to pesticides (eg. DDT)

(f) Reproductive and endocrine damage

(g) Bathing in polluted water causes rashes, ear aches and pink eyes.

Water can be treated by many ways, i.e. denitrification, industrial treatment, Septic tank and Ozone waste water treatment. Raw sewage should be treated in water treatment plant before releasing it in environment. In water treatment plant sewage goes through many chambers and chemical processes which reduce its toxicity. Denitrification is an ecological method to prevent the discharge of nitrates in soil, and stops ground water pollution with nutrients. Septic tanks treat sewage at the place where it is located and used to treat sewage from an individual building. Untreated sewage from a property streams into the septic tank and the solids are separated from the liquid. Breaking of pollutants into water sources is done by ozone generator. By using Ultraviolet radiation and Electric discharge field oxygen is converted into ozone by the generators.

## BOD (Biochemical Oxygen Demand)

BOD (Biochemical Oxygen Demand), is a test performed to measure the potential of wastewater and other waters to deplete the oxygen level of receiving waters. In other words, the BOD test is performed to determine what effect dirty water, containing bacteria and organic materials, will have on animal and plant life when released into a stream or lake. When there is an abundance of bacteria and organic materials, the bacteria will take in oxygen in order to breakdown these molecules. If bacteria are taking in large amounts of oxygen, this will have a detrimental effect on the surrounding ecosystem. On the contrary, when there are low levels of organic waste in the water, there are fewer bacteria present, the BOD will be lower and the dissolved oxygen levels higher. In wastewater treatment plants, they often calculate the percentage removal of BOD to determine the efficiency of the treatment process. For this reason, BOD is sometimes referred to as a water contaminant.

A BOD level of 1-2 ppm is considered very good. There will not be much organic waste present in the water supply. A water supply with a BOD level of 3-5 ppm is considered moderately clean. In water with a BOD level of 6-9 ppm, the water is considered somewhat polluted because there is usually organic matter present and bacteria are decomposing

this waste. At BOD levels of 100 ppm or greater, the water supply is considered very polluted with organic waste.

A **pH** of 6.5 to 8.2 is optimal for most organisms. Rapidly growing algae or submerged aquatic vegetation remove $CO_2$ from the water during photosynthesis, significantly increasing pH levels. pH levels > 9.0 begin to be harmful to salmonids (trout) and perch. Rainwater naturally has a pH of 5.5; pH < 5.5 is harmful to freshwater shrimp, snails, and clams; metals normally trapped in sediments may be released into the acidified water.

**Acidic < 6.5 pH**                    **Basic > 7.5 pH**

# Sound Pollution

In India, the **Air (Prevention and control of pollution) Act** came into force in 1981 and in 1987 it was amended to include Noise as an Air pollutant.

Unwanted sounds created by humans, animals and machines which disturbs the environment and humans is called as sound pollution. The word noise comes from the Latin word *nausea* meaning *seasickness*.

## Sources of Sound

The main source of noise is transportation system including rail noise, aircraft noise and vehicle noise. People leaving near factories experience sound pollution because of the unwanted sounds coming from factories. Other sources of sound pollution are car alarms, emergency service sirens, office equipment, factory machinery, construction work, grounds keeping equipment, barking of dogs, appliances, power tools, lighting hum, audio entertainment systems, loudspeakers, and noisy people. Use of loudspeakers for political purposes and other purposes is also the cause of sound pollution.

## Measurement of sound

Sound pollution is measured in *decibels*. Humans can't sleep at 45 decibels; hearing begins to damage in 85 decibels and pain in ears start at 120 decibels.

According to '**Central pollution control board**', the permissible ambient noise levels are

|  | Day time | Night time |
| --- | --- | --- |
| Industrial | 75 dB | 70 dB |
| Commercial | 65 dB | 55 dB |
| Residential | 55 dB | 45 dB |
| Silent zone | 50 dB | 40 dB |

A brief exposure to extremely high level of sound ($\geq$ 150 dB ), generated by taking off of a jet- plane or rocket, may damage ear drums and hence can impair hearing ability permanently. The same may also happen from prolonged exposure to even lower noise level.

## Effects of sound pollution

Health and behaviour of humans are disturbed by the noise pollution. Unwanted sounds can damage physiological and psychological health. Sound pollution can cause annoyance and aggression, hypertension, high stress levels, tinnitus, hearing loss, sleep disturbances, and other harmful effects. Due to increase in sound level there can be lack of concentration at work which can lead to low productivity and performance. High sound levels can increase in cardiovascular effects in humans which is very dangerous for health.

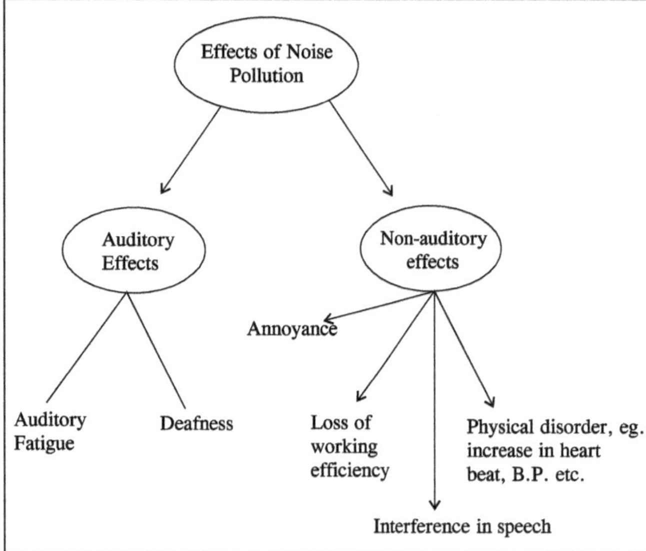


## Control of Noise Pollution

- For reducing industrial sound the Mufflers or the sound absorbent materials can be used.
- The Horn free zones around hospitals and schools can be created.
- Low level of sound can be permitted for crackers and loudspeakers.
- Fixing the time for playing loud speakers, after which they cannot be played.
- Stringent laws should be framed to implement and observe the noise level.
- Planting the trees or dense hedge plants, that act as noise barriers.
- Proper maintenance or lubrication of machines.

## Agro-chemicals & Its effect

Agro chemicals are developed by the use of modern technology that depends on inorganic fertilizers and pesticides. Excess use of these fertilizers can lead to immediate harmful effect or can also be long lasting. Although many benefits are there by the use of agro chemicals which are related to increase yield of plants and animal crops and less wastage during storing. These profits are substantial. In combination with genetically enhanced varieties of crop species, agrochemicals have made significant contributions to the accomplishments of the "green revolution." However there are certain environmental and ecological damages also related to the use of agro chemicals. For example excess use of fertilizers can contaminate the ground water with nitrate, making it unfit for the consumption of humans and livestock. If there is large concentration of nitrogen in water

it can poison animals by immobilizing some hemoglobin in blood and hence reducing the ability to transport oxygen. However if the fertilizers are in the water such as streams, lakes, etc. can cause an increased productivity of those aquatic ecosystems, a problem known as eutrophication. Due to eutrophication there can be excessive growth of algae, wide mortality of fish and other aquatic animals and a bad taste of water.

There are global contaminators of environment with pesticides such as *DDT*, *Dieldrin*, and *Aldrin*. This contamination includes the extensive presence of pesticide residues in almost all wildlife, well water, food, and even in humans. Residues of some of the chemicals used in animal husbandry are also thought by some people to be a problem, for example, when traces of antibiotics and bovine growth hormones arise in consumer products such as meat or milk.

The worst examples of the use of pesticides are the use of DDT. Modern use of pesticides includes the use of pesticides that are less persistent than DDT and related chlorinated hydrocarbon.

However humans are also at the risk of the use of some pesticides. There are about almost one million pesticides poisoning all over the world with nearly 20,000 fatalities. About one-half of the human poisonings happen in poorer, less-developed countries, even though these places account for only 20% of the world's use of pesticides. This is due to the illiteracy in these countries and to negligent enforcement of regulations about the use of pesticides.

Researchers are continuously searching for non-chemical means of dealing with several of these agricultural requirements. Organic methods are been invented in enhancing the soil fertility and dealing with pests. Therefore, modern agricultural industries will continue to depend on heavily on the use of agrochemicals to achieve their problems of fertility, soil quality, and pests.

## Acid Rain

Acid rain is a rain or any other form of precipitation that is unusually acidic, meaning that it possesses elevated levels of hydrogen ions (low pH). The term **"acid rain"** was coined in *1872* by **Robert Angus Smith,** after a link was established between *sulfur dioxide* ($SO_2$) emissions from the burning of coal in Manchester and acidification of nearby rainfall. *Rainfall with pH less than 5.6 is called Acid rain.*

### Sources of Acid Rain

- Acid rain is caused by a chemical reaction that starts when sulfur dioxide and nitrogen oxides are released into the air.
- These compounds can rise very high into the atmosphere, where they mix and react with water, oxygen, and other chemicals to form more acidic pollutants, called as acid rain. Sulfur dioxide and nitrogen oxides are highly soluble in water and can be carried very far by the wind.
- Consequently, the two compounds can travel long distances where they become part of the rain, sleet, snow, and fog that humans experience on specific days.
- Though there are few natural causes also for acid rain, but still human activities are considered to be the main cause of acid rain.

- During last few decades, human beings have released various chemicals into the air, which has altogether changed the composition of gases in the atmosphere. Power plants release huge amount of sulfur dioxide and nitrogen oxides when they burn fossil fuels, like coal, to produce electricity. Additionally, the exhaust from light and heavy vehicles releases nitrogen oxides and sulfur dioxide into the air. These pollutants are the main cause of acid rain.

## Effects of Acid Rain

- Acid rain leads to acidification of water bodies such as lakes and streams. It contributes to the damage of trees at high elevations (e.g. red spruce trees at the height of 2,000 feet and above) and many sensitive forest soils.
- Additionally, acid rain stimulates the decay of building materials and paints. Before reaching the earth, sulfur dioxide and nitrogen oxide gases and their particulate matter derivatives (**sulfates** and **nitrates**) lead to visibility degradation and harm people health.
- Acid rain has been held responsible for ruining the marble walls and pillars of one of the Seven Wonders of the World, *Taj Mahal* in India.
- Acid rain reacts with calcium to form calcium bicarbonate, which can be easily washed away.
- **St. Paul's Cathedral in London** and the Statue of Liberty in New York are known to be few victims of acid rain. As the concentration of Sulphur dioxide is increasing in the air of Delhi, there may be a danger of corrosion of the Red Fort and similar other historical buildings and monuments made up of stones.
- In Calcutta also, architectures such as the marble-built Victoria Memorial Hall may be in similar danger in the near future.

## Measures to control Acid Rain

Some of the major procedures that must be followed to control acid rain are as follows:
- Reduce amount of sulphur dioxide and oxides of nitrogen released into the atmosphere.
- Use cleaners fuels
- Flue (waste) gas desulphurisation (FGD)
- Use other sources of electricity (i.e. nuclear power, hydro-electricity, wind energy, geothermal energy, and solar energy).
- Reduce the effects of Acid Rain by liming the soil and water.

# Soil Pollution

- Soil is a thin layer of organic and inorganic materials that covers the Earth's rocky surface. Soil pollution is defined as the 'addition of substances to the soil, which adversely affect physical, chemical and biological properties of soil and reduces its productivity.'
- It is build-up of persistent toxic compounds, chemicals, salts, radioactive materials, or disease causing agents in soil which have adverse effects on plant growth, human and animal health.

- A soil pollutant is any factor which deteriorates the quality, texture and mineral content of the soil or which disturbs the biological balance of the organisms in the soil.

## Source of Soil Pollution

- **Industrial Wastes:** Industrial waste includes chemicals such as mercury, lead, copper, zinc, cadmium, cynides, thiocynates, chromates, acids, alkalies, organic substances etc.
- **Pesticides:** Pesticides are chemicals that include insecticides, fungicides, algicides, rodenticides, weedicides sprayed in order to improve productivity of agriculture, forestry and horticulture.
- **Fertilizers and manures:** Chemical fertilizers are added to the soil for increasing crop yield. Excessive use of chemical fertilizers reduces the population of soil borne organism and the crumb structure of the soil, productivity of the soil and increases salt content of the soil.
- **Discarded materials:** It includes concrete asphalt, rungs, leather, cans plastics, glass, discarded food paper and carcasses.
- **Radioactive wastes:** Radioactive elements from mining and nuclear power plants, find their way into water and then into the soil.
- **Other pollutants:** Many air pollutants (acid rain) and water pollutants ultimately become part of the soil and the soil also receives some toxic chemicals during weathering of certain rocks.

| Types of Soil Pollution |
| --- |
| - Agricultural Soil Pollution |
| - Pollution due to industrial effluents and solid wastes |
| - Pollution due to urban activities |

# Solid Waste Management

Solid waste management is one of the major challenges faced by many countries around the globe. Inadequate collection, recycling or treatment and uncontrolled disposal of waste in dumps can lead to severe hazards, such as *health risks* and *environmental pollution*.

No other pollutant is discussed about more vociferously among environmentalists, politicians and the people at large than the garbage which is the *bulky plastic* and refuse heap variety trash that accumulates in different corners of the cities. These piles are quite often taller than the city halls. What we throw away is the closest we come to the pollution problem as we rarely see the acid rain or spot those CFCs.

The growing accumulation of garbage reduces the land values, increases truck traffic, and ruins health, aesthetics and the necessities of life - the air we breathe and the water we drink.

## Sources

*Solid waste refers to the non-liquid waste materials* arising from domestic (*garbage debris* and night soil) activities, trade and commercial activities (hazardous and non-hazardous) industrial activities, agricultural activities, mining and public services (office and hospital wastes).

## Effects

It may be emphasized that unsanitary disposal and utilization of wastes result in high incidence of illness and death from *faecal borne diseases*. The faecal borne diseases are *bacillary dysentery*, *typhoid fever* and *enteritis*. Therefore, it is necessary to provide adequate and sanitary measures of disposal of wastes.

## E-waste

- "E-waste" is a popular, informal name for electronic products nearing the end of their "useful life. "E-wastes are considered dangerous, as certain components of

some electronic products contain materials that are hazardous, depending on their condition and density. The hazardous content of these materials pose a threat to human health and environment. Discarded computers, televisions, VCRs, stereos, copiers, fax machines, electric lamps, cell phones, audio equipment and batteries if improperly disposed can leach lead and other substances into soil and groundwater. Many of these products can be reused, refurbished, or recycled in an environmentally sound manner so that they are less harmful to the ecosystem. This paper highlights the hazards of e-wastes, the need for its appropriate management and options that can be implemented.

### Effects of E Waste constituent on health

| Source of e-wastes | Constituent | Health effects |
|---|---|---|
| Solder in printed circuit boards, glass panels and gaskets in computer monitors | Lead (PB) | • Damage to central and peripheral nervous systems, blood systems and kidney damage.<br>• Affects brain development of children. |
| Chip resistors and semiconductors | Cadmium (CD) | • Toxic irreversible effects on human health.<br>• Accumulates in kidney and liver.<br>• Causes neural damage.<br>• Teratogentic. |
| Relays and switches printed circuit boards | Mercury (Hg) | • Chronic damage to the brain.<br>• Respiratory and skin disorders due to bioaccumulation in fishes. |
| Corrosion protection of untreated and galvanized steel plates decorator or hardner for steel housing | Hexavalent chromium (Cr) VI | • Asthmatic bronchitis.<br>• DNA damage. |
| Cabling and computer housing | Plastics including PVC | Burning produces dioxin. It causes<br>• Reproductive and developmental problems;<br>• Immune system damage;<br>• Interfere with regulatory hormones |
| Plastic housing of electronic equipments and circuit boards | Brominated flame retardants (BFR) | • Disrupts endocrine system functions |
| Front panel of CRTs | Barium (Ba) | Short term exposure causes;<br>• Muscle weakness;<br>• Damage to heart, liver and spleen. |
| Motherboard | Beryllium (Be) | • Carcinogenic (lung cancer)<br>• Inhalation of fumes and dust. Causes chronic beryllium disease or beryllicosis.<br>• Skin diseases such as warts. |

## Management of E-waste

It is estimated that 75% of electronic items are stored due to uncertainty of how to manage it. These electronic junks lie unattended in houses, offices, warehouses etc. and normally mixed with household wastes, which are finally disposed off at landfills. This necessitates implementable management measures.

In industries management of e-waste should begin at the point of generation, this can be done by waste minimization techniques and by sustainable product design. Waste minimization in industries involves adopting:

- inventory management,
- production-process modification,
- volume reduction,
- recovery and reuse.

## Radioactive Waste Management

Radioactive waste which arises from civil nuclear activities as well as from defense related nuclear weapon activities, poses a terrible problem for handling and keeping the environment to be safe to the present and future generations. The techniques used emphasizes on waste minimization and volume reduction. Nuclear waste is categorized into high, intermediate and low levels depending on the level of radioactivity in it.

Spent fuel is stored for long time to reduce the level of radioactivity in it and then reprocessed at reprocessing plants for gathering fissile elements. The generation of high level waste is at reprocessing plants. The amount of this waste in our country is much lesser due to our adoption of the closed fuel cycle. High level waste produced from the reprocessing plant is vitrified into a glassy form, enclosed in multiple barrier vessels and stored for a temporary period of three to four decades in engineered vaults with essential observation services. After cooling down in these storage facilities, waste vessels will be stored for long term in deep geological repositories.

Reprocessing and Waste Management plants are currently being operated by Bhabha Atomic Research Centre (BARC).

## Harmful Effects

Initially the use of nuclear energy was considered to be a non-polluting way for generating electricity. Soon it proved to have 2- serious problems-

- Problem of leakage
- Problem of storage and safe disposal

The *accidental leakage* occurred in the **'Three Mile Island'** and **'Chernobyl'**.

The nuclear waste is extremely potent pollutant. The radiation given off by nuclear waste is extremely damaging to biological organisms since it causes mutations at a very high rate. In lower doses, it creates various disorders, the most frequent of which is Cancer. In higher doses the nuclear radiation becomes lethal.

Radioactive wastes have the harmful effects in the following ways:

(i) Pollutes the earth to a dangerous level of toxicity.
(ii) Are absorbed in water and then enter in living beings through food chains.
(iii) Emit harmful radiations which damage cells, tissues and Red blood corpuscles (RBC).
(iv) Can cause cancer, leukemia, etc.
(v) Are threats for aquatic life.

## Control Measures for Radioactive wastes

With respect to control of the materials composition radioactive waste can be grouped into:

(i) The treatment and packaging has to be performed according to a qualified process.
(ii) Conditioned waste products being qualified with respect to the radiological requirements.
(iii) Legacy waste products need to be qualified by sport checking according to composition requirements.

## Plastic Waste Management

Plastics have become an indispensable part of our daily lives. Invented in 1935, they are wonderful products of polymer chemistry produced from the by- products of petroleum refining. They are classified as into two main categories:

- **Thermoplastics:** They are substances that become plastic on heating. A plastic material can be repeatedly melted or softened by heat without change of properties. This property makes it possible to recycle the used plastic articles.
- **Thermosetting plastics:** Plastics that have once been subjected to heat and pressure, lose their plasticity.

## Environmental aspects of Plastic Manufacturing

All the varieties of plastics are manufactured from *petrochemical* based *hydrocarbons*. These hydrocarbons, and the plastic manufacturing processes involved possess environmentally critical characteristics.

The raw materials and intermediate products used in the manufacture of *Polyvinyl chloride* (PVC) - Ethylene, Chlorine, Hydrogen chloride, Vinyl Chloride Monomer (VCM), and Ethylene Dichloride (EDC) — are known hazardous materials. Additives, fillers, and coloring pigments used in plastic goods can also exhibit hazardous properties.

## Heavy-Metal Pollution from Plastics

*Lead* and *cadmium* compounds are added as stabilizers in PVC. Manufacturing these chemicals are used in the manufacture of soft plastic items such as vinyl flooring sheets, soft toys, etc. to increase their durability. Lead and cadmium can leach out during human contact, or when disposed in land-fills. Incineration of such rejected plastic items produces ash with high heavy metal content. Use of lead compounds in the manufacturing process can be a potential hazard to workers in the PVC industry. *Lead and cadmium are known neurotoxins* and *nephrotoxins respectively*. Neurotoxins damage the *nervous system*, whereas nephrotoxins affect the kidneys. Strict adherence to process controls in industry, and quality control of products can greatly reduce the risk of heavy-metal pollution.

## Nature of Plastics

Articles made of plastics are environment friendly if properly used and handled. Plastics are *non-biodegradable* because of their chemical structure. They cannot be bio-chemically decomposed by the microbes and as such, there is no threat of pollution. Being non-biodegradable they become virtually inert materials and remain in the environment for very long periods. They obstruct the natural and man-made activities in a physical way and do not easily participate in any reactions. These activities can be avoided by little care and common sense while discarding used plastics. That proves the fact that plastic, an 'environment friendly' product has been made an enemy by the callousness of humans. It is the misuse or abuse of plastic that is creating problems and not the plastics that are derived from the depths of Mother Earth.

The importance of plastic should be seen in their utility some of their uses and contributions to the environment are presented below.

## Prevention of Plastic-Disposal -Related Problems

Do not burn the plastics. They are valuable resource. Also gaseous emissions from combustion of plastics pollute the air and some of them are considered to be toxic. Combustion of plastics, particularly in high temperature incinerators produces **(Dioxins)** and **(Furan)** as by-products. **(Dioxins)** are a family of more than 75 different chlorinated hydrocarbons while Plastic or PVC – polyvinyl chloride is a chlorinated hydrocarbon. Some of them are highly toxic and are persistent chemicals that stay in the environment for a very long period. **(Furans)** (e.g. Furfuran) a colorless liquid, with a low boiling point of 320°C- used as an intermediate chemical in manufacture of synthetic resins are also toxic in nature.

## Recycling

The best way to tackle the plastic-disposal problem is to adopt suitable methods for collection and conveyance of plastic articles and practice recycling. With proper quality control, reprocessed plastics can be made as good as first-generation products are cheaper than good reprocessed plastic goods. Methods should be devised to make up this extra cost through taxes or subsidy. The extra monetary expenses involved in purifying the used plastic may become small compared to the environmental burden imposed by indiscriminate discarding of plastics.

## Government Regulations on Manufacture and Use of Recycled Plastics

The Ministry of Environment and Forests issued the Recycled Plastics Manufacture and Usage Rules 1999, and amended it in 2003 under the Environment (Protection) Act, 1986 for regulating and managing plastic carry bags and containers. **Salient features of the Rules are:-**

- No vendor shall use carry bags and containers of recycled plastics for storing carrying and or packaging of foodstuffs.
- Carry bags and container used for packaging of foodstuff shall be made of virgin plastic and of natural shade or white.
- Carry bags and container made from recycled plastics must be manufactured using pigments and colorants as per IS: 9833/ 1981 notified by the Bureau of Indian Standards (BIS);
- Minimum thickness of carry bags made of virgin or recycled plastics must not be less than 20 microns.
- Manufactures of recycled carry bag shall code/ mark carry bags and containers as per IS: 14534: 1998 and mark them as "recycled "along with percentage of recycled material.
- Manufactures shall print on words packet containing carry bags the words "Recycled marital" or "virgin plastics' as the case may be.
- No vendor shall use carry bags made of virgin or recycled plastic below 8 × 12 inches {20 × 30 cm} in size; and 50 bags of such will have minimum weight of 105 grams; and proportionate increase in weight to the increased size of the carry bags; for selling any commodity.
- Every occupier manufacturing carry bags or containers shall apply in prescribed form to the State Pollution Control Board/Pollution Control Committee for grant of Registration and renewal of Registration.

- The State Pollution Control Board / Pollution Committee shall issue and renew the Registration after ascertaining that  the unite meets the norms prescribed under these rules and also  possesses a valid cosset under Air and Water Act as per requirements of the State Pollution Control  Board / Pollution Control Committee.
- The prescribed authority of enforcement of provisions relating to use, collection, segregation, transpiration and disposal is with District collector, Deputy Commissioner of the concerned district, where no such Authority has been constituted by the State Government/Union Territory administration under any law regarding non-biodegradable garbage.
- SPCB's / PCC's are the prescribed authority for enforcement of provisions relating to manufacture and recycling.

## Difficulties in Recycling

Almost the entire content of the discarded plastics is made up of thin carry bags and small food-packaging pouches. Laminations made on books, electronic goods, compact discs, cassettes, and many consumer goods add to this problem.

- The tendency of people particularly house wives is to preserve the thick large bags and discard the thin carry bags with the domestic garbage. Once they get mixed up with the garbage these carry bags are difficult to separate. Cost of retrieval becomes more. Even the rag pickers do not find it attractive to collect the carry bags. If housewives, shopkeepers, and other users discard the carry bags in a container for periodic collection by some designated agency for recycling, the problem of plastics in environment can be greatly reduced.

## Bio-degradable Plastics

- An alternative to the plastic disposal problem has evolved in the form of 'Bio-degradable plastics'. It is possible to collect these items along with the municipal solid waste (MSW) for suitable disposal.
- MSW collection and disposal is not satisfactory in most of the towns in India. The bio-degradable plastics will add to the already piling up municipal garbage. The immediate benefits of recovery and recycle of normal plastics is also lost if bio-degradable plastics are introduced.
- As of now, compared to normal plastic, the bio-degradable plastics are expensive and the technology for manufacture is not easily available. It may be possible to treat bio-degradable plastics in countries where solid waste management systems are working satisfactorily and extensively.

## Reuse of Plastics

Mixing shredded PVC bags with asphalt for *road making* has been experimented with reasonable success. *Rope-making* using fiber removed from knitted cement bags is done in rural areas. These ropes are used in farming activities.

## Mercury Pollution

Mercury is one of the most harmful pollutants faced by fish and wildlife.

- Mercury pollution arises from a variety of sources. There is mercury mining although this is overwhelmingly now only in China and some Central Asian countries such as Kyrgyzstan. It is also very heavily used in artisanal and small-scale gold mining to separate gold from the ore.

- Mercury is used in the chemical and petrochemical industries and also in household products like compact fluorescent lamps (CFLs) and thermometers. Mercury emissions to the atmosphere also take place from coal-fired power plants.

- Mercury is present in industrial effluents that are let into water bodies and the sea and enters the human food chain through the consumption of fish. This is, in fact, what caused the disaster at Minamata in the 1950s. Contaminated sites including old mines, landfills and waste disposal locations are also important sources of mercury pollution.

- India dragged its feet a bit, but in the end signed up to the Minamata Convention on Mercury on 30 September, a year after it was adopted. The Minamata Convention gives India five years to control and, where feasible, to reduce emissions from new power plants and 10 years to do so for existing power plants.

- The Minamata Convention on Mercury is a global treaty to protect human health and the environment from the adverse effects of mercury. It was agreed at the fifth session of the Intergovernmental Negotiating Committee in Geneva, Switzerland at 7 a.m. on the morning of Saturday, 19 January 2013.

- The major highlights of the Minamata Convention on Mercury include a ban on new mercury mines, the phase-out of existing ones, control measures on air emissions, and the international regulation of the informal sector for artisanal and small-scale gold mining.

## DEGRADATION OF NATURAL RESOURCES

The degradation of natural resources has occurred not only by pollution but also by Improper utilization of natural resources

### Soil Erosion and Desertification

The development of fertile, top soil, takes centuries but the following human – practices can remove or erode this soil easily

- Over-cultivation
- Urbanization
- Deforestation
- Unrestricted grazing
- Poor irrigation

When large barren patches extend and meet over time, a desert is created. Now-a- days the desertification is occurring mainly because of urbanization, by human activities.

### Water-Logging and Soil Salinity

These problems have come-up due to Green revolution. When irrigation is done and there is no proper drainage of water, it leads to water-logging in the soil.

Besides, affecting the crops, the water logging draws down salt to soil surface. This soil is deposited as a thin crust and also accumulates in the roots of plants. This increased salt content (Soil- salinity) is injurious to the growth of crops and damages agriculture.

---

### EARTH HOUR

WWF's Earth Hour is an annual global celebration where people switch off their lights for one hour to show they care about the future of our planet. This year's celebrations will be on Saturday 19 March from 8.30 pm to 9.30 pm.

Since it first began in Sydney Australia in 2007, the number of countries taking part in Earth Hour has grown to an incredible 172 countries and territories.

India joined the Earth Hour campaign in 2009 and over the years has seen an exponential growth in participation across cities, towns and even far-flung villages of rural India. Iconic monuments of the country like the Rashtrapati Bhawan, Gateway of India, India Gate, Howrah Bridge and the Victoria Memorial, among others, switch off their non-essential lights in support of this global campaign.

# Exercise -1

1. A wetland ecosystem has a very high Biological Oxygen Demand (BOD). Which of the following statement about such a wetland is correct ?
   (a) It has high level of microbial pollution.
   (b) It has very low level of microbial pollution.
   (c) There is no microbial pollution.
   (d) It is highly turbid.

2. Desertification is the process of
   (a) increase in desert area
   (b) sand dune movement
   (c) land degradation
   (d) arid zone management

3. The dominant dissolved carbon dioxide species in sea water is :
   (a) Bicarbonate ion
   (b) Carbonate ion
   (c) Carbonic acid
   (d) Aquated carbon dioxide

4. Identify the incorrect statement with regard to saline and alkaline soil :
   (a) These show white incrustation of salts of calcium, magnesium and sodium on the soil surface.
   (b) These soils are infertile.
   (c) These soils are poor in drainage.
   (d) These soils are pervious.

5. Green house effect is warming due to
   (a) infra-red rays reaching earth
   (b) moisture layer in atmosphere
   (c) increase in temperature due to increase in carbon dioxide concentration of atmosphere
   (d) ozone layer of atmosphere.

6. Acid rain is due to increase in atmospheric concentration of
   (a) ozone and dust    (b) $CO_2$ and $CO$
   (c) $SO_2$ and $CO$    (d) $SO_2$ and $NO_2$.

7. The two great industrial tragedies namely, MIC and Chernobyl tragedies respectively occurred where and at which time?
   (a) Bhopal 1984, Ukrain 1986
   (b) Bhopal 1986, Russia 1988
   (c) Bhopal 1984, Ukrain 1990
   (d) Bhopal 1984, Ukrain 1988

8. If there was no $CO_2$ in the earth's atmosphere, the temperature of earth's surface would be
   (a) higher than the present
   (b) dependent on the amount of oxygen in the atmosphere
   (c) same as present
   (d) less than the present.

9. How carbon monoxide, emitted by automobiles, prevents transport of oxygen in the body tissues?
   (a) by forming a stable compound with haemoglobin
   (b) by obstructing the reaction of oxygen with haemoglobin
   (c) by changing oxygen into carbon dioxide
   (d) by destroying the haemoglobin.

10. What is B.O.D.?
    (a) The amount of $O_2$ utilized by organisms in water
    (b) The amount of $O_2$ utilized by micro-organisms for decomposition
    (c) The total amount of $O_2$ present in water
    (d) All of the above.

11. one of the following pairs is mismatched?
    (a) fossil fuel burning – release of $CO_2$
    (b) nuclear power – radioactive wastes
    (c) solar energy – greenhouse effect
    (d) biomass burning – release of $CO_2$.

12. Acid rain concentrated in the eastern portions of the United States is primarily the result of
    (a) nuclear power plants in the region
    (b) coal-burning power plants in the Midwest
    (c) hydro electric power plants in northeastern Canada
    (d) off-shore oil drilling rigs along the east coast of the United States

13. Alien species that cause the most harm are those that
    (a) struggle to fit into new ecosystems and eventually die out.
    (b) eventually become naturalized
    (c) become invasive
    (d) become agricultural products

14. Harmful algal booms appear to be linked to unusually high levels of nutrient pollution. Which of the following is the most likely source of nutrient pollution in a river drainage system associated with an algal bloom?
    (a) a coal-fired power plant
    (b) a nuclear power plant
    (c) chicken and hog farms
    (d) a large shopping mall

15. Health problems associated with indoor air pollution in developing countries is most commonly associated with:
    (a) chlorine gas released from tap water.
    (b) the use of biofuels for cooking and heating.
    (c) poor hygiene and sanitation inside the home.
    (d) the widespread use of pesticides to control disease vectors.

16. The formation of ozone hole in the Antarctic region has been a cause of concern. What could be the reason for the formation of this hole ?
    (a) Presence of prominent tropo-spheric turbulence; and inflow of chlorofluorocarbons.
    (b) Presence of prominent polar front and stratospheric clouds; and inflow of chlorofluorocarbons.

   (c)  Absence of polar front and stratospheric clouds; and inflow of methane and chlorofluorocarbons.

   (d)  Increased temperature at polar region due to global warming.

17. Recent studies indicate that two of the most dangerous components of air pollution around major cities in the developed nations are:
   (a)  fine particles and sulfur pollution.
   (b)  carbon monoxide and ozone.
   (c)  lead and volatile organic compounds.
   (d)  *radon* and carbon monoxide.

18. The decline of the polar ice caps because of increasing temperatures at the poles will
   (a)  increase the amount of fresh water available for human use.
   (b)  decrease the largest reserve of fresh water on Earth.
   (c)  increase the amount of fresh water available in aquifers.
   (d)  decrease global sea levels.

19. The developed countries of the world have contributed the most to global climate change. By applying the polluter pays and equity principles, we would expect that the:
   (a)  developed countries will provide funds for adaptations in the developing countries.
   (b)  developing countries will provide funds for adaptations in the developed countries.
   (c)  precautionary principle will guide the payment of compensation to developed countries.
   (d)  stabilization wedge approach to global climate change will help to equalize the funds for adaptations.

20. The evolution of pesticide resistance resurgence, and secondary-pest outbreaks are only some of the problems that result from reliance on
   (a)  crop rotation and biological controls, which disrupt the natural dynamics of ecosystems.
   (b)  pesticides, creating the need to alternate between a pesticide and an herbicide every other year.
   (c)  rodenticides to kill weeds and insect pests and prevent the spread of viral diseases.
   (d)  pesticides, creating a never-ending pesticide treadmill requiring new pest-fighting strategies.

21. The most effective way to reduce GHG emissions is to increase
   (a)  the production of electric cars.
   (b)  energy efficiency and renewable energy.
   (c)  our reliance on widely available natural gas
   (d)  the use of coal gasification plants and scrubber technologies to reduce sulfur emissions.

22. The most likely sustainable solutions of ecological problems are
   (a)  Incorporate the concerns of economists, ecologists, and sociologists.
   (b)  emphasize ecology over all other fields.
   (c)  emphasize economics over all other fields.
   (d)  emphasize ecological and social is - "Use over economic concerns.

23. The negative impacts of ozone pollution on forests are expected to increase as
   (a)  ocean levels rise and wind patterns shift.
   (b)  organisms spread northward because of warming climate conditions.
   (c)  the increasing demand for timber further stresses the growth of trees,
   (d)  temperatures increase and precipitation becomes more unpredictable.

24. The pesticide that directly attacks the nervous system is
   (a)  Aldrin         (b)  DDT
   (c)  Organic Phosphates   (d)  None of the above

25. The pesticides that also function as endocrine disruptors cause disease by
   (a)  causing excessive secretion of stomach acids.
   (b)  mimicking the effects of estrogenic hormones.
   (c)  causing muscle spasms and cramping in major muscle groups.
   (d)  greatly reducing the ability of the intestines to absorb nutrients.

26. The quality of the final treated wastewater effluent from a modern treatment plant is typically:
   (a)  lower in organic and nutrient content than the body of water into which it is discharged.
   (b)  lower in organic content but higher in nutrient content than the body of water into which it is discharged.
   (c)  higher in organic and nutrient content than the body of water into which it is discharged.
   (d)  higher in organic content but lower in nutrient content than the body of water into which it is discharged.

27. Brightly colored antique children's toys from before 1970 may be colored with paints that are contaminated with:
   (a)  heavy metals
   (b)  toxic plastic compounds.
   (c)  synthetic organic compounds.
   (d)  synthetic inorganic compounds.

28. By design, the molecules that resist biodegradation and include some of the most problematic persistent organic pollutants are the :
   (a)  synthetic organic compounds
   (b)  synthetic inorganic compounds
   (c)  recycled heavy metals
   (d)  chlorinated heavy metals

29. Carcinogens arc dangerous because they affect
   (a)  oxygen-carrying red blood cells.
   (b)  the ability of the lining of the lungs to absorb oxygen.
   (c)  DNA molecules inside cells.
   (d)  the ability to absorb nutrients in the wall of the intestines.

30. CFCs primarily contribute to the destruction of the ozone by:
   (a)  producing chlorinated gases that reflect back a significant amount of ultraviolet light.
   (b)  releasing carbon monoxide into the stratosphere, which reacts with the oxygen in ozone.
   (c)  releasing gases into the stratosphere that block the enzymes that create ozone.
   (d)  contributing chlorine, which acts as a catalyst in the breakdown of ozone.

31. Freshwater becomes polluted:
    (a) by oil spills in ocean water moving inland.
    (b) primarily by contaminants from aquifers moving to surface waters.
    (c) as a result of eutrophication.
    (d) from runoff associated with urban areas chemicals used in farming in rural areas.

32. In developing countries, contaminated water is responsible for the deaths of more than 1.6 million people. Contributing to this problem is the use of
    (a) groundwater for consumption and the disposal of human sewage.
    (b) groundwater for consumption and the disposal of human sewage in surface waters.
    (c) surface waters for consumption and the disposal of human sewage.
    (d) surface waters for consumption and the disposal of human sewage in groundwater.

33. In general, temperatures along an ocean coastline vary less than temperatures 100 miles inland. This moderation of temperatures along coastlines is because
    (a) as the oceans evaporate it cools off the coastlines.
    (b) the sun shines more intensely away from the ocean coastlines
    (c) ocean temperatures change more quickly than air temperatures.
    (d) ocean temperatures do not change as quickly as air temperatures.

34. Ozone levels increase in the atmosphere when volatile organic compounds (VOCs) are present because:
    (a) less nitric oxide is available to react with ozone.
    (b) VOCs react with atmospheric nitrogen to form ozone.
    (c) VOCs release ozone when they are broken apart by solar energy.
    (d) more carbon dioxide is available to contribute additional oxygen for ozone formation.

35. The greatest progress in reducing atmospheric levels of lead pollution resulted from
    (a) the elimination of leaded gas.
    (b) the switch from lead to graphite in pencils.
    (c) the development of new types of batteries that use lithium instead of lead.
    (d) new types of lead scrubbers on smokestacks that removed lead from the air.

36. The inside of a car or greenhouse would not heat up as much in the presence of sunshine if
    (a) air was circulated within the car or within the greenhouse.
    (b) infrared radiation passed through glass as easily as sunlight.
    (c) infrared radiation could not pass through glass as easily as sunlight.
    (d) sunlight could pass through glass more easily than through air.

37. Villagers living in a heavily forested region surrounding a remote district in Punjab decided to reduce air pollution in their village. In the autumn season, after the leaves had fallen from the trees, the villagers blew all of the dead leaves into the village pond. About 8 months later, they noticed a large number of dead fish in the pond. What is the most likely cause of the fish kill?
    (a) the dead leaves released poisons that killed the fish.
    (b) the decomposing leaves depleted the levels of oxygen.
    (c) bacteria fed on the leaves and then the bacteria infected the fish.
    (d) carbon dioxide from the decaying leaves reached toxic levels and killed the fish.

38. Which of the following represents an alarming positive feedback loop of global warming ?
    (a) increasing temperature raise humidity, which further increases temperatures.
    (b) decreased pH of the ocean increases the rate at which carbon dioxide is absorbed by the oceans from the atmosphere.
    (c) increased use of fossil fuels adds sulfate aerosols into the atmosphere, which traps more heat.
    (d) increased levels of atmospheric carbon dioxide increases photosynthesis, which further increases carbon dioxide atmospheric levels.

39. Which one of the following generally increases the pollution of the air?
    (a) bright sunlight.
    (b) generation of hydroxyl radicals.
    (c) sea salt aerosols entering the air over an ocean.
    (d) gases released by a volcanic eruption.

40. Wood pellets are produced from the waste sawdust of lumber and paper mills. Home-heating stoves burning these pellets can heat homes directly, instead of relying on other energy sources. Heating your home with wood pellets is :
    (a) sustainable, less polluting, and about 3 times as efficient as heating a home using electricity from a coal-fired power plant.
    (b) sustainable, slightly more polluting, and is about 30% more efficient than using electricity from a coal-fired power plant.
    (c) not sustainable but is less polluting and is about as efficient as using electricity from a coal-fired power plant.
    (d) not sustainable and actually pollutes more than using electricity from a coal-fired power plant.

41. The Clean Development Mechanism (CDM), a mechanism to reduce greenhouse gas emission as per Kyoto Protocol implies that
    (a) industrial countries receive carbon credits by funding carbon saving projects in another relatively affluent nation
    (b) industrial countries reduce their carbon emission by using environment friendly technology in production
    (c) developed countries invest in carbon reduction in developing countries and receive carbon credit in return
    (d) developed nations purchase carbon credit from other nations

42. A gardener applied heavy doses of the same insecticide to his garden for two consecutive years to kill squash bugs. During the third year, the man called in an expert to explain why he had an abundance of new pests that were destroying her garden. The expert explained that the abundant new pests were largely due to his previous use of a insecticide in a phenomenon known as
    (a) pesticide resistance
    (b) secondary-pest outbreak
    (c) triennial pest emergence
    (d) bounce back resurgence

43. A gardener has a large garden and decides this year he will not let the pests get beyond control. At the earliest sign of insect pests, he applies an organic insecticide and continues to apply it every month throughout the growing season. The next year he decides not to use any insecticides, thinking that he must have eliminated the pests with the prior year's treatments. Unfortunately, the pests reappear in numbers greater than he has ever seen before, and his plants are destroyed. Investigating this phenomenon, he learns that he has just experienced a phenomenon known as
    (a) resurgence         (b) pesticide resistance
    (c) natural selection   (d) emergence

44. Moss invades and establishes itself on bare rock, accumulating the beginnings of soil. After several years, enough soil has become established that grasses begin to grow where there was once bare rock.
    Without the moss building up soil, the grasses would have had no chance. The mosses changed the environment enough to permit grasses to grow in a process called:
    (a) sublimation.      (b) facilitation.
    (c) regeneration.     (d) improvisation.

45. Most of the wheat, rice and corn raised in the world has resulted from genetic engineering of one sort or another, either by crossing certain varieties or deliberately transferring genes using transgenic techniques. These methods select for plants that produce their own defenses against pests with chemicals or physical barriers. Helping to feed the world, this represents an example of :
    (a) cultural control
    (b) natural enemies control
    (c) genetic control
    (d) natural chemical control

46. The eagle predators, the amount of acorns produced annually, nesting sites in the trees, and cold winter temperatures limits the squirrel population in the Punjab region. The many factors listed above that can affect the squirrel population represent:
    (a) environmental resistance.
    (b) the carrying capacity of the squirrel population.
    (c) the squirrel's life history.
    (d) the biotic potential of the squirrel population.

47. The most widespread negative health impact of air pollution is the
    (a) destruction of the cellular component of the immune system.
    (b) loss of the ability to absorb vital nutrients by the digestive system.
    (c) disruption of the signaling processes of the endocrine system.
    (d) chronic stress that weakens many systems of the body.

48. The population of a particular type of fish, called Kubani found and in the Chilka lake only, is under heavy fishing pressure. If too many Kubians are caught, its population will crash and future years of fishing Kubani will suffer. Kubani can exhibit logistic growth under certain circumstances. Assuming logistic growth, it would be best to manage Kubani population by permitting the harvesting of just enough fish to keep the Kubani population.
    (a) at 1/10 of its carrying capacity.
    (b) at half its carrying capacity.
    (c) at its full carrying capacity.
    (d) above its carrying capacity.

49. In the lower regions of Uttaranchal, a toxic weed called leafy spurge was accidentally introduced and has grown and spread rapidly, covering millions of acres of grasslands. Leafy spurge is generally avoided by cattle and horses and may be toxic to them. Thus, grasslands where leafy spurge has spread has been damaged by the invasion of this plant. Plants such as leafy spurge can double their population size every year in part because of their efficient production of large amounts of seeds. Populations that can double every year, such as leafy spurge.
    (a) can do so endlessly, eventually covering all of the land on Earth.
    (b) exhibit constant growth increasing by the same amount every year.
    (c) exhibit a state of equilibrium when they are spreading.
    (d) exhibit exponential growth as they spread to new regions.

50. Which one of the following statements best reflects the overall position of current science on the role of biodiversity in ecosystems?
    (a) The more species in an ecosystem, the greater the biomass production.
    (b) The more species in an ecosystem, the greater the drought resistance.
    (c) The effects of biodiversity on the functioning of an ecosystem are not consistent.
    (d) Almost every species in an ecosystem is essential to maintain the overall ecosystem.

51. Widely applying pesticides may lead to resurgence and secondary-pest outbreak because:
    (a) the insecticide also killed the natural predators of the pests.
    (b) the plants have now lost their ability to fight the pests.
    (c) pesticides typically harm plants in ways that take several years to appear.
    (d) new species that are more resistant to insecticides have evolved.

52. Protection of endangered species by preserving the entire ecosystem is known as:
    (a) In-situ conservation
    (b) Ex-situ conservation
    (c) Biodiversity conservation
    (d) None of the above

53. Ramsar Convention 1971 aimed at the conservation of
    (a) Wasteland      (b) Wetland
    (c) Desert      (d) All of the above

54. Building on scientific research and careful measurements, the 1987 Montreal Protocol represented :
    (a) global stewardship to limit the destruction of the ozone.
    (b) agreements to maintain sustainable levels of agricultural productivity.
    (c) sound science to better understand the impact of acid precipitation.
    (d) stewardship by the Canadian government to limit the production of greenhouse gases.

55. Over the past 20 years, vultures in India and Pakistan have declined by more than 95% due to :
    (a) increased hunting and fear from villagers that the vultures will kill their domestic cattle.
    (b) the destruction of their nesting habitat in cliffs bordering the Indus River.
    (c) the spread of respiratory viruses common in domestic chickens.
    (d) the widespread use of an anti-inflammatory drug in cattle that were eaten by vultures.

56. 'El Nino' associated with the formation of the South West Monsoon of India is
    (a) an abnormally warm ocean current
    (b) a periodic warm air-mass
    (c) a periodic warm wind
    (d) a periodic low pressure centre

57. Ozone holes are more pronounced at the
    (a) Equator      (b) Tropic of Cancer
    (c) Tropic of Capricorn (d) Poles

58. Acid rains are produced by
    (a) excess $NO_2$ and $SO_2$ from burning fossil fuels
    (b) excess production of $NH_3$ by industry and coal gas
    (c) excess release of carbon monoxide by incomplete combustion
    (d) excess formation of $CO_2$ by combustion and animal respiration. (1988, 89)

59. 'BioCarbon Fund Initiative for Sustainable Forest Landscapes' is managed by the      **(IAS Prelims 2015)**
    (a) Asian Development Bank
    (b) International Monetary Fund
    (c) United Nations Environment Programme
    (d) World Bank

60. Which one of the following is associated with the issue of control and phasing out of the use of ozone-depleting substances?      **(IAS Prelims 2015)**
    (a) Bretton Woods Conference
    (b) Montreal Protocol
    (c) Kyoto Protocol
    (d) Nagoya Protocol

61. What is Rio+20 Conference, of ten mentioned in the news?      **(IAS Prelims 2015)**
    (a) It is the United Nations Conference on Sustainable Development
    (b) It is a Ministerial Meeting of the World Trade Organization
    (c) It is a Conference of the Inter-governmental Panel on Climate Change
    (d) It is a Conference of the Member Countries of the Convention on Biological Diversity

# Exercise -2



1. The Global Warming Potential (GWP) of a substance depends on
   1. the spectral band of its absorbing wavelengths.
   2. its residence time in atmosphere.
   3. its number of carbon molecules.
   4. concentration of the substance.

   **Choose the correct answer :**
   (a) 1, 2 and 3 only    (b) 2, 3 and 4 only
   (c) 1, 3 and 4 only    (d) 2, 4 and 1 only

2. Which of the following air pollutants are responsible for photochemical smog ?
   (1) Oxides of nitrogen
   (2) Ozone
   (3) Unburnt hydrocarbons
   (4) Sulphur dioxide

   **Choose the correct code :**
   (a) (1), (2) and (4) only    (b) (1), (2) and (3) only
   (c) (3) and (4) only    (d) (1) and (3) only

3. Biomass gasification is considered to be one of the sustainable solutions to the power crisis in India. In this context, which of the following statements is/are correct?
   1. Coconut shells, groundnut shells and rice husk can be used in biomass gasification.
   2. The combustible gases generated from biomass gasification consist of hydrogen and carbon dioxide only.
   3. The combustible gases generated from biomass gasification can be used for direct heat generation but not in internal combustion engines.

   Select the correct answer using the codes given below :
   (a) 1 only    (b) 2 and 3
   (c) 1 and 3    (d) 1, 2 and 3

4. Eutrophication in the Chesapeake Bay along the eastern edge of Maryland bas resulted in low oxygen levels in the water and alteration of food webs. The cause of this eutrophication appears to be pollution that contains high levels of:
   1. nitrogen    2. carbon
   3. phosphorus    4. sulphur
   Which of the above is/are correct?
   (a) 1 and 3    (b) 2 and 4
   (c) 1, 2 and 3    (d) All of these

5. Consider the following statements:
   1. Kyoto protocol came into force in the year 2005.
   2. Kyoto protocol deals primarily with the depletion of the ozone layer.
   3. Methane as a green house gas is more harmful than carbon dioxide.
   Which of the statements given above is/are correct?
   (a) 1 and 2    (b) 1 and 3
   (c) 1 only    (d) 3 only

6. Compared to 50 years ago, the thinning ozone layer has produced dramatic increases in cases of :
   1. asthma    2. color blindness
   3. cataracts    4. skin cancer
   Which of the above is/are correct?
   (a) 1 and 2    (b) 3 and 4
   (c) 1, 2 and 3    (d) All of these

7. If atmospheric carbon dioxide was eliminated from our atmosphere, we would expect that :
   1. the Earth would cool considerably
   2. photosynthesis would dramatically increase
   3. the Earth would heat up considerably
   4. photosynthesis would dramatically decrease
   Which of the above is/are correct?
   (a) 1 and 2    (b) 2 and 3
   (c) 1 and 4    (d) 2 and 4

8. Due to their extensive rice cultivation, some regions may be contributing to global warming. To what possible reason/reasons is this attributable ?
   1. The anaerobic conditions associated with rice cultivation cause the emission of methane.
   2. When nitrogen based fertilizers are used, nitrous oxide is emitted from the cultivated soil.
   Which of the statements given above is / are correct ?
   (a) 1 only    (b) 2 only
   (c) Both 1 and 2    (d) Neither 1 nor 2

9. Gases commonly referred as green house gases are :
   1. $CH_4$    2. $CO_2$
   3. CFC    4. $NH_3$
   Which of the above is/are correct?
   (a) 1 and 4    (b) 2 and 3
   (c) 1, 2 and 3    (d) All of these

10. Fertilizers cause
    1. eutrophication of water bodies
    2. survival of most microorganisms
    3. destruction of crumb structure of soil
    4. all the above
    Which of the above is/are correct?
    (a) 1 and 3    (b) 2 and 4
    (c) 1, 2 and 3    (d) All of these

11. Eutrophication of a lake most likely is the result of
    1. Elevated nitrogen gas level in water.
    2. Elevated phosphorus levels in water.
    3. Excessive concentration of $CO_2$.
    4. A decrease in oxygen content of the water.

Which of the above is/are correct?

(a)  1 only            (b)  1 and 3

(c)  1 and 2         (d)  1 and 4

12. Ozone layer can be destroyed by pollutants such as

1. Hydro carbons     2. Carbon mono oxide

3. Sulphur dioxide     4. Nitrogen oxides

(a)  1 and 2         (b)  2 and 3

(c)  1 and 3         (d)  1 and 4

13. Climatologist warm of a tipping point when global temperature trigger catastrophic events and rise levels rise more than 50 feets. What would cause the sea level rise so greatly and how much warmer does the world need to get for this tripping point to happen

1. $1°C$

2. $3°C$

3. Melting of Greenland ice sheet

4. thermal expansion of oceans

Which of the above is/are correct?

(a)  1 and 3         (b)  1 and 3

(c)  2 and 3         (d)  2 and 4

14. One Carbon Credit is defined as _____ .

1. Credit permit to release one ton of carbon dioxide.

2. providing loans to establish a unit which produces carbon dioxide for industrial use.

3. Finding out one new business which can use and recycle greenhouse gases.

Which of the following statements(s) is/are correct?

(a)  3 only         (b)  2 only

(c)  1 only         (d)  All 1, 2 and 3

15. Humans have contributed to habitat destruction by

1. clearing land for farming

2. excessive use of chemicals

3. producing green-house gases through use of fossil fucls

4. exploitation of land and water for mining of scarce resources

Which of the above is/are correct?

(a)  1 and 2         (b)  2 and 3

(c)  1, 2 and 3       (d)  All of these

16. Global climate change threatens coral reefs by

1. increasing the temperature

2. decreasing the temperature

3. increasing the pH of the oceans

4. decreasing the pH of the oceans

Which of the above is/are correct?

(a)  1 and 2         (b)  2 and 3

(c)  1 and 4         (d)  2 and 4

17. The acidification of oceans is increasing. Why is this phenomenon a cause of concern?

1. The growth and survival of calcareous phytoplankton will be adversely affected.

2. The growth and survival of coral reefs will be adversely affected.

3. The survival of some animals that have phytoplanktonic larvae will be adversely affected.

4. The cloud seeding and formation of clouds will be adversely affected.

Which of the statements given above is /are correct?

(a)  1, 2 and 3       (b)  2 only

(c)  1 and 3         (d)  1, 2, 3 and 4

18. Which of the following countries suffer from the acid rains?

1. Canada           2. France

3. Norway          4. Germany

Select the correct answers from the codes given below:

**Codes:**

(a)  1 and 2         (b)  1 and 3

(c)  2 and 3         (d)  3 and 4

19. Which of the following statements about Radioactive pollution are correct?

1. It causes genetic changes in the animals.

2. It causes disbalance among different minerals in the soil.

3. It hinders blood circulation.

4. It causes cancers.

Select the correct answer from the codes given below:

**Codes:**

(a)  1 and 2         (b)  1 and 4

(c)  1, 3 and 4      (d)  2, 3 and 4

20. Which of the following conditions indicate the impact of global warming?

1. Melting of glaciers

2. Rise in sea level

3. Changes in weather conditions

4. Rise in global temperature

Select the correct answer from the codes given below:

**Codes:**

(a)  1 and 2         (b)  1, 2 and 3

(c)  2, 3 and 4      (d)  1, 2, 3 and 4

21. As per National Aeronautics and Space Adminis-tration (NASA) research scientists found that concentrations of mercury near the ground level had increased in the Arctic Sea by mercury-pumping reaction which takes place because -

1. of open water in a lead is much warmer than the air above it.

2. of the temperature difference, the air above the lead churns like the air above a boiling pot.

3. the mixing is so strong that it actually pulls down mercury from a higher layer of the atmosphere to near the surface.

Select the answer from the codes given below-

(a)  1 only         (b)  1 and 2 only

(c)  2 and 3 only    (d)  All of the above

22. A new nuclear waste disposal strategy announced by United States include-

1. a "pilot interim store" will become operational in 2021

2. a larger "full-scale interim store" will open be open by 2025

3. an underground disposal facility to be established by 2048 to permanently dispose of the material.

4.  a new organisation will be established to manage the siting, development and operation of the future waste stores.
Select the answer from the codes given below-
(a)  1, 2 and 3                   (b)  2, 3 and 4
(c)  1, 3 and 4                   (d)  All of the above

23. Which of the following statements are correct ?
1.  A new study has found that changes in solar activity contributed no more than 10 per cent to global warming in the 20th century published in the journal Environmental Research Letters.
2.  It has been proposed that cosmic rays may have a role in cooling the earth by encouraging clouds to form, which subsequently reflect the sun's rays back into space.
3.  Researchers found high correlation between cosmic rays and global temperatures occurring every 22 years.
Select the answer from the codes given below-
(a)  1 only                       (b)  1 and 2 only
(c)  2 and 3 only                 (d)  All of the above

24. There is a concern, over the increases in harmful algal blooms in the seawaters of India. What could be the causative factors for this phenomenon?
1.  Discharge of nutrients from the estuaries.
2.  Run-off from the land during the monsoon.
3.  Upwelling in the seas.
Select the correct answer from the codes given below:
(a)  1 only                       (b)  1 and 2
(c)  2 and 3                      (d)  1, 2 and 3

25. Biomass gasification is considered to be one of the sustainable solutions to the power crisis in India. In this context, which of the following statements is/are correct?
1.  Coconut shells, groundnut shells and rice husk can be used in biomass gasification.
2.  The combustible gases generated from biomass gasification consist of hydrogen and carbon dioxide only.
3.  The combustible gases generated from biomass gasification can be used for direct heat generation but not in internal combustion engines.
Select the correct answer using the codes given below :
(a)  1 only                       (b)  2 and 3
(c)  1 and 3                      (d)  1, 2 and 3

26. The safest method for biomedical waste disposal is:
1.  Incineration
2.  Autoclaving
3.  Sharp pit encapsulation
4.  Precipitation
Which of the above is/are correct?
(a)  1 and 2                      (b)  1 and 3
(c)  1, 2 and 3                   (d)  1, 2, 3 and 4

27. Forests that experience high levels of acid precipitation expose trees to soil that has :
1.  more dissolved calcium
2.  more dissolved aluminium
3.  less dissolved calcium
4.  less dissolved aluminium
Which of the above is/are correct?
(a)  1 and 2                      (b)  2 and 3
(c)  1 and 4                      (d)  2 and 4

28. Excessive exposure of humans to UV-rays results in
1.  damage to immune system
2.  damage to lungs
3.  skin cancer
4.  peptic ulcers
Which of the above is/are correct?
(a)  1 and 2                      (b)  2 and 3
(c)  1 and 3                      (d)  2 and 4

29  Gases commonly referred as green house gases are :
1.  $CH_4$                        2.  $CO_2$
3.  CFC                           4.  $NH_3$
Which of the above is/are correct?
(a)  1 and 4                      (b)  2 and 3
(c)  1, 2 and 3                   (d)  1, 2, 3 and 4

30. Climatologist warn of a tipping point when global temperature trigger catastrophic events and rise levels rise more than 50 feets. What would cause the sea level rise so greatly and how much warmer does the world need to get for this tripping point to happen
1.  $1°C$
2.  $3°C$
3.  Melting of Greenland ice sheet
4.  thermal expansion of oceans
Which of the above is/are correct?
(a)  1 and 3                      (b)  1 and 3
(c)  2 and 3                      (d)  2 and 4

31. Due to improper/ indiscriminate disposal of old and used computers or their parts, which of the following are released into the environment as e-waste?
1.  Beryllium                     2.  Cadmium
3.  Chromium                      4.  Heptachlor
5.  Mercury                       6.  Lead
7.  Plutonium
Select the correct answer using the codes given below.
(a)  1, 3, 4, 6 and 7 only        (b)  1, 2, 3, 5 and 6 only
(c)  2, 4, 5 and 7 only           (d)  1, 2, 3, 4, 5, 6 and 7

32. Which of the following can be found as pollutants in the drinking water in some parts of India?
1.  Arsenic                       2.  Sorbitol
3.  Fluoride                      4.  Formaldehyde
5.  Uranium
Select the correct answer using the codes given below.
(a)  1 and 3 only                 (b)  2, 4 and 5 only
(c)  1, 3 and 5 only              (d)  1, 2, 3, 4 and 5

33. With reference to a conservation organization called "Wetlands International', which of the following statements is/ are correct?
1.  It is an intergovernmental organization formed by the countries which are signatories to Ramsar Convention.
2.  It works at the field level to develop and mobilize knowledge, and use the practical experience to advocate for better policies.

Select the correct answer using the code given below.

(a) 1 only            (b) 2 only

(c) Both 1 and 2      (d) Neither 1 nor 2

34. Brominated flame retardants are used in many household products like mattresses and upholstery. Why is there some concern about their use?

     1. They are highly resistant to degradation in the environment.

     2. They are able to accumulate in humans and animals.

Select the correct answer using the code given below.

(a) 1 only            (b) 2 only

(c) Both 1 and 2      (d) Neither 1 nor 2

35. With reference to 'Eco-Sensitive Zones', which of the following statements is/are correct?

     1. Eco-Sensitive Zones are the areas that are declared under the Wildlife (Protection) Act, 1972.

     2. The purpose of the declaration of Eco-Sensitive Zones is to prohibit all kinds of human activities in those zones except agriculture.

Select the correct answer using the code given below.

(a) 1 only            (b) 2 only

(c) Both 1 and 2      (d) Neither 1 nor 2

36. In India, the problem of soil erosion is associated with which of the following?

     1. Terrace cultivation

     2. Deforestation

     3. Tropical climate

Select the correct answer using the code given below.

(a) 1 and 2 only      (b) 2 only

(c) 1 and 3 only      (d) 1, 2 and 3

37. The scientific view is that the increase in global temperature should not exceed 2 °C above pre-industrial level. If the global temperature increases beyond 3 °C above the pre-industrial level, what can be its possible impact/impacts on the world?

     1. Terrestrial biosphere tends toward a net carbon source.

     2. Widespread coral mortality will occur.

     3. All the global wetlands will permanently disappear.

     4. Cultivation of cereals will not be possible anywhere in the world.

Select the correct answer using the code given below.

(a) 1 only            (b) 1 and 2 only

(c) 2, 3 and 4 only    (d) 1, 2, 3 and 4

38. Which of the following are some important pollutants released by steel industry in India?

     1. Oxides of sulphur     2. Oxides of nitrogen

     3. Carbon monoxide     4. Carbon dioxide

Select the correct answer using the code given below.

(a) 1, 3 and 4 only    (b) 1and 3 only

(c) 1 and 4 only      (d) 1, 2, 3 and 4

39. Global climate change threatens coral reefs by

     1. increasing the temperature

     2. decreasing the temperature

     3. increasing the pH of the oceans

     4. decreasing the pH of the oceans

Which of the above is/are correct?

(a) 1 and 2          (b) 2 and 3

(c) 1 and 4          (d) 2 and 4

40. With reference to 'Forest Carbon Partnership Facility', which of the following statements is/ are correct?

     1. It is a global partnership of governments, businesses, civil society and indigenous peoples.

     2. It provides financial aid to universities, individual scientists and institutions involved in scientific forestry research to develop eco-friendly and climate adaptation technologies for sustainable forest management.

     3. It assists the countries in their 'REDD+ (Reducing Emissions from Deforestation and Forest Degradation+)' efforts by providing them with financial and technical assistance.

Select the correct answer using the code given below.

(a) 1 only            (b) 2 and 3 only

(c) 1 and 3 only      (d) 1, 2 and 3

41. With reference to 'dugong', a mammal found in India, which of the following statements is/an; correct?

     1. It is a herbivorous marine animal.

     2. It is found along the entire coast of India.

     3. It is given legal protection under Schedule I of the Wildlife (Protection) Act, 1972.

Select the correct answer using the code given below.

(a) 1 and 2          (b) 2 only

(c) 1 and 3          (d) 3 only

42. What are the effects that IPCC has predicted regarding global warming?

     I. Earth's temperature will rise by 1-30°C in next few decades, leading to extreme weather changes (heat waves, hurricanes and severe winters), changes in ocean currents and marine life.

     II. If $CO_2$ concentration doubles, Earth's temperature may rise by 50°C.

     III. The biggest glacier in the Peruvian Andes was retreating by 5 meters per year some 20 years ago; today it is shrinking by 33 meters per year.

     IV. The Arctic Sea ice has thinned by 40% in the last two decades, while Mount Everest is losing height at the rate of 1.5 meters per year.

(a) Only I          (b) I & II

(c) Only III        (d) All the above

43. Which statement is correct regarding the steps taken to reduce global warming?

     I. Cleaning up and gasification of coal (for which technology is available) will result in lesser pollution.

     II. Increased use of natural gas contains only half of the carbon and no Sulphur.

     III. Renewable energy sources, such as wind, solar, photo-voltaic and fuel cells, tidal, etc.

     IV. Manufacture of fuel-efficient vehicles.

(a) I & II          (b) Only III

(c) Only II         (d) All the above

44. Which statement is correct regarding greenhouse gases?
    I.   A greenhouse gas (GHG) is a gas in an atmosphere that absorbs and emits radiation within the thermal infrared range
    II.  Water vapour contributes to 36-72% of Greenhouse effect
    III. Nitrous Oxide contributes to about 10% of Greenhouse effect
    IV.  Ozone contributes to 3-7% of Greenhouse effect
    (a) I & II                (b) I, II & III
    (c) I, II & IV            (d) All the above

45. Ozone layer in the outer atmosphere helps in:
    I.   Reflecting radio waves and makes radio communication possible
    II.  Absorbing U-V radiations
    III. Regulating the temperature of atmosphere
    IV.  Absorbing cosmic ray particles
    (a) I & II                (b) Only II
    (c) Only III              (d) All the above

46. Ozone depletion would impact the plant community in several ways. These include :
    I.   Increase in photosynthesis
    II.  Decline in water use efficiency
    III. Decline in yield of plants
    (a) I & II                (b) Only III
    (c) II & III              (d) All the above

47. Nitrogen Oxide is responsible for the depletion of Ozone layer, which of following is source of Nitrogen Oxide?
    I.   Industrial emission
    II.  Fertilizers which are used in agricultural activities
    III. Thermonuclear weapons
    (a) I & II                (b) Only III
    (c) Only II               (d) All the above

48. Which of the following statement is correct regarding CFC's and HCFC's?
    I.   These chemicals are inert, non-flammable, non-toxic, and lighter than air and can remain intact for years
    II.  CFCs are commonly used in Air-conditioners and the Refrigeration industry (Freon gas), aerosol propellants (in perfumes and deodorants), in the foam packaging industry (Styropor, Thermocol) and as solvents for greases and glues.
    III. They contain Chlorine and Fluorine, common being CFC-ll, CFC-12, CFC-22 and CFC- 13.
    (a) I & II                (b) II & III
    (c) Only III              (d) All the above

49. Which statement is correct regarding deforestation?
    I.   The process of clearance of forest by burning or logging is called deforestation
    II.  The main reasons for deforestation are trees or derived charcoal are used as, or sold, for fuel or as a commodity, while cleared land is used as grassland for livestock, plantations of commodities, and settlements.

III. Deforested areas usually sustain extensive adverse soil erosion and regularly damage into wasteland.
    (a) I & II                (b) II & III
    (c) Only III              (d) All the above

50. Deforestation includes which of the following?
    I.   Felling, and removal of forest litter
    II.  Browsing
    III. Grazing and trampling of seedlings
    IV.  Repeated lopping
    Select the correct answer:
    (a) Only I                (b) I and III
    (c) III and IV            (d) All the above

51. Consider the following statements
    I.   As a greenhouse gas (GHG) methane is even more harmful than carbon dioxide
    II.  Methane has been included in the list of six GHGs in Kyoto Protocol.
    Which of the statements given above is/are correct?
    (a) Only I                (b) Only II
    (c) Both I & II           (d) All the above

52. Increased level of carbon dioxide in the atmosphere would impact the plants in many ways. These can be:
    I.   Decrease in photosynthetic productivity of plants
    II.  Proliferation of weeds
    III. Increase in number of insects and other pests.
    (a) I & II                (b) II only
    (c) II & III              (d) All the above

53. Relative contributions of $CO_2$, $CH_4$, CFCs and N2O towards global warming  are:
    I.   50 %, 30 % , 10 % , and  10 % respectively
    II.  60%, 20%, 14%,  and 6% respectively
    III. 40 %, 30%, 20% and 10% respectively
    IV.  None of the above
    (a) Only II               (b) Only III
    (c) Only I                (d) None of the above

54. What is denitrification?
    I.   It prevents the discharge of nitrates in soil, and stops ground water pollution with nutrients.
    II.  In this solids are separated from the liquid
    III. In this sewage goes through many chambers and chemical processes which reduce its toxicity.
    (a) I & II                (b) Only I
    (c) II & III              (d) All the above

55. Which statement is correct regarding noise pollution?
    I.   The word noise comes from the Latin word nausea meaning seasickness.
    II.  The main source of noise is transportation system including rail noise, aircraft noise and vehicle noise
    III. Sound pollution is measured in decibels
    (a) I & II                (b) II & III
    (c) Only III              (d) All the above

56. Chlorofluorocarbons, known as ozone-depleting substances, are used:
    I.   In the production of plastic foams
    II.  In the production of tubeless tyres

III. In cleaning certain electronic components

IV. As pressurizing agents in aerosol cans

(a) Only I        (b) I, III & IV

(c) II & III       (d) All the above

57. Which of the following gases are responsible for acid rain in environment?

I. Carbon dioxide and nitrogen

II. Carbon monoxide and carbon dioxide

III. Ozone and carbon dioxide

IV. Nitrous oxide and Sulphur dioxide

(a) I & II        (b) Only II

(c) Only IV      (d) All the above

58. Spraying of DDT on crops causes pollution of:

I. Soil and Water

II. Air and Soil

III. Crops and Air

IV. Air and Water

(a) I & II        (b) II & III

(c) Only I       (d) All the above

59. Which statement is correct regarding Agro-Chemicals?

I. Agro chemicals are developed by the use of modern technology that depends on inorganic fertilizers and pesticides

II. Excess use of these fertilizers can lead to immediate harmful effect or can also be long lasting.

III. In combination with genetically enhanced varieties of crop species, agrochemicals have made significant contributions to the accomplishments of the "green revolution."

(a) I & II        (b) Only II

(c) Only III      (d) All the above

60. Which statement is correct regarding acid rain?

I. Acid rain is caused by a chemical reaction that starts when sulfur dioxide ($SO_2$) and nitrogen oxides ($NO_2$) are released into the air

II. Sulfur dioxide and nitrogen oxides are highly soluble in water and can be carried very far by the wind

III. Power plants release huge amount of sulfur dioxide and nitrogen oxides when they burn fossil fuels, like coal, to produce electricity which can cause acid rain

(a) I & II        (b) II & III

(c) Only III      (d) All the above

61. Acid rain reacting with calcium forms:

I. Calcium bicarbonate

II. Calcium Nitrate

III. Calcium Sulphate

IV. Calcium Carbonate

(a) I & IV       (b) Only I

(c) Only II       (d) Only III

62. What among the below is/are the cause of ground water contamination?

I. Septic tanks      II. Septic tanks

III. Landfills

(a) Only II       (b) I & III

(c) II & III       (d) All the above

63. Which statement is correct regarding Ozone Hole?

I. Ozone destruction rate is equal to the its formation rate

II. Ozone formation and destruction keep on happening

III. Ozone destruction rate is higher than its formation rate

(a) I & II        (b) II & III

(c) Only III      (d) Only I

64. Which statement is not true regarding Ozone?

I. Ozone is covered under Montreal Protocol.

II. Montreal protocol binds countries to adopt measures to curb ozone depleting substances.

III. HFC was used to replace ozone depleting substances.

IV. Ozone is also covered under Kyoto Protocol.

(a) I & II        (b) Only III

(c) Only IV      (d) II & III

65. Which of the following is not the feedback of the example in which human activity is responsible for the global climatic changes in the temperature?

I. Global warming causes snow to melt in polar regions

II. Global warming causes increased rainfall, plant growth and photosynthesis

III. Global warming causes increased $CO_2$ release from biomass decomposition

IV. Tropical deforestation causes warming and drying so that remaining forests begin to decline

(a) I & II        (b) Only iii

(c) Only II       (d) II & IV

66. What is effluent waste?

I. This category of waste, contains, hazardous wastes that are harmful to human beings and hence should be stored and treated separately.

II. These wastes include a high proportion of paper, cardboards and plastics.

III. Domestic as well as industrial effluents that contaminate river water if allowed to flow unchecked.

IV. All the waste resulting from the maintenance of streets, roads, parks, and schools, paper, dry leaves, animal wastes, sludge, carcasses of small animals and slaughter house wastes.

(a) I & II        (b) Only III

(c) Only IV      (d) II & IV

67. What are the methods of collection of solid wastes?

I. Refuse storage which may sometimes require delivery of refuse by the householder over a considerable distance

II. Door-to-door collection, where the collector enters the premises and collects the refuse and the householder is not involved in the collection process.

III. Dumping in river or stream

(a) I & II        (b) Only II

(c) Only I        (d) All the above

68. Which statement is correct regarding radioactive waste material?

I. This arises from civil nuclear activities as well as from defense related nuclear weapon activities

II. The techniques used emphasizes on waste minimization and volume reduction

III. Nuclear waste is categorized into high, intermediate and low levels depending on the level of radioactivity in it
(a) I & III     (b) Only III
(c) Only I     (d) All the above

69. Which statement is correct regarding the disposal of High level waste produced from radioactive material?
I. High level waste produced from the reprocessing plant is vitrified into a glassy form, enclosed in multiple barrier vessels
II. They are stored for a temporary period of three to four decades in engineered vaults with essential observation services
III. After cooling down in these storage facilities, waste vessels will be stored for long term in deep geological repositories
(a) I & II     (b) Only II
(c) Only III     (d) All the above

70. Which statement is correct regarding plastic waste management?
I. Plastic was invented in 1960
II. They are the products of polymer chemistry produced from the by- products of petroleum refining
III. They are characterized into thermoplastics and thermosetting plastics
(a) I & II     (b) II & III
(c) Only III     (d) All the above

71. What are the advantages of using PVC in Water supply pipes and Industrial piping over GI pipes?
I. They are heavy and plumbing work is difficult
II. Corrosion problem is eliminated and hence corrosion related contamination of water is avoided and life of the pipes increases
III. Inner surface of pipes may be made smooth to reduce friction losses, thus saving on electricity bills and conserving energy
(a) I & II     (b) II & III
(c) Only III     (d) All the above

72. What are the problems from Indiscriminate Discarding of used Plastics?
I. They choke storm water drains, often causing overflow of storm water on roads.
II. Being non-biodegradable they remain in the soil for a very long time, thus affecting the farm economy
III. Direct transfer of molecular oxygen into water is also affected
(a) I & II     (b) Only II
(c) Only III     (d) All the above

73. Which statement is correct regarding the rule of the Forests issued the Recycled Plastics Manufacture and Usage Rules 1999 which was amended in 2003 under the Environment (Protection) Act, 1986?
I. No vendor shall use carry bags and containers of recycled plastics for storing carrying and / or packaging of foodstuffs
II. Carry bags and Container used for packaging of foodstuff shall be made of virgin plastic and of natural shade or white
III. Minimum thickness of Carry bags made of virgin or recycled plastics must not be less than 20 microns
(a) I & II     (b) II & III
(c) Only III     (d) All the above

74. What is the main health risks associated with greater UV radiation through the atmosphere due to depletion of stratospheric ozone?
I. Increased skin cancer
II. Damage to eyes
III. Increased liver cancer
IV. Reduced immune system
(a) I & II     (b) III
(c) II & III     (d) All the above

75. What are the negative effect regarding bio degradable plastics?
I. The bio-degradable plastics will add to the already piling up municipal garbage
II. bio-degradable plastics are expensive and the technology for manufacture is not easily available
(a) only I     (b) only II
(c) Both I & II     (d) only III

76. Which of the following reasons does not help regulate global carbon dioxide concentrations?
I. Alterations in rainfall patterns
II. Storing carbon in the soil and biomass
III. Absorbing carbon dioxide for photosynthesis
IV. Releasing carbon dioxide following decay
(a) I & II     (b) II & III
(c) Only I     (d) All the above

77. The main function of ozone layer is:
I. Heating the stratosphere
II. Maintaining the temperature of atmosphere
III. Absorbing the ultraviolet solar radiation
(a) I & II     (b) Only II
(c) Only III     (d) All the above

78. Which statement is correct regarding methane?
I. Methane ($CH_4$), also called "Marsh gas"
II. It arises from rice paddies, wetlands, enteric fermentation in cattle, burning of wood, and landfills
III. It is responsible for about 4-9% of Greenhouse effect.
(a) I & II     (b) II & III
(c) Only III     (d) All the above

79. Which statement is correct regarding CFC's?
I. They are 1000 times more heat absorbent than carbon dioxide
II. They reach the atmosphere from refrigeration & air conditioning, aerosol sprays, and foam packaging industry.
III. They are responsible for 30% of greenhouse effect
(a) I & II     (b) II & III
(c) Only III     (d) All the above

80. Consider the following statements regarding Ozone:
I. Ozone contributes to 3-7% of Greenhouse effect
II. The largest net source of tropospheric ozone is influx from the stratosphere
III. Large amounts of ozone are also produced in the troposphere by photochemical reactions, the amounts increasing with high levels of air pollution.
(a) I & II     (b) II & III
(c) Only III     (d) All the above

81. What are the causes of deforestation?
I. Population growth and overpopulationand urbanization
II. Globalization
III. Dishonesty of government institutions

(a) Only I      (b) Only II
(c) I & II      (d) All the above

82. Which statement is correct regarding acid rain?
   I. The term "acid rain" was coined in 1972 by Robert Angus Smith
   II. Rainfall with pH less than 5.6 is called Acid rain.
   III. Acid rain is caused by a chemical reaction that starts when sulfur dioxide ($SO_2$) and nitrogen oxides (NOX) are released into the air
   (a) I & II      (b) Only II
   (c) II & III      (d) All the above

83. Lead and cadmium compounds are added as stabilizers in PVC. Which statement is correct regarding lead and cadmium?
   I. Lead and cadmium can leach out during human contact, or when disposed in land-fills
   II. Lead and cadmium are known neurotoxins and nephrotoxins respectively
   III. These chemicals are used in the manufacture of soft plastic items such as vinyl flooring sheets, soft toys etc. to increase their durability
   (a) I & II      (b) II & III
   (c) Only III      (d) All the above

84. Consider the following pairs : **(IAS Prelims 2016)**

| Terms sometimes seen in the news | Their origin |
| --- | --- |
| 1. Annex—I Countries | Cartagena Protocol |
| 2. Certified Emissions Reductions | Nagoya Protocol |
| 3. Clean Development Mechanism | Kyoto Protocol |

Which of the pairs given above is/are correctly matched?
(a) 1 and 2 only      (b) 2 and 3 only
(c) 3 only      (d) 1, 2 and 3

85. What is 'Greenhouse Gas Protocol'? **(IAS Prelims 2016)**
   (a) It is an international accounting tool for government and business leaders to understand, quantify and manage greenhouse gas emissions
   (b) It is an initiative of the United Nations to offer financial incentives to developing countries to reduce greenhouse gas emissions and to adopt eco-friendly technologies
   (c) It is an inter-governmental agreement ratified by all the member countries of the United Nations to reduce greenhouse gas emissions to specified levels by the year 2022
   (d) It is one of the multilateral REDD+ initiatives hosted by the World Bank

86. Consider the following statements: **(IAS Prelims 2016)**
   (1) The International Solar Alliance was launched at the United Nations Climate Change Conference in 2015.
   (2) The Alliance includes all the member countries of the United Nations.
   Which of the statements given above is/are correct?
   (a) 1 only      (b) 2 only
   (c) Both 1 and 2      (d) Neither 1 nor 2

87. With reference to the Agreement at the UNFCCC Meeting in Paris in 2015, which of the following statements is/are correct? **(IAS Prelims 2016)**
   1. The Agreement was signed by all the member countries of the UN and it will go into effect in 2017.
   2. The Agreement aims to limit the greenhouse gas emissions so that the rise in average global temperature by the end of this century does not exceed 2 °C or even 1.5 °C above pre-industrial levels.
   3. Developed countries acknowledged their historical responsibility in global warming and committed to donate $ 1000 billion a year from 2020 to help developing countries to cope with climate change.
   Select the correct answer using the code given below.
   (a) 1 and 3 only      (b) 2 only
   (c) 2 and 3 only      (d) 1, 2 and 3

88. 'Net metering' is sometimes seen in the news in the context of promoting the **(IAS Prelims 2016)**
   (a) production and use of solar energy by the households/consumers
   (b) use of piped natural gas in the kitchens of households
   (c) installation of CNG kits in motor-cars
   (d) installation of water meters in urban households

89. On which of the following can you find the Bureau of Energy Efficiency Star Label? **(IAS Prelims 2016)**
   1. Ceiling fans
   2. Electric geysers
   3. Tubular fluorescent lamps
   Select the correct answer using the code given below.
   (a) 1 and 2 only      (b) 3 only
   (c) 2 and 3 only      (d) 1, 2 and 3

90. In the cities of our country, which among the following atmospheric gases are normally considered in calculating the value of Air Quality Index? **(IAS Prelims 2016)**
   1. Carbon dioxide      2. Carbon monoxide
   3. Nitrogen dioxide      4. Sulfur dioxide
   5. Methane
   Select the correct answer using the code given below.
   (a) 1, 2 and 3 only
   (b) 2, 3 and 4 only
   (c) 1, 4 and 5 only
   (d) 1, 2, 3, 4 and 5

91. Which of the following statements regarding 'Green Climate Fund' is/are correct? **(IAS Prelims 2016)**
   1. It is intended to assist the developing countries in adaptation and mitigation practices to counter climate change.
   2. It is founded under the aegis of UNEP, OECD, Asian Development Bank and World Bank.
   Select the correct answer using the code given below.
   (a) 1 only      (b) 2 only
   (c) Both 1 and 2      (d) Neither 1 nor 2

92. In the context of mitigating the impending global warming due to anthropogenic emissions of carbon dioxide, which of the following can be the potential sites for carbon sequestration? **[CDS 2017-I]**
   1. Abandoned and uneconomic coal seams
   2. Depleted oil and gas reservoirs
   3. Subterranean deep saline formations
   Select the correct answer using the code given below:
   (a) 1 and 2 only      (b) 3 only
   (c) 1 and 3 only      (d) 1, 2 and 3

# Hints and Explanations

## EXERCISE-1

1. (b)　2. (b)　3. (a)　4. (d)
5. (c) The mean global temperature rise by 2° – 6°c and the concentration of carbon dioxide increases in the troposphere upto 600 ppm. Hence, the surface of the earth becomes warm which causes global warming. The phenomenon is similar to that of green house in which the glass enclosed atmosphere gets heated up due to its insulation from the rest of the environment. Hence, global warming is also known as green house effect and the gases responsible for it are called green house gases e.g $CH_4$, $CO_2$ etc.
6. (d) $SO_2$ and NO when present in large quantities dissolved in water vapour form sulphuric acid and nitric acid which dissolve in rain water resulting in acid rain $(H_2SO_4)$ and $(HNO_3)$ which in turn causes great damage to forests and vegetation.
7. (a) The Bhopal gas tragedy occurred on 3rd Dec. 1984 in which methyl isocyanate gas was released from a fertilizer manufacturing plant of Union Carbide causing death of approximately 2500 persons. Chernobyl disaster occurred on April 26, 1986, from an explosion at the chernobvl power station which released a huge radioactive cloud into the atmosphere in Ukrain.
8. (d) Carbon dioxide is one of the important green house gas. It allows the shorter wavelength of infra red radiations to pass through it but does not allow these radiations to leave the earth's atmosphere. This results in warming of the atmosphere. If the amount of $CO_2$ decreases then there will not be any increase in temperature.
9. (a)
10. (b) Strength of sewage or degree of water pollution is measured in terms of BOD (Biochemical Oxygen Demand) value. BOD may be defined as, 'number of milligrams of $O_2$ required for decomposition of one litre of waste or water by decomposing microorganisms (bacteria)'.
11. (c) Due to heavy industrilization and transportation (modernization), $CO_2$ concentration is increasing day by day in the atmosphere. $CO_2$ has capacity for absorbing heat radiations and thus increases temperature. This increase in global temperature (global warming) is mainly due to $CO_2$ concentration is called green house effect. Complete combustion of fossil fuels and biomass releases carbon dioxide. Nuclear power plants releases radioactive wastes.
12. (b)　13. (c)　14. (c)　15. (b)　16. (b)
17. (a)　18. (b)　19. (a)　20. (d)　21. (b)
22. (a)　23. (d)　24. (a)　25. (b)　26. (a)
27. (a)　28. (a)　29. (c)　30. (d)　31. (d)

32. (c)　33. (d)　34. (a)　35. (a)　36. (b)
37. (b)　38. (a)　39. (d)　40. (a)
41. (b) The Kyoto protocol is a protocol to the United Nations Framework convention on climate change aimed at fighting global warming. This protokol adopted on 11 December 1997 in Kyoto, Japan. Under the protocol 37 countries commit themselves to a reduction of four greenhouse gases and two groups of gases.
42. (b)　43. (a)　44. (b)　45. (c)　46. (a)
47. (d)　48. (b)　49. (d)　50. (c)　51. (a)
52. (b)　53. (b)　54. (a)　55. (d)
56. (a) 'El Nino' is a warm ocean current. The term El Niño refers to the large-scale oceanatmosphere climate interaction linked to a periodic warming in sea surface temperatures across the central and east-central Equatorial Pacific.
57. (d) Ozone holes are more pronounced at the polar regions especially over Antarctica.
58. (a) Acid rain refers to the precipitation with a pH of less than 5. It is a mixture of $H_2SO_4$ and $HNO_3$, the ratio of the two acids vary depending on the relative quantities of sulphur oxides and nitrogen oxides present in the atmosphere. These oxides are mainly produced by combustion of fossil fuels, smelters, industries, power plants, automobile exhausts etc.
59. (d) Housed within the Carbon Finance Unit of the World Bank, the Bio Carbon Fund is a public-private sector initiative mobilizing financing to help for development of projects that sequester or conserve carbon in forest and agro-ecosystems. It was created in 2004.
60. (b) The Montreal Protocol is an international treaty designed to protect the ozone layer by phasing out the production of numerous substances that are responsible for ozone depletion.
61. (a) The United Nations Conference on Environment and Development (UNCED), also known as the Rio Summit or Earth Summit. It was a major United Nations conference held in Rio de Janeiro from 3 to 14 June 1992. In 2012, the United Nations Conference on Sustainable Development was also held in Rio, and is also commonly called Rio+20 or Rio Earth Summit 2012.

## EXERCISE-2

1. (d)　2. (b)
3. (c) Coconut shells, groundnut shells and rice husk can be used in biomass gassfication.
Combustible gases generated from biomass gasification can be used for direct heat generation but not in internal combustion engines.

4. (a)

5. (c)

6. (b) The protocol was initially adopted on 11th December 1997. But it entered into force on 16th February 2005, after Kyoto, Japan. So, it is called Kyoto protocol.

   Kyoto protocol deals with reducing the green house gases emission to a level at least 5% below 1990 level. Methane is more effective or harmful green house gas than carbon dioxide.

7. (b)    8. (c)

9. (c) Methane and nitrous oxide are the two green house gases emitted from rice field. In rice field, the flooding a field cuts off the oxygen supply from atmosphere resulting anaerobic condition which emittes methane and nitrogen fertilizer which generally used in rice field for high production, emits nitrous oxide by the reaction with atmospheric oxygen.

10. (c)    11. (a)    12. (d)    13. (c)    14. (c)

15. (d)    16. (c)    17. (a)

18. (b) United States and Canada are the countries which are mostly affected by acid rain because of high number of factories, power plants and large number of automotive plants. Europe, Poland, Germany, Czech Republic, Sweden, Norway and Finland are affected because of British and European factories. In Asia, India and China are mostly affected mainly because of the large number of factories.

19. (b) Radioactive contamination or pollution causes severe life- threatening consequences in organisms. Because of the radioactive decay of the contaminants, which emit harmful ionising radiation such as alpha or beta particles, gamma rays or neutrons, genetic mutations occur which are hereditary. Carcinogenic contaminants cause cancers.

20. (d) Global warming is the increase in the global temperature. It has put many negative impacts on glaciers causing them to start melting, so, rise of sea level. Unpredictable weather conditions prevailing in some geographical areas are some of the other effects of global warming.

21. (d) Almost all of the mercury in the Arctic atmosphere is transported there in gaseous form from sources in areas farther south, from sources such as wildfires, coal burning and gold mining. Scientists have long known that mercury in the air near ground level undergoes complex chemical reactions that deposit the element on the surface. Once the mercury is completely removed from the air, these reactions stop. However, this newly discovered mixing ice forces down additional mercury to restart and sustains the reactions.

22. (d) The schedule is meant to reduce the growth of the US government's liabilities under the 1982 Nuclear Waste Policy Act, under which it was to begin taking spent reactor fuel from power companies in 1998. About 68,000 tonnes of used reactor fuel remains at 72 different power plant sites across the country, with the Department of Energy (DoE) reimbursing power companies the cost. The current production rate of spent fuel is 2,000 tonnes a year. The two interim facilities will accept used reactor fuel at a rate faster than this in order to reduce gradually the inventory at power companies.

23. (b) The Researchers found a small correlation between cosmic rays and global temperatures occurring every 22 years; however, the changing cosmic ray rate lagged behind the change in temperatures by between one and two years, suggesting that the cause might not be down to cosmic rays and cloud formation but might be due to the direct effects of the sun. By comparing the small oscillations in the cosmic ray rate, which were taken from data from two neutron monitors, and temperature with the overall trends in both since 1955, the research team found that less than 14 per cent of the global warming seen during this period could be attributable to solar activity.

24. (d) There is no single factor which cause an algal bloom. A combination of optimum factors such as the presence of good nutrients, warm temperatures, surface runoff, upwelling in the sea can all contribute harmfull algal blooms.

25. (c) Coconut shells, groundnut shells and rice husk can be used in biomass gasification.

   Combustible gases generated from biomass gasification can be used for direct heat generation but not in internal combustion engines.

26. (b) Autoclaves use pressurized steam to destroy microorganisms, and are the most dependable systems available for the decontamination of laboratory waste and the sterilization of laboratory glassware, media, and reagents. For efficient heat transfer, steam must flush the air out of the autoclave chamber. Before using the autoclave, check the drain screen at the bottom of the chamber and clean if blocked. If the sieve is blocked with debris, a layer of air may form at the bottom of the autoclave, preventing efficient operation.

27. (b) Forests that experience high levels of acid precipitation expose trees to soil that has more dissolved aluminum and less dissolved calcium.

28. (c) Prolonged human exposure to solar UV radiation may result in acute and chronic health effects on the skin, eye and immune system. Over the longer term, UV radiation induces degenerative changes in cells of the skin, fibrous tissue and blood vessels leading to premature skin aging, photodermatoses and actinic keratoses.

29. (c) Greenhouse gases are those that can absorb and emit infrared radiation, but not radiation in or near the visible spectrum. In order, the most abundant greenhouse gases in Earth's atmosphere are:

- Water vapor ($H_2O$)
- Carbon dioxide ($CO_2$)
- Methane ($CH_4$)
- Nitrous oxide ($N_2O$)
- Ozone ($O_3$)
- CFCs

30. (c) Greenland ice sheet melt water, which moves to the sea under the ice in contact with the land surface, may transport solids or dissolved material such as iron to the ocean. Measurements of the amount of available iron in melt water from the Greenland ice sheet shows that extensive melting of the ice sheet might add an amount of iron to the Atlantic Ocean equivalent to that added by airborne dust. This would increase biological activity in the Atlantic.

31. (b) Electronic waste or E-waste has ferrous and non-ferrous metals both. Non-ferrous metals like copper, aluminium, silver, gold, platinum, palladium etc. The presence of elements like lead, mercury arsenic, cadmium, selenium and hexavalent chromium are classified as hazardous waste.

32. (a) Drinking water in some parts of India has contaminants like Arsenic, Fluoride other than many other contaminants. The sources of Arsenic are run off from orchards. The sources of fluoride are erosion of natural deposits, discharge from fertilizers and aluminum factories.

33. (b) This organization is in partnership but not formed by Ramsar convention. The organization was formed in 1954 and Ramsar convention was signed in 1971. "Wetlands International", It is an intergovernmental organization formed by the countries which are signatories to Ramsar Convention.It works at the field level to develop and mobilize knowledge, and use the practical experience to advocate for better policies.

34. (c) Brominated flame retardants used in many household products are highly resistant to degradation in the environment and they are able to accumulate in humans and animals.

35. (d) Eco-sensitive zones are the ecologically important areas designated to be protected from industrial pollution and unregulated development under the Environment Protection Act of 1986. Only environmentally hazardous human activities are prohibited in those areas. Therefore, both the statements are incorrect.

36. (b) In India, the problem of soil erosion is associated with deforestataion .Terace cultivation helps in less erosion of soil.

37. (b) If the global temperature increases beyond $3°C$ above the pre-industrial level then Terrestrial biosphere tends toward a net carbon source and Widespread coral mortality will occur.

38. (d) In steel furnace coke reacts with iron to release pollutants like Oxides of sulphur, Oxides of nitrogen, Carbon monoxide & Carbon dioxide.

39. (c) Global climate change threatens coral reef by increasing the temperature and decreasing the ph level of the ocean. Much of the carbon dioxide that enters the atmosphere dissolves into the ocean. In fact, the oceans have absorbed about 1/3 of the carbon dioxide produced from human activities since 1800 and about 1/2 of the carbon dioxide produced by burning fossil fuels (Sabine et al. 2004). As carbon dioxide in the ocean increases, ocean pH decreases or becomes more acidic.

40. (c) The Forest Carbon Partnership Facility is a global partnership of governments, businesses, civil society, and Indigenous Peoples focused on reducing emissions from deforestation and forest degradation, forest carbon stock conservation, the sustainable management of forests, and the enhancement of forest carbon stocks in developing countries (activities commonly referred to as REDD+).

41. (c) The dugong is a medium-sized marine mammal. Dugong is listed under schedule 1 of India Wildlife Protection Act, 1972. In 2008, a MoU was signed between the Ministry of Environment and Forests and the Government of India, in order to conserve dugongs. In fact the highest level of legal protection is accorded to dugongs in India.

42. (d) 43. (d)

44. (c) Nitrous Oxide (NO2) (5%) arises from coal burning, biomass burning, and breakdown of chemical fertilizers.

45. (b)

46. (c) Photosynthesis would decrease as increased UV radiations (due to ozone depletion) would make it difficult for leaves of green plants to exchange gases with the atmosphere. Due to increased temperature consequent upon increased UV radiation, the evaporation rate of surface water will increase and soil moisture would decrease leading to drying of agricultural crops and hence reduced yield.

47. (d)

48. (d) CFCs and HCFCs destroy ozone in the stratosphere. These chemicals are inert, non-flammable, non-toxic, and lighter than air and can remain intact for years. They contain Chlorine and Fluorine, common being CFC-ll, CFC-12, CFC-22 and CFC- 13.

49. (d) The process of clearance of forest by burning or logging is called deforestation. The main reasons for deforestation are trees or derived charcoal are used as, or sold, for fuel or as (a) commodity, while cleared land is used as grassland for livestock, plantations of commodities, and settlements. Deforested areas usually sustain extensive adverse soil erosion and regularly damage into wasteland.

50. (d) Deforestation is the removal of vegetation in (a) forest to the extent that it no longer supports its natural flora and fauna. Deforestation is (a) very broad term, which consists of cutting of trees

including repeated lopping, felling, and removal of forest litter, browsing, grazing and trampling of seedlings.

51. (c) The six main greenhouse gases are – • Carbon dioxide ($CO_2$); • Methane ($CH_4$); • Nitrous oxide ($N_2O$); • Hydrofluorocarbons (HFCs); • Perfluorocarbons (PFCs); and • Sulphur hexafluoride ($SF_6$). Methane ($CH_4$) is the second most important greenhouse gas. $CH_4$ is more potent than $CO_2$ because the radiative forcing produced per molecule is greater. In addition, the infrared window is less saturated in the range of wavelengths of radiation absorbed by $CH_4$, so more molecules may fill in the region.

52. (c)

53. (a) $CO_2$ is largest contributor towards global warming.

54. (b)      55.   (d)   56.   (b)      57.   (c)

58. (c) spraying of DDT in soil results in the pollution of soil and water.

59. (d) Agro chemicals are developed by the use of modern technology that depends on inorganic fertilizers and pesticides. Excess use of these fertilizers can lead to immediate harmful effect or can also be long lasting. Although many benefits are there by the use of agro chemicals which are related to increase yield of plants and animal crops and less wastage during storing. These profits are substantial.

60. (d)

61. (b) Acid rain reacts with calcium to form calcium bicarbonate, which can be easily washed away.

62. (d)   63.   (b)      64.   (c)      65.   (c)

66. (c) Domestic as well as industrial effluents that contaminate river water if allowed to flow unchecked.

67. (a) Refuse storage: which may sometimes require delivery of refuse by the householder over (a) considerable distance. Where the householder delivers the refuse to the vehicle at the time of collection. Door-to door collection, where the collector enters the premises and collects the refuse and the householder is not involved in the collection process.

68. (d) Radioactive waste which arises from civil nuclear activities as well as from defense related nuclear weapon activities, poses a terrible problem for handling and keeping the environment to be safe to the present and future generations. The techniques used emphasizes on waste minimization and volume reduction. Nuclear waste is categorized into high, intermediate and low levels depending on the level of radioactivity in it.

69. (d) High level waste produced from the reprocessing plant is vitrified into a glassy form, enclosed in multiple barrier vessels and stored for a temporary period of three to four decades in engineered vaults with essential observation services. After cooling down in these storage facilities, waste vessels will be stored for long term in deep geological repositories.

70. (d) Plastics have become an indispensable part of our daily lives. Invented in 1935, they are wonderful products of polymer chemistry produced from the by- products of petroleum refining. They are classified as into two main categories

71. (b)   72.   (d)

73. (d) No vendor shall use carry bags and containers of recycled plastics for storing carrying and / or packaging of foodstuffs, Carry bags and Container used for packaging of foodstuff shall be made of virgin plastic and of natural shade or white, Carry bags and Container made from recycled plastics must be manufactured using pigments and colorants as per IS: 9833/ 1981 notified by the Bureau of Indian Standards (BIS), Minimum thickness of Carry bags made of virgin or recycled plastics must not be less than 20 microns.

74. (b)

75. (c) The bio-degradable plastics will add to the already piling up municipal garbage. The immediate benefits of recovery and recycle of normal plastics is also lost if bio-degradable plastics are introduced. As of now, compared to normal plastic, the bio-degradable plastics are expensive and the technology for manufacture is not easily available. It may be possible to treat bio-degradable plastics in countries where solid waste management systems are working satisfactorily and extensively.

76. (c)

77. (c) The main function of the ozone gas found in the ozonosphere is to absorb the ultraviolet solar radiation. Ozone absorbs the ultraviolet solar radiation and through this process, the most harmful ultraviolet radiation is effectively filtered, thus safeguarding life at earth.

78. (d) Methane ($CH_4$), also called "Marsh gas", arises from rice paddies, wetlands, enteric fermentation in cattle, burning of wood, and landfills. It is responsible for about 4-9% of Greenhouse effect.

79. (a) Chlorofluorocarbons (CFCs) and their replacements (15%) are 1000 times more heat absorbent than carbon dioxide. They reach the atmosphere from refrigeration & air conditioning, aerosol sprays, and foam packaging industry

80. (d) Ozone contributes to 3-7% of Greenhouse effect. The largest net source of tropospheric ozone is influx from the stratosphere. Large amounts of ozone are also produced in the troposphere by photochemical reactions, the amounts increasing with high levels of air pollution.

81. (d) There are numerous causes of current deforestation such as dishonesty of government institutions, the imbalanced distribution of wealth and power, population growth and overpopulation, and urbanization. Globalization is also main cause of deforestation, though there are cases in which the effects of globalization have supported localized forest recuperate.

82. (c) Acid rain is a rain or any other form of precipitation that is unusually acidic, meaning that it possesses elevated levels of hydrogen ions (low pH). The term "acid rain" was coined in 1872 by Robert Angus Smith, after a link was established between sulfur dioxide ($SO_2$) emissions from the burning of coal in Manchester and acidification of nearby rainfall. Rainfall with pH less than 5.6 is called Acid rain.

83. (d) Lead and cadmium compounds are added as stabilizers in PVC. These chemicals are used in the manufacture of soft plastic items such as vinyl flooring sheets, soft toys etc. to increase their durability. Lead and cadmium can leach out during human contact, or when disposed in land-fills. Incineration of such rejected plastic items produces ash with high heavy metal content. Use of lead compounds in the manufacturing process can be (a) potential hazard to workers in the PVC industry. Lead and cadmium are known neurotoxins and nephrotoxins respectively

84. (c) (i) The Kyoto Protocol separates countries into two groups. Annex I includes developed nations, while Non-Annex I refers to developing countries.
A CER is a certificate which is issued every time the United Nations prevents one tonne of CO2 equivalent being emitted through carbon projects registered with the Clean Development Mechanism (CDM).
(ii) All three terms are associated with Kyoto Protocol. Therefore, answer "c" 3 only.

85. (a) (i) The Greenhouse Gas Protocol (GHG Protocol) is the most widely used international accounting tool for government and business leaders to understand, quantify, and manage greenhouse gas emissions. A decade-long partnership between the World Resources Institute (WRI) and the World Business Council for Sustainable Development (WBCSD), the GHG Protocol is working with businesses, governments, and
(ii)              A is correct according to their "ABOUT US" page
Ref : http://www.ghgprotocol.org/about-ghgp

86. (a) (i) The COP-21 Climate Conference was held in Paris, France from 30 November to 12 December 2015. During this conference, India and France have launched the International Solar Alliance (ISA). International Solar Alliance includes an alliance of 121 countries located between Tropic of Cancer and Tropic of Capricorn.
(ii) While ISA was launched on Sidelines of Paris Summit, therefore first statement right but it includes only the 121 countries between Capricorn and Cancer receiving sunlight for 300 days or more. Hence 2nd statement wrong.

87. (b) (i)   The agreement emphasized on urgent need to address the significant gap between the aggregate effect of Parties' mitigation pledges in terms of global annual emissions of greenhouse gases by 2020 and aggregate emission pathways consistent with holding the increase in the global average temperature to well below 2°C above preindustrial levels and pursuing efforts to limit the temperature increase to 1.5°C above preindustrial levels.
(ii) Paris Summit - not all nations have signed the agreement and there is no deadline to ratify it. hence, statement 1 is wrong. This eliminates a and b. And developed countries committed to give $100 billion by 2020. But, for future, there is no mention of giving $1,000 billion dollars. Therefore, third statement wrong. We are left with Answer (b) only.

88. (a) (i) A Net metering is a billing mechanism that credits solar energy system owners for the electricity they add to the grid. Net metering allows residential and commercial customers who generate their own electricity from solar power to feed electricity they do not use back into the grid.
(ii) Under Net-metering system, Customer installs a solar or windpower plant on his premise, gets it grid-connected with the electricity distribution company (DISCOM) Hence (a) is the apt choice.

89. (d) (i) The Bureau of Energy Efficiency is an agency of the Government of India, under the Ministry of Power created in March 2002 under the provisions of the nation's 2001 Energy Conservation Act. The agency's function is to develop programs which will increase the conservation and efficient use of energy in India. The government has proposed to make it mandatory for all appliances in India to have ratings by the BEE starting in January 2010.
(ii) According to centre for science and environment (CSE), both 1 and 3 are correct. There is only option (d) whether such combination is possible.
Ref:http://cseindia.org/content/energy-efficient-appliances

90. (b) (i) The API level is based on the level of 6 atmospheric pollutants, namely sulfur dioxide (SO2), nitrogen dioxide (NO2), suspended particulates smaller than 10 $\mu$m in aerodynamic diameter (PM10), suspended particulates smaller than 2.5 $\mu$m in aerodynamic diameter (PM2.5), carbon monoxide (CO), and ozone (O3) measured at the monitoring stations throughout.
So by elimination we are left with option "b".
Ref: Thehindu newspaper/ April 9, 2015;
http://www.thehindu.com/opinion/blogs/blog-datadelve/article7083985.ece

91. (a) The Green Climate Fund (GCF) is a fund within the framework of the UNFCCC founded as a mechanism to redistribute money from the developed to the developing world, in order to assist the developing countries in adaptation and mitigation practices to counter climate change. The Fund is governed by the GCF Board. The assets of the GCF will be administered by a trustee only for the purpose of, and in accordance with, the relevant decisions of the GCF Board. The World Bank was invited by the COP to serve as the interim trustee of the GCF, subject to a review three years after operation of the Fund.

92. (d) Carbon sequestration may be carried out by pumping carbon into carbon sinks of two types:
A. Natural sinks- ocean, forest, soil etc.
B. Artificial sink- depleted oil reserve, unminable mines.
So statement 1 and 2 are correct.
And deep Saline Formations infact have highest capacity for this. So accordingly, answer is "D".

<table>
<tr><td>

# 3
# Chapter

</td><td>

# BIODIVERSITY

</td></tr>
</table>

## Introduction

Biodiversity mean us diversity of heterogeneity at all levels of biological organisation, i.e from micro molecules of the cells to the biomass. The word biodiversity was postulated by the sociologist E.D. Wilson. Biodiversity is commonly used to replace the more clearly and long established terms, species diversity and species richness. Biologist define biodiversity in "totality of genes", species and ecosystems of region.

This results in existence of a wide variety of plant and animal species in their natural environments, which is the aim of conservationists Who are mainly concerned about indiscriminate destruction of rainforests and other habitats.

## LEVELS OF BIODIVERSITY

### 1. Genetic diversity

It is the diversity at genetic level, or at sub-species level i.e. below species level, in a single species.

The genetic diversity helps the population to adapt. If a population has more diversity which means, it can adapt better to the changed environmental conditions. The low diversity leads to uniformity. The genetic variability is therefore, considered to be the raw material for speciation.

### 2. Species diversity

The measurement of species diversity is its richness, i.e. the number of species per unit area. Greater the species richness, more will be the species diversity. In nature, the number and kind of species, as well as the number of individual per species, vary, and this leads to greater diversity.

### 3. Ecological diversity

It is the diversity at community level. It can be of three types :

(a) **Alpha ($\alpha$) diversity** : It is the diversity of organisms within the same community or habitat.

(b) **Beta ($\beta$) diversity** : It is the diversity in between communities or different habitats. Higher the heterogenecity in the altitude, humidity and temperature of a region, the greater will be the dissimilarity between communities and higher will be the diversity.

(c) **Gamma ($\gamma$) diversity** : It is the diversity of organisms over the entire geographical area, covering several ecosystems or habitats and various trophic levels and food webs. Such diversity is most stable and productive in nature.

## Number of species on earth

It is difficult to believe that there are 20,000 species of orchids, 20,000 species of ants, 28,000 species of fishes and about 3,00,000 species of beetles on earth. According to IUCN (International Union for Conservation of Nature and Natural resources) estimates, the total number of animal and plant species, described so far, is more than 1.5 million. Due to project **'Species 2000'** and **'Global Biodiversity Information'**, the new species are being discovered faster than ever before. However, the discovery and description of species is more complete in temperate than in tropical countries. A large number of species are waiting to be discovered from tropics. According to estimates of **Robert May**

- The global species diversity is about 7 million (1.5 million, i.e. 22% reported till now and 78% are yet to be discovered).

- More than 70% of all the species recorded are animals. Plants are not more than 22% of the total.

- Among animals also, about 70% are insects.

- The Fungi have more species than all the vertebrates species combined.

- In case of vertebrates, the species of fishes are more than that of birds, and of latter, more than reptiles.

- In case of plant species, the species of fungi > species of angiosperms > species of algae.

The all above estimates do not give any idea for the number of species of prokaryotes, whose species diversity may run in millions.

## Number of species in India

India is one of the 12 mega divesity country of the world. It has 2.4%, i.e., 1/40 of world land area, but global species diversity is 8.1 %, i.e. 1/12. In India the number of animal and plant species recorded so far is 90,000 and 45,000 respectively.

According to **May**'s global estimates, about 3,00,000 animal species and 1,00,000 plant species are yet to be discovered from India.

(A large number of species are facing the threat of extinction even before they are discovered, i.e. 'Nature's biological library is burning even before we catalogue the titles of all the books stocked there').

# Pattern of Biodiversity

Biodiversity varies with the change of altitude and latitude. *The species diversity is maximum in plains (low altitude) and equator (low latitude).* As we move from lower to higher latitude (from equator to poles) or from lower to higher altitutde, the biological diversity decreases. The diversity also depends upon seasonal variability and physical environment like temperature, humidity etc.

Thus the diversity of animals and plants is not uniform throughout the world and shows uneven pattern. There are 2 specific patterns of biodiversity.

1. **Latitudial pattern**

   The species diversity is the maximum at equator and decreases as one moves towards poles. The tropical diversity is highest between lititudinal ranges of 23.5°N to 23.5°S. For example, Columbia, near equator, has about 1400 species of birds, while New York (41°N) and Greenland (71°N) have 105 and 56 species only.

   A forest of tropical regions, like Ecuador, has ten times more species of vascular plants as compared to the forest of temperate region, like mid-west USA,

   The tropical Amazonian rain forest of, S. America, has the greatest biodiversity on earth, and has about 30,000 species of fishes, 1300 species of birds, about 400 each of amphibians, reptiles and mammals, and 1,25,000 species of invertebrates. There are about 2 million species of insects and about 40,000 species of plants.

   There are *3 explanations or hypothesis* for the greater biodiversity in tropics

   1. The tropics have remained relatively undisturbed for million of years. There have been no frequent glaciations as in temperate and hence, long evolution time for species diversification.
   2. The tropic environments are more constant or less seasonal
   3. Tropics have more solar energy, contributing to higher productivity, hence greater diversity.

2. **Species - Area relationship**

   The German naturalist and geographer, **Alexander Von Humboldt,** while exploring SouthAmerican jungles, observed that species - richness increased with increasing explored area, but only up to a limit. This relationship between species richness and explored area is a rectangular hyperbola, described by the equation —

   $$S = C \, A^z$$

   Where S is species richness; C is Y-intercept; A is area and z is the slope to the line (regression coefficient).

# Relationship between species diversity and ecosystem

Most of the ecologists believe that

- The communities with more species are more stable than those with lesser species.
- The stable community means lesser variations in productivity from year to year.
- The community with more species, is more resistant to occasional (natural or man made) disturbances.
- Such communities are resistant to invasions by alien or exotic species.

  **David Tilman,** in his long-term ecosystem experiments, found that plots with more species showed less – year to year variation in total biomass and the increased diversity contributed to higher productivity.

  Thus the rich biodiversity is not only essential for the health of the ecosystem but also for the survival of human race on this planet.

# Loss of biodiversity

There is continuous loss of the earth' treasure of species. For example, the colonization of tropical pacific Islands hy human has led to extinction of more than 2000 species of native birds.

The Red list of IUCN documented the extinction of 784 species in last 500 years. The last 20 years witnessed the disappearance of 27 species.

Some important examples of recent extinctions are

*Dodo* (Mauritius), *Quagga* (Africa), *Thylacine* (Australia), *Steller Sea-cow* (Russia), and subspecies of Tiger, like *bali, javan* and *caspian.*

Presently, more than 15,500 species world–wide are facing the threat of extinction. This includes 32% of amphibian species, 23% of mammalian species and 12% of birds' species. About 31% of the gymnosperms species are also facing the extinction. The amphibians are however, more vulnerable in such cases.

From origin to evolution of life on earth, i.e. duration about 3 billion yrs., there have been 5-episodes of mass extinction, but the present, the 6th, mass extinction is 100 to 1000 times faster than the pre-human extinctions. The ecologists now warn that in next 100 years about 50% of all the species on earth will be wiped out. The loss in biodiversity of a region leads to

1. Lowered resistance to environmental changes
2. Decline in the plant production
3. Increased variability in certain ecosystem, pest disease cycles and water use etc.

# Causes of loss of biodiversity

The accelerated rate of species-extinction is largely due to human activities. There are 4-major causes, called **'The Evil Quartet',** for the loss of biodiversity –

1. Habitat loss and fragmentation
2. Overexploitation
3. Invasion of Alien or exotic species
4. Co-extinctions

1. **Habitat loss and fragmentation**

The cutting trees and burning of forest destroys the natural habitat of a species. The construction of mines, dams, harbors, industries and buildings for human settlement has also affected the biodiversity. *The Habitat destruction is the primary and major reason for the loss of biodiversity.* The tropical rain forest is the example of the habitat loss where forest covering has been reduced from 14% of land surface to 6%.

The Amazon rain forest, called *'The Lungs of the Planet'*, which harbors millions of species, is being cleared for cultivating soybean or developing grasslands for raising cattle. The pollution is also the factor for degradation of habitat.

When large habitats are broken into small fragments due to various human activities, the population of migratory animals, mammals and birds, that require a large territory, are adversely affected.

2. **Overexploitation**

When human need turns to human greed, for food and shelter, it leads to overexploitation of natural resources. Many species – extinction, like that of Stellar sea-cow and Passenger pigeon, in last 500 years, are due to overexploitation by humans. Many marine fishes are also being over harvested. Over fishing from a water body, or over harvesting a product is just like *'killing a goose laying golden eggs'*.

3. **Invasion of Alien or exotic species**

When alien species are introduced into an explored area, some of the species turn invasive and cause decline or extinction of indigenous species. For example –

- Introduction of **Nile perch** into lake Victoria (E. Africa) led to the extinction of more than 200 species of Cichlid fish in the lake
- Introduction of weed species, like **Carrot grass** (*Parthenium*), Lantana and **water hyacinth** (*Eicchornia*) has posed threat to the native species and damage to environment.
- The illegal introduction of **African cat fish** (*Clarias gariepinus*) for aquaculture purposes into the river has threatened indigenous cat fishes.

4. **Co-extinctions**

Whenever a plant or animal species becomes extinct, its obligatory-associated species also becomes extinct. For example, when a host species becomes extinct, the parasite also meets the same fate. In case of *'plant pollinator mutualism'* the extinction of one species leads to the extinction of the other.

# Processes of extinction of biodiversity –

1. **Natural extinction**

With the change of environmental conditions some species have disappeared and the more adaptive species have appeared. This extinction is slow and is called 'Background extinction'.

2. **Mass extinction**

It is extinction of large number of species due to natural calamities/catastrophies. The extinction of *Dinosaurs* is one such example.

3. **Anthropogenic extinction**

It is the disappearance of species due to human activities. This man-made extinction represents a severe depletion of biodiversity in terms of time. The current rate of extinction is thousand times higher than the background extinction.

If the current rate of losses continues the earth may lose up to 50% of the species by the end of 21$^{st}$ Century.

# Susceptibility to extinction –

The species with the following features are more susceptible (vulnerable) to extinction than the other species.

1. Larger body size (eg. Elephant, Bengal Tiger and Lion etc.)
2. Smaller population with low reproductive rate (eg. Blue whale and Giant panda )
3. Fixed habitat or migratory routes (eg. Whooping cranes and Blue whales ).
4. Feeding at higher trophic level in the food chain. (eg. Bengal tiger and Bald Eagle ).
5. Narrow range of distribution (eg. Island species and woodland caribou).

# Conservation of Biodiversity

Conservation means management of human-use of the biosphere so that it may yield greatest long term (sustainable) benefits for the present generation by maintaining its potential to meet the needs and aspiration of future generations.

**Strategies of conservation -**

1. The threatened species should be protected *in-situ* or *ex-situ*
2. Critical habitats should be safe guarded.
3. Unique ecosystems should be protected.
4. Planning and Management of the land and water use.
5. Utilization should not exceed the productive capacities.
6. The international trade of wild life organisms or their products should be regulated by legislature and administrative measures.

The reasons for conservation of biodiversity can be grouped into three categories

1. Narrowly utilitarian
2. Broadly utilitarian
3. Ethical reasons

1. **Narrowly utilitarian**

   According to them, the conservation is obvious since human directly derives several economic benefits from biodiversity/ nature, like food (cereal, pulses, and fruits), industrial products (lubricants, dyes, resins, perfumes, tannins etc), medicinal products, firewood and fibres etc.

   About 25% of the drugs in the world market are derived from plants

   No body knows how many medicinal plants are still unexplored in tropical rain forest.

2. **Broadly utilitarian**

   They believe that biodiversity plays major role in ecosystem or nature. For example, the Amazon rain forest, through photosynthesis, produces 20% of total oxygen in the earth's atmosphere. The economic value of such services can not be estimated in money.

   The Pollination, without which the plants can not give fruits or seeds, through pollinators like bees, bumble bees, birds and bats, is another such service that ecosystem provides.

   We also get aesthetic pleasure when we walk through full bloom flowers in spring and listen to the melodious songs of bulbul or cockoo.

3. **Ethical reasons**

   There is spiritual and philosophical need for the conservation of biodiversity. It is our moral duty to take care for the well being of each and every species.

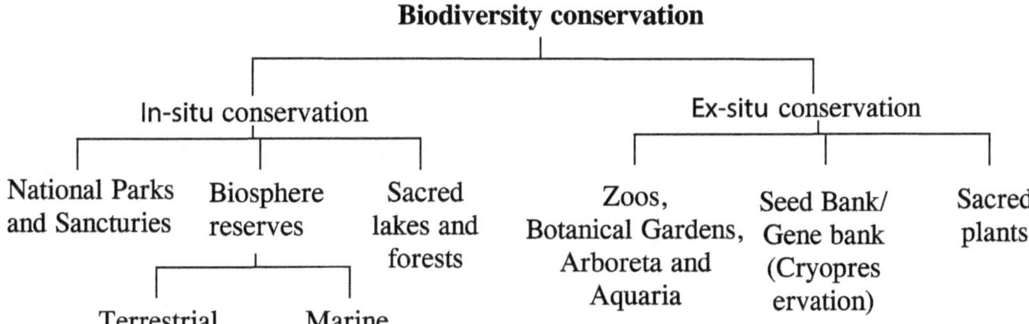


## In situ conservation

In such conservation the endangered species are protected in their natural habitat with entire ecosystem. The conservationists, on global basis, have identified certain *Biodiversity Hot Spots* (with high level of species richness and high degree of endemism).

The endemic species are the ones which are confined to a particular region and are not found any where else. The hot spots are also the regions of accelerated habitat loss.

Hot spots are the areas with high density of biodiversity or mega diversity which are most threatened at present. The concept was developed by environmental scientist **Norman Myers** of Oxford University in the United Kingdom in an attempt to identify priority areas for biodiversity conservation. Around the world, 35 areas qualify as hotspots. They represent just 2.3% of earth's land surface,but they support more than half of the world's plant species as endemics — *i.e.*, species found no place else — and nearly 43% of bird, mammal, reptile and amphibian species as endemics.

The number of such hot spots is now 34. These hot spots cover only 1 to 2 percent of earth's land area,

To qualify as a biodiversity hotspot, a region must meet two strict criteria:

- It must have at least 1,500 vascular plants as endemics — which is to say, it must have a high percentage of plant life found nowhere else on the planet. A hotspot, in other words, is irreplaceable.

- It must have 30% or less of its original natural vegetation. In other words, it must be threatened.

The *in situ* conservation, in India, is done through 18–**Biosphere reserves, 103-National Parks,** more than 543 **sanctuaries** and several **Sacred Groves** or the tracts of forests.

1. **Biosphere reserves**

   They represent natural biomes which contain unique biological communities. They include land as well as coastal environment. Biosphere reserves were created under **MAB** (Man and Biosphere) programme of **UNESCO** in 1971. Till May 2000 there were 408 biosphere reserves in 94 countries of the world. In India there are 15 biosphere reserves. There are three zones in a biosphere reserve:

   **(a)** **Core (natural) zone** – It is inner most zone which is legally protected and completely undisturbed from human interference,

   **(b)** **Buffer zone** - In this zone limited human activity is allowed for research and education purposes.

   **(c)** **Transition (manipulation) zone** – It is the outermost zone of biosphere reserve in which large number of human activities are permitted, eg. Cultivation, domestication, harvesting of natural product, grazing, forestry, settlement and recreation etc. In this zone the traditional life style of tribals is protected with their live-stock.

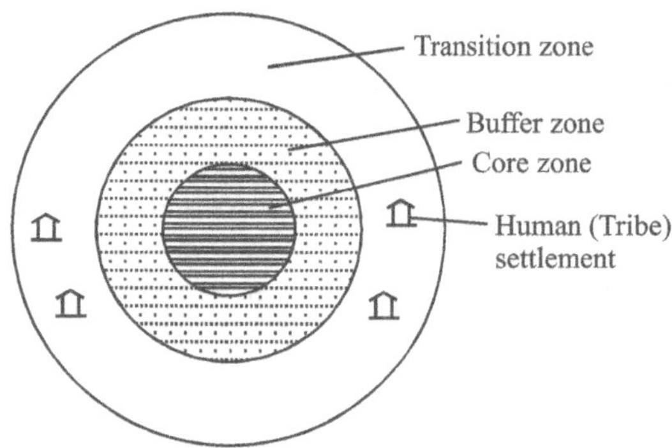


Different zones of a Terrestrial Biosphere reserve

### Functions of biosphere reserves

1. For conservation of landscape, ecosystem and genetic resources.
2. For economic development.
3. For scientific research, education and for exchange of information at national and global level.

### 2. National Parks

They are reserved for the betterment of wild life, both **fauna and flora.** In national parks private ownership is not allowed. The grazing, cultivation, forestry etc. is also not permitted. The first national park of the world, Yellow stone, in U.S.A., was founded in 1872.

### 3. Sanctuaries

In sanctuaries the protection is given to **fauna** only. The activities like harvesting of timber, collection of forest products and private ownership rights are permitted so long as they do not interfere with the well being of the animals. The important wild life sanctuaries are Chilka Wild Life Sanctuary (**Orissa**), Bharatpur Bird Sanctuary (**Rajasthan**), Sultanpur Bird sanctuary (**Haryana**) and Jalpara Sanctuary (**West Bengal**). Maximum sanctuaries belong to Andaman and Nicobar.

The **Project Tiger** was launched in India in year **1973** with the assistance of **WWF** (World Wild life Fund) after the recommendation of **IBWL** (Indian Board of Wild Life). At present there are more than 20 tiger projects. (**WWF** after its silver jubilee in 1986 has been renamed as **World Fund for Nature (WFN)**. The symbol of **WWF** is **Giant Panda.**

In India National Parks and Sanctuaries were created after formulation of **Wild life (protection) act** in **1972**. (This act was amended in 1991).

The sacred groves are found in Khasi and Jaintia hills (Meghalaya), Aravalli hills (Rajasthan), Western ghats (Karnataka and Maharashtra) and Sarguja, Chanda and Bastar areas of Madhya Pradesh.

## Major National Parks in India

| Name | State | Notability |
|---|---|---|
| Bandipur National Park (1974) | Karnataka | Chital, gray langurs, Indian giant squirrel, Gaur, leopard, Sambar deer, indian elephants, honey buzzard, red-headed vulture and other animals. |
| Bannerghatta National Park (Bannerghatta Biological Park) (1974) | Karnataka | White Tiger, Royal Bengal Tiger, Bear, other animals |
| Betla National Park (1986) | Jharkhand | Tiger, Sloth Bear, Peacock, Elephant, Sambar deer, mouse deer and other animals. |
| Bhitarkanika National Park (1988) | Odisha | Mangroves, Saltwater crocodile, white crocodile, Indian python, black ibis, wild pigs, rhesus monkeys, chital and other animals |
| Buxa Tiger Reserve (1992) | West Bengal | Tiger |
| Dachigam National Park (1981) | J&K | Only area where Kashmir stag is found |
| Dudhwa National Park (1977) | U.P | Swamp deer, sambar deer, barking deer, spotted deer, hog deer, tiger, Indian rhinoceros, |
| Gir Forest National Park (1965) | Gujarat | Asiatic lion |
| Great Himalayan National Park (1984) | Himachal Pradesh | UNESCO World Heritage Site |
| Gulf of Mannar Marine National Park (1980) | Tamil Nadu | Green turtles and Olive Ridley turtles and whales. |
| Indravati National Park (1981) | Chhattisgarh | Wild Asian Buffalo, Tiger Reserve, Hill Mynas |
| Jaldapara National Park (2012) | West Bengal | Indian one horned rhinoceros |
| Jim Corbett National Park (1936) | Uttarakhand | Tiger |
| Kanha National Park (1955) | M. P. | Swamp Deer, Tigers |
| Kaziranga National Park (1905) | Assam | Indian rhinoceros, UNESCO World Heritage Site |
| Keibul Lamjao National Park (1977) | Manipur | Only floating park in the world |
| Keoladeo National Park (1981) | Rajasthan | UNESCO World Heritage Site |
| Manas National Park (1990) | Assam | UNESCO World Heritage Site |
| Mandla Plant Fossils National Park (1983) | M. P | Plant Fossils National Park |

| | | |
|---|---|---|
| Marine National Park, Gulf of Kutch (1980) | Gujarat | 70 species of sponges, Coral 52 species along with puffer fishes, sea horse and sting ray |
| Namdapha National Park (1974) | Arunachal Pradesh | Snow Leopards, Clouded Leopards, Common Leopards and Tigers |
| Nanda Devi National Park (1982) | Uttarakhand | UNESCO World Heritage Site |
| Neora Valley National Park (1986) | West Bengal | Clouded leopard, red panda and musk deer |
| Nokrek National Park (1986) | Meghalaya | UNESCO World Biosphere Reserve |
| Periyar National Park (1982) | Kerala | Tigers |
| Ranthambore National Park (1981) | Rajasthan | Tigers, Leopards, Striped Hyenas, Sambar deer and Chital. |
| Sariska Tiger Reserve (1955) | Rajasthan | Tiger |
| Simlipal National Park (1980) | Odisha | Tiger, Leopard, Asian elephant, Sambar, Barking deer, Gaur, Jungle cat, Wild boar, and other animals. |
| Sultanpur National Park (1989) | Haryana | Siberian crane, greater flamingo, ruff, black-winged stilt, common teal, northern pintail, and yellow wagtail. |
| Sundarbans National Park (1984) | West Bengal | UNESCO World Heritage Site |
| Valley of Flowers National Park (1982) | Uttarakhand | Flying squirrel, Himalayan black bear, red fox, Himalayan weaseland Himalayan yellow-throated marten, and Himalayan goral |

## Wild Life Sanctuaries

India has total 543 animal sanctuaries referred to as wildlife sanctuaries category IV protected areas. Among these, the 48 tiger reserves are governed by Project Tiger and are of special significance in terms of conservation of the tiger.

### WILD LIFE SANCTUARIES IN INDIA

| Name of the Sanctuaries | Location | Major Species |
|---|---|---|
| Gir Wild Life Sanctuary | Sasan Gir, Junagadh, Amreli | Lion, Leopard, Chausinga, Chital, Hyena, Sambar, Chinkara, Herpetofauna, Crocodiles and birds |
| Wild Ass Sanctuary | Little Rann of Kachchh | Wild Ass, Chinkara, Blue bull, Houbara bustard, Wolf, Waterfowls, Herpetofauna |
| Hingolgadh Sanctuary | Hingolgadh, Rajkot | Chinkara, Blue bull, Wolf, Hyena, Fox, Birds, Herpetofauna |
| Marine Sanctuary | Gulf of Kachchh, Jamnagar | Sponges, Corals, Jellyfish, Sea horse, Octopus, Oyster, Pearloyster, Starfish, Lobster, Dolphin, Dugong, waterfowls |
| Simlipal Sactuary | Odisha | Elephant, Tiger, Leopard, Gaur, Cheetal |
| Kutch Desert Sanctuary | Great Rann of Kachchh | Chinkara, Hyena, Fox, Flamingo, Pelicans & other waterfowls, Herpetofauna |
| Rampara Sanctuary | Rampara, Rajkot | Blue bull, Chinkara, Wolf, Fox, Jackal, Birds, Herpetofauna |
| Ghana Bird Sanctuary | Rajasthan | Water Bird, Black-buck, Cheetal, Sambar |
| Panchmarhi | Madhya Pradesh | Tiger, Panther, Sambhar, Nilgai, Baskeng, Deer |
| Dandeli Sanctuary | Karnataka | Tiger, Panther, Elephant, Cheetal, Sanbhar, Wild Boar |
| Kutch Bustard Sanctuary | Near Naliya, Kachchh | Great Indian Bustard, Lesser Florican, Houbara bustard, Chinkara, Blue bull, Herpetofauna |

# Biosphere reserves in India

## Nilgiri Biosphere Reserve

This is the first Biosphere Reserve established in the country.

| Year of Establishment | States | Coverage | Type | Area (sq kilometres) | Key Fauna |
|---|---|---|---|---|---|
| 1-Aug-1986 | Tamil Nadu, Karnataka, Kerala | Parts of Wayanad, Nagarhole, Bandipur and Mudumalai, Nilambur, Silent Valley and Siruvani hills | Western Ghats | 5,520 | Nilgiri Tahr, Lion-tailed macaque |

## Gulf of Mannar

| Year of Establishment | States | Coverage | Type | Area (sq kilometres) | Key Fauna |
|---|---|---|---|---|---|
| 18-Feb-1989 | Tamil Nadu | Rameswaram in the north to Kanyakumari in the south | Coastal | 10,500 | Dugong or Sea Cow |

## Sunderbans

| Year of Establishment | States | Coverage | Type | Area (sq kilometres) | Key Fauna |
|---|---|---|---|---|---|
| 29-Mar-1989 | West Bengal | Parts of delta of Ganges & Brahamaputra river | Gangetic Delta | 9,630 | Royal Bengal Tiger |

## Nanda Devi National Park & Biosphere Reserve

| Year of Establishment | States | Coverage | Type | Area (sq kilometres) | Key Fauna |
|---|---|---|---|---|---|
| 18-Jan-1988 | Uttarakhand | Parts of Chamoli, Pithoragarh and Almora districs in Uttarakhand | Western Himalayas | 5,860 | Himalayan Snow Leopard |

## Nokrek

| Year of Establishment | States | Coverage | Type | Area (sq kilometres) | Key Fauna |
|---|---|---|---|---|---|
| 1-Sep-1988 | Meghalaya | Parts of East, West and South Garo Hill districts | Eastern Himalayas | 820 | Red Panda |

## Pachmarhi Biosphere Reserve

| Year of Establishment | States | Coverage | Type | Area (sq kilometres) | Key Fauna |
|---|---|---|---|---|---|
| 03-Mar-1999 | Madhya Pradesh | Parts of Betul, Hoshangabad and chhindwara | Semi-Arid | 4,981 | Giant Squirrel, Flying Squirrel |

## Similipal

| Year of Establishment | States | Coverage | Type | Area (sq kilometres) | Key Fauna |
|---|---|---|---|---|---|
| 21-Jun-1994 | Odisha | Parts of Mayurbhanj district | Deccan Peninsula | 4,374 | Gaur, Royal Bengal Tiger, Wild Elephant |

## Achanakmar-Amarkantak

| Year of Establishment | States | Coverage | Type | Area (sq kilometres) | Key Fauna |
|---|---|---|---|---|---|
| 30-Mar-2005 | Madhya Pradesh and Chhattisgarh | Parts of Anuppur and Dindori district and Bilaspur district | Maikala Hills | 3,835 | Leopards, gaur, chital |

## Great Nicobar Island Biosphere Reserve

| Year of Establishment | States | Coverage | Type | Area (sq kilometres) | Key Fauna |
|---|---|---|---|---|---|
| 06-Jan-1989 | Andaman and Nicobar Islands | Southernmost islands of Andaman & Nicobar | Island | 885 | Saltwater Crocodile |

## Agasthyamalai Biosphere Reserve

| Year of Establishment | States | Coverage | Type | Area (sq kilometres) | Key Fauna |
|---|---|---|---|---|---|
| 12-Nov-2001 | Tamil Nadu, Kerala | Parts of Thirunelveli and Kanyakumari districts and Thiruvanthapuram, Kollam, and Pathanmthitta districts | Western Ghats | 3,500 | Nilgiri Tahr, Elephants |

## Manas

| Year of Establishment | States | Coverage | Type | Area (sq kilometres) | Key Fauna |
|---|---|---|---|---|---|
| 14-Mar-1989 | Assam | Parts of Kokrajhar, Bongaigaon, Barpeta, Nalbari, Kamprup and Darang districts | East Himalayas | 2,837 | Golden Langur, Red Panda |

## Dibru-Saikhowa

| Year of Establishment | States | Coverage | Type | Area (sq kilometres) | Key Fauna |
|---|---|---|---|---|---|
| 28-Jul-1997 | Assam | Parts of Dibrugarh and Tinsukia districts | East Himalayas | 765 | Golden Langur |

## Dehang-Dibang

| Year of Establishment | States | Coverage | Type | Area (sq kilometres) | Key Fauna |
|---|---|---|---|---|---|
| 02-Sep-1998 | Arunachal Pradesh | Parts of Upper Siang, West Siang and Dibang Valleys | East Himalayas | 5,111 | N/A |

## Khangchendzonga

| Year of Establishment | States | Coverage | Type | Area (sq kilometres) | Key Fauna |
|---|---|---|---|---|---|
| 7-Feb-2000 | Sikkim | Parts of North and West Sikkim districts | East Himalayas | 2,931 | Snow Leopard, Red Panda |

## Great Rann of Kutch

| Year of Establishment | States | Coverage | Type | Area (sq kilometres) | Key Fauna |
|---|---|---|---|---|---|
| 29-Jan-2008 | Gujarat | Parts of Kutch, Rajkot, Surendranagar and Patan districts | Desert | 12,454 | Indian Wild Ass |

## Cold Desert

| Year of Establishment | States | Coverage | Type | Area (sq kilometres) | Key Fauna |
|---|---|---|---|---|---|
| 28-Aug-2009 | Himachal Pradesh | Pin Valley National Park and its surroundings; Chandratal & Sarchu and Kibber Wildlife Sanctuary | Western Himalayas | 7,770 | Snow Leopard |

## Seshachalam Hills

| Year of Establishment | States | Coverage | Type | Area (sq kilometres) | Key Fauna |
|---|---|---|---|---|---|
| 20-Sep-2010 | Andhra Pradesh | Seshachalam hill ranges in Eastern Ghats encompassing part of Chittoor and Kadapa districts | Eastern Ghats | 4,755 | N/A |

## Panna

| Year of Establishment | States | Coverage | Type | Area (sq kilometres) | Key Fauna |
|---|---|---|---|---|---|
| 25-Aug-2011 | Madhya Pradesh | Parts of Panna and Chhattarpur districts | River Valley | 2,998 | Tiger, Chital, Chinkara, Sambhar and Sloth Bear |

### Differences between wildlife sanctuary and national park

| Wildlife Sanctuary | National Park |
|---|---|
| Refers to the geographical area which is reserved exclusively for the conservation of bio-diversity | National park is another protected area kept apart for the conservation of wild life |
| Limited human activity is allowed | No human activity is allowed |
| Usually, not as well marked as in the case of a national park | Properly marked |
| A good level of permanency | A higher level of permanency |
| Usually through a competent authority like chief conservator of forests, etc. | Usually by the national or federal government |

### Ex situ conservation

In such type of conservation the threatened animals and plants are taken out of their natural habitat and are protected in special parks or areas like, **Zoological parks, Wild life safari parks** and **Botanical gardens*** etc. The *ex situ* conservation also includes:

- **Cryopreservation** of gametes of threatened species in viable and fertile form.
- Fertilization of eggs *in vitro* and propagation of plants through '**Tissue culture methods**'
- Preservation of seeds through **Seed banks**

The historic conservation on Biodiversity, '**The Earth Summit**' was held in **Rio de Janeiro** (Brazil) in 1992. In a follow-up, in 2002, through '**World Summit on Sustainable Development**' in **Johannesburg** (South Africa), 190 countries pledged their commitment for a significant reduction in current rate of biodiversity-loss at global, regional and local level by 2010. The next summit for the cause of biodiversity is to be held in 2012.

(***Botanical gardens** – There are about 1500 botanical gardens and **arboreta** (a place where specific species of trees or shrubs are cultivated for research or display) in the world. They contain more than 80000 species. Some botanical gardens also have facilities of seed bank and tissue culture.)

# BIODIVERSITY OF INDIA

As per the available data, the varieties of species living on the earth are around 1753739. Out of the above total number of species, 134781 are residing in India although the surface area of India is only 2.42% of the earth's surface. Wild life the Institute of India has divided it into ten biogeographical regions and twenty five biotic provinces.

## Biogeographical regions are:

(i) Trans Himalayas
(ii) Gangetic plain
(iii) Desert
(iv) Semiarid zone
(v) Western Ghats
(vi) Deccan peninsula
(vii) North eastern zone
(viii) Coastal lands
(ix) Himalayas
(x) Islands

## India is one of the twelve mega diversity nations of the world due to the following reasons:

(i) It has 7.3% of the global fauna and 10.88% of global flora as per the data collected by Ministry of Environment and forest.

(ii) It has 350 different mammals, 1200 species of birds- 453 different reptiles, 182 amphibians and 45,000 plants species.

(iii) It has 50,000 known species of insects which include 13,000 butterflies and moths.

(iv) It has 10 different biogeographical regions and 25 biotic provinces having varieties of lands and species.

## IUCN at a glance

- Founded in 1948 as the world's first global environmental organisation
- Today, IUCN (International Union for conservation of Nature) the largest professional global conservation network. Work together to forge and implement solutions to environmental challenges.
- A leading authority on the environment and sustainable development
- As per the IUCN data more than 1,200 member organizations including 200+ governments and 900+ non-government organizations
- Almost 11,000 voluntary scientists and experts, grouped in six Commissions in some 160 countries harnessing the experience and reaching out to its members.
- IUCN's work is supported by over 1,000 staff in 45 offices and hundreds of partners in public, NGO and private sectors around the world. The Union's headquarters are located in Gland, near Geneva, in Switzerland.
- A neutral forum for governments, NGOs, scientists, business and local communities to find practical solutions to conservation and development challenges
- IUCN is funded by governments, bilateral and multilateral agencies, foundations, member organisations and corporations
- Official Observer Status at the United Nations General Assembly

The **IUCN Red List** of 'Threatened Species' provides taxonomic, conservation status and distribution information on plants, fungi and animals that have been globally evaluated using the IUCN Red List categories and criteria. This system is designed to determine the relative risk of extinction, and the main purpose of the IUCN Red List is to catalogue and highlight those plants and animals that are facing a higher risk of global extinction (i.e. those listed as **Critically Endangered, Endangered and Vulnerable**). The IUCN Red List also includes information on plants, fungi and animals that are categorized as **Extinct** or **Extinct in the Wild**; on taxa that cannot be evaluated because of insufficient information (i.e., are **Data Deficient**); and on plants, fungi and animals that are either close to meeting the threatened thresholds or that would be threatened were it not for an ongoing taxon-specific conservation programme (i.e., are **Near Threatened**).

The IUCN Red List of Threatened Species is widely recognized as the most comprehensive, objective global approach for evaluating the conservation status of plant and animal species. The IUCN Red List was updated three times in 2015. The IUCN Red List now includes 79,837 assessed species, of which 23,250 are threatened with extinction, with habitat loss and degradation identified as the main threat to more than 80% of species assessed.

## Red data book

A Red Data Book contains lists of species whose continued existence is threatened. Species are classified into different categories of perceived risk. Each Red Data Book usually deals with a specific group of animals or plants (e. reptiles, insects, mosses). They are now being published in many different countries and provide useful information on the threat status of the species.

By the end of 2014 India had 988 threatened species on the list, which lists critically endangered, endangered and vulnerable species. while 2013, the number was 973. In 2008, there were 659 species only which increased by 50 percent in seven years due to better research identifying more threatened species and deforestation.

Indian elephant, Bengal tiger, Indian lion, Indian rhino, Gaur, lion tailed macaque, Tibetan antelope, ganga river dolphin, the Nilgiri tahr, snow leopard, dhole, black buck, great Indian bustard, forest owlet, white – winged duck and many more are the most endangered animals in India.

## Endangered Species in India

### Birds

- White-bellied heron
- Great Indian bustard (Ardeotis nigriceps)
- Forest owlet (Athene blewitti)
- Baer's pochard (Aythya baeri)
- Spoon-billed sandpiper (Eurynorhynchus pygmeus)
- Siberian crane (Grus leucogeranus)
- White-rumped vulture (Gyps bengalensis)
- Indian vulture (Gyps indicus)
- Slender-billed vulture (Gyps tenuirostris)
- Bengal florican (Houbaropsis bengalensis)
- Himalayan quail (Ophrysia superciliosa)
- Jerdon's courser (Rhinoptilus bitorquatus)
- Pink-headed duck (Rhodonessa caryophyllacea)
- Red-headed vulture (Sarcogyps calvus)
- Sociable lapwing (Vanellus gregarius)
- Bugun liocichla (Liocichla bugunorum)

### Fish

- Knifetooth sawfish (Anoxypristis cuspidata)
- Pondicherry shark (Carcharhinus hemiodon)
- Ganges shark (Glyphis gangeticus)
- Deccan labeo (Labeo potail)
- Largetooth sawfish (Pristis microdon)
- Longcomb sawfish (Pristis zijsron)
- Humpback mahseer

### Reptiles and Amphibians

- Northern river terrapin (Batagur baska)
- Red-crowned roofed turtle (Batagur kachuga)
- Hawksbill sea turtle (Eretmochelys imbricata)
- Gharial (Gavialis gangeticus)
- Ghats wart frog (Fejervarya murthii)
- Gundia Indian frog (Indirana gundia)
- Toad-skinned frog (Indirana phrynoderma)
- Charles Darwin's frog (Ingerana charlesdarwini)
- Rao's torrent frog (Micrixalus kottigeharensis)
- Amboli bush frog (Pseudophilautus amboli)
- White-spotted bush frog (Raorchestes chalazodes)
- Griet bush frog (Raorchestes griet)
- Munnar bush frog (Raorchestes munnarensis)
- Ponmudi bush frog (Raorchestes ponmudi)
- Sacred Grove bush frog (Raorchestes sanctisilvaticus)
- Shillong bubble-nest frog (Raorchestes shillongensis)
- Resplendent shrubfrog (Raorchestes resplendens)
- Anaimalai flying frog (Rhacophorus pseudomalabaricus)
- Patinghe Indian gecko (Geckoella jeyporensis)

### Mammals

- Asiatic cheetah (Acinonyx jubatus venaticus)
- Namdapha flying squirrel (Biswamoyopterus biswasi)
- Himalayan wolf (Canis himalayensis)
- Andaman Shrew (Crocidura andamanensis)
- Jenkins' shrew (Crocidura jenkinsi)
- Nicobar shrew (Crocidura nicobarica)
- Northern Sumatran rhinoceros (Dicerorhinus sumatrensis lasiotis)
- Kondana soft-furred rat (Millardia kondana)
- Pygmy hog (Porcula salvania)
- Indian Javan rhinoceros (Rhinoceros sondaicus inermis)
- Malabar large-spotted civet (Viverra civettina)
- Elvira rat (Cremnomys elvira)
- Chinese pangolin (Manis pentadactyla)
- Kashmir stag (Cervus canadensis hanglu)

### Coral

- Fire corals (Millepora boschmai)
- Spiders
- Rameshwaram Ornamental or Parachute Spider (Poecilotheria hanumavilasumica)
- Gooty Tarantula, Metallic Tarantula or (Poecilotheria metallica)

# GLOBAL BIODIVERSITY HOTSPOTS

He British biologist Norman Myers coined the term "biodiversity hotspot" in 1 988 as a biogeographic region characterized both by exceptional levels of plant endemism and by serious levels of habitat loss. In 1990 Myers added a further eight hotspots, including four Mediterranean-type ecosystems. Conservation International (C1) adopted Myers' hotspots as its institutional blueprint in 1989, and in 1996, the organization made the decision to undertake a reassessment of the hotspots concept. Three years later an extensive global review was undertaken, which introduced quantitative thresholds for the designation of biodiversity hotspots.

According to CI, to qualify as a hotspot a region must meet two strict criteria: it must contain at least 1,500 species of vascular plants ($> 0.5\%$ of the world's total) as endemics, and it has to have lost at least 70% of its original habitat. In 1999, Cl identified 25 biodiversity hotspots in the book "Hotspots: Earth's Biologically Richest and Most Endangered Terrestrial Ecoregions".

Collectively, these areas held as endemics about 44% of the world's plants and 35% of terrestrial vertebrates in an area that formerly covered only 11.8% of the planet's land surface. The habitat extent of this land area had been reduced by 87.8% of its original extent, such that this wealth of biodiversity was restricted to only 1.4% of Earth's land surface. In 2005 CI published an updated titled "Hotspots Revisited: Earth's Biologically Richest and Most Endangered Terrestrial Ecoregions".

## AFRICA

A total of 8 Hotspots in African continent hold a diversity of plant and animal life, many of which are found nowhere else on Earth.

## ASIA-PACIFIC

Composed of large land areas as well as islands dotting the Pacific seas, these 14 Hotspots represent important biodiversity.

## EUROPE AND CENTRAL ASIA

From the Mediterranean Basin to the Mountains of Central Asia, these four Hotspots are unique in their diversity.

## NORTH AND CENTRAL AMERICA

North and Central America play host to thousands of acres of important habitat.

## SOUTH AMERICA

From Brazil's Cerrado to the Tropical Andes, South America has some of the richest and most diverse life on Earth.

The biodiversity hotspots hold especially high numbers of endemic species, yet their combined area of remaining habitat covers only 2.3% of the Earth's land surface. Each hotspot faces extreme threats and has already lost at least 70% of its original natural vegetation. Over 50% of the world's plant species and 42% of all terrestrial vertebrate species are endemic to the 35 biodiversity hotspots.

## World's 35 Biodiversity Hotspots

| I. Africa | II. Asia-Pacific | III. Europe and Central Asia | IV. North and Central America | V. South America |
|---|---|---|---|---|
| 1. Cape Floristic Region | 1. East Melanesian Islands | 1. Caucasus | 1. California Floristic Province | 1. Atlantic Forest |
| 2. Coastal Forests of Eastern Africa | 2. Himalaya | 2. Irano-Anatolian | 2. Caribbean Islands | 2. Cerrado |
| 3. Eastern Afromontane | 3. Indo-Burma | 3. Mediterranean Basin | 3. Mediterranean Pine - Oak Woodlands | 3. Chilean Winter Rainfall-Valdivian Forests |
| 4. Guinean Forests of West Africa | 4. Japan | 4. Mountains of Central Asia | 4. Mesoamerica | 4. Tumbes-Choco-Magdalena |
| 5. Horn of Africa | 5. Mountains of Southwest China | | | 5. Tropical Andes |
| 6. Madagascar and the Indian Ocean Islands | 6. New Caledonia | | | |
| 7. Maputaland-Pondoland-Albany | 7. New Zealand | | | |
| 8. Succulent Karoo | 8. Philippines | | | |
| | 9. Polynesia-Micronesia | | | |
| | 10. Southwest Australia | | | |
| | 11. Forests of Eastern Australia (new) | | | |
| | 12. Sundaland | | | |
| | 13. Wallacea | | | |
| | 14. Western Ghats and Sri Lanka | | | |

# BIODIVERSITY HOTSPOTS IN INDIA

1. **Himalaya:** Includes the entire Indian Himalayan region (and that falling in Pakistan, Tibet, Nepal, Bhutan, China and Myanmar)
2. **Indo-Burma:** Includes entire North-eastern India, except Assam and Andaman group of Islands (and Myanmar, Thailand, Vietnam, Laos, Cambodia and southern China)
3. **Sundalands:** Includes Nicobar group of Islands (and Indonesia, Malaysia, Singapore, Brunei, Philippines)
4. **Western Ghats and Sri Lanka:** Includes entire Western Ghats (and Sri Lanka)

## Endemism

It is the ecological state of a species belonging to the particular or specific geographical area such as an island, nation, country or other defined zones. Hence, there are endemic and are not found in any other regions.

## CITES

CITES (the Convention on International Trade in Endangered Species of Wild Fauna and Flora) is an international agreement between governments. Its aim is to ensure the international trade in specimens of wild animals and plants does not threaten their survival.

For many years, CITES has been among the conservation agreements with the largest membership, with now 181 parties. Roughly 5,600 species of animals and 30,000 species of plants are protected by CITES against over-exploitation through international trade. They are listed in the three CITES Appendices. The species are grouped in the appendices according to how threatened they are by international trade. They include some whole groups, such as primates, cetaceans (whales, dolphins and tortoises), sea turtles, parrots, corals, cacti and orchids. However, in some cases only a subspecies or geographically separate population of a species (for example the population of just one country) is listed.

## Ministry of Environment, Forests and Climate Change (INDIA)

The Ministry of Environment & Forests (MoEF) is the nodal agency in the Central Government for overseeing the implementation of India's environment and forest policies and programmes relating to conservation of the country's natural resources including lakes and rivers, its biodiversity, forests and wildlife, ensuring the welfare of animals and prevention and abatement of pollution. While implementing these policies and programmes, the Ministry is guided by the principle of sustainable development. The Ministry is also the nodal agency for the United Nations Environment Programme (UNEP), South Asia Co-operative Environment Programme (SACEP), International Centre for Integrated Mountain Development (ICIMOD) and the United Nations Conference on Environment and Development (UNCED). The Ministry also coordinates with multilateral bodies such as the Commission on Sustainable Development (CSD), Global Environment Facility (GEF) and regional bodies such as Economic and Social Council for Asia and Pacific (ESCAP) and South Asian Association for Regional Cooperation (SAARC) on matters pertaining to environment.

The broad objectives of the Ministry are:

- Conservation and survey of flora, fauna, forests and wildlife
- Prevention and control of pollution
- Afforestation and regeneration of degraded areas
- Protection of environment, and
- Ensuring the welfare of animals.

## National biodiversity authority (NBA)

The Biological Diversity Act 2002 came into force in 2003. The Act extents to the whole of India. The objectives of the Act are conservation, sustainable utilization and fair and equitable sharing of benefits arising out of the use of biological resources and associated knowledge. The Act is being implemented in a three tiered institutional structures (NBA at National level, State Biodiversity Board at State level and Biodiversity Management Committee at local level).

The NBA is a body corporate established in accordance with the provisions of Sec.8 of the Biological Diversity Act, 2002, at Chennai w.e.f. 1st October 2003. It is an autonomous, statutory and regulatory organization which is intended to implement the provisions of Biological Diversity Act, 2002. The main objectives of NBA are: –

- To regulate access to biological resources of the country to conserve and sustainable use of biological diversity.
- To respect and protect the knowledge of local communities related to biodiversity.
- To secure sharing of benefits with the local people as conservers of biological resources and holders of knowledge and information relating to the use of biological resources.
- Conservation and development of area of importance from the view point of biological diversity by declaring them as biological diversity heritage sites.
- Protection and rehabilitation of threatened species; involvement of institutions of state government in the broad scheme of implementation of the Biological Diversity Act through constitution of committees.

## Centres of Excellence ( in India)

- Centre for Environment Education (CEE), Ahmedabad .
- CPR Environmental Education Centre (CPREEC), Chennai.

- Centre for Ecological Sciences (CES), Indian Institute of Science (IISc), Bengaluru.
- Centre of Mining Environment (CME), Indian School of Mines, Dhanbad.
- Salim Ali Centre for Ornithology and Natural History (SACON), Coimbatore.
- Centre for Environment Management of Degraded Ecosystem (CEMDE), University of Delhi, Delhi.
- Madras School of Economics (MSE), Chennai.
- Foundation for Revitalization of Local Health Traditions (FRLHT), Bengaluru.

The Tropical Botanic Garden and Research Institute (TBGRI), Thiruvananthapuram .

Centre for Animals and Environment, CARTMAN, Bengaluru.

# Animal Welfare

## People for the Ethical Treatment of Animals (PETA)

It is a non-profitable American animal rights organization based in Norfolk, Virginia. The organisation is led by Ingrid Newkirk, the international president, founded in 1980 with a slogan "Animals are not ours to eat, wear, experiment on, use for entertainment, or abuse in any other way." It focuses its attention on the four areas in which the largest numbers of animals suffer the most intensely for the longest periods of time-on factory farms, in the clothing trade, in laboratories, and in the entertainment industry.

## World Wide Fund for Nature

The organisation was conceived in Morges, Switzerland (29, April, 1961). It is an international non-governmental organization in nature. Works in the field related to biodiversity conservation, and the reduction of humanity's footprint on the environment. It is the world's largest conservation organization with the slogan of "For a Living Planet." The method of its working involves Lobbying Research and Consultancy. Basically it's a charitable trust. WWF's giant panda logo originated from a panda named Chi Chi. It has been designed by Sir Peter Scott from preliminary sketches made by Gerald Watterson.

The main missions of WWF are as follows:
- Conserving the world's biological diversity
- ensuring that the use of renewable natural resources is sustainable.
- Promoting the reduction of pollution and wasteful consumption.

At present WWF's current strategy of achieving its mission which is related to restoring populations of 36 species (species or species groups that are important for their ecosystem or to people, including elephants, tunas, whales, dolphins and porpoises). and ecological footprint in 6 areas (carbon emissions, cropland, grazing land, fishing, forestry and water).

**Animal Welfare Board of India**
**Functions**

- To keep the law in force in India for the Prevention of Cruelty to Animals under constant study and to advise the government on the amendments to be undertaken in any such law from time to time.
- To advise the Central Government on the making of rules under the Act with a view to preventing unnecessary pain or suffering to animals and transported.
- To advise in the design of vehicles so as to lessen the burden on draught animals.
- To take all such steps as the Board may think fit for amelioration of animals by encouraging, or providing for the construction of sheds, water troughs and the like and by providing for veterinary assistance to animals.
- To advise in the design of slaughter houses or its maintenance.

## India Initiative towards Animal protection

**Project Tiger** an government of India  initiative for conserving its national animal, the tiger. The project was launched in 1973. Since then the no of tiger reserve has been increased from 9 to 47 which accounts for 2.08% the total geographical area of our country. The area of tiger projects have been developed on core/ buffer strategy. The core areas are legally termed as National Parks and the buffering areas are a mixture of forest and non-forest land managed as a multiple used area. The project aims at fostering an exclusive tiger agenda in the core areas of tiger reserves, with an inclusive people oriented agenda in the buffer

**Project Rhino** was joint venture of the Assam Forest Department and Wildlife Trust of India - InternationalFund for Animal Welfare (WTI-IFAW) and initiated in February 2006 with the trans location of a hand-raised rhino calf to Manas Wildlife Sanctuary. The projects aims at repopulatimg the one horn rhino by displacing them to Manas wild life sanctuary from Kaziranga National Park. The whole project is supported by Bodoland Territorial Council and the Assam Forest Department.

## Indian Rhino Vision 2020

- Indian rhino vision 2020 implemented by the department of environment and forests, Assam with The Bodo autonomous council as a active partner. The programme will be supported by WWF - India, WWF areas (Asian rhino and elephant action strategy) programme, the international rhino foundation (IRF), save the rhino's campaign of zoological institutions worldwide and a number of local NGOs.
- The vision of this program is to increase the total rhino foundation in Assam from about 2000 to 3000 by the year 2020 and to ensure that these rhinos are distributed over at least 7 protected areas (PA) to provide long term viability of the one horned rhino population.

**Project Crocodile Conservation** was launched in 1975 in different States for protecting the endangered crocodile species like Gharial, Gavialis gangeticus; Mugger crocodile, Crocodylus palustris and Saltwater crocodile, Crocodylus were on the verge of extinction by the seventies. The funds and technical support for the project came from UNDP/ FAO through the Government of India.

## Vulture

**4.** **India has nine species of vultures in the wild.**

(i)   Indian Griffon **vulture** (Gyps fulvus),

(ii)  Himalayan **Griffon** (Gyps himalayensis),

(iii) Cinereous **Vulture** (Aegypius monachus) and

(iv)  Bearded Vulture or **Lammergeier** (Gypaetus barbatus),

(v)   Oriental White-**backed Vulture** (Gyps bengalensis),

(vi)  Slender billed **Vulture** (Gyps tenuirostris),

(vii) Long billed **Vulture** (**Gyps** indicus),

(viii) Egyptian **Vulture** (**Neophron** percnopterus),

(ix)  Red Headed **Vulture** (Sarcogyps calvus).

- Decline of vulture populations in India was first recorded at the Keoladeo Ghana National Park, Rajasthan

- The decline of Gyps genus in India has been put at 97% (over a 12 year period) oy 2005.

- Similar declines have occurred in other countries in Asia, including Nepal and Pakistan.

- In India the population of three species i.e. White backed Vulture, Slender billed Vulture and Long billed Vulture in the wild has declined drastically over the past decade.

- Red-headed vulture or king vulture, Slender billed Vulture and Long billed Vulture are listed as critically endangered.

- Populations of Egyptian vultures and White-backed Vulture have also undergone decline in India and are now classified as Endangered.

- It is initially thought the drastic decline in population was due to non-availability of food (dead livestock) or an unknown viral epidemic disease, but later on confirmed that decline in population was due to the drug diclofenac.

### Causes of Vultures extinction

- Diclofenac is a non-steroidal anti-inflammatory drug (NSAID) administered to reduce inflammation and to reduce pain in certain conditions.

- NSAIDs are associated with adverse kidney (renal) failure which is caused due to the reduction in synthesis of renal prostaglandins.

- Vultures which were unable to break down the chemical diclofenac, suffer from kidney failure when they eat the carcass of animals which have been administered with the drug - Diclofenac

- Visceral gout, an accumulation of uric acid within tissues and on the surfaces of internal organs, was observed in 85% of dead vultures found. Death caused by renal failure, which is known to occur as a result of metabolic failure or toxic disease.

- "Neck drooping-vulture exhibit this behaviour for protracted periods over several weeks before collapsing and falling out of trees or just prior to death. It is the only obvious behavioural indication that birds are ill. Neck drooping is also reported in healthy birds under hot conditions.



| SIGNIFICANCE OF VULTURES IN INDIA |
|---|

- Scavenging on animal carcasses of animals and thereby helping keep the environment clean.

- Disposal of dead bodies as per the religious practices of the Parsi community.

- Vultures are the primary removers of carrion in India and Africa.

**Vulture Safety Zones**

- The concept of a VSZ is unique for the Asian continent but similar VSZ are in operation in both Europe and Africa.

- Aim of developing VSZs is to establish targeted awareness activities surrounding 150 km radius of vultures colonies so that no diclofenac or the veterinary toxic drugs are found in cattle carcasses, the main food of vultures (to provide safe food).

- The VSZ is spread around in several hundred kilometers covering the Jim Corbett in Uttarakhand, Dudhwa and Kartarniaghat forest reserves in UP which is adjoining the Indo-Nepal border. Nepal has already set up VSZ on the Indian borders.

**Project Elephant (PE)** is a central government initiative to provide financial and technical support to major elephant bearing states of India. It was launched in February 1992. It aims at protecting the elephants, their habitat and corridor. It also looks after the human elephant issues. It is implemented in 13 States / UTs, viz. Andhra pradesh, Arunachal Pradesh, Assam, Jharkhand, Karnataka, Kerala, Meghalaya, Nagaland, Orissa, Tamil Nadu, Uttranchal, Uttar Pradesh and West Bengal.

**SAVE** (Saving Asia's Vultures from Extinction) is a consortium of regional and international organization to co-ordinate conservation, campaigning and fundraising activities to help the plight of south Asia's vultures. The key strategies of vulture conservation SAVE is involved in a wide range of conservation activities across South Asia including:

- Breeding vultures in captivity so that their offspring can be released back in to the wild when the environment is free from diclofenac.

- An active advocacy programme targeting the vets and farmers using diclofenac.

- Legislation controlling the manufacture and sale of veterinary drugs.

- In-situ conservation actions focused around the small but key remaining vulture populations in the wild.

- An active research programme that underpins these activities and monitors their effectiveness.

**Project Dolphin–** Gangetic river dolphins is India's national aquatic animal and is often known as the 'Tiger of the Ganges'. This dolphin species is an indicator animal which represent healthy river ecosystem in a same position as a tiger in a forest. Their population is estimated to be less than 2,000 in the country. Some of the major threats are habitat fragmentation due to construction of dams and barrages, direct killing, indiscriminate fishing and pollution of rivers.

For conservation of dolphins, India's first Dolphin Community Reserve established in West Bengal to protect the endangered mammal, Gangetic river dolphins. The reserve would be set up in the Hooghly River between Malda and Sundarbans as per provisions of Wildlife Protection Act, 1972. State Forest department also has announced that it would also conduct a census to estimate the population of dolphins.

## SEA TURTLE PROJECT

- A significant proportion of world's Olive Ridley Turtle population migrates every winter to Indian coastal waters for nesting mainly at eastern coast.

- With the objective of conservation of olive ridley turtles and other endangered marine turtles, Ministry of Environment & Forests initiated the Sea Turtle Conservation Project in collaboration of UNDP in November, 1999 with Wildlife Institute of India, Dehradun as the Implementing Agency.

- The project is being implemented in 10 coastal States of the country with special emphasis in State of Orissa.

- The project has helped in preparation of inventory map of breeding sites of Sea Turtles, identification of nesting and breeding habitats along the shore line, and migratory routes taken by Sea Turtles, development of guidelines to safeguard and minimize turtle mortality, development of national and international cooperative and collaborative action for Sea Turtle Conservation, developing guideline plans for tourism in sea turtle areas and developing infrastructure and human resources for Sea Turtle Conservation.

- One of the important achievements have been demonstration of use of Satellite Telemetry to locate the migratory route of Olive Ridley Turtles in. the sea and sensitizing the fishermen and State Government for the use of Turtle Exclusion Device (TED) in fishing trawlers to check turtle mortality in fishing net.

## Steps Taken By Indian Government to Protect Biodiversity

Along with above specified conservation projects of the wild animals, GOI has also initiated few schemes that are worked upon to protect the biodiversity and minimize the mortality of critically endangered, endangered and threatened animals. Here are few important steps that Government of India has taken for the wildlife protection:

- In the Wildlife Protection Act of 1972. GOI created Protected Areas like National Parks, Sanctuaries, Conservation Reserves and Community Reserves for the wildlife and imposed punishments on those indulged in illegal act of hunting.

- Wetland (Conservation and Management) Rules 2010 have been drafted to protect of wetlands in India The Central Government has also initiated the scheme. National Plan for Conservation of Aquatic Eco-System that lends assistance to the states for the sound management of all wetlands.

- In order to curb the illegal trade of wildlife and that of endangered species, Wildlife Crime Control Bureau has been established.

- Special organizations like Wildlife Institute of India, Bombay Natural History' society and Salim Ali Centre for Ornithology and Natural History are formed to conduct research on conservation of wildlife.

- To check the dwindling population of Gyps vulture in India, Government of India has banned the veterinary use of diclofenac drug.

- For restocking of the endangered species, the Central Government first initiated Integrated Development of Wildlife Habitat Scheme and later modified it by including a new component, Recovery of Endangered Species which included animals like Hangul/stag deer in Jammu & Kashmir, Vultures in Punjab, Haryana and Gujarat Snow Leopard in Jammu & Kashmir, Himachal Pradesh, Uttarakhand and Arunachal Pradesh, Swiftlet in Andaman & Nicobar Islands, Niigiri Tahr in Tamil Nadu, Sangai Deer in Manipur. Financial and technical assistance is also extended to the state government to provide better means of protection and conservation for the specified species.

- The State Governments have been asked to strengthen the field formations and increase patrolling in and around the Protected Areas.

- GOI intensified anti-poaching activities and initiated special patrolling strategy for monsoon season. Also, deployment of anti-poaching squad.

- In order to strengthen tiger conservation, National Tiger Conservation Authority is constituted by Government of India.

- A Special Tiger Protection Force (STPF) has also been constituted and is deployed in Karnataka, Maharashtra and Odisha

- E-Surveillance has been started in Kaziranga National Park in Assam and borders of Ratapani Wildlife Sanctuary in Madhya Pradesh.

# Exercise -1

1. Degradation of different categories of pesticides by soil microorganism is called
   - (a) Biotransformation
   - (b) Biomineralization
   - (c) Bioaugmentation
   - (d) Biomagnification

2. A species having a dominating influence on the structure and function of a community or ecosystem is known is
   - (a) Fundamental species
   - (b) Functional species
   - (c) Keystone species
   - (d) Indicator species

3. According to ZSI (GOI), which one of the following birds declined by 99%?
   - (a) Sparrow
   - (b) Pink-headed Duck
   - (c) Pond heron
   - (d) White backed Vulture

4. Taxonomic diversity of a region with several ecosystems is:
   - (a) Alpha diversity
   - (b) Beta diversity
   - (c) Gamma diversity
   - (d) Sigma diversity

5. In which of the following ecosystems, the food web involves more species and more trophic levels?
   - (a) Rain forest
   - (b) Ocean
   - (c) Desert
   - (d) Glacier

6. A keystone species
   - (a) has a disproportionately large impact on an ecosystem.
   - (b) typically reduces overall diversity of an ecosystem.
   - (c) is typically an herbivore.
   - (d) is an example of amensalism.

7. Extinction of a weaker species by an aggressive alien species is the results of
   - (a) Endemism of weaker species
   - (b) Habitat loss
   - (c) The Domino Effect
   - (d) All of the above.

8. In the Lower Himalayan Mountains, several species of salamander, an amphibian, live in or near a stream. The largest species lives in the stream and along its edges, a smaller species lives on land within a meter or two of the stream, and a smaller species lives about 3-5 meters away from the stream. In this region, these three salamander species are using
   - (a) different niches within the same habitat
   - (b) the same niche and microhabitat
   - (c) the same landscape but different ecosystems
   - (d) the same habitat but different niches

9. Invasive species are dangerous because
   - (a) they are almost all predators, disturbing ecological relationships by eating other species.
   - (b) they carry viruses that spread disease in new ecosystems.
   - (c) the native species have not evolved with these organisms.
   - (d) they tend to be secretive, going unnoticed in their new ecosystems.

10. Protection and preservation of endangered species away from their natural habitat under human care in zoos, nurseries and laboratories is known as
    - (a) In-situ conservation
    - (b) Ex-situ conservation
    - (c) Biodiversity conservation
    - (d) None of the above

11. Protection of biodiversity around the world requires:
    - (a) basic science to produce government policies and laws that then must be enforced.
    - (b) changes to social structure and political organizations that drive basic science.
    - (c) new technologies and techniques that are still being developed.
    - (d) the introduction of new species into new regions to spread a species range.

12. Within biological communities, some species are important in determining the ability of a large number of other species to persist in the community. Such species are called
    - (a) Keystone species
    - (b) Allopatric species
    - (c) Sympatric species
    - (d) Threatened species

13. The diversity and productivity or coral reefs is most similar to that of
    - (a) desert environments
    - (b) a natural prairie.
    - (c) tropic rain forests
    - (d) a river system.

14. The risk of introducing a natural enemy to control an invasive species is that
    - (a) it might drive the invasive species to extinction.
    - (b) the natural enemy might also become a pest.
    - (c) the natural enemy might evolve into a new species
    - (d) the natural enemy may introduce genetic diversity into the invasive species.

15. Biodiversity is important because:
    - (a) it is necessary to maintain ecosystems.
    - (b) humans can use new sources of food.
    - (c) without certain species, photosynthesis may not be possible.
    - (d) certain species are necessary to provide oxygen in the atmosphere.

16. Endemic species are:
    - (a) secure groups that show the least risk of extinction.
    - (b) limited to just one habitat.
    - (c) widely distributed, found especially on large continents.
    - (d) usually the dominant species within an ecosystem.

17. The greatest loss of biodiversity in the last two centuries has resulted from:
    - (a) the introduction of alien species to new ecosystems.
    - (b) the use of fossil fuels to power transportation and electrical production.
    - (c) the physical alteration of habitats.
    - (d) the use of rivers, lakes, and oceans for transportation.

18. Which one of the following groups of animals belongs to the category of endangered species ?
    (a) Great Indian Bustard, Musk Deer, Red Panda and Asiatic Wild Ass
    (b) Kashmir Stag, Cheetal, Blue Bull and Great Indian Bustard
    (c) Snow Leopard, Swamp Deer, Rhesus Monkey and Saras (Crane)
    (d) Lion-tailed Macaque, Blue Bull, Hanuman Langur and Cheetal

19. Which one of the following is included in the world list of biosphere reserves by UNESCO?
    (a) Kinnaur region       (b) Spiti Valley
    (c) Nallamalai Hills      (d) Sunderbans

20. Which one of the following is a global biodiversity hotspot in India?
    (a) Western Ghats
    (b) Western Himalayas
    (c) Eastern Ghats
    (d) Northern Himalayas

21. Which one of the following is the correct sequence of the given tiger reserves of India from North to South?
    (a) Dudwa-Kanha-Indravati-Bandipur
    (b) Kanha-Bandipur-Dudwa-Indravati
    (c) Indravati-Kanha-Dudwa-Bandipur
    (d) Dudwa-Kanha-Bandipur-Indravati

22. Kanha National Park belongs to which one among the following biogeographical areas in the world?
    (a) Tropical Sub-humid Forests
    (b) Tropical Humid Forests
    (c) Tropical Dry Forests
    (d) Tropical Moist Forests

23. Veliconda hills, which is a part of Eastern Ghats, is situated in
    (a) Odisha            (b) Tamil Nadu
    (c) Karnataka         (d Andhra Pradesh

24. Biodiversity is richer in
    (a) tropical regions   (b) polar regions
    (c) temperate regions  (d) oceans

25. The biodiversity is the study of diversity
    (a) Below species level
    (b) At species level
    (c) At community level
    (d) At all levels of biological organization

26. The term 'Biodiversity' was popularized by
    (a) Edward Wilson     (b) Alexander Von Humboldt
    (c) Paul Ehrlich      (d) Robert May

27. According to IUCN 2004, the total number of plant and animal species described so far is slightly more than
    (a) 5 million         (b) 7 million
    (c) 1.5 million       (d) 0.5 million

28. More than 70% of all the species recorded so far, are
    (a) Insects           (b) Plants
    (c) Animals           (d) Invertebrates

29. Mark the correct statement
    (a) Amazonian rain forest has greatest biodiversity on earth
    (b) According to Robert May estimates, the global species diversity is 7 million
    (c) Biodiversity is the greatest in tropics
    (d) All of these

30. Amongst vertebrates, the species diversity is the maximum in
    (a) Birds             (b) Fishes
    (c) Reptiles          (d) Mammals

31. Following arrangement is correct from the point of view of decreasing biodiversity in angiosperms (N), fungi (F), pteridophytes (P) and algae(A)
    (a) $N > F > P > A$    (b) $N > F > A > P$
    (c) $F > N > P > A$    (d) $F > N > A > P$

32. India's share in global species diversity is around
    (a) 8%                (b) 14 %
    (c) 17 %              (d) 2.4 %

33. The number of plant species recorded from India, is
    (a) 30,000           (b) 45,000
    (c) 70,000           (d) 90,000

34. If S is species richness, A is area, Z is slope of the line, and the C is Y-intercept, then the species richness will be shown as
    (a) $S = C + A^z$     (b) $S = C + AZ$
    (c) $S = C. AZ$       (d) $S = C. A^z$

35. The 'Increased diversity contributes to higher productivity' was the idea of
    (a) Robert May        (b) David Tilman
    (c) Edward Wilson     (d) A V Humboldt

36. The Evil Quartet of biodiversity loss, does not include
    (a) Habitat loss
    (b) Introduction of alien species
    (c) Overexploitation
    (d) Hunting

37. Amazon rain forest, called the 'Lungs of the planet', contribute following percentage of oxygen by photosynthesis, to earth atmosphere
    (a) 20%              (b) 35%
    (c) 42%              (d) 50%

38. The following is not the approach for *in situ* conservation
    (a) Biosphere reserve  (b) Sanctuary
    (c) Wild life safari park (d) Sacred grove

39. The 'Earth summit' for biodiversity was held in
    (a) China             (b) Brazil
    (c) Germany           (d) S. Africa

40. The Indian Rhinoceros is a natural inhabitant of which one of the Indian states?
    (a) Uttarakhand       (b) Uttar Pradesh
    (c) Himachal Pradesh  (d) Assam

**41.** Which of the following is a native of Rajasthan and Gujarat and is presently an endangered animal
  (a)  Wild Ass
  (b)  Rhinoceros
  (c)  Great Indian Bustard
  (d)  Black buck (Antelope)

**42.** Bandhavgarh national park is situated in
  (a)  Karnataka        (b)  Orissa
  (c)  Madhya Pradesh   (d)  Gujrat

**43.** Two places in India show maximum biological diversity. One of them is the Western Ghats, another is
  (a)  Eastern Ghats    (b)  North – East India
  (c)  Coastal region   (d)  Foot hill of Himalaya

**44.** First National Park of India was established in 1935 and was named as
  (a)  Kanha National Park
  (b)  Hailey's National Park
  (c)  Rajaji National Park
  (d)  None of these

**45.** Which of the following set of National Park and the State is wrongly matched?
  (a)  Dudhwa – U.P.
  (b)  Bandipur - Karnataka
  (c)  Nokrek - Meghalaya
  (d)  Simlipal – Bihar

**46.** Match the column -I with column -II

| *Column I* | | *Column II* |
| --- | --- | --- |
| (i)   | Bihar | (a)  Indian elephant |
| (ii)  | Rajasthan | (b)  Gazello |
| (iii) | Madhya Pradesh | (c)  Leopard |
| (iv)  | Uttar Pradesh | (d)  Barasingha |
| (v)   | Gujarat | (e)  Sloth Bear |
|       |  | (f)  Asiatic Lion |

  (a)  (i) a (ii) c (iii) e (iv) b (v) d
  (b)  (i) e (ii) b (iii) d (iv) c (v) f
  (c)  (i) c (ii) e (iii) b (iv) d (v) a
  (d)  (i) f (ii) e (iii) d  (iv) c (v) b

**47.** Main reason behind the destruction of Bio-diversity is :
  (a)  Hunting
  (b)  Soil erosion
  (c)  Green house effect
  (d)  Destruction of natural habitat

**48.** Project tiger was launched by the recommendation of Indian board of Wildlife (IBWL) in
  (a)  1971          (b)  1975
  (c)  1973          (d)  1972

**49.** Which of the following natural bounty is used for giving protection to fauna only?
  (a)  Botanical garden   (b)  National Park
  (c)  Biosphere Reserve  (d)  Sanctuary

**50.** The four Biosphere Reserves, i.e. Nanda Devi (N), Gulf of Mannar (G), Sundarbans (S) and Manas (M) belong to four different states. Mark the incorrect statement in the following
  (a)  S.M. & G. do not belong to U.P.
  (b)  G and N do not belong to Assam
  (c)  None of these belong to Tamil Nadu.
  (d)  M.S.G. belong to Eastern states

**51.** Out of 25 hot spots in the world, how many appear in the tropical forest
  (a)  25            (b)  15
  (c)  9             (d)  5

**52.** Which resource is non-renewable
  (a)  Wild life          (b)  Aquatic animals
  (c)  Biological species (d)  Fresh water plants

**53.** Anthropogenic extinction means
  (a)  The extinction of apes
  (b)  Extinction due to introduction of exotic species
  (c)  Catastrophic extinction
  (d)  Extinction due to human activities

**54.** How many of the following can not be included in wild life – Human, Cultivated plants, Microorganisms, Fossils and Domesticated animals
  (a)  Two            (b)  Three
  (c)  Four           (d)  Five

**55.** An example of biological conservation *in situ* is
  (a)  Biosphere reserve   (b)  Zoo
  (c)  Botanical garden    (d)  All of these

**56.** Which group of the vertebrates comprises the highest number of endangered species?
  (a)  Birds           (b)  Mammals
  (c)  Fishes          (d)  Reptiles

**57.** The number of critically endangered animal and plant species in India is respectively :
  (a)  5 & 10          (b)  18 & 44
  (c)  31 & 14         (d)  54 & 113

**58.** Following organization is associated with the Red – Data book
  (a)  National wild life action plan
  (b)  International union for conservation of nature and natural resources
  (c)  Bombay natural history
  (d)  Man and Biosphere

**59.** Which of the following species is critically endangered in India?
  (a)  Red Panda       (b)  Pigmy hog
  (c)  Black buck      (d)  Reindeer

**60.** The following is not the major threat category of wild life
  (a)  Critically endangered
  (b)  Vulnerable
  (c)  Endangered
  (d)  Extinct in the wild

**61.** Following number of terrestrial Hot Spots for conservation of biodiversity have been identified worldwide
  (a)  9             (b)  15
  (c)  25            (d)  40

**62.** In cryopreservation germplasm is maintained at:
  (a)  – 196° F       (b)  0° F
  (c)  – 100° F       (d)  None

**63.** The maximum number of species have extincted from
  (a)  Islands        (b)  Mainland
  (c)  Oceans         (d)  Fresh water bodies

64. The 'Earth Summit' held at Rio de Janeiro in 1992 resulted into
    (a) Compilation of Red list
    (b) Establishment of Biosphere Reserves
    (c) Convention on Biodiversity
    (d) Development of Hot Spots of Biodiversity

65. Buffer zone, Core zone and the Transition zone are three subdivisions of the Biosphere reserves. The transition zone
    (a) Covers the Buffer zone and lies in between Buffer zone and the Core zone
    (b) Covers the Core zone and lies in between the Core zone and the Buffer zone
    (c) Is the innermost zone of the Biosphere reserve
    (d) Is the outermost zone of the Biosphere reserve

66. Which one of the following National Parks has a climate that varies from tropical to subtropical, temperate and arctic?                **[IAS Prelims 2015]**
    (a) Khangchendzonga National Park
    (b) Nandadevi National Park
    (c) Neora Valley National Park
    (d) Namdapha National Park

67. In India, in which one of the following types of forests is teak a dominant tree species?    **[IAS Prelims 2015]**
    (a) Tropical moist deciduous forest
    (b) Tropical rain forest
    (c) Tropical thorn scrub forest
    (d) Temperate forest with grasslands

68. Which of the following National Parks is unique in being a swamp with floating vegetation that supports a rich biodiversity?                **[IAS Prelims 2015]**
    (a) Bhitarkanika National Park
    (b) Keibul Lamjao National Park
    (c) Keoladeo Ghana National Park
    (d) Sultanpur National Park

69. Which one of the following is the national aquatic animal of India?                **[IAS Prelims 2015]**
    (a) Saltwater crocodile      (b) Olive ridley turtle
    (c) Gangetic dolphin      (d) Gharial

70. What is/are unique about 'Kharai camel', a breed found in India?                **[IAS Prelims 2016]**
    1. It is capable of swimming up to three kilometers in seawater.
    2. It survives by grazing on mangroves.
    3. It lives in the wild and cannot be domesticated.
    Select the correct answer using the code given below.
    (a) 1 and 2 only      (b) 3 only
    (c) 1 and 3 only      (d) 1, 2 and 3

71. Recently, our scientists have discovered a new and distinct species of banana plant which attains a height of about 11 metres and has orange-coloured fruit pulp. In which part of India has it been discovered?
    (a) Andaman Islands        **[IAS Prelims 2016]**
    (b) Anaimalai Forests
    (c) Maikala Hills
    (d) Tropical rain forests of northeast

72. With reference to 'Red Sanders', sometimes seen in the news, consider the following statements:
                        **[IAS Prelims 2016]**
    1. It is a tree species found in a part of South India.
    2. It is one of the most important trees in the tropical rain forest areas of South India.
    Which of the statements given above is/are correct?
    (a) 1 only      (b) 2 only
    (c) Both 1 and 2      (d) Neither 1 nor 2

73. Recently, for the first time in our country, which of the following States has declared a particular butterfly as 'State Butterfly'?                **[IAS Prelims 2016]**
    (a) Arunachal Pradesh      (b) Himachal Pradesh
    (c) Karnataka      (d) Maharashtra

74. In which of the following regions of India are you most likely to come across the 'Great Indian Hornbill' in its natural habitat?                **[IAS Prelims 2016]**
    (a) Sand deserts of northwest India
    (b) Higher Himalayas of Jammu and Kashmir
    (c) Salt marshes of western Gujarat
    (d) Western Ghats

75. With reference to an initiative called 'The Economics of Ecosystems and Biodiversity (TEEB)', which of the following statements is/are correct? **[IAS Prelims 2016]**
    1. It is an initiative hosted by UNEP, IMF and World Economic Forum.
    2. It is a global initiative that focuses on drawing attention to the economic benefits of biodiversity.
    3. It presents an approach that can help decision-makers recognize, demonstrate and capture the value of ecosystems and biodiversity.
    Select the correct answer using the code given below.
    (a) 1 and 2 only      (b) 3 only
    (c) 2 and 3 only      (d) 1, 2 and 3

76. Which of the following statements is/are correct?
    Proper design and effective implementation of UN-REDD+ Programme can significantly contribute to
    1. protection of biodiversity
    2. resilience of forest ecosystems
    3. poverty reduction
    Select the correct answer using the code given below.
                        **[IAS Prelims 2016]**
    (a) 1 and 2 only      (b) 3 only
    (c) 2 and 3 only      (d) 1, 2 and 3

77. What is/are unique about 'Kharai camel', a breed found in India?                **[IAS Prelims 2016]**
    1. It is capable of swimming up to three kilometers in seawater.
    2. It survives by grazing on mangroves.
    3. It lives in the wild and cannot be domesticated.
    Select the correct answer using the code given below.
    (a) 1 and 2 only      (b) 3 only
    (c) 1 and 3 only      (d) 1, 2 and 3

**78.** Recently, our scientists have discovered a new and distinct species of banana plant which attains a height of about 11 metres and has orange-coloured fruit pulp. In which part of India has it been discovered?

**[IAS Prelims 2016]**

(a) Andaman Islands

(b) Anaimalai Forests

(c) Maikala Hills

(d) Tropical rain forests of northeast

**79.** The Mahatma Gandhi Marine National Park is located in:

**[CDS 2016]**

(a) Pirotan Island      (b) Rameswaram

(c) Ganga Sagar Island      (d) Port Blair

**80.** If you want to see gharials in their natural habitat, which one of the following is the best place to visit?

(a) Bhitarkanika Mangroves     **[IAS Prelims 2017]**

(b) Chambal River

(c) Pulicat Lake

(d) DeeporBeel

**81.** In India, if a species of tortoise is declared protected under Schedule I of the Wildlife (Protection) Act, 1972, what does it imply ?     **[IAS Prelims 2017]**

(a) It enjoys the same level of protection as the tiger.

(b) It no longer exists in the wild, a few individuals are under captive protection; and now it is impossible to prevent its extinction.

(c) It is endemic to a particular region of India.

(d) Both (b) and (c) stated above are correct in this context.

**82.** Recently there was a proposal to translocate some of the lions from their natural habitat in Gujarat to which one of the following sites ?     **[IAS Prelims 2017]**

(a) Corbett National Park

(b) KunoPalpur Wildlife Sanctuary

(c) Mudumalai Wildlife Sanctuary

(d) Sariska National Park

**83.** In which one of the following States is Pakhui Wildlife Sanctuary located?     **[IAS Prelims 2018]**

(a) Arunachal Pradesh

(b) Manipur

(c) Meghalaya

(d) Nagaland

# Exercise -2

## Statement Based MCQ

**1.** Biodiversity :
1. Increase towards the Arctic region
2. Decrease towards the Arctic region
3. Increase towards the equator
4. Decrease towards the equator

Choose the correct code:

(a) 1 and 4      (b) 1 and 2

(c) 1 and 3      (d) 2 and 3

**2.** Consider the following pairs

| Protected area | Well-known for |
|---|---|
| 1. Bhiterkanika, Odisha | — Salt Water Crocodile |
| 2. Desert National Park, Rajasthan | — Great Indian Bustard |
| 3. Eravikulam, Kerala | — Hoolak Gibbon |

Which of the pairs given above is / are correctly matched ?

(a) 1 only      (b) 1 and 2

(c) 2 only      (d) 1, 2 and 3

**3.** Three of the following criteria have contributed to the recognition of Western Ghats , Sri Lanka and Indo Burma regions as hotspots of biodiversity
1. Species richness
2. Vegetation density
3. Endemism
4. Ethno-botanical importance
5. Threat perception
6. Adaption of flora and fauna to warm and humid conditions

Which three of the above are correct criteria in this context?

(a) 1, 2 and 6      (b) 2, 4 and 6

(c) 1, 3 and 5      (d) 3, 4 and 6

**4.** Consider the following statements
1. Biodiversity hotspots are located only in tropical regions.
2. India has four biodiversity hotspots i.e., Eastern Himalayas, Western Himalayas, Western Ghats and Andaman and Nicobar Islands.

Which of the statements given above is / are correct?

(a) 1 only      (b) 2 only

(c) Both 1 and 2      (d) Neither 1 nor 2

**5.** The "Red Data Books'' published by the International Union for Conservation of Nature and Natural resources (IUCN) contain lists of ?
1. Endemic plant and animal species present in the biodiversity hotspots.
2. Threatened plant and animal species.
3. Protected sites for conservation of nature and natural resources in various countries.

Select the correct answer using the codes given below:

(a) 1 and 3      (b) 2 only

(c) 2 and 3      (d) 3 only

**6.** Consider the following protected areas:
1. Bandipur
2. Bhitarkanika
3. Manas
4. Sunderbans
Which of the above are declared Tiger Reserves?
(a) 1 and 2 only
(b) 1, 3 and 4 only
(c) 2, 3 and 4 only
(d) 1, 2, 3 and 4

**7.** Which of the following can be threats to the biodiversity of a geographical area?
1. Global warming
2. Fragmentation of habitat
3. Invasion of alien species
4. Promotion of vegetarianism
Select the correct answer using the codes given below:
(a) 1 and 2 only
(b) 2 and 3 only
(c) 1, 2 and 3 only
(d) 1, 2, 3 and 4 only

**8.** Biodiversity forms the basis for human existence in the following ways:
1. Soil formation
2. Prevention of soil erosion
3. Recycling of waste
4. Pollination of crops
Select the correct answer using the codes given below:
(a) 1, 2 and 3 only
(b) 2, 3 and 4 only
(c) 1 and 4 only
(d) 1, 2, 3 and 4

**9.** Which of the following regions of India have been designated as biodiversity hotspots?
Select the correct answer from the codes given below:
1. Eastern Himalaya
2. Eastern Ghat
3. Western Ghat
4. Western Himalaya
**Codes:**
(a) 1 and 2 only
(b) 1 and 3 only
(c) 2 and 4 only
(d) 3 and 4 only

**10.** The steps taken by the Government of India for conversion endangered species are
1. The Central Government has enacted the Wild Life (Protection) Act, 1972 for protection of wildlife including birds.
2. Wetland (Conservation and Management) Rules 2010 have been framed for protection of wetlands, in the States, which are habitats of birds.
3. Wildlife Crime Control Bureau has been established for control of illegal trade in wildlife, including endangered species of birds and their parts and products.
4. The Centrally Sponsored Scheme of National Plan for Conservation of Aquatic Eco-System also provides assistance to the States for management of wetlands including Ramsar sites in the country.
Select the answer from the codes given below-
(a) 1, 2, and 3
(b) 2, 3, and 4
(c) 1, 3, and 4
(d) All of the above

**11.** Consider the following statements
1. Tree Foundation, an NGO engaged in conservation of the sea turtle found more than 100 dead Olive Ridley Turtles in the shores of Nagapattinam.
2. The Olive Ridley turtles find the coastline of Nagapattinam as a favourable nesting habitat and that's why they reach to the shore from December to March every year.
3. The Olive Ridley looks very similar to the Kemp's Riddle, but has a deeper body and slightly up-turned edges to its carapace (shell).
4. Olive Ridley weighs around 45 kilograms and are 70cm in size and this makes them the smallest of the sea turtles along with Kemp riddles.
Which of the following statements are correct?
(a) 1, 2 and 3
(b) 2, 3 and
(c) 1, 3 and 4
(d) All of the above

**12.** Which of the following two criteria have to be met in order to qualify as a 'biodiversity hotspot' on the world hotspots map?
1. The region must contain at last 0.5% or 1500 species of vascular plants as endemic species.
2. The region has to have lost at least 70% of its primary vegetation.
Which of the statements given above is/are correct?
(a) 1 only
(b) 2 only
(c) 1 and 2 both
(d) None

**13.** Sumatran rhino populations have declined steadily to a point near extinction. Because of its population decline, this unusual forest dwelling rhino is near its :
1. carrying capacity
2. officially listed as threatened
3. critical number
4. officially listed as endangered
Which of the above is/are correct?
(a) 1 and 2
(b) 3 and 4
(c) 1 and 3
(d) 2 and 3

**14.** Which of the following can be threats to the biodiversity of a geographical area?
1. Global warming
2. Fragmentation of habitat
3. Invasion of alien species
4. Promotion of vegetarianism
Select the correct answer using the codes given below:
(a) 1, 2 and 3
(b) 2 and 3
(c) 1 and 4
(d) 1, 2, 3 and 4

**15.** The "Red Data Books" published by the International Union for Conservation of Nature and Natural resources (IUCN) contain lists of ?
1. Endemic plant and animal species present in the biodiversity hotspots.
2. Threatened plant and animal species.
3. Protected sites for conservation of nature and natural resources in various countries.
Select the correct answer using the codes given below:
(a) 1 and 3
(b) 2 only
(c) 2 and 3
(d) 3 only

**16.** Consider the following statements:

1. The boundaries of a National Park are defined by legislation.
2. A Biosphere Reserve is declared to conserve a few specific species of flora and fauna.
3. In a Wildlife Sanctuary, limited biotic interference is permitted.

Which of the statements given above is / correct ?

(a) 1 only             (b) 2 and 3
(c) 1 and 3          (d) 1, 2 and 3

**17.** One Carbon Credit is defined as _____ .

1. Credit permit to release one ton of carbon dioxide.
2. providing loans to establish a unit which produces carbon dioxide for industrial use.
3. Finding out one new business which can use and recycle greenhouse gases.

Which of the following statements(s) is/are correct?

(a) 3 only           (b) 2 only
(c) 1 only          (d) 1, 2 and 3

**18.** How does National Biodiversity Authority (NBA) help in protecting the Indian agriculture?

1. NBA checks the biopiracy and protects the indigenous and traditional genetic resources.
2. NBA directly monitors and supervises the scientific research on genetic modification of crop plants.
3. Application for Intellectual Property Rights related to genetic/biological resources cannot be made without the approval of NBA.

Which of the statements given above is /are correct?

(a) 1only          (b) 2 and 3
(c) 1 and 3        (d) 1, 2 and 3

**19.** Three of the following criteria have contributed to the recognition of Western Ghats , Sri Lanka and Indo Burma regions as hotspots of biodiversity

1. Species richness
2. Vegetation density
3. Endemism
4. Ethno-botanical importance
5. Threat perception
6. Adaption of flora and fauna to warm and humid conditions

Which three of the above are correct criteria in this context?

(a) 1, 2 and 6      (b) 2, 4 and 6
(c) 1, 3 and 5      (d) 3, 4 and 6

**20.** Biodiversity forms the basis for human existence in the following ways

1. Soil formation
2. Prevention of soil erosion
3. Recycling of waste
4. Pollination of crops

Select the correct answer using the codes given below:

(a) 1,2 and 3      (b) 2, 3 and 4
(c) 1 and 4        (d) 1, 2, 3 and 4

**21.** Which of the following can be threats to the biodiversity of a geographical area?

1. Global warming
2. Fragmentation of habitat
3. Invasion of alien species
4. Promotion of vegetarianism

Select the correct answer using the codes given below :

(a) 1, 2 and 3     (b) 2 and 3
(c) 1 and 4       (d) 1, 2, 3 and 4

**22.** Consider the following statements :

1. The boundaries of a National Park are defined by legislation.
2. A Biosphere Reserve is declared to conserve a few specific species of flora and fauna.
3. In a Wildlife Sanctuary, limited biotic interference is permitted.

Which of the statements given above is / correct ?

(a) 1 only            (b) 2 and 3
(c) 1 and 3          (d) 1, 2 and 3

**23.** In which of the following States is lion-tailed macaque found in its natural habitat?

1. Tamil Nadu      2. Kerala
3. Karnataka       4. Andhra Pradesh

Select the correct answer using the codes given below.

(a) 1, 2 and 3 only    (b) 2 only
(c) 1, 3 and 4 only    (d) 1, 2, 3 and 4

**24.** Consider the following:

1. Star tortoise       2. Monitor lizard
3. Pygmy hog        4. Spider monkey

Which of the above are naturally found in India?

(a) 1, 2 and 3 only    (b) 2 and 3 only
(c) 1 and 4 only      (d) 1, 2, 3 and 4

**25.** Consider the following fauna of India:

1. Gharial          2. Leatherback turtle
3. Swamp deer

Which of the above is/are endangered?

(a) 1 and 2 only     (b) 3 only
(c) 1, 2 and 3       (d) None

**26.** If you walk through countryside, you are likely to see some birds stalking alongside the cattle to seize the insects disturbed by their movement through grasses. Which of the following is/are such bird/birds?

1. Painted Stork     2. Common Myna
3. Black-necked Crane

Select the correct answer using the code given below.

(a) 1 and 2        (b) 2 only
(c) 2 and 3        (d) 3 only

**27.** With reference to the International Union for Conservation of Nature and Natural Resources (IUCN) and the Convention on International Trade in Endangered Species of Wild Fauna and Flora (CITES), which of the following statements is/are correct?   **[UPSC Prelims 2015]**

1. IUCN is an organ of the United Nations and CITES is an international agreement between governments.
2. IUCN runs thousands of field projects around the world to better manage natural environments.
3. CITES is legally binding on the States that have joined it, but this Convention does not take the place of national laws.

Select the correct answer using the code given below.

(a) 1 only           (b) 2 and 3 only
(c) 1 and 3 only     (d) 1, 2 and 3

**28.** With reference to an organization known as 'Birdlife International', which of the following statements is/are correct? **[UPSC Prelims 2015]**
1. It is a Global Partnership of Conservation Organizations.
2. The concept of 'biodiversity hotspots' originated from this organization.
3. It identifies the sites known/referred to as 'Important Bird and Biodiversity Areas'.

Select the correct answer using the code given below.
(a) 1 only     (b) 2 and 3 only
(c) 1 and 3 only     (d) 1, 2 and 3

**29.** Consider the following sanctuaries of India
1. Periyar     2. Dachigam
3. Sariska     4. Kanha

Which one among the following is the correct sequence of location of the above sanctuaries from South to North?
(a) 1, 4, 2, 3     (b) 4, 1, 3, 2
(c) 1, 4, 3, 2     (d) 3, 1, 4, 2

**30.** Which of the following are UNESCO recognised world heritage sites?
1. Caves of Ajanta.
2. Temple and Caves at Ellora.
3. Mandapas of Mahabalipurarn.
4. Caves of Kanheri.

Select the correct answer using the codes given below
(a) 1 and 4     (b) 1, 2 and 3
(c) 1, 3 and 4     (d) 2, 3 and 4

**31.** Consider the following statements
1. Jim Corbett National Park is the oldest national park of india.
2. It was one of the nine tiger reserves created at the launch of the Project Tiger in 1973.
3. Initially it was named as 'Hailey National Park'.

Which of the statements given above are correct?
(a) 1 and 2     (b) All of these
(c) 2 and 3     (d) 1 and 3

---

**Directions (Q. 31 to 34):** Match List-I with List-II and select the correct answer using the codes given below the lists.

**32.**

| | List-I | | List-II |
|---|---|---|---|
| A. | Biodiversity | 1. | G. Tansley |
| B. | Wildlife | 2. | E.O. Wilson |
| C. | Ecosystem | 3. | E. Haeckel |
| D. | Ecology | 4. | W.T. Hornaday |

Codes:

| | A | B | C | D |
|---|---|---|---|---|
| (a) | 2 | 4 | 3 | 1 |
| (b) | 2 | 4 | 1 | 3 |
| (c) | 4 | 2 | 3 | 1 |
| (d) | 4 | 2 | 1 | 3 |

**33.** Consider the following pairs:
1. Nokrek Bio-sphere Reserve : Garo Hills
2. Logtak (Loktak) Lake : Barail Range
3. Namdapha National Park : Dafla Hills

Which of the above pairs is/are correctly matched?
(a) 1 only     (b) 2 and 3 only
(c) 1, 2 and 3     (d) None

**34.** Consider the following pairs :
1. Dampa Tiger Reserve : Mizoram
2. Gumti Wildlife Sanctuary : Sikkim
3. Saramati Peak : Nagaland

Which of the above pairs is/are correctly matched?
(a) 1 only     (b) 2 and 3 only
(c) 1 and 3 only     (d) 1, 2 and 3

**35.**

| | List-I (Major Biome) | | List-II (Physical characterstics) |
|---|---|---|---|
| A. | The Northern most of the Temperate Formations | 1. | Foristically poor (i.e., a continuous belt across North America and Northern Eurasia) |
| B. | Arctic Tundra Vegetation | 2. | Boreal Forest |
| C. | Marine | 3. | Pelagic division |
| D. | The Terrestrial Biomes of the Tropics | 4. | Savanna woodland |
| | | 5. | Soviet Steppe and North American Prairie |

Select the correct option from the codes given below:

| | A | B | C | D |
|---|---|---|---|---|
| (a) | 2 | 4 | 3 | 1 |
| (b) | 2 | 1 | 3 | 4 |
| (c) | 4 | 3 | 5 | 2 |
| (d) | 4 | 1 | 3 | 2 |

**36.** Read the two statements A and B
Statement A : Diversity observed in the entire geographical area is called gamma diversity.
Statement B : Biodiversity decreases from high altitude to low altitude.
Identify the correct choice from those given below :
(a) statement A is correct, B is wrong
(b) statement B is correct, A is wrong
(c) both the statements A and B are correct
(d) both the statements A and B are wrong

**37.** Read the statement regarding a stable community and choose the correct option:
A. Must be resistant to occasional disturbances
B. Should show much variation in productivity from year to year
C. Must be resistant to invasions by alien species
(a) A and B are correct    (b) A, B and C are correct
(c) Only A is correct    (d) A and C are correct

**38.** Find the wrongly matched pair:
(a) Endemism- Species confined to a region and not found anywhere else
(b) Hot spots- Western Ghats
(c) Sacred groves- Jaintia Hills of Rajasthan
(d) Ex situ conservation- Zoological park

**39.** Conservation of flora and fauna in its natureel habitat is :
(a) In-situ conservation
(b) Ex-situ conservation
(c) In vivo conservation
(d) In vitro conservation

**40.** Which of the following represent maximum number of species among global biodiversity?
(a) Lichens
(b) Fungi
(c) Mosses and Ferns
(d) Algae

**41.** With reference to 'Red Sanders', sometimes seen in the news, consider the following statements: **[IAS Prelims 2016]**
1. It is a tree species found in a part of South India.

2. It is one of the most important trees in the tropical rain forest areas of South India.

Which of the statements given above is/are correct?

(a) 1 only      (b) 2 only
(c) Both 1 and 2      (d) Neither 1 nor 2

**42.** Recently, for the first time in our country, which of the following States has declared a particular butterfly as 'State Butterfly'? **[IAS Prelims 2016]**

(a) Arunachal Pradesh    (b) Himachal Pradesh
(c) Karnataka      (d) Maharashtra

**43.** In which of the following regions of India are you most likely to come across the 'Great Indian Hornbill' in its natural habitat? **[IAS Prelims 2016]**

(a) Sand deserts of northwest India
(b) Higher Himalayas of Jammu and Kashmir
(c) Salt marshes of western Gujarat
(d) Western Ghatsw

**44.** Consider the following statements:

1. The definition of "Critical Wildlife Habitat" is incorporated in the Forest Rights Act, 2006.
2. For the first time in India, Baigas have been given Habitat Rights.
3. Union Ministry of Environment, Forest and Climate Change officially decides and declares Habitat Rights for Primitive and Vulnerable Tribal Groups in any part of Indi(a)

Which of the statements given above is/are correct ?

(a) 1 and 2 only      (b) 2 and 3 only
(c) 3 only      (d) 1, 2 and 3

**45.** According to the Wildlife (Protection) Act, 1972, which of the following animals cannot be hunted by any person except under some provisions provided by law?

**[IAS Prelims 2017]**

1. Gharial      2. Indian wild ass
3. Wild buffalo

Select the correct answer using the code given below:

(a) 1 only      (b) 2 and 3 only
(c) 1 and 3 only      (d) 1, 2 and 3

# Hints and Explanations

## EXERCISE-1

| | | | | | | | | | |
|---|---|---|---|---|---|---|---|---|---|
| 1. | (a) | 2. | (d) | 3. | (d) | 4. | (c) | 5. | (b) |
| 6. | (a) | 7. | (a) | 8. | (a) | 9. | (c) | 10. | (d) |
| 11. | (a) | 12. | (a) | 13. | (c) | 14. | (b) | 15. | (a) |
| 16. | (b) | 17. | (c) | | | | | | | |

**18.** (a) Red Panda and Asiatic Wild Ass, are endangered species.

**19.** (d) The Sundarbans is the largest single block of tidal halophytic mangrove forest in the world. The Sundarban forest lies in the vast delta on the Bay of Bengal formed by the super confluence of the Ganges, Padma, Brahmaputra and Meghna rivers across southern Bangladesh. It is a UNESCO World Heritage Site.

**20.** (a) Western Ghats are UNESCO World Heritage Site and is one of the eight "hottest hotspots" of biological diversity in the world.

**21.** (a) 1. Dudwa National park - Uttar Pradesh
2. Kanha National Park- Madhya Pradesh
3. Indravati National Park - Chattisgarh
4. Bandipur National Park- Karnataka

**22.** (c) Kanha National Park belongs to tropical moist dry deciduous forest. It is a tiger reserve of India and the largest national park of Madhya Pradesh.

**23.** (d) Veliconda Hills are situated in southeastern Andhra Pradesh state. They form the eastern flank of the Eastern Ghats.

**24.** (a) Biodiversity is richer in tropical regions. Biodiversity is a measure of the health of ecosystems. Greater biodiversity implies greater health. Biodiversity is in part a function of climate. In terrestrial habitats, tropical regions are typically rich whereas Polar Regions support fewer species.

| | | | | | | | | | |
|---|---|---|---|---|---|---|---|---|---|
| 25. | (d) | 26. | (a) | 27. | (c) | 28. | (c) | 29. | (d) |
| 30. | (b) | 31. | (d) | 32. | (a) | 33. | (b) | 34. | (d) |
| 35. | (b) | 36. | (d) | 37. | (a) | 38. | (c) | 39. | (b) |
| 40. | (d) | 41. | (c) | 42. | (c) | | | | | |

**43.** (b) Western Ghats and Eastern Himalayas are the hot spots of India.

**44.** (b) Hailey's National park is now known as Corbett N P, and is located in Uttaranchal.

**45.** (d) Simlipal is the National park of Orissa.

| | | | | | |
|---|---|---|---|---|---|
| 46. | (b) | 47. | (d) | 48. | (c) |

**49.** (d) National parks give protection to fauna and flora both.

**50.** (c) Gulf of Mannar is the biosphere reserve of Tamil Nadu

| | | | | | |
|---|---|---|---|---|---|
| 51. | (b) | 52. | (c) | 53. | (d) |

**54.** (c) Out of these categories only micro-organisms are covered in wild life.

**55.** (a) Zoo/ Zoological gardens and botanical gardens provide ex situ conservation.

**56.** (b)

**57.** (b)

**58.** (b) IUCN is now known as WCU (World Conservation Union).

**59.** (b) The Zoological name of this hog is Sus salvanius.

**60.** (d)

**61.** (c) Out of 25 terrestrial hot spots of the world, Tropics appear in 16 and Islands in 9.

**62.** (d) The germ plasm is maintained at $-196°C$ (not $°F$).

| | | | |
|---|---|---|---|
| 63. | (a) | 64. | (c) |

**65.** (d) The transition zone of biosphere reserve is also known as manipulation zone.

66. (d) Namdapha National Park is located in Arunachal Pradesh. The climate of this area varies from tropical to subtropical, temperate and arctic. It is tropical and subtropical in southern regions and arctic type found in northern part of the park.

67. (a) The tropical moist deciduous forests are found in Sahyadris, the north-eastern parts of the peninsula and along the foothills of the Himalayas. Teak and sal are found in these forests.

68. (b) The Keibul Lamjao National Park is a national park located in Manipur. It is 40 km in area and the only floating park in the world which is located in North East India, and an integral part of Loktak Lake.

69. (c) The Gangetic dolphins have been declared as the National Aquatic Animal of India .River Dolphin is the National Aquatic Animal of India. The Ministry of Environment and Forests notified the Ganges River Dolphin as the National Aquatic Animal on 18th May 2010. This mammal is also said to represent the purity of the holy Ganga as it can only survive in pure and fresh water.

70. (a) These camels can swim up to three kilometers into the sea in search of mangroves - So, 1 and 2 are correct.Most families in Jatt and Rabari communities of Kachchh, are traditional rearers of Kharai camels. So, third statement also correct. Kharai camels found in the Kutch region are very unique. They can can swim through deep sea waters and it feeds on mangroves and other saline plants. The breeders have meticulously followed the traditional grazing pattern in the coastal districts. They do not provide special housing or shelter to the camels.Given the breed's ability to survive both on land and sea, the Kharai camel is one of the most preferred choices of graziers in the arid coastal region of Kachchh. People consume its milk, while male calves are sold for economic returns (females are not sold because they are considered sacred). A male calf fetches anywhere between Rs. 6,000 and Rs.14,000, says Ramesh Bhatti of Sahjeevan, an NGO working on livelihood issues of graziers in Kachchh. It can be domesticated also – so its not wild. They are reared in four blocks of Abdasa, Bundra, Lakhpat and Bachau of Gujarat.

Ref : DOWN TO EARTH (An important source for Env)

Rare Kharai camel species, found in Kutch district, is under threat due to the onslaught of industrialisation, post-2001 earthquake.

71. (a) Scientists at the Botanical Survey of India (BSI) have discovered a new species of banana from a remote tropical Krishna Nalah rain forest on the Little Andaman islands. The new species is about 11 metres high, whereas as the usual banana species is about three to four meters high. The fruit pulp is orange in colour, distinctive from the white and yellow color of regular bananas. Hence (a) is the correct answer.
Ref: TheHindu/October 11, 2015
http://www.thehindu.com/news/national/other-states/andamans-yield-a-sweet-banana-with-orange-pulp/article7750316.ece

72. (a) (i) Pterocarpus santalinus, with the common names red sanders, red sandalwood, and saunderswood, is a species of Pterocarpus endemic to the southern Eastern Ghats mountain range of South India. This tree is valued for the rich red color of its wood. The wood is not aromatic.
(ii) It was in national media during April 2015, when Andhra Pradesh police killed 20 Red Sander smugglers in an encounter. So first statement is right.
(iii) Red Sanders is associated with Tropical dry deciduous forest, as per environment ministry website, Hence 2nd statement wrong.

73. (d) In June 2015, Maharashtra government has declared the Blue Mormon (Papilio polymnestor) as the State butterfly.
Ref: The Hindu newspaper (http://www.thehindu.com/news/national/other-states/maharashtra-gets-state-butterfly/article7342955.ece MUMBAI, June 22, 2015)

74. (d) Frontline/ENVIRONMENT "WILDLIFE
Print edition : February 6, 2015
http://www.frontline.in/environment/wild-life/cry-from-the-ghats/article6805391.ece

75. (c) (i) The Economics of Ecosystems and Biodiversity (TEEB) is a study led by Pavan Sukhdev. It is an international initiative to draw attention to the global economic benefits of biodiversity. Its objective is to highlight the growing cost of biodiversity loss and ecosystem and to draw together expertise from the fields of science, economics and policy to enable practical actions.
(ii) As per the official page of the organization. 2 and 3 are correct, but there is no mention of their association with UNEP, IMF. Hence 1st statement is wrong. Accordingly answer is "c"

76. (a) (i) Reducing emissions from deforestation and forest degradation (REDD) is a mechanism that has been under negotiation by the United Nations Framework Convention on Climate Change (UNFCCC) since 2005, with the objective of mitigating climate change through reducing net emissions of greenhouse gases through enhanced forest management in developing countries.

(ii) Under REDD+ Developing country will have to prove the 'result' they have fought deforestation without harming local communities or biological diversity. Only then, they'll get the Money. Therefore, 1 and 2 are correct.

Although REDD+ has galvanized significant support internationally, among both developed and developing countries, its implications for poverty alleviation at the local level remain unclear. hence 3rd statement is wrong. Therefore Answer (a).

77. (a) These camels can swim up to three kilometers into the sea in search of mangroves - So, 1 and 2 are correct.Most families in Jatt and Rabari communities of Kachchh, are traditional rearers of Kharai camels. So, third statement also correct.

Kharai camels found in the Kutch region are very unique. They can can swim through deep sea waters and it feeds on mangroves and other saline plants. The breeders have meticulously followed the traditional grazing pattern in the coastal districts. They do not provide special housing or shelter to the camels.Given the breed's ability to survive both on land and sea, the Kharai camel is one of the most preferred choices of graziers in the arid coastal region of Kachchh. People consume its milk, while male calves are sold for economic returns (females are not sold because they are considered sacred). A male calf fetches anywhere between Rs. 6,000 and Rs.14,000, says Ramesh Bhatti of Sahjeevan, an NGO working on livelihood issues of graziers in Kachchh. It can be domesticated also – so its not wild. They are reared in four blocks of Abdasa, Bundra, Lakhpat and Bachau of Gujarat.
Ref : DOWN TO EARTH (An important source for Env)
Rare Kharai camel species, found in Kutch district, is under threat due to the onslaught of industrialisation, post-2001 earthquake.

78. (a) Scientists at the Botanical Survey of India (BSI) have discovered a new species of banana from a remote tropical Krishna Nalah rain forest on the Little Andaman islands. The new species is about 11 metres high, whereas as the usual banana species is about three to four meters high. The fruit pulp is orange in colour, distinctive from the white and yellow color of regular bananas. Hence (a) is the correct answer.
Ref: TheHindu/October 11, 2015
http://www.thehindu.com/news/national/other-states/andamans-yield-a-sweet-banana-with-orange-pulp/article7750316.ece

79. (d) Mahatma Gandhi Marine National Park is a national park in Wandoor on the Andaman Islands situated 29 km. from Port Blair.

80. (b) Gharials are river dwelling fish-eaters and their only viable population is in the Chambal Sanctuary. So "B" should be the answer

81. (a) Tiger is given as Schedule I animal. So "A" is correct.

82. (b) Even if you eliminate Corbett (Uttrakhand) and Mudumalai (Tamilnadu) for climatic reasons for Lion relocation, still you're left with Sariska (Rajasthan). Sariska being a tiger reserve, would sound unfit for lion immigration. So by elimination answer would be "B". and Indianexpress report confirm it.

83. (a) "Pakhui / Pakke Tiger reserve" is in Arunanchal Pradesh, so if there is a wildlife sanctuary in Pakhui, it should be in "A" for Arunanchal Pradesh.

## EXERCISE-2

1. (d)

2. (b) • Bhiterkanika, Odisha is a protected area for salt water crocodile, where breeding is the main purpose of that protected area.
   • Great Indian Bustard is protected in desert area of Rajasthan.
   • The Eravikulam National Park was established to protect the Nilgiri tahir (wild goat) species.

3. (c) To qualify as a hotspot, a region must meet two strict criteria: it must contain at least 1,500 species of vascular plants (> 0.5 percent of the world's total) as endemics, and it has to have lost at least 70 percent of its original habitat. So we choose Species richness as well as Endemism. Along with this Threat perception is necessary to take, because it makes the base of this concept. Adaptation of flora is an arbitrary option, Ethno-botanical importance does nothing with the Biodiversity Hotspot selection criteria, vegetation Density is also discarded.

4. (d) Biodiversity hot spots are located in temperate regions and hotspots are present in eastern Himalayas, Western Ghats and Andaman Islands.

5. (b) The red data book is contain only 8 lists of threatened plant and animal species.

6. (b) Bandipur National Park, a tiger reserve is located in the south Indian state of Karnataka.
   Manas National Park or Manas Wildlife Sanctuary is a National Park, UNESCO Natural World Heritage site, a Project Tiger Reserve, an Elephant Reserve and a Biosphere Reserve in Assam. The Sundarban National Park is a National Park, Tiger Reserve, and a Biosphere Reserve in India. It is a part of the Sundarbans on the Ganges Delta of India and Bangladesh.
   Bhitarkanika National Park is a national park located in the Kendrapara District Odisha, which is not specifically for Tiger reserve.

7. (a) Global Warming, fragmentation of habitat and invasion of alien species can be threats to the bio-diversity of a geographical area.

8. (d) Biological diversity helps in the formation and maintenance of soil structure and the retention of

moisture and nutrient levels. Trees on the other hand, lower the water table and remove deposited salt from the upper soil horizons.

9. (b) A biodiversity hotspot is a biogeographic region with a significant reservoir of biodiversity that is under threat from humans. Around the world, as many as 25 areas qualify to be the hotspots. Out of which India has 2 hotspots: Eastern Himalayas and Western Ghats.

10. (d) For conversion endangered species Wildlife Crime Control Bureau has been established for control of illegal trade in wildlife, including endangered species of birds and their parts and products. Research and monitoring activities on birds are promoted by the Government through reputed research organizations. Wildlife Institute of India, Bombay Natural History society and Salim Ali Centre for Ornithology and Natural History are some of the research organizations undertaking research on conservation of birds. The Indian government has banned the veterinary use of diclofenac drug that has caused rapid decline in vulture population across the Indian Subcontinent. Conservation Breeding Programmes to conserve these vulture species have been initiated at Pinjore (Haryana), Buxa (West Bengal) and Rani, Guwahati (Assam) by the Bombay Natural History Society.

11. (d) The Olive Ridley turtles are rusty coloured carapace and have slightly smaller head and shell than the Kemp turtles. These Olive Ridley turtles generally occur through the Antilles, around the north coast of South America, in West Africa, the Indian Ocean, Australia and Southeast Asia. As per the reports the populations of Olive Riddles have declined in Pakistan, Myanmar, Malaysia and Thailand, and possibly on the east coast of India, south of Orissa and in the Andaman and Nicobar islands.

12. (c) To qualify as a biodiversity hotspot on Myers 2000 edition of the hotspot-map, a region must meet two strict criteria: it must contain at least 0.5% or 1,500 species of vascular plants as endemics, and it has to have lost at least 70% of its primary vegetation.

13. (b) The Sumatran Rhino Crisis Summit opened with the shocking news that rather than 130-190 Sumatran rhinos as previously estimated, there are in fact fewer than 100 individual animals.

14. (a) Except promotion of vegetarianism all other acts are threats to the biodiversity of a geographical area.

15. (b) The red data book contains only 8 lists of threatened plant and animal species.

16. (c) The fix boundary of national park is described in Wild Life Protection Act, 1972 and the actual area of the national park is notified by state government.

A biosphere reserve conserves an ecosystem and not just few specific species of plants and animals.

17. (c) A carbon credit is a generic term for any tradable certificate or permit representing the right to emit one tonne of carbon dioxide or the mass of another greenhouse gas with a carbon dioxide equivalent $(CO_2)$ equivalent to one tonne of carbon dioxide.

18. (d) National Biodiversity Authority (NBA) checks the biopiracy and protects the indigeneous and traditional genetic resources. It directly monitors and supervises the scientific research on genetic modification of crop plants application for intellectual property Rights related to genetic biological resources cannot be made without the approval of NBA.

19. (c) To qualify as a hotspot, a region must meet two strict criteria: it must contain at least 1,500 species of vascular plants ($>$ 0.5 percent of the world's total) as endemics, and it has to have lost at least 70 percent of its original habitat. So we choose Species richness as well as Endemism. Along with this Threat perception is necessary to take, because it makes the base of this concept. Adaptation of flora is an arbitrary option, Ethno-botanical importance does nothing with the Biodiversity Hotspot selection criteria, vegetation Density is also discarded.

20. (d) Biological diversity helps in the formation and maintenance of soil structure and the retention of moisture and nutrient levels. Biodiversity supports ecosystem services including air quality, climate water purification, pollination, and prevention of erosion.

21. (a) Except promotion of vegetarianism all other acts are threats to the biodiversity of a geographical area.

22. (c) The fix boundary of national park is described in Wild Life Protection Act, 1972 and the actual area of the national park is notified by state government. A biosphere reserve conserves an ecosystem and not just few specific species of plants and animals.

23. (a) Lion-tailed Macaques are found in the mountain forests scattered across three Indian states stated above. The lion-tailed Macaques are endangered as per IUCN.

24. (a) Star tortoise is found in India in the dry and scrub forests. Pygmy Hog is an endangered species found in Assam. Only 150 animals are left. Monitor Lizard is found in India, Sri Lanka and Pakistan. Spider Monkey is the inhabitant of tropical forests of Central and South America.

25. (c) Gharial is critically endangered according to IUCN. Overhunting for skin and trophies, habitat loss due to construction of dams and barrages has been the reason for their decline. Leather back turtles are endangered due to human carelessness. Swamp deer

occupies a place in the list of the endangered species of the world. Deforestation, draining of swamps and marshes for farming has led to the destruction of their natural habitat.

26. (b) Common Myna are birds stalking alongside the cattle to seize the insects disturbed by their movement through grasses. The common myna is readily identified by the brown body, black hooded head and the bare yellow patch behind the eye.

27. (b) IUCN is not an organ of UN. It has observer and consultative status at the United Nations.

28. (c) Bird Life international is a global partnership of conservation organisations that strives to conserve birds, their habitats and global biodiversity. It is working with people towards sustainability in the use of natural resources. It is the World's largest partnership of conservation organisations, with over 120 partner organizations. An Important Bird and Biodiversity Area (IBA) is an area recognized as being globally important habitat for the conservation of bird populations. The program was developed and sites are identified by Bird Life International.

29. (c) Periyar National Park and Wildlife Sanctuary is a protected area in the districts of Idukki and Pathanamthitta in Kerala.
Kanha National Park is one of the tiger reserves of India and the largest national park of Madhya Pradesh.
The Sariska Tiger Reserve is an Indian national park located in the Alwar district of Rajasthan.
Dachigam National Park is located in Jammu and Kashmir.

30. (b)

31. (b) All statements are correct.

32. (b) The concept of biodiversity was propounded by E.O. Wilson. The concept of wildlife was propounded by W. Hornaday. The concept of Ecosystem propounded by G. Tansley. The concept of Ecology was propounded by E. Haeckel.

33. (a) Nokrek Biosphere Reserve is situated in Garo Hills in Meghalaya. Logtak Lake is in Manipur. Barail Range is in Assam. Though Namdapha National Park and Dafla Hill both are in Arunachal Pradesh, the two are separate entities.

34. (c) Dampa Tiger Reserve, the largest wildlife sanctuary in Mizoram. Saramati peak is in Nagaland. It is located near Tuensang town with a height of 3,826 m. Gumti Wildlife Sanctuary is famous wildlife reserve in Tripura.

35. (b)  36. (a)  37. (d)  38. (c)  39. (a)
40. (b)

41. (a) (i) Pterocarpus santalinus, with the common names red sanders, red sandalwood, and saunderswood, is a species of Pterocarpus endemic to the southern Eastern Ghats mountain range of South India. This tree is valued for the rich red color of its wood. The wood is not aromatic.
(ii) It was in national media during April 2015, when Andhra Pradesh police killed 20 Red Sander smugglers in an encounter. So first statement is right.
(iii) Red Sanders is associated with Tropical dry deciduous forest, as per environment ministry website, Hence 2nd statement wrong.

42. (d) In June 2015, Maharashtra government has declared the Blue Mormon (Papilio polymnestor) as the State butterfly.
Ref: TheHindu newspaper(http://www.thehindu.com /news/national/other-states/maharashtra-gets-state-butterfly/article7342955.ece MUMBAI, June 22, 2015)

43. (d) Frontline/ENVIRONMENT "WILDLIFE
Print edition : February 6, 2015
http://www.frontline.in/environment/wild-life/cry-from-the-ghats/article6805391.ece

44. (b) This plant is a native of Mexico, and spread throughout Indi(a) It's an aggressive colonizer, common weed of wastelands, scrublands and degraded forests. Since it's mention under the head of invasive alien species so it'd reduce biodiversity in the area, Hence Option (B)

45. (d) The schedule 5 vermin- crow, fruitbat, mice and rat can be killed. Since the animals given in above MCQ are outside that list hence answer is "D".

# 4 Chapter

# HAZARDS AND DISASTER MANAGEMENT

## Introduction to Disaster Management

### Objectives of this chapter

*The main objective of this chapter is to have a basic understanding of various concepts used in disaster management. The concepts explained here are: Disaster, Hazard, Vulnerability, Capacity, Risk and Disaster Management Cycle. Apart from the terminologies, the chapter also tries to explain various types of disasters. After reading this chapter students will have a basic understanding about the concepts and should be able to differentiate between them with suitable examples.*

### Background

#### The global context

Disasters are as old as human history but the dramatic increase and the damage caused by them in the recent past have become a cause of national and international concern. Over the past decade, the number of natural and manmade disasters has climbed inexorably. From 1994 to 1998, reported disasters average was 428 per year but from 1999 to 2003, this figure went up to an average of 707 disaster events per year showing an increase of about 60% over the previous years. The biggest rise was in countries of low human development, which suffered an increase of 142%.

The figure A shows the deadliest disasters of the decade (1992 – 2001). Drought and famine have proved to be the deadliest

disasters globally, followed by flood, technological disaster, earthquake, windstorm, extreme temperature and others. Global economic loss related to disaster events average around US $880 billion per year.

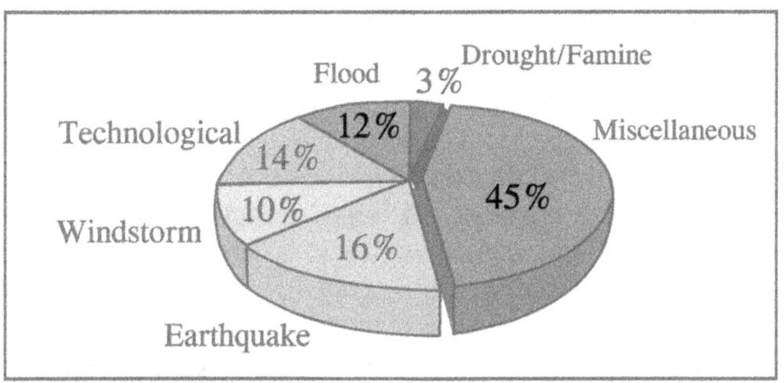


**A World Scenario: Reported Deaths from all Disasters (1992-2001)**

#### Indian scenario

The scenario in India is no different from the global context. The super cyclone of Orissa (1999), the Gujarat earthquake (2001) and the recent Tsunami (2004) affected millions across the country leaving behind a trail of heavy loss of life, property and livelihood. Table given below shows a list of some of the major disasters that have caused colossal impact on the community.

**Table: Major Disasters in India since 1970**

| SI. No. | Disaster | Impact |
|---------|----------|--------|
| | **Cyclone** | |
| 1. | 29, October, 1971, Odisha | Cyclone and tidal waves killed 10,000 people |
| 2. | 19, November 1977, Andhra Pradesh | Cyclone and Tidal waves killed 20,000 people |
| 3. | 29th and 30th October, 1999, Odisha | Cyclone and Tidal waves killed 9,000 and 18 million people were affected |
| | **Earthquake** | |
| 4. | 20th October, 1991, Uttarkashi | An earthquake of magnitude 6.6 killed 723 people. |
| 5. | 30th September, 1993, Latur | Approximately 8000 people died and there was heavy loss to infrastructure. |
| 6. | 22, May, 1997, Jabalpur | 39 people died. |

| 7. | 29th March 1997 | Chamoli 100 people dead |
|---|---|---|
| 8. | 26th January, 2001 | Bhuj, More than 10,000 dead and heavy loss Gujarat to infrastructure |
| | **Landslide** | |
| 9. | July 1991, Assam | 300 people killed, heavy loss to roads and infrastructure |
| 10. | August 1993 | Nagaland 500 killed and more than 200 houses destroyed and about 5kms. Road damaged. |
| 11. | 18th August 1998, Malpa | 210 people killed. Villages were washed away |
| | **Flood** | |
| 12. | 1978 Floods in North East India | 3,800 people killed and heavy loss to property. |
| 13. | 1994 Floods in Assam, Arunachal Pradesh, Jammu Kashmir, Himachal Pradesh, Punjab, Uttar Pradesh, Goa, Kerala and Gujarat. | More than 2000 people killed and thousands affected |

## What is a Disaster?

Almost every day, newspapers, radio and television channels carry reports on disaster striking several parts of the world. But what is a disaster? The term disaster owes its origin to the French word **"Desastre"** which is a combination of two words '*des*' meaning *bad* and '*aster*' meaning *star*. Thus the term refers to '*Bad or Evil star*'. A disaster can be defined as "*A serious disruption in the functioning of the community or a society causing wide spread material, economic, social or environmental losses which exceed the ability of the affected society to cope using its own resources*". A disaster is a result from the combination of hazard, vulnerability and insufficient capacity or measures to reduce the potential chances of risk. A disaster happens when a hazard impacts on the vulnerable population and causes damage, casualties and disruption would give a better illustration of what a disaster is. Any hazard – flood, earthquake or cyclone which is a triggering event along with greater vulnerability (inadequate access to resources, sick and old people, lack of awareness etc) would lead to disaster causing greater loss to life and property. For example; an earthquake in an uninhabited desert cannot be considered a disaster, no matter how strong the intensities produced.

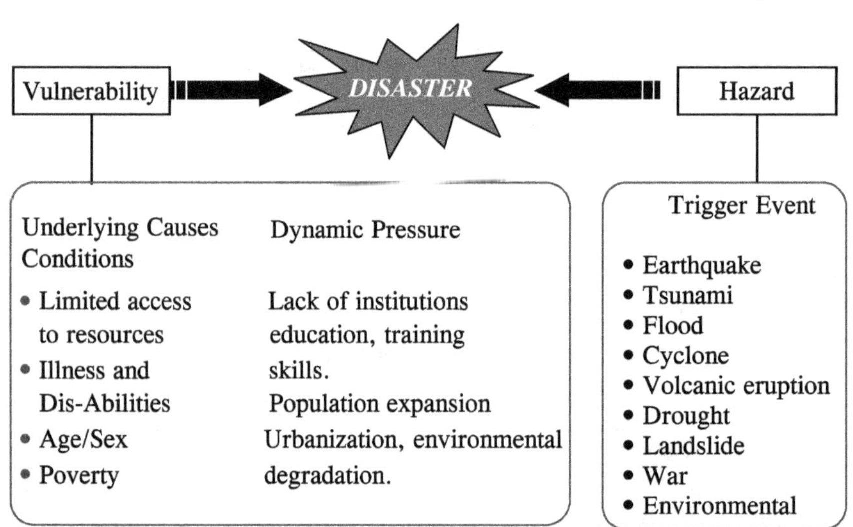


An earthquake is disastrous only when it affects people, their properties and activities. Thus, disaster occurs only when hazards and vulnerability meet. But it is also to be noted that with greater capacity of the individual/community and environment to face these disasters, the impact of a hazard reduces. Therefore, we need to understand the three major components namely hazard, vulnerability and capacity with suitable examples to have a basic understanding of disaster management.

## What is a Hazard? How is it classified?

Hazard may be defined as "*a dangerous condition or event, that threat or have the potential for causing injury to life or damage to property or the environment.*" The word '*hazard*' owes its origin to the word '*hasard*' in old French and '*az-zahr*' in *Arabic* meaning '*chance*' or '*luck*'. Hazards can be grouped into two broad categories namely natural and manmade.

## 1.  Natural Hazards

Natural hazards are hazards which are caused because of natural phenomena (hazards with meteorological, geological or even biological origin). Examples of natural hazards are cyclones, tsunamis, earthquake and volcanic eruption which are exclusively of natural origin. Landslides, floods, drought, fires are socio-natural hazards since their causes are both natural and manmade. For example flooding may be caused because of heavy rains, landslide or blocking of drains with human waste.

## 2.  Manmade Hazards

Manmade hazards are hazards which are due to human negligence. Manmade hazards are associated with industries or energy generation facilities and include explosions, leakage of toxic waste, pollution, dam failure, wars or civil strife etc. The list of hazards is very long. Many occur frequently while others take place occasionally. However, on the basis of their genesis, they can be categorized as follows:

| Types | Types of Hazards |
|---|---|
| Geological Hazards | 1. Earthquake<br>2. Tsunami<br>3. Volcanic Eruption<br>4. Landslides<br>5. Dam Burst<br>6. Mine Fire |
| Water & Climatic Hazards | 1. Tropical Cyclone<br>2. Tornado and hurricane<br>3. Flood<br>4. Drought<br>5. Hailstorm<br>6. Cloud Burst<br>7. Landslide<br>8. Heat and Cold Wave<br>9. Snow Avalanche<br>10. Sea Erosion |
| Environmental Hazards | 1. Environmental Pollution<br>2. Deforestation<br>3. Desertification<br>4. Pest Infection |
| Biological Hazards | 1. Human/Animal Epidemics<br>2. Pest attacks<br>3. Food Poisoning<br>4. Weapons of mass destruction. |
| Chemical, Industrial and Nuclear Accidents | 1. Chemical disasters<br>2. Nuclear disasters<br>3. Oil Spills/Fires<br>4. Nuclear |
| Accident Related | 1. Transportation Urban fires bomb blast, Forest fires, Air Crash<br>2. Building collapse<br>3. Electrical accidents<br>4. Festival related disasters |

# Vulnerability

Vulnerability may be defined as *"The extent to which a community, structure, services or geographic area is likely to be damaged or disrupted by the impact of particular hazard, on account of their nature, construction and proximity to hazardous terrains or a disaster prone area."* Vulnerabilities can be categorized into physical and socio-economic vulnerability.

## Physical Vulnerability

It includes notions of whom and what may be damaged or destroyed by natural hazard such as earthquakes or floods. It is based on the physical condition of people and elements at risk, such as buildings, infrastructure etc; and their proximity, location and nature of the hazard. It also relates to the technical capability of building and structures to resist the forces acting upon them during a hazard event. Unchecked growth of settlements in unsafe areas exposes the people to the hazard. In case of an earthquake or landslide the ground may fail and the houses on the top may topple or slide and affect the settlements at the lower level even if they are designed well for earthquake forces.

## Socio-economic Vulnerability

The degree to which a population is affected by a hazard will not merely lie in the physical components of vulnerability but also on the socioeconomic conditions. The socio-economic condition of the people also determines the intensity of the impact. For example, people who are poor and living in the sea coast don't have the money to construct strong concrete houses. They are generally at risk and lose their shelters whenever there is strong wind or cyclone. Because of their poverty they too are not able to rebuild their houses.

## Capacity

Capacity can be defined as *"resources, means and strengths which exist in households and communities and which enable them to cope with, withstand, prepare for, prevent, mitigate or quickly recover from a disaster"*. People's capacity can also be taken into account.

## What is risk?

Risk is a *"measure of the expected losses due to a hazard event occurring in a given area over a specific time period. Risk is a function of the probability of particular hazardous event and the losses each would cause."* The level of risk depends upon:
❖ **Nature of the hazard**
❖ **Vulnerability of the elements which are affected**
❖ **Economic value of those elements**
A community/locality is said to be at 'risk' when it is exposed to hazards and is likely to be adversely affected by its impact. Whenever we discuss 'disaster management' it is basically 'disaster risk management'.

---

### Disaster Risk Reduction can take place in the following ways:

**1. Preparedness:** This protective process embraces measures which enable governments, communities and individuals to respond rapidly to disaster situations to cope with them effectively. Preparedness includes the formulation of viable emergency plans, the development of warning systems, the maintenance of inventories and the training of personnel. It may also embrace search and rescue measures as well as evacuation plans for areas that may be at risk from a recurring disaster. Preparedness therefore encompasses those measures taken before a disaster event which are aimed at minimizing loss of life, disruption of critical services, and damage when the disaster occurs.

**2. Mitigation:** Mitigation embraces measures taken to reduce both the effect of the hazard and the vulnerable conditions to it in order to reduce the scale of a future disaster. Therefore mitigation activities can be focused on the hazard itself or the elements exposed to the threat. Examples of mitigation measures which are hazard specific include water management in drought prone areas, relocating people away from the hazard prone areas and by strengthening structures to reduce damage when a hazard occurs. In addition to these physical measures, mitigation should also aim at reducing the economic and social vulnerabilities of potential disasters.

---

# Disaster Risk Management

Disaster Risk Management includes sum total of all activities, programmes and measures which can be taken up before, during and after a disaster with the purpose to avoid a disaster, reduce its impact or recover from its losses. The three key stages of activities that are taken up within disaster risk management are:

## 1. Before a disaster (pre-disaster).

Activities taken to reduce human and property losses caused by a potential hazard. For example carrying out awareness campaigns, strengthening the existing weak structures, preparation of the disaster management plans at household and community level, etc. Such risk reduction measures taken under this stage are termed as *mitigation* and *preparedness activities*.

## 2. During a disaster (disaster occurrence).

Initiatives taken to ensure that the needs and provisions of victims are met and suffering is minimized. Activities taken under this stage are called *emergency response activities*.

## 3. After a disaster (post-disaster)

Initiatives taken in response to a disaster with a purpose to achieve early recovery and rehabilitation of affected communities, immediately after a disaster strikes. These are called as *response and recovery activities*.

### Earthquake & Its Risk Management

An **earthquake** (also known as a **quake, tremor** or **temblor**) is the shaking of the surface of the Earth, resulting from the sudden release of energy in the Earth's lithosphere that creates seismic waves. Earthquakes can range in size from those that are so weak that they cannot be felt to those violent enough to toss people around and destroy whole cities. The seismicity or **seismic activity** of an area refers to the frequency, type and size of earthquakes experienced over a period of time. Earthquakes are measured using measurements from seismometers. The moment magnitude is the most common scale on which earthquakes larger than approximately 5 are reported for the entire globe. The more numerous earthquakes smaller than magnitude 5 reported by national seismological observatories are measured mostly on the local magnitude scale, also referred to as the **Richter magnitude scale**. These two scales are numerically similar over their range of validity. Magnitude 3 or lower earthquakes are mostly imperceptible or weak and magnitude 7 and over potentially causes serious damage over larger areas, depending on their depth. The largest earthquakes in historic times have been of magnitude slightly over 9, although there is no limit to the possible magnitude. Intensity of shaking is measured on the modified **Mercalli scale**. The shallower an earthquake, the more damage to structures it causes, all else being equal.

## Earthquakes and volcanic activity

Earthquakes often occur in volcanic regions and are caused there, both by tectonic faults and the movement of magma in volcanoes. Such earthquakes can serve as an early warning of volcanic eruptions, as during the 1980 eruption of Mount St. Helens. Earthquake swarms can serve as markers for the location of the flowing magma throughout the volcanoes. These swarms can be recorded by seismometers and telemeters (a device that measures ground slope) and used as sensors to predict imminent or upcoming eruptions.

## Cause of Earthquake

The earth's crust is a rocky layer of varying thickness ranging from a depth of about 10 kilometers under the sea to 65 kilometers under the continents. The crust is not one piece but consists of portions called *'plates'* which vary in size from a few hundred to thousands of kilometers. The *'theory of plate tectonics'* holds that the plates ride up on the more mobile mantle, and are driven by some yet unconfirmed mechanisms, perhaps thermal convection currents. When these plates contact each other, stress arises in the crust. These stresses can be classified according to the type of movement along the plate's boundaries:

(a) Pulling away from each other,

(b) Pushing against one another and

(c) Sliding sideways relative to each other. All these movements are associated with earthquakes.

Earthquakes can be of three types based on the focal depth:

- Deep: - 300 to 700 kms from the earth surface
- Medium: - 60 to 300 kms
- Shallow: - less than 60 kms

## Measuring and locating Earthquakes

The instrumental scales used to describe the size of an earthquake began with the *Richter magnitude scale* in the 1930s. It is a relatively simple measurement of an event's amplitude, and its use has become minimal in the 21st century. Seismic waves travel through the Earth's interior and can be recorded by seismometers at great distances. The surface wave magnitude was developed in the 1950s as a means to measure remote earthquakes and to improve the accuracy for larger events. The moment magnitude scale measures the amplitude of the shock, but also takes into account the seismic moment (total rupture area, average slip of the fault, and rigidity of the rock). The Japan Meteorological Agency seismic intensity scale, the Medvedev–Sponheuer–Karnik scale, and the Mercalli intensity scale are based on the observed effects.

## Distribution pattern of Earthquakes in India

India falls quite prominently on the *'Alpine - Himalayan Belt'*. This belt is the line along which the Indian plate meets the Eurasian plate. This being a convergent plate, the Indian plate is thrusting underneath the Eurasian plate at a speed of 5 cm per year. The movement gives rise to tremendous stress which keeps accumulating in the rocks and is released from time to time in the form of earthquakes.

The seismic zoning map of India is divided into four zones namely Zone II, III, IV and V, with zone V shown in above figure being most vulnerable to earthquakes. Much of India lies in zone III. New Delhi the capital city of India lies in zone IV where as big cities like Mumbai and Chennai are in zone III.

| Year | Location | Magnitude |
|---|---|---|
| 1950 | Arunachal Pradesh-China Border | 8.5 |
| 1956 | Anja, Gujarat | 7.0 |
| 1967 | Koyna, Maharshtra | 6.5 |
| 1975 | Kinnaur-Himachal Pradesh | 6.2 |
| 1988 | Manipur-Myanmar Border | 6.6 |
| 1988 | Bihar-Nepal Border | 6.4 |
| 1991 | Uttarkashi-Uttar Pradesh Hills | 6.0 |
| 1993 | Latur-Maharashtra | 6.3 |
| 1997 | Jabalpur, Madhya Pradesh | 6.0 |
| 1999 | Chamoli, Himachal Pradesh | 6.8 |
| 2001 | Bhuj, Gujarat | 6.9 |
| 2005 | Muzaffarabad (Pakistan) impact in J&K | 7.4 |
| 2015 | Nepal impact in different parts of India (Delhi, Bihar, Uttar Pradesh, Rajasthan | 7.8 |
| 2016 | North-East India | 6.7 |

## Possible risk reduction measures

### Community preparedness

Community preparedness is vital for mitigating earthquake impact. The most effective way to save you even in a slightest shaking is 'DROP, COVER and HOLD'.

### Planning

The *Bureau of Indian Standards* has published building codes and guidelines for safe construction of buildings against earthquakes. Before the buildings are constructed the building plans have to be checked by the Municipality, according to the laid down bylaws. Many existing lifeline buildings such as hospitals, schools and fire stations may not be built with earthquake safety measures. Their earthquake safety needs to be upgraded by retrofitting techniques.

### Public education

Public education is educating the public on causes and characteristics of an earthquake and preparedness measures. It can be created through sensitization and training programme for community, architects, engineers, builders, masons, teachers, government functionaries teachers and students. Engineered structures: Buildings need to be designed and constructed as per the building by laws to withstand ground shaking. Architectural and engineering inputs need to be put together to improve building design and construction practices. The soil type needs to be analyzed before construction. Building structures on soft soil should be avoided. Buildings on soft soil are more likely to get damaged even if the magnitude of the earthquake is not strong as shown in Figure. Similar problems persist in the buildings constructed on the river banks which have alluvial soil.

## Tsunami

The term Tsunami has been derived from a Japanese term *'Tsu'* meaning *'harbor'* and *'nami'* meaning *'waves'*. Tsunamis are popularly called tidal waves but they actually have nothing to do with the tides. These waves which often affect distant shores, originate by rapid displacement of water from the lake or the sea either by seismic activity, landslides, volcanic eruptions or large meteoroid impacts. Whatever the cause may be sea water is displaced with a violent motion and swells up, ultimately surging over land with great destructive power. The effects of a tsunami can be unnoticeable or even destructive.

## Causes of a Tsunami

The geological movements that cause tsunamis are produced in three major ways. The most common of these are fault movements on the sea floor, accompanied by an earth-quake. They release huge amount of energy and have the capacity to cross oceans. The degree of movement depends on how fast the earthquake occurs and how much water is displaced. Fig shows how an earthquake causes tsunami. The second most common cause of the tsunami is a landslide either occurring under water or originating above the sea and then plunging into the water. The largest tsunami ever produced by a landslide was in Lituya Bay, Alaska 1958. The massive rock slide produced a wave that reached a high water mark of 50 - 150 meters above the shoreline. The third major cause of tsunami is volcanic activity. The flank of a volcano located near the shore or under water may be uplifted or depressed similar to the action of a fault, or, the volcano may actually explode. In 1883, the violent explosion of the famous volcano, Krakotoa in Indonesia, produced tsunami measuring 40 meters which crushed upon Java and Sumatra. Over 36,000 people lost their lives in this tyrant waves.

**Picture of a Tsunami Wave**

### Predictability of Tsunami

There are two distinct types of tsunami warning:

(a)  International tsunami warning systems and

(b)  Regional warning systems.

Tsunamis have occurred in all the oceans and in the Mediterranean Sea, but the great majority of them have occurred in the Pacific Ocean. Since scientists cannot exactly predict earthquakes, they also cannot exactly predict when a tsunami will be generated.

**(a)  International Tsunami Warning Systems**

Shortly after the Hilo Tsunami (1946), the Pacific Tsunami Warning System (PTWS) was developed with its operational center at the Pacific Tsunami Warning Center (PTWC) near Honolulu, Hawaii. The PTWC is able to alert countries several hours before the tsunami strikes. The warning includes predicted arrival time at selected coastal communities where the tsunami could travel in few hours. A tsunami watch is issued with subsequent arrival time to other geographic areas.

**(b)  Regional Warning Systems**

Usually use seismic data about nearby earthquakes to determine if there is a possible local threat of a tsunami. Such systems are capable enough to provide warnings to the general public in less than 15 minutes.

In India, the Survey of India maintains a tide gauge network along the coast of India.

### Typical adverse effects

Local tsunami events or those less than 30 minutes from the source cause the majority of damage. The force of the water can raze everything in its path. It is normally the flooding affect of the tsunami that causes major destruction to the human settlements, roads and infrastructure thereby disrupting the normal functioning of the society. Withdrawal of the tsunami causes major damage. As the waves withdraw towards the ocean they sweep out the foundations of the buildings, the beaches get destroyed and the houses carried out to sea. Damage to ports and airports may prevent importation of needed food and medical supplies. Apart from the physical damage, there is a huge impact on the public health system. Deaths mainly occur because of drowning as water inundates homes. Many people get washed away or crushed by the giant waves and some are crushed by the debris. There are very few evidences which show that tsunami flooding has caused large scale health problem. Availability of drinking water has always been a major problem in areas affected by a disaster. Sewage pipes may be damaged causing major sewage disposal problems. Open wells and other ground water may be contaminated by salt water and debris and sewage. Flooding in the locality may lead to crop loss, loss of livelihood like boats and nets, environmental degradation, etc.

### Distribution pattern of Tsunami in India

Even though India has not faced frequent Tsunamis but there is a need to identify the areas that are generally affected by Tsunamis. The whole of the Indian coastal belt is prone to Tsunami.

## Cyclone

Cyclone is a region of low atmospheric pressure surrounded by high atmospheric pressure resulting in swirling atmospheric disturbance accompanied by powerful winds blowing in anticlockwise direction in the Northern Hemisphere and in the clockwise direction in the Southern Hemisphere. They occur mainly in the tropical and temperate regions of the world.

### General Characteristics

Cyclones in India are moderate in nature. Some of the general characteristics of a cyclone are:

1.  Strong winds
2.  Exceptional rain
3.  Storm surge Cyclones are generally accompanied by strong winds which cause a lot of destruction. In some cases it is accompanied by heavy downpour and also the rise in the sea which intrudes inland thereby causing floods.

**CYCLONES ARE KNOWN BY DIFFERENT NAMES IN DIFFERENT PARTS OF THE WORLD:**

- Typhoons: in the Northwest Pacific Ocean west of the dateline
- Hurricanes: in the North Atlantic Ocean, the Northeast Pacific Ocean east of the dateline, or the South Pacific Ocean.
- Tropical cyclones: the Southwest Pacific Ocean and Southeast Indian Ocean.
- Severe cyclonic storm" (the North Indian Ocean)
- Tropical cyclone (the Southwest Indian Ocean)
- Willie-Willie in Australia
- Tornado in South America

| CYCLONE IN ODISHA (1999) |
| --- |

29th October 1999, Super-cyclone with wind speed of 260-300 km/hour hit the 140 kilometer coast of Orissa with a storm surge created in the Bay-of-Bengal with water level 9 metres higher than normal. The superstorm travelled more than 250 km inland and within a period of 36 hrs ravaged more than 200 lakh hectares of land, devouring trees and vegetation, leaving behind a huge trail of destruction.

## Indian Cyclones

Cyclones vary in frequency in various parts of the world. The 7516.6 kilometers long Indian coastline is the earth's most cyclone battered stretch of the world. Around 8% of the total land area in India is prone to cyclones. About two-third of the cyclones that occur in the Indian coastline occur in the Bay of Bengal. The states which are generally affected in the east coast are West-Bengal, Orissa, Andhra Pradesh; Tamil Nadu and on the west coast Gujarat, Maharashtra, Goa, Karnataka and Kerala.

| SI No. | Year | Area | Death Toll |
| --- | --- | --- | --- |
| 1 | 1971 | Eastern Coast | 9658 |
| 2 | 1972 | Andhra Pradesh and Orissa | 100 |
| 3 | 1977 | Chennai, Kerala & Andhra Pradesh | 14,204 |
| 4 | 1979 | Andhra Pradesh | 594 |
| 5 | 1981 | Gujarat | 470 |
| 6 | 1982 | Gujarat & Maharashtra | 500 |
| 7 | 1984 | Tamil Nadu & Andhra Pradesh | 512 |
| 8 | 1985 | Andhra Pradesh | 5000 |
| 9 | 1990 | Andhra Pradesh | 957 |
| 10 | 1990 | Orissa | 250 |
| 11 | 1999 | Orissa | 8913 |

## Warning

Low pressure and the development can be detected hours or days before it causes damage. The satellites track the movement of these cyclones based on which the people are evacuated from areas likely to be affected. It is difficult to predict the accuracy. Accurate landfall predictions can give only a few hours' notice to threatened population. India has one of the best cyclone warning systems in the world. The India Meteorological Department (IMD) is the nodal department for wind detection, tracking and forecasting cyclones.

Cyclone tracking is done through INSAT satellite. Cyclone warning is disseminated by several means such as satellite based disaster warning systems, radio, television, telephone, fax, high priority telegram, public announcements and bulletins in press. These warnings are disseminated to the general public, the fishing community especially those in the sea, port authorities, commercial aviation and the government machinery.

## Typical Adverse effect

First, in a sudden, brief onslaught, high winds cause major damage to infrastructure and housing, in particular fragile constructions. They are generally followed by heavy rains and floods and, in flat coastal areas by storm surge riding on tidal waves and inundating the land over long distances of even up to 15 kilometer inland.

## Possible Risk Reduction Measures

**Coastal belt plantation -** green belt plantation along the coastal line in a scientific interweaving pattern can reduce the effect of the hazard. Providing a cover through green belt sustains less damage. Forests act as a wide buffer zone against strong winds and flash floods. Without the forest the cyclone travel freely inland. The lack of protective forest cover allows water to inundate large areas and cause destruction. With the loss of the forest cover each consecutive cyclone can penetrate further inland. Cyclones can be predicted several days in advance. The map is prepared with data inputs of past climatological records, history of wind speed, frequency of flooding etc.

**Land use control** designed so that least critical activities are placed in vulnerable areas. Location of settlements in the floodplains is at utmost risk. Majority of the buildings in coastal areas are built with locally available materials and have no engineering inputs. Good construction practice should be adopted such as:

- **Cyclonic** wind storms inundate the coastal areas. It is advised to construct on stilts or on earth mound. - **Houses** can be strengthened to resist wind and flood damage. All elements holding the structures need to be properly anchored to resist the uplift or flying off of the objects. For example, avoid large overhangs of roofs, and the projections should be tied down.

- **A row** of planted trees will act as a shield. It reduces the energy.

- **Buildings** should be wind and water resistant.

- **Buildings** storing food supplies must be protected against the winds and water.

-**Protect** river embankments. Communication lines should be installed underground.

- **Provide** strong halls for community shelter in vulnerable locations.

**Flood management** – Torrential rains, strong wind and storm range leads to flooding in the cyclone affected areas. There are possibilities of landslides too. Flood mitigation measures could be incorporated (see section on floods for additional information).

**Improving vegetation cover** – The roots of the plants and trees keep the soil intact and prevent erosion and slow runoff to prevent or lessen flooding. The use of tree planted in rows will act as a windbreak. Coastal shelterbelt plantations can be developed to break severe wind speeds. It minimizes devastating effects. The Orissa calamity has also highlighted the need for urgent measures like shelterbelt plantation along cyclone-prone coastal areas. Species chosen for this purpose should not only be able to withstand the impact of strong cyclonic winds, but also check soil erosion.

# Flood

Flood is a state of high water level along a river channel or on the coast that leads to inundation of land, which is not usually submerged. Floods may happen gradually and also may take hours or even happen suddenly without any warning due to breach in the embankment, spill over, heavy rains etc.

There are different types of floods namely: flash flood, riverine flood, urban flood, etc. Flash floods can be defined as floods which occur within six hours of the beginning of heavy rainfall, and are usually associated with cloud bursts, storms and cyclones requiring rapid localized warnings and immediate response to reduce damage. Wireless network and telephone connections are used to monitor flood conditions. In case of flash floods, warnings for timely evacuation may not always be possible.

## Causes

There are several causes of floods and differ from region to region. The causes may vary from a rural area to an urban area. Some of the major causes are:

(a) Heavy rainfall

(b) Heavy siltation of the river bed reduces the water carrying capacity of the rivers/stream.

(c) Blockage in the drains leads to flooding of the area.

(d) Landslides blocking the flow of the stream.

(e) Construction of dams and reservoirs

(f) In areas prone to cyclone, strong winds accompanied by heavy down pour along with storm surge leads to flooding.

## Adverse Effects

The most important consequence of floods is the loss of life and property. Structures like houses, bridges; roads etc. get damaged by the gushing water, landslides triggered on account of water getting saturated, boats and fishing nets get damaged. There is huge loss to life and livestock caused by drowning. Lack of proper drinking water facilities, contamination of water (well, ground water, piped water supply) leads to outbreak of epidemics, diarrhea, viral infection, malaria and many other infectious diseases. Flooding also leads to a large area of agricultural land getting inundated as a result there is a huge crop loss. This results in shortage of food, and animal fodder. Floods may also affect the soil characteristics. The land may be rendered infertile due to erosion of top layer or may turn saline if sea water floods the area.

## Distributional Pattern of floods in India

Floods occur in almost all the river basins of the country. The Vulnerability Atlas of India shows pictorially the areas liable to floods. Around 12% (40 million hectare) of land in India is prone to floods. Map showing Flood Zones in India Most of the flood affected areas lie in the Ganga basin, Brahmaputra basin (comprising of Barak, Tista, Torsa, Subansiri, Sankosh, Dihang and Luhit), the northwestern river basin (comprising Jhelum, Chenab, Ravi, Sutlej, Beas and the Ghagra), peninsular river basin (Tapti, Narmada, Mahanadi, Baitarani, Godavari, krishna, Pennar and the Kaveri) and the coastal regions of Andhra Pradesh, Tamilnadu, orissa and Kerela. Assam, Uttar Pradesh, Bihar and Orissa are some of the states who have been severely prone to floods. Our country receives an annual rainfall of 1200 mm, 85% of which is concentrated in 3-4 months i.e. June to September. Due to the intense and periodic rain, most of the rivers of the country are fed with huge quantity of water, much beyond their carrying capacity.

## Benefits

Floods (in particular more frequent or smaller floods) can also bring many benefits, such as recharging ground water, making soil more fertile and increasing nutrients in some soils. Flood waters provide much needed water resources in arid and semi-arid regions where precipitation can be very unevenly distributed throughout the year and kills pests in the farming land. Freshwater floods particularly play an important role in maintaining ecosystems in river corridors and are a key factor in maintaining floodplain biodiversity. Flooding can spread nutrients to lakes and rivers, which can lead to increased biomass and improved fisheries for a few years.

# Drought

Drought is either absence or deficiency of rainfall from its normal pattern in a region for an extended period of time leading to general suffering in the society. It is interplay between demand that people place on natural supply of water and natural event that provides the water in a given geographical region. The state of Kerala which receives more than 3000 mm of rainfall every year is declared drought affected as it is insufficient to have two good crops. The more the imbalance in supply the higher is the drought. The following will help explaining this general definition of the drought further.

- It is a slow on-set disaster and it is difficult to demarcate the time of its onset and the end.
- Any unusual dry period which results in a shortage of useful water. Drought is a normal, recurrent feature of climate.
- Drought can occur by improper distribution of rain in time and space, and not just by its amount.
- Drought is negative balance between precipitation and water use (through evaporation, transpiration by plants, domestic and industrial uses etc) in a geographical region. The effects of drought accumulate slowly over a considerable period of time.

## Causes of Drought

Though drought is basically caused by deficit rainfall, which is a meteorological phenomenon, it manifests into different spheres because of various vulnerability factors associated with them (see the box). Some of these factors are human induced. Though drought is a natural disaster, its effects are made worst in developing countries by over population, over grazing, deforestation, soil erosion, excessive use of ground and surface water for growing crops, loss of biodiversity.

## Adverse effects

Drought, different from any other natural disaster, does not cause any structural damages. As the meteorological drought turns into hydrological drought, the impacts start appearing first in agriculture which is most dependants on the soil moisture. Irrigated areas are affected much later than the rain fed areas. However, regions surrounding perennial rivers tend to continue normal life even when drought conditions are prevailing around. The impacts slowly spread into social fabric as the availability of drinking water diminishes, reduction in energy production, ground water depletion, food shortage, health reduction and loss of life, increased poverty, reduced quality of life and social unrest leading to migration.

## Distribution Pattern

Around 68% of India's total area is drought prone to drought.
- 315 out of a total of 725 Talukas in 99 districts are drought prone.
- 50 million people are annually affected by drought.
- In 2001 more than eight states suffered the impact of severe drought.
- In 2003 most parts of Rajasthan experienced the fourth consecutive year of drought.

## Possible Risk Reduction Measures

There are various mitigation strategies to cope up with drought.

1. *Public Awareness and education:* If the community is aware of the dos and don'ts, then half of the problem is solved. This includes awareness on the availability of safe drinking water, water conservation techniques, agricultural drought management strategies like crop contingency plans, construction of rain water harvesting structure.

2. *Drought Monitoring:* It is continuous observation of the rainfall situation, availability of water in the reservoirs, lakes, rivers etc and comparing with the existing water needs in various sectors of the society.

3. *Water supply augmentation and conservation*: Through rainwater harvesting in houses and farmers' fields increases the content of water available. Water harvesting by either allowing the runoff water from all the fields to a common point or allowing it to infiltrate into the soil where it has fallen (in situ) (e.g. contour bunds, contour cultivation, raised bed planting etc) helps increase water availability for sustained agricultural production.

4. *Expansion of irrigation*: Facilities reduces the drought vulnerability. Land use based on its capability helps in optimum use of land and water and can avoid the undue demand created due to their misuse.

5. *Livelihood planning*: Identifies those livelihoods which are least affected by the drought. Some of such livelihoods include increased off-farm employment opportunities, collection of non-timber forest produce from the community forests, raising goats, carpentry etc.

6. *Drought planning:* The basic goal of drought planning is to improve the effectiveness of preparedness and response efforts by enhancing monitoring, mitigation and response measures

---

### CASE STUDY

A success story the people of Ralegan Siddhi in Maharashtra transformed the dire straits to prosperity. Twenty years ago the village showed all traits of abject poverty. It practically had no trees, the topsoil had blown off, there was no agriculture and people were jobless. Anna Hazare, one of the India's most noted social activists, started his movement concentrating on trapping every drop of rain, which is basically a drought mitigation practice. So the villagers built check dams and tanks. To conserve soil they planted trees. The result: from 80 acres of irrigated area two decades ago, Ralegan Siddhi has a massive area of 1300 acres under irrigation. The migration for jobs has stopped and the per capita income has increased ten times from ₹225 to 2250 in this span of time. The entire effort was only people's enterprise and involved no funds or support from the Government.

# Landslides

The term '*landslide*' includes all varieties of mass movements of hill slopes and can be defined as the downward and outward movement of slope forming materials composed of rocks, soils, artificial fills or combination of all these materials along surfaces of separation by falling, sliding and flowing, either slowly or quickly from one place to another. Although the landslides are primarily associated with mountainous terrains, these can also occur in areas where an activity such as surface excavations for highways, buildings and open pit mines takes place. They often take place in conjunction with earthquakes, floods and volcanoes. At times, prolonged rainfall causing landslide may block the flow of river for quite some time. The formation of river blocks can cause havoc to the settlements downstream on its bursting.

## Causes of Landslide

There are several causes of landslide. Some of the major causes are as follows:

1. **Geological Weak material**: Weakness in the composition and structure of rock or soil may also cause landslides.
2. **Erosion**: Erosion of slope toe due to cutting down of vegetation, construction of roads might increase the vulnerability of the terrain to slide down.
3. **Intense rainfall:** Storms that produce intense rainfall for periods as short as several hours or have a more moderate intensity lasting several days have triggered abundant landslides. Heavy melting of snow in the hilly terrains also results in landslide.
4. **Human Excavation** of slope and its toe, loading of slope/toe, draw down in reservoir, mining, deforestation, irrigation, vibration/blast, Water leakage from services.
5. **Earthquake** shaking has triggered landslides in many different topographic and geologic settings. Rock falls, soil slides and rockslides from steep slopes involving relatively thin or shallow dis-aggregated soils or rock, or both have been the most abundant types of landslides triggered by historical earthquakes.
6. **Volcanic eruption** Deposition of loose volcanic ash on hillsides commonly is followed by accelerated erosion and frequent mud or debris flows triggered by intense rainfall.

## Adverse Effects

The most common elements at risk are the settlements built on the steep slopes, built at the toe and those built at the mouth of the streams emerging from the mountain valley. All those buildings constructed without appropriate foundation for a given soil and in sloppy areas are also at risk. Roads, communication lines are vulnerable.

## Risk reduction measures

Hazard mapping locates areas prone to slope failures. This will help to avoid building settlements in such areas. These maps will also serve as a tool for mitigation planning. Land use practices such as:

- Areas covered by degraded natural vegetation in upper slopes are to be afforested with suitable species. Existing patches of natural vegetation (forest and natural grass land) in good condition should be preserved.
- Any developmental activity initiated in the area should be taken up only after a detailed study of the region has been carried out.
- In construction of roads, irrigation canals etc. proper care is to be taken to avoid blockage of natural drainage. Total avoidance of settlement in the risk zone should be made mandatory.
- Relocate settlements and infrastructure that fall in the possible path of the landslide.
- No construction of buildings in areas beyond a certain degree of slope Retaining Walls can be built to stop land from slipping (these walls are commonly seen along roads in hill stations).

# Volcanic Eruptions

A **volcano** is a rupture in the crust of a planetary-mass object, such as Earth, that allows hot lava, volcanic ash, and gases to escape from a magma chamber below the surface.

Earth's volcanoes occur because its crust is broken into 17 major, rigid tectonic plates that float on a hotter, softer layer in its mantle. Therefore, on Earth, volcanoes are generally found where tectonic plates are diverging or converging. For example, a mid-oceanic ridge, such as the Mid-Atlantic Ridge, has volcanoes caused by divergent tectonic plates pulling apart; the Pacific Ring of Fire has volcanoes caused by convergent tectonic plates coming together. Volcanoes can also form where

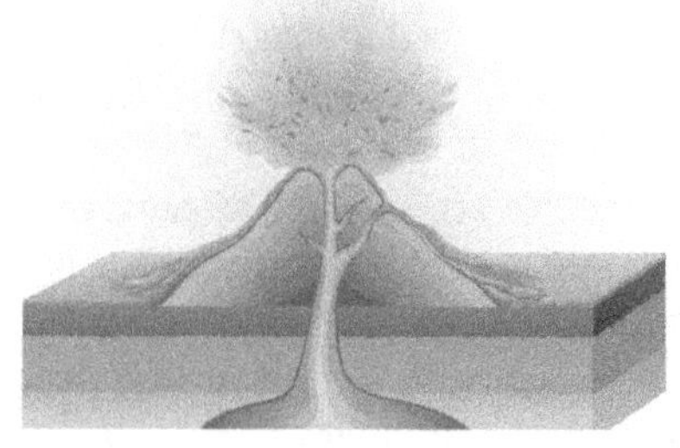

## Causes of Volcano

Volcanoes are caused by movement of tectonic plates deep within the earth's surface and along its ocean floors. Volcanoes are classified in two distinct categories: composite volcanoes and shield volcanoes. Composite volcanoes form from sticky and acidic lava; shield volcanoes, in contrast, form from basic lava. Over time, both types of volcanoes gradually increase in size. Inside their domes, gases and hot air accumulates and leads to increasing pressure. Eventually, volcanoes relieve themselves of these burdens through volcanic eruptions, which produce primary and secondary effects.

## Distribution Pattern

### India

One active volcano in India is the Barren Island volcano, located in the Indian possession of the Andaman Islands. The volcano reaches a height of 1,161 feet above sea level. It is classified as a strato-volcano.

### World

**Volcanic belts** are found above zones of unusually high temperature (700-1400 °C) where magma is created by partial melting of solid material in the Earth's crust and upper mantle. These areas usually form along tectonic plate boundaries at depths of 10–50 km.

**Pacific Ring of Fire:** The Ring of Fire is a major area in the basin of the Pacific Ocean where a large number of earthquakes and volcanic eruptions occur.

- It is associated with a nearly continuous series of oceanic trenches, volcanic arcs, and volcanic belts and/or plate movements.
- It has 452 volcanoes (more than 75% of the world's active and dormant volcanoes).
- The Ring of Fire is sometimes called the **circum-Pacific belt**. About 90% of the world's earthquakes and 81% of the world's largest earthquakes occur along the Ring of Fire.

## ANTHROPOGENIC HAZARD MANAGEMENT

**Anthropogenic hazards** are those hazards caused directly or indirectly by human action or inaction. They can be contrasted with natural hazards. Anthropogenic hazards may adversely affect humans, other organisms and biomes and eco-systems. The frequency and severity of hazards are key elements in some risk analysis methodologies. Hazards may also be described in relation to the impact that they have. Environmental hazards may be very different from human hazards. A hazard only exists if there is a pathway to exposure. As an example the center of the earth consists of molten material at very high temperatures which would be a severe hazard if contact was made with the core. However, there is no feasible way of making contact with the core; therefore the center of the earth currently poses no hazard.

## Industrial Hazard

Industrial accidents resulting in releases of hazardous materials usually occur in a commercial context, such as mining accidents. They often have an environmental impact but also can be hazardous for people living in proximity. The *Bhopal disaster* saw the release of Dioxins into the neighbouring environment seriously affecting large numbers of people.

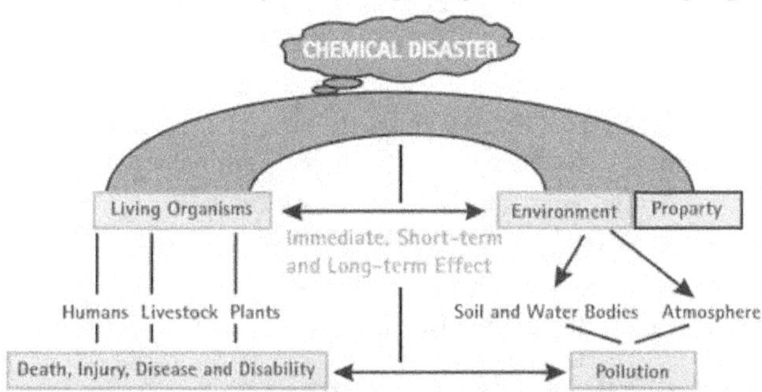


| **Bhopal Disaster** |
| --- |
| The Bhopal disaster, also referred to as the Bhopal gas tragedy, was a gas leak incident in India, considered the world's worst industrial disaster. |
| It occurred on the night of 2–3 December 1984 at the Union Carbide India Limited (UCIL) pesticide plant in Bhopal, Madhya Pradesh. Over 500,000 people were exposed to methyl isocyanate (MIC) gas and other chemicals. The highly toxic substance made its way into and around the shanty towns located near the plant. |

## Disaster Risk Reduction

Disaster Risk Reduction (DRR) aims to reduce the damage caused by natural hazards like earthquakes, floods, droughts and cyclones, through an ethic of prevention. Disasters often follow natural hazards. A disaster's severity depends on how much impact a hazard has on society and the environment. The scale of the impact in turn depends on the choices we make for our lives and for our environment. These choices relate to how we grow our food, where and how we build our homes, what kind of government we have, how our financial system works and even what we teach in schools. Each decision and action makes us more vulnerable to disasters - or more resilient to them.

### The Seven Global Targets

(a) Substantially reduce global disaster mortality by 2030, aiming to lower average per 100,000 global mortality rates in the decade 2020-2030 compared to the period 2005-2015.

(b) Substantially reduce the number of affected people globally by 2030, aiming to lower average global figure per 100,000 in the decade 2020 -2030 compared to the period 2005-2015.

(c) Reduce direct disaster economic loss in relation to global gross domestic product (GDP) by 2030.

(d) Substantially reduce disaster damage to critical infrastructure and disruption of basic services, among them health and educational facilities, including through developing their Resilience by 2030.

(e) Substantially increase the number of countries with national and local disaster risk reduction strategies by 2020.

(f) Substantially enhance international cooperation to developing countries through adequate and sustainable support to complement their national actions for implementation of this Framework by 2030.

Substantially increase the availability of and access to multi-hazard early warning systems and disaster risk information and assessments to the people by 2030.

## The Four Priorities for Action

### *Priority 1. Understanding disaster risk*

Disaster risk management should be based on an understanding of disaster risk in all its dimensions of vulnerability, capacity, exposure of persons and assets, hazard characteristics and the environment. Such knowledge can be used for risk assessment, prevention, mitigation, preparedness and response.

### *Priority 2. Strengthening disaster risk governance to manage disaster risk*

Disaster risk governance at the regional; national and global levels is very important for prevention, mitigation, preparedness, response, recovery, and rehabilitation. It fosters collaboration and partnership.

### *Priority 3. Investing in disaster risk reduction for resilience*

Public and private investment in disaster risk prevention and reduction through structural and non-structural measures are essential to enhance the economic, social, health and cultural resilience of persons, communities, countries and their assets, as well as the environment.

### *Priority 4. Enhancing disaster preparedness for effective response and to "Build Back better" in recovery, rehabilitation and reconstruction*

The growth of disaster risk means there is a need to strengthen disaster preparedness for response, take action in anticipation of events, and ensure capacities are in place for effective response and recovery at all levels. The recovery, rehabilitation and reconstruction phase is a critical opportunity to build back better, including through integrating disaster risk reduction into development measures.

# Exercise -1

1. According to the Hazardous Waste (Management and Handling) Rules, 1989, the limit for Polyaromatic Hydrocarbons (PAH) in waste oil suitable for recycling should be less than
   - (a) 8%
   - (b) 10%
   - (c) 6%
   - (d) 15%

2. Landscape mosaic comprises
   - (a) matrices and patches
   - (b) patches and corridors
   - (c) matrices, patches and corridors
   - (d) matrices and corridors

3. A place where an earthquake originates is called _____?
   - (a) Focus
   - (b) Fault line
   - (c) Epicenter
   - (d) S- Wave

4. Earthquakes occur when there is a sudden release of stored up energy in Earth's
   - (a) inner core
   - (b) outer core
   - (c) upper mantle
   - (d) lower crust

5. Tremors that have occurred in Earth's crust are known as
   - (a) Earthquakes
   - (b) Volcanic eruptions
   - (c) Bed eruptions
   - (d) Volcano-Earth Quake

6. Instrument used to measure earthquake is known as
   - (a) quake meter
   - (b) quake graph
   - (c) seismograph
   - (d) typanicgraph

7. Another name for Earthquakes is
   - (a) nektons
   - (b) temblors
   - (c) blusters
   - (d) flickers

8. An example of composite volcanoes is
   - (a) Mount Everest
   - (b) Puy de Dome
   - (c) Mauna Loa
   - (d) Mount Merapi

9. A reference to process by which materials such as magma and gases from inside Earth are forced onto Earth's surface is
   - (a) Eruption
   - (b) Lava
   - (c) Volcanism
   - (d) Earthquake

10. Tropical cyclones are intense low pressure areas confined to the area lying between?
    - (a) 30 degree north and 30 degree south
    - (b) 50 degree north and 50 degree south
    - (c) 50 degree north and 30 degree south
    - (d) 50 degree south and 30 degree north

11. The instrument that measures the wind speed in a cyclone is?
    - (a) Anemometer
    - (b) Barometer
    - (c) Thermometer
    - (d) Ammeter

12. Which one of the following places is unlikely to be affected by a cyclone?
    - (a) Chennai
    - (b) Mangalore
    - (c) Amritsar
    - (d) Puri

13. Droughts are formed by which of the following methods?
    - (a) lack of precipitation
    - (b) Temperature variations
    - (c) Atmospheric pressure
    - (d) All of the above

14. The term Tsunami is coined from
    - (a) Chinese term
    - (b) Japanese term
    - (c) Hawaiian term
    - (d) German Term

15. National institute for Disaster management is located at?
    - (a) Bangalore
    - (b) New Delhi
    - (c) Pune
    - (d) Hyderabad

16. Landslides occur because of?
    - (a) Intensity of rainfall
    - (b) Steep sloped
    - (c) Deforestation leading to soil erosion
    - (d) All of the above

17. Out of the total 35 state/ union territories of India, how many are disaster prone?
    - (a) 22
    - (b) 24
    - (c) 25
    - (d) 23

18. Bhopal Gas Disaster occurred with the release of which of the following gas.
    - (a) Methyl-isocynate
    - (b) Methyl –isocynide
    - (c) Sulphur dioxide
    - (d) Nitrous oxide

19. In an open ocean Tsunami can travel __________miles per hour with the periods up to____ minutes?
    - (a) 50; 20
    - (b) 50;60
    - (c) 485;20
    - (d) 485;60

20. Which of the following events produces biggest tsunami?
    - (a) Earthquake
    - (b) Underwater landslides
    - (c) Hurricanes
    - (d) Impacts of asteroids and comets

21. Powerful tsunamis are most frequently produced by?
    - (a) Volcanoes
    - (b) Underwater landslides
    - (c) Earthquake
    - (d) Impact of comets

22. Which of the following is the location of super volcano?
    - (a) Yellowstone National Park
    - (b) Mt. Rainier
    - (c) Iceland
    - (d) Mt. Kilimanjaro

23. Which was the deadliest hurricane in US history?
    - (a) Katrina
    - (b) Gavelston hurricane of 1990
    - (c) Andrew
    - (d) Camille

24. Other than boundaries of crustal plates, earthquakes may occur within areas with
    - (a) frequent civil activities
    - (b) frequent explosive activities
    - (c) frequent deforestation activities
    - (d) frequent volcanic activities

**25.** Magma which is forced onto Earth's surface is known as
   (a) Vent         (b) Cone
   (c) Lava         (d) Magma Chamber

**26.** When volcanoes eject basic lava, eruption is mainly?
   (a) Loud'         (b) Violent
   (c) Silent         (d) Hard

**27.** The Indian Tsunami Early Warning centre is located in which of the following places?
   (a) Chennai         (b) Kochi
   (c) Hyderabad         (d) Goa

**28.** _____________ helps us announce a cyclone alert
   (a) Satellite         (b) Stars
   (c) Sun         (d) moon

**29.** Which of the following activities is covered by disaster management before, during and after disaster?
   (a) Reconstruction and Rehabilitation
   (b) Mitigation
   (c) Emergency Response
   (d) All of the above

**30.** Landslides occur because of?
   (a) Intensity of rainfall
   (b) Steep sloped
   (c) Deforestation leading to soil erosion
   (d) All of the above

**31.** U.N. Disaster Management Team UNDMT is responsible for solving problems resulting from disasters in which of the following countries?
   (a) India
   (b) Iran
   (c) Bangladesh
   (d) All countries of the world

**32.** The disaster management act was enacted in India in which of the following year?
   (a) 2006         (b) 2005
   (c) 2008         (d) 2007

**33.** Which of the following is not a waste disposal method?
   (a) Landfill         (b) Regenration
   (c) Recycling         (d) Incineration

**34.** Which of the following plant is used for the treatment of oil spills?
   (a) Skimmers         (b) Jatropa
   (c) Eucalyptus         (d) Cycas

**35.** Pacific Ring of Fire is associated with which one of the following disasters?
   (a) Earthquake         (b) Volcanic Eruption
   (c) Landslides         (d) Cyclones

**36.** Arunachal Pradesh is located in which of the following seismic zones?
   (a) Zone II         (b) Zone III
   (c) Zone IV         (d) Zone V

**37.** Tsunami waves are the undersea occurrence of earthquake exceeding 7.5 on Richter scale. Which one of the following statements regarding this is not correct?

**[CDS 2017-I]**

   (a) It often generates strong waves.
   (b) The Pacific coasts are most vulnerable to Tsunami waves.
   (c) Tsunami waves are also called high-energy tidal waves or seismic sea waves.
   (d) Tsunami is a Latin word.

# Exercise -2

## Statement Based MCQ

**1.** Which of these is/are flood prevention and mitigation strategy?
1. Construction flood prevention embracement's
2. Depopulating flood plains
3. Afforestation
4. Decongesting the river channels
Select the following options below
(a) 1 and 2 only
(b) 1, 2 and 3
(c) 2, 3 and 4
(d) 1, 2, 3 and 4

**2.** Consider the following statements:
1. natural hazards are the elements of circumstances in the natural environment that have the potential to cause harm to people and property or both
2. natural disasters are relatively sudden and cause large scale, wide spared death and loss of property and disturbance to social systems and life over, which people have more to little or no control.
Which of the following statements is/are correct?
(a) 1 only
(b) 2 only
(c) Both 1 & 2
(d) Neither 1 or 2

**3.** Which of the following statement is/are correct?
1. Indian National Centre for Ocean Information Services (INCOIS) works under Ministry of Environment at Hyderabad.
2. Indian Tsunami Early Warning System (TWES) was established in INCOIS.
Which of the following is/are correct?
(a) Only 1
(b) Only 2
(c) Both 1 and 2
(d) None of the above

**4.** The preparedness for prevention of chemical accidents and emergency in industry should be made according to the statutory framework of
1. The National Environmental Tribunal Act, 1975
2. The Public Liability Insurance Act, 1991
3. The Factories Act, 1948
4. The Water (Prevention and Control of Pollution) Act, 1974
Choose the correct answer :
(a) 1,2 and 3 only
(b) 2,3 and 4 only
(c) 2 and 3 only
(d) 1,2,3 and 4

# Hints and Explanations

## EXERCISE-1

| | | | | | | | | | |
|---|---|---|---|---|---|---|---|---|---|
| 1. | (a) | 2. | (c) | 3. | (a) | 4. | (c) | 5. | (a) |
| 6. | (c) | 7. | (b) | 8. | (d) | 9. | (c) | 10. | (a) |
| 11. | (a) | 12. | (c) | 13. | (d) | 14. | (b) | 15. | (b) |
| 16. | (d) | 17. | (c) | 18. | (a) | 19. | (d) | 20. | (d) |
| 21. | (c) | 22. | (a) | 23. | (b) | 24. | (d) | 25. | (c) |
| 26. | (c) | 27. | (c) | 28. | (a) | 29. | (d) | 30. | (d) |
| 31. | (d) | 32. | (b) | 33. | (b) | 34. | (b) | 35. | (b) |
| 36. | (d) | | | | | | | | |

37. (d) Tsunami, a Japanese word, is a series of waves generated in a water body due to the displacement of a large volume of water. It is also called seismic sea wave (gravitational water waves) and can generate strong water waves. About 80% of tsunamis are witnessed in the Pacific Ocean.

## EXERCISE-2

| | | | | | | | |
|---|---|---|---|---|---|---|---|
| 1. | (d) | 2. | (c) | 3. | (b) | 4. | (b) |

# 5
## Chapter

# CLIMATE CHANGE

The year 2015-16 was important for climate change both at domestic and global level. It was started with the groundwork of the third National Communication (NATCOM) under the United Nations Framework Convention on Climate Change (UNFCCC) and the release of the Biennial Update Reports (BURs). It has been clear that human influence is there in the climate system and the recent anthropogenic emissions of greenhousegases are the highest in history. Recent climate changes have had widespread impacts on human and natural systems.

## CHANGES IN THE CLIMATE SYSTEM

- Warming of the climate system is clear and since the 1950s, many of the observed changes are:
  - atmosphere and ocean have warmed
  - the amounts of snow and ice have diminished
  - sea level has risen
- Each of the last three decades has been successively warmer at the Earth's surface than any preceding decade since 1850.
- The period almost 30 years from 1983 to 2012 was likely the warmest 30-year period of the last 1400 years in the Northern Hemisphere, where such assessment is possible.

## Causes of Climate Change

- The anthropogenic greenhouse gas (GHG) emissions have amplified since the pre-industrial era, driven largely by economic and population growth, and are now higher than ever which led to atmospheric concentrations of carbon dioxide ($CO_2$), methane ($CH_4$) and nitrous oxide ($N_2O$) that are unprecedented in at least the last 800,000 years.
- The effects of GHG together with those of other anthropogenic drivers, have been observed throughout the climate system and are extremely likely to have been the dominant cause of the detected warming since the mid-20th century.
- Between the years 1750 and 2011, the cumulative anthropogenic $CO_2$ emissions to the atmosphere were $2040 \pm 310$ $GtCO_2$ (Giga tonnes of $CO_2$) out of which about 40% of these emissions have remained in the atmosphere ($880 \pm 35$ $GtCO_2$); the rest was removed from the atmosphere and stored on land (in plants and soils) and in the ocean.

- The ocean alone has absorbed about 30% of the emitted anthropogenic $CO_2$, causing ocean acidification.
- About half of the anthropogenic $CO_2$ emissions between 1750 and 2011 have occurred in the last 40 years.

## Impacts of Climate Change

- In the last few decades, severe changes in climate have caused impacts on human natural eco-systems on all continents and across the oceans.
- Impacts are due to observed climate change, irrespective of its cause, indicating the sensitivity of natural and human systems to changing climate.
- Evidence of observed climate change impacts is strongest and most comprehensive for natural systems while in many regions in the world, changing pattern of precipitation or melting snow and ice are altering hydrological balancing systems, affecting water resources in terms of both quantity and quality.
- Some impacts on human systems have also been ascribed to climate change, with a major or minor impact of climate change discernable from other influences.
- In response to ongoing climate change much fresh water, terrestrial and marine species have shifted their geographic ranges, migration patterns, seasonal activities, abundances and species interactions in response to ongoing climate change.
- As per the assessment of many studies, which covers a wide range of regions and crops shows that negative impacts of climate change on crop produces have been more conjoint than positive impacts.
- Some impacts of ocean acidification on marine organisms have been attributed to human influence.

## Some Examples of impact of climate change

- Sub-Arctic *boreal* forests are likely to be particularly badly affected, with tree lines gradually retreating north as temperatures rise.
- In tropical forests such as the **Amazon**, where there is abundant biodiversity, even modest levels of climate change can cause high levels of extinction.
- If global warming remains on its upward path, by 2050 just 5% of **Australia's Great Barrier Reef**- the world's largest coral reef- will remain.
- Global warming in the Himalayas has already occurred at three times the global average which is prime **snow leopard** habitat and continued warming will cause their range to shrink as the tree-line moves higher up the mountains. This will not only fragment and isolate snow leopard populations, but it will severely affect their prey too.

## India's Stand on Climate Change

- Under the Prime Minister's **Council on Climate Change** (PMCCC) all country's missions under the **National Action Plan on Climate Change** (NAPCC) were asked to revisit their plans.
- The new mission on wind energy, health, waste to energy and coastal areas was also taken up. It also redesigned the **National Water Mission** and **National Mission** on **Sustainable Agriculture** in India.
- The **National Adaptation Fund for Climate Change** (NAFCC) was made operational in the financial year 2015-16.
- To develop its institutional capacities and implement state-level activities to address the climate change the **State Action Plan on Climate change** (SAPCCC) is being prepared.
- To create and strengthen the scientific and analytical capacity for assessment of climate change in the country different studies under Climate change action programme (CCAP) has been started.
- During the same financial year 2015-16, many significant bilateral and multilateral meetings and international negotiations on climate change were held.
- India also submitted its Intended **Nationally Determined Contribution** (INDC) to the UNFCCC.
- During **COP21** Summit in Paris, **India Pavilion** was set up to showcase and share information on India's act on climate change.
- In addition, a new online **Management Information System** (MIS) was launched by the **National Clean Development Mechanism Authority** (NCDMA).
- Also, the **National Designated Entity** (NDE) for **Reducing Emissions from Deforestation and Forest Degradation** (REDD+) has been established in the climate change division along with the National Designated Entity for Climate Technology Centre and Network (CTCN) and Technology Executive Committee (TEC).

## National Communication Submitted to the UNFCCC

- In an enactment of the reporting obligations under the UNFCCC, India has started to communicate information about the implementation and execution of the convention, taking into account the common but distinguished responsibilities and respective capabilities and specific regional and national development priorities, objectives and circumstances.
- The elements of information provided in the communication include a national inventory of anthropogenic emissions by sources and removals by sinks of all greenhouse gases, a general description of steps taken to implement the Convention including an assessment of impacts and vulnerability, and any other relevant information.
- The communication is meant to provide the context and the national circumstances inter alia India's geography, imperative of development needs, climate and economy; based on which India would be addressing and responding to the challenges of climate change.
- India has submitted its *second* **National Communication** (NATCOM) to the UNFCCC in 2012 and the second NATCOM provides information of the emissions of Green House Gases (GHG) for the years 2000 and 2007.
- The Ministry is currently preparing India's *third* **National Communication** (TNC) and in this connection a workshop on **National Inventory Management System** (NIMS) was organized in July 2015.
- The purpose of this workshop was to provide inputs for establishment of **National Inventory Management System** (NIMS) and increased accuracy of Green House Gas Inventory preparation with use of higher tier methods.
- The **Biennial Update Reports** (BURs) are new reporting obligation under the transparency arrangement of sharing information on implementation of the Convention.
- The BUR is a form of enhanced reporting, containing updates of national greenhouse gas inventories and information on mitigation actions, financial, technical needs and support received and an update to India's second National Communication.
- The *first* BUR encompassing information on National Circumstance, GHG Inventories for the year 2010, Mitigation Actions, Analysis of Constraints, Gaps and related financial, technical and capacity needs and other related information along with information on domestic **Monitoring, Reporting and Verification** (MRV) arrangements has been released.

## National and State Action Plans on Climate Change

- Indbia's domestic strategy for addressing climate change is reflected in many of its social and economic development programmes like the **National Action Plan on Climate Change** (NAPCC) which is coordinated by the Ministry of Environment, Forest & Climate Change (MoEF & CC) is being implemented through the Nodal Ministries in specific sectors/ areas.

- Eight national missions in the area of solar energy, enhanced energy efficiency, sustainable agriculture, sustainable habitat, water, Himalayan eco-system, Green India and strategic knowledge for climate change form the core of NAPCC.

- All National missions were approved by the Prime Minister's Council on Climate change (PMCCC) and are at different stages of implementation and the Missions are under constant review of the Prime Minister's Council on Climate Change.

- An **Executive Committee** on Climate Change under the Chairmanship of Principal Secretary to Prime Minister has been set up for assisting the Prime Minister's Council on Climate Change in evolving a coordinating response to issues relating to climate change at national level with regular monitoring of the eight national missions along with other initiatives on climate change and coordinating with various agencies on issues relating to climate change.

- Prime Minister's office has entrusted the responsibility of convening and servicing the Prime Minister's Council on Climate Change as well as the Executive Committee on Climate Change to MoEF & CC.

- The Ministry has also motivated state governments to prepare **State Action Plan on Climate Change** (SAPCC) which has the aim to create institutional capacities and implement state level activities to address climate change.

- Till date, 33 states/UTs namely Andaman and Nicobar, Andhra Pradesh including Telangana, Arunachal Pradesh, Assam, Bihar, Chandigarh Chhattisgarh, Delhi, Gujarat, Haryana, Himachal Pradesh, Jammu & Kashmir, Jharkhand, Kerala, Karnataka, Lakshadweep, Madhya Pradesh, Manipur, Meghalaya, Mizoram, Nagaland, Odisha, Puducherry, Punjab, Rajasthan, Sikkim, Tamil Nadu, Tripura, Uttarakhand, West Bengal, Uttar Pradesh, Maharashtra, Goa have prepared and submitted document on SAPCC.

- The MoEF & CC is also closely following up with the remaining two states which have not submitted their SAPCCs.

## National Adaptation Fund for Climate Change

- The National Adaptation Fund for Climate Change (NAFCC) came into force in 2015-16.

- The fund is meant to assist *national* and *state level* activities to meet the cost of adaptation measures in areas that are particularly vulnerable to the adverse effects of climate change.

- This scheme has been taken as **Central Sector Scheme** with the **National Bank for Agriculture and Rural Development** (NABARD) as **National Implementing Entity** (NIE).

- The overall aim of the fund is to support concrete *adaptation* activities which are not covered under ongoing schemes of State and National Government that reduce the adverse *effects* of climate change facing community sector and states.

---

### NATIONAL WATER MISSION

**Mission Objective**: To conserve water, minimise wastage and ensure equitable distribution both across and within states through integrated water resources development and management.

**Mission Targets and Timeline**: To achieve its objective, the mission targets are:

- Development of comprehensive water database in public domain and assessment of impact of climate change on water resources.
- Promotion of citizen and state actions for water conservation, augmentation and preservation.
- Focused attention to vulnerable areas including over-exploited areas.
- Increase water use efficiency by 20%.
- Promotion of basin level integrated water resources management.

---

## Climate Change Action Programme

- The National Action Plan on Climate Change was launched in 2008 which identifies a number of measures that simultaneously advance the country's development and climate change related objectives of adaptation and mitigation.

- The Ministry is implementing a scheme titled '**Climate Chance Action Programme**' (CCAP) since January, 2014, with an objective to create and strengthen the scientific and analytical capacity for assessment of climate change in the country, putting in place appropriate institutional framework for scientific and policy initiatives and implementation of climate change related actions in the context of sustainable development.

- Total budget for the scheme is 290 crore for the 12th Plan period.

- In order to enhance understanding of climate change the CCAP includes **National Carbonaceous Aerosols Programme** (NCAP), **Long Term Ecological Observatories** (LTEO) and **Coordinated Studies on Climate Change for North East Region** (CSCCNER).

- The NCAP is a major activity involving multi-institutional and multi-agency study under which the MoEF & CC will collaborate with the Ministry of Earth Sciences, the Indian Space Research Organization (ISRO), the Ministry of Science and Technology and other associated agencies to enhance the understanding the role of **Black Carbon** in climate change through monitoring and assessment of the impacts of Black Carbon using modeling techniques.

- The work programme envisages three Working Groups namely **Long Term Monitoring of Aerosol** (Working Group-I), **Impact of Aerosol on Himalayan Glaciers** (Working Group-II) and **Modeling of Black Carbon emissions** in India and assessment of its impacts (Working Group-III).

- **International Negotiations on Climate Change** under the **United Nations Framework Convention on Climate Change** during the financial year 2015-16 many important bilateral and multilateral meetings and international negotiations on climate change were held. These meetings were crucial in the run up to the 21st Conference of Parties (COP 21).

- The key contributions envisaged in India's INDCs are as follows:
  - to put forward and further propagate a healthy and sustainable way of living based on traditions and values of conservation and moderation;
  - to adopt a climate friendly and a cleaner path than the one followed hitherto by others at corresponding level of economic development;
  - to reduce the emissions intensity of its GDP by 33 to 35% by 2030 from 2005 level, etc.

# Forest Carbon Partnership Facility

- The Forest Carbon Partnership Facility (FCPF) is a global partnership focused on reducing emissions from deforestation and forest degradation, forest carbon stock conservation, sustainable management of forests, and enhancement of forest carbon sotcks (REDD+).

- FCPF was originially developed as a concept by the World Bank and The Nature Conservancy (TNC). It was then launched at the negotiations of the UNFCCC in Bali in 2007 (COP13) by the World Bank, nine donor governments and TNC. FCPF has 36 REDD country participants. The FCPF has created a framework and processes to assist countries in their REDD+ readiness; helping countries prepare for future financial incentive systems for REDD+.

- FCPF is made up of two separate, but complementary, funds that support countries in their REDD+ preparations. Firstly, the Readiness fund, which assists participant countries prepare for REDD+ by developing policies and systems, in particular national REDD+ strategies; developing reference emission levels (RELs); designing measurement, reporting and verification (MRV) systems; and establishing national management arrangements, including safeguards, for REDD+. Contributors to the Readiness Fund are known as Donor Participants.

- Secondly, it consists of the Carbon Fund. This became operational in May 2011 and will provide payments for verified emissions reductions from REDD+ programmes. Contributors to the Carbon Fund are calles Carbon Fund Participants. Developing countries participating in the FCPF in both funds are known as REDD Country Participants. About five REDD Country Participants will be supported by the Carbon Fund, dependent on a progress assessment made by the FCPF Participants Committee.

# REDD & REDD+ (Reducing Emissions from Deforestation & Forest Degradation)

- REDD (Reducing Emissions from Deforestation and Forest Degradation) is the global endeavour to create an incentive for developing countries to protect, better manage and save their forest resources, thus contributing to the global fight against climate change.

- REDD+ goes beyond merely checking deforestation and forest degradation, and includes incentives for positive elements of conservation, sustainable management of forests and enhancement of forest carbon stocks.

- REDD+ conceptualizes flow of positive incentives for demonstrated reduction in deforestation or for enhancing quality and expanse of forest cover.

- It works on the basis of creating a financial value for the carbon stored and enhanced in biomass and soil of standing forests. Countries that reduce emissions and undertake sustainable management of forests will be entitled to receive funds and resources as incentives.

- REDD+ approach incorporates important benefits of livelihoods improvement, biodiversity conservation and food security services.

## India's Position on Redd And Redd+

- India believes REDD needs to be seen in the broader context of REDD+, not in isolation or in a truncated form since reduction of deforestation, and conservation and improvement of forests are two sides of the same coin, and so should be treated at par.

- India's stand was finally accepted in 13th Meeting of the Conference of the Parties (COP 13) at Bali when elements of conservation, sustainable management of forests and enhancement of forest carbon stocks were added to the then existing text of reducing deforestation and forest degradation as part of Bali Action Plan.

- It has presented an ambitious Green India Mission programme under its National Action Plan on Climate Change.

## India initiatives related to REDD+

- India has made a submission to UNFCCC on "REDD, Sustainable Management of Forest(SMF) and Afforestation and Reforestation (A&R)" in December 2008

- A Technical Group has been set up to develop methodologies and procedures to assess and

- monitor contribution of REDD+ actions

- A National REDD+ Coordinating Agency is being established

- A National Forest Carbon Accounting Programme is being institutionalized
- India is hosting the Conference of Parties (COP-11) of the Convention on Biological Diversity (CBD) in 2012, to coincide with twenty years of Rio convention.
- Study on the impact of climate change on India's forests assigned to the Indian Network for Climate Change Assessment (INCCA), has been released in November 2010.
- There is likely to be an increase in Net Primary Productivity (NPP) ranging from 20 - 57%.

## Climate Technology Centre & Network and Technology Executive Committee

- The National Designated Entity (NDE) for Climate Technology Centre and Network (CTCN) and Technology Executive Committee (TEC) [NDE (CTCN & TCE)] has been established in the Climate Change Division of this Ministry.
- The key function will include:
    - leading and coordinating the formulation, selection and submission of requests for technology needs assessment and support;
    - facilitating and monitoring the implementation of CTCN response assistance;
    - foster collaboration and access to information and knowledge to accelerate climate technology transfer in the country;
    - strengthen network, partnership and capacity building for climate technology transfer.
- Ozone Layer Protection Ozone, a triatomic molecule of oxygen is formed from oxygen naturally in the upper levels of the earth's atmosphere by high energy Ultraviolet (UV) radiation from the Sun.
- The UV radiation breaks down oxygen molecules, releasing free atoms, some of which bond with other oxygen molecule to form ozone.
- About 90% of ozone formed in this way lies between 10 and 50 kilometers above the earth's surface, called the Stratosphere.
- The **Vienna Convention** for the Protection of the Ozone Layer and its Montreal Protocol on substances that deplete the Ozone Layer are the international treaties specific for the protection of the Stratospheric Ozone (Ozone layer).
- The **Montreal Protocol** has been recognized as the most successful international environmental treaty in history. It has been universally ratified and all the 197 United Nations member countries of the world are the parties to the Vienna Convention and its Montreal Protocol.
- In the 29 years of operation of the Montreal Protocol, extraordinary international cooperation under this agreement has led to phase-out of production and consumption of several major **Ozone Depleting Substances** (ODSs) such as **Chlorofluorocarbons** (CFCs), **Carbon tetrachloride** (CTC) and halons globally from 1st January, 2010.
- The production and consumption of **Methyl chloroform** has been phased out globally by 2015, with possible essential use exemptions.
- The production and consumption of **Methyl bromide** was phased out globally in 2016, except use in quarantine and pre-shipment applications.
- Global systematic observations have confirmed that atmospheric levels of key ODSs are declining and it is estimated that with continued, full implementation of the Montreal Protocol's provisions, the global ozone layer should return to pre-1980 levels by around the middle of this century and the **Antarctic ozone** around 15 years later.
- The Montreal Protocol has also delivered substantial climate benefits.

## INDIA'S INDC: CLIMATE CHANGE CONTRIBUTIONS

1. To put forward and further propagate a healthy and sustainable way of living based on traditions and values of conservation and moderation.
2. To adopt a climate friendly and cleaner path than the one hitherto followed by others at a corresponding level of economic development.
3. To reduce the emissions intensity of its GDP by 33 to 35% of the 2005 level by 2030.
4. To achieve about 40% cumulative electric power installed capacity from non-fossil fuel- based energy resources by 2030 with the help of transfer of technology and low cost international finance including from the Green Climate Fund (GCF).
5. To create an additional carbon sink of 2.5 to 3 billion tonnes of $CO_2$ equivalent ($CO_2$eq.) through additional forest and tree cover by 2030.
6. To better adapt to climate change by enhancing investments in development programmes in sectors vulnerable to climate change, particularly agriculture, water resources, the Himalayan region, coastal regions, health and disaster management.
7. To mobilize domestic and new and additional funds from developed countries for implementing these mitigation and adaptation actions in view of the resources required and the resource gap.
8. To build capacities, create a domestic framework and an international architecture for quick diffusion of cutting-edge climate technology in India and for joint collaborative R&D for such future technologies.

# Carbon Footprint

A carbon footprint is the amount of greenhouse gases—primarily carbon dioxide- released into the atmosphere by a particular human activity. A carbon footprint can be a broad measure or be applied to the actions of an individual, a family, an event, an organization, or even an entire nation. It is usually measured as tons of $CO_2$ emitted per year, a number that can be supplemented by tons of $CO_2$-equivalent gases, including methane, nitrous oxide, and other greenhouse gases.

## Climate Fiction(Cli-Fi)

Cli-Fi refers to "climate fiction;" it is a term coined by journalist Dan Bloom. These are fictional books that somehow or someway bring real climate change science to the reader. What is really interesting is that Cli-Fi books often present real science in a credible way. They become fun teaching tools. There are some really well known authors such as Paolo Bacigalupi and Margaret Atwood among others. A list of other candidate Cli-Fi novels was provided by Sarah Holding in the Guardian.

Cli-Fi stories are vehicles that can help us imagine. The authors get us to think about these what ifs – these future Earths. Cli-Fi novels (and movies for that matter) can make experiences far more real than endless graphs or plots of temperature variations. And that, perhaps, is the most important contribution Cli-Fi can make to the discussion of climate change in our everyday lives. These authors get us to imagine what experiences are or would be like.

## Carbon Credit

In step with the dramatic rise in $CO_2$ emissions and other pollutants in recent years, a variety of new financial markets have emerged, offering businesses key incentives — aside from taxes and other punitive measures — to slow down overall emissions growth and, ideally, global warming itself.

A key feature of these markets is emissions trading, or cap-and-trade schemes, which allow companies to buy or sell "credits" that collectively bind all participating companies to an overall emissions limit. While markets operate for specific pollutants such as greenhouse gases and acid rain, by far the biggest emissions market is for carbon. In 2007, the trade market for $CO_2$ credits hit $60 billion worldwide—almost double the amount from 2006.

### How It Works

Emissions limits and trading rules vary country by country, so each emissions-trading market operates differently. For nations that have signed the Kyoto Protocol, which holds each country to its own $CO_2$ limit, greenhouse gas-emissions trading is mandatory. In the United States, which did not sign the environmental agreement, corporate participation is voluntary for emissions schemes such as the Chicago Climate Exchange. Yet a few general principles apply to each type of market.

Under a basic cap-and-trade scheme, if a company's carbon emissions fall below a set allowance, that company can sell the difference — in the form of credits — to other companies that exceed their limits. Another fast-growing voluntary model is carbon offsets. In this global market, a set of middlemen companies, called offset firms, estimate a company's emissions and then act as brokers by offering opportunities to invest in carbon-reducing projects around the world. Unlike carbon trading, offsetting isn't yet government regulated in most countries; it's up to buyers to verify a project's environmental worth. In theory, for every ton of $CO_2$ emitted, a company can buy certificates attesting that the same amount of greenhouse gas was removed from the atmosphere through renewable energy projects such as tree planting.

### Why It Matters Now

Industry watchers say carbon markets will continue to grow at a fast clip—especially in the United States, where Fortune 500 powerhouses such as DuPont, Ford, and IBM are voluntarily capping and trading their emissions. Even though a national cap on carbon emissions doesn't yet exist in the United States, most consider it inevitable, and legislators are already pushing the issue in Congress.

It's not just governments who are demanding emissions compliance—consumers want it, too. The commitment a company makes to curb its pollutant output is an increasingly public aspect of strategy. More and more employees are taking these factors into account when deciding where to work. A recent study from MonsterTRAK found that 80 percent of young professionals want their work to impact the environment in a positive way, and 92 percent prefer to work for an environmentally friendly company.

## Carbon Trading

**Carbon trading is a market-based system aimed at reducing greenhouse gases that contribute to global warming, particularly carbon dioxide emitted by burning fossil fuels.**

### How does It work?

There have been attempts to allow richer countries to cut their emissions by paying for the development of carbon lowering schemes in poorer nations. However, the effectiveness of these schemes has been questioned, with research indicating that some have created more emissions than they have actually curtailed.

Of greater significance have been the so called cap and trade schemes, at regional, national and international levels. They work by setting an overall limit or cap on the amount of emissions that are allowed from significant sources of carbon, including the power industry, automotive and air travel.

Governments then issue permits up to the agreed limit, and these are either given free or auctioned to companies in the sector. If a company curbs its own carbon significantly it can trade the excess permits on the carbon market for cash. If it's not able to limit its emissions it may have to buy extra permits.

Schemes are up and running in the European Union and in several regions of the United States, but attempts at a national scheme in the US foundered in the Senate in 2010.

# Carbon Budget

The Carbon Budget is the expected amount of carbon dioxide ($CO_2$) the world can emit while still having a likely chance of limiting global temperature rise to $2^0C$ above pre-industrial levels. The international scientific community estimates this budget to be 1 trillion tonnes of carbon.

One of the studies appointed by **WWF** from Ecofys chose to set the anticipated concentration limit at 400 ppm $CO_2e$, so as to have a better chance (66% likelihood) of staying below 2°C of global warming. The study translates this ppm limit into a global carbon budget for the period 1990–2100. (1990 was chosen as the start year because the **Kyoto Protocol** allows for emission reduction targets against 1990 emissions levels).The study concludes that collectively we can emit no more than about 1600 $GtCO_2e$ over the period 1990–2100. We have already emitted a significant portion of this global carbon budget in the last 20 years, leaving us with about 870 Gt $CO_2e$ from 2009–2100. After that we need to approach no net emissions.

If we divide this total budget up per year, globally we can emit on average 9.5 Gt $CO_2e$ per year for the 91 years from 2009. This is about 20% of our current annual global emissions. If we continue our current global 47 $GtCO_2e$ emissions per year, we will use up our remaining budget by about 2030.

# Paris Agreement

- The $21^{st}$ Conference of Parties (COP 21) under the United Nations Framework Convention on Climate Change (UNFCCC) successfully concluded in **Paris** from 30 November to 11 December 2015 after intense negotiations by the Parties followed by the adoption of the Paris Agreement on post-2020 actions on climate change.

- This universal agreement will succeed the Kyoto Protocol. Unlike the Kyoto Protocol, it provides a framework for all countries to take action against climate change.

- Placing emphasis on concepts like climate justice and sustainable lifestyles, the Paris Agreement for the first time brings together all nations for a common cause under the UNFCCC.

- One of the main focuses of the agreement is to hold the increase in the global average temperature to well below 2°C above pre-industrial level and on driving efforts to limit it even further to 1.5°C. The Paris Agreement comprises of 29 articles.

## Salient Features of the Paris Agreement

- The Paris Agreement acknowledges the development imperatives of developing countries by recognizing their right to development and their efforts to harmonize it with the environment, while protecting the interests of the most vulnerable.

- The Agreement seeks to enhance the '**implementation of the Convention**' while reflecting the principles of equity and CBDR-RC, in the light of different national circumstances.

- Countries are required to communicate to the UNFCCC climate action plans known as **nationally determined contributions** (NDCs) every five years. Each Party's successive NDC will represent a progression beyond the Party's then current NDC thereby steadily increasing global effort and ambition in the long term.

- The agreement is not mitigation-centric and includes other important elements such as adaptation, loss and damage, finance, technology development and transfer, capacity building and transparency of action and support.

- Climate action will also be taken forward in the period before 2020. Developed countries are urged to scale up their level of financial support with a complete road map towards achieving the goal of jointly providing US$ 100 billion by 2020. At the same time, a new collective quantified goal based on US$ 100 billion floor will be set before 2025.

- The Agreement mandates that developed countries provide financial resources to developing countries. Other Parties may also contribute, but on a purely voluntary basis.

- Developed countries are urged to take the lead in mobilization of climate finance, while noting the significant role of public funds in the mobilization of finance which should represent a progression beyond their previous effort.

- The Agreement includes a robust transparency framework for both action and support.

- Starting in 2023, a global stock take covering all elements will take place every five years to assess the collective progress towards achieving the purpose of the Paris Agreement and its long term goals.

- The Paris Agreement establishes a compliance mechanism, overseen by a committee of experts that operates in a non-punitive way, and is facilitative in nature.

## India Pavilion at COP-21

- An India Pavilion was set up in COP-21 to showcase and share information on India's actions on climate change.

- The Indian Pavilion in Paris was inaugurated by the Indian Prime Minister on $30^{th}$ November 2015 and the pavilion hosted 25 sessions, 150 speakers, 130 presentations, over 80 films, 13 book/reports/CDs/films/brochure releases.

- Pavilion was appreciated and viewed by nearly 6,500 visitors from different countries.

- Information on India's initiatives was also shared in the form of books or brochures and digital material. India Pavilion was one of the centres of attraction in COP-21 due to its water screen, 360 degree film, ipad forest e-book on India's culture and sustainable living.

## GREEN FINANCE

The term 'green finance' has come in the view in the past few years with the increased focus on green development. The Rio+20 document clearly states what green economy policies should result in and what they should not. While there is no universal definition of green finance, it mostly refers to financial investments flowing towards sustainable development projects and initiatives that encourage the development of a more sustainable economy. Green finance includes different elements like greening the banking system, the bond market and institutional investment. Several working definitions and sets of criteria of green finance have also been developed. Examples include the China's Green Credit Guidelines, the Climate Bonds Taxonomy of Green Bonds, the International Development Finance Club's (IDFC) approach to reporting on green investment, the World Bank/International Finance Corporation's (IFC) Sustainability Framework and the UK Green Investment Bank Policies. An initial review of the current definitions in use reveals sizeable intersections of the various definitions in thematic areas such as clean energy, energy efficiency, green buildings, sustainable transport, water and waste management, as well as areas of controversy such as nuclear and large-scale hydro energy, biofuels and efficiency gains in conventional power. Over the past decade there have been advances in mainstreaming of green finance within financial institutions and financial markets. Voluntary standards such as the Equator Principles have enhanced environmental risk management for many financial institutions. The World Bank Group has set up an informal "Sustainable Banking Network" of banking regulators, led by developing countries, to promote sustainable lending practices. In 2015, green bonds issued by governments, banks, corporates and individual projects amounted to US$42 billion. Globally, more than 20 stock exchanges have issued guidelines on environmental disclosure, and many green indices and green ETFs (exchange-traded funds) have been developed. The Financial Stability Board (FSB) has established a climate-related financial disclosures task force that was expected to complete its first stage of the work by end-March 2016. A growing number of institutions, including the Bank of England and Bank of China (Industrial and Commercial Bank of China); have begun to assess the financial impact of climate and environmental policy changes. Germany, the US and the UK have developed interest subsidy and guarantee programmes for green financing, and over a dozen government-backed green investment banks are operating globally. The G-20 has also recently set up a green finance study group (GFSG).

One topical issue in the context of green finance is that of enhancing the ability of the financial system to mobilize private green finance, thereby facilitating the green transformation of the global economy which has been widely discussed in different fora including the G20. However, for developing countries like India, private finance will not readily be forthcoming and public finance both international and domestic needs to be used to leverage private finance. Green development is also important for India though green finance is yet to pick up. Attaining the ambitious solar energy target, development of solar cities, setting up wind power projects, developing smart cities, providing infrastructure which is considered as a green activity and the sanitation drive under the 'Clean India' or 'Swach Bharath Abhiyan' are all activities needing green finance. India has created a corpus called the National Clean Energy Fund (NCEF) in 2010-11 out of the cess on coal produced/imported ('polluter pays' principle) for the purpose of financing and promoting clean energy initiatives and funding research in the area of clean energy. Some of the projects financed by this fund include innovative schemes like a green energy corridor for boosting the transmission sector, the Jawaharlal Nehru National Solar Mission's (JNNSM) installation of solar photovoltaic (SPV) lights (see Figure 3 (b)) and small capacity lights, installation of SPiV water pumpwing systems, SPV power plants, grid-connected rooftop SPV (see Figure 3(c)) power plants and a pilot project to assess wind power potential. So far four banks have issued green bonds in India.

Proceeds from these bonds are mostly used for funding renewable energy projects such as solar, wind and biomass projects and other infrastructure sectors, with infrastructure and energy efficiency being considered as green in their entirety. The Securities and Exchange Board of India (SEBI) has also recently approved the guidelines for green bonds. While mobilization and effective use of green finance is of primary importance, there are some issues which need to be taken note of:

- For a developing country like India, poverty alleviation and development are of vital importance and resources should not be diverted from meeting these development needs. Green finance should not be limited only to investment in renewable energy, as, for a country like India, coal based power accounts for around 60% of installed capacity. Emphasis should be on greening coal technology. In fact, green finance for development and transfer of green technology is important as most green technologies in developed countries are in the private domain and are subject to intellectual property rights (IPR), making them cost prohibitive.
- Green bonds are perceived as new and attach higher risk and their tenure is also shorter. There is a need to reduce risks to make them investment grade.
- There is also a need for an internationally agreed upon definition of green financing as its absence could lead to over-accounting.
- While environmental risk assessment is important, banks should not overestimate risks while providing green finance.
- Green finance should also consider unsustainable patterns of consumption as a parameter in deciding finance, particularly conspicuous consumption and unsustainable lifestyles in developed countries.

## Intergovernmental Panel on Climate Change (IPCC)

The Intergovernmental Panel on Climate Change (IPCC) is the international body for assessing the science related to climate change. The IPCC was set up in 1988 by the World Meteorological Organization (WMO) and United Nations Environment Programme (UNEP) to provide policymakers with regular assessments of the scientific basis of climate change, its impacts and future risks, and options for adaptation and mitigation.

IPCC assessments provide a scientific basis for governments at all levels to develop climate related policies, and they underlie negotiations at the UN Climate Conference — the United Nations Framework Convention on Climate Change (UNFCCC). The assessments are policy-relevant but not policy-prescriptive: they may present projections of future climate change based on different scenarios and the risks that climate change poses and discuss the implications of response options, but they do not tell policymakers what actions to take.

The IPCC embodies a unique opportunity to provide rigorous and balanced scientific information to decision-makers because of its scientific and intergovernmental nature. Participation in the IPCC is open to all member countries of the WMO and United Nations. It currently has 195 members. The Panel, made up of representatives of the member states, meets in Plenary Sessions to take major decisions. The IPCC Bureau, elected by member governments, provides guidance to the Panel on the scientific and technical aspects of the Panel's work and advises the Panel on related management and strategic issues

IPCC assessments are written by hundreds of leading scientists who volunteer their time and expertise as Coordinating Lead Authors and Lead Authors of the reports. They enlist hundreds of other experts as Contributing Authors to provide complementary expertise in specific areas.

IPCC reports undergo multiple rounds of drafting and review to ensure they are comprehensive and objective and produced in an open and transparent way. Thousands of other experts contribute to the reports by acting as reviewers, ensuring the reports reflect the full range of views in the scientific community. Teams of Review Editors provide a thorough monitoring mechanism for making sure that review comments are addressed

IPCC Assessment Reports cover the full scientific, technical and socio-economic assessment of climate change, generally in four parts — one for each of the Working Groups plus a Synthesis Report. Special Reports are assessments of a specific issue. Methodology Reports provide practical guidelines for the preparation of greenhouse gas inventories under the UNFCCC.

### Assessment Reports

- In accordance with its mandate and as reaffirmed in various decisions by the Panel, the IPCC prepares at regular intervals comprehensive Assessment Reports of scientific, technical and socio-economic information relevant for the understanding of human induced climate change, potential impacts of climate change and options for mitigation and adaptation.

- Assessment Reports are normally published in several volumes, one for each of the Working Groups of the IPCC and, subject to the decision by the Panel, a Synthesis Report.

- They are written in a non-technical style suitable for policymakers. They are composed of a longer report and a Summary for Policymakers.

- Five Assessment Reports have beea completed in 1990, 1995, 2001 and 2007, 2014.

### $AR_5$ Contents

- Compared with previous reports, the $AR_5$ has put greater emphasis on assessing the socio-economic aspects of climate change and implications for sustainable development, risk management and the framing of a response through both adaptation and mitigation.

- The $AR_5$ comprise the full reports prepared by the Working Groups (I, II and III) as well as the Synthesis Report.

- Key $AR_5$ cross-cutting themes are:

- Water and the Earth System: Changes, Impacts and Responses;

- Carbon Cycle including Ocean Acidification;

- Ice Sheets and Sea-Level Rise;

- Mitigation, Adaptation and Sustainable Development and

- Article 2 of the UNFCCC (see UNFCCC for definition).

### Special Reports

- Special Reports have been prepared on topics such as aviation, regional impacts of climate change, technology transfer, emissions scenarios, land use, land use change and forestry, carbon dioxide capture and storage and on the relationship between safeguarding the ozone layer and the global climate system.

## The Climate Change Performance Index 2018

Recognizing the urgency to take immediate action in protecting the global climate, the 21st Conference of the Parties, held in December 2015 in Paris, made a groundbreaking achievement in adopting the goal to limit global warming to "well below" 2°C and to pursue efforts to limit warming to 1.5°C. Under the Paris Agreement, for the first time ciimate action was anchored in the context of international law. This requires countries to make their own unique contribution to the prevention of dangerous climate change. The next crucial step to follow this agreement is the rapid implementation by the signing parties of concrete measures to make their individual contributions to the global goal. For the past 13 years, the Climate Change Performance Index (CCPI) has been keeping track of countries' efforts in combating climate change. The varying initial positions, interests and strategies of the numerous countries make it difficult to distinguish their strengths and weaknesses and the CCPI has been an important tool in contributing to a clearer understanding of national and international climate policy.

To demonstrate existing measures more accurately and to encourage steps toward effective climate policy, we evaluated the design of the CCPI this year with several achievements: For the first time, it is monitoring the development of all greenhouse gas emissions of the 56 countries and the EU that are assessed in the CCPI. In addition to that, the index now is suited even better to measure how well countries are on track to the global goals of the Paris Agreement. It does so by not only comparing countries by their development and recent trends in the three categories "GHG Emissions", "Renewable Energy" and "Energy Use", but also the 2°C-compatibility of their current status and future targets in each of these categories. The index also continues to evaluate countries' ambition and progress in the field of climate policy.

The following publication is issued by Germanwatch, the New Climate Institute and the Climate Action Network. However, only with the help of around 300 energy and climate experts from all over the world we are able to include a review of each country's national and international policies. The review charts the efforts that have been made to avoid dangerous climate change, and also evaluates the various countries' current efforts regarding the implementation of the Paris Agreement. We greatly appreciate these experts for their time, efforts and knowledge in contributing to this publication. The experts are mainly representatives of NGOs who work within their respective countries, fighting for the implementation of the climate policy that we all so desperately need.

| Rank | Country | Score |
|------|---------|-------|
| 1. | - | - |
| 2. | - | - |
| 3. | - | - |
| 4. | Sweden | 74.32 |
| 5. | Lithuania | 69.20 |
| 6. | Morocco | 68.22 |
| 7. | Norway | 67.99 |
| 8. | United Kingdom | 66.79 |
| 9. | Finland | 66.55 |
| 10. | Latvia | 63.02 |
| 11. | Malta | 61.87 |
| 12. | Switzerland | 61.20 |
| 13. | Croatia | 61.19 |
| 14. | India | 60.02 |
| 15. | France | 59.80 |
| 16. | Italy | 59.65 |
| 17. | Denmark | 59.49 |
| 18. | Portugal | 59.16 |
| 19. | Brazil | 57.86 |
| 20. | Ukraine | 57.49 |
| 21. | European Union (28) | 56.89 |
| 22. | Germany | 56.58 |
| 23. | Belarus | 56.38 |
| 24. | Slovak Republic | 56.04 |
| 25. | Luxembourg | 55.54 |
| 26. | Romania | 55.32 |
| 27. | Mexico | 54.77 |
| 28. | Egypt | 54.02 |
| 29. | Cyprus | 52.29 |
| 30. | Estonia | 52.02 |
| 31. | Slovenia | 50.54 |
| 32. | Belgium | 49.60 |
| 33. | New Zealand | 49.57 |
| 34. | Netherlands | 49.49 |
| 35. | Austria | 49.49 |
| 36. | Thailand | 49.07 |
| 37. | Indonesia | 48.94 |
| 38. | Spain | 48.19 |
| 39. | Greece | 47.86 |
| 40. | Poland | 46.53 |
| 41. | China | 45.84 |
| 42. | Bulgaria | 45.35 |
| 43. | Czech Republic | 45.13 |
| 44 | Hungary | 44.00 |
| 45. | Algeria | 43.61 |
| 46. | Argentina | 41.21 |
| 47. | Turkey | 41.02 |
| 48. | South Africa | 40.61 |
| 49. | Ireland | 38.74 |
| 50. | Japan | 35.76 |
| 51. | Canada | 33.98 |
| 52. | Malaysia | 32.61 |
| 53. | Russian Federation | 29.85 |
| 54. | Chinese Taipei | 29.43 |
| 55. | Kazakhstan | 28.17 |
| 56. | United States | 25.86 |
| 57. | Australia | 25.03 |
| 58. | Korea | 25.01 |
| 59. | Islamic Republic of Iran | 23.05 |
| 60. | Saudi Arabia | 11.20 |

# Exercise -1

1. Ministry for water resources, river development and Ganga rejuvenation has announced to celebrate the birth anniversary of Dr. Bhim Rao Ambedkar held on 14th April as which day?
   (a) Health Day
   (b) Water Day
   (c) Conservation Day
   (d) Food Day

2. Which country issued its first Green Bonds with a record sale of USD 7.5 billion in January, 2017?
   (a) Britain
   (b) France
   (c) Germany
   (d) Mauritius

3. The National Physical Laboratory (NPL)-CSIR has dedicated the first pristine air-quality monitoring station to the Nation at:
   (a) Palampur
   (b) Srinagar
   (c) Nanital
   (d) Shimla

4. Considering climate change, melting of ice sheets and glaciers causes the
   (a) destruction of infrastructure
   (b) endangering of species
   (c) desertification
   (d) destruction of human settlements

5. Considering climate change, increased global temperatures causes the
   (a) desertification
   (b) destruction of human settlements
   (c) destruction of infrastructure
   (d) endangering of species

6. Considering climate change, rise in water level in oceans and seas due to melted ice sheets and glaciers causes
   (a) desertification
   (b) destruction of human settlements
   (c) destruction of infrastructure
   (d) endangering of species

7. Long period of time without water is classified as
   (a) flood
   (b) drought
   (c) desertification
   (d) endangering

8. Human activities that causes climate change on Earth includes
   (a) burning of forests
   (b) agricultural activities
   (c) use of aerosol cans
   (d) all of above

9. Which of the following contributes the maximum to the greenhouse effect?
   (a) Carbon dioxide
   (b) Water vapour
   (c) Methane
   (d) Nitrous oxide

10. What was Montreal Protocol concerned with?
    (a) Checking ozone layer depletion
    (b) Checking Global warming
    (c) Protecting Biodiversity
    (d) Increasing forest cover

11. Consider the following statements
    (i) Ramsar Convention is an intergovernmental treaty to maintain the ecological character of Wetlands of international importance.
    (ii) 26 sites in India is covered under Ramsar Convention for wildlife conservation.
    Which of the following statement(s) is\are true?
    (a) i)
    (b) ii)
    (c) both i) and ii)
    (d) None

12. Earth's temperatures are stable because we are surrounded by ________ which allows the right amount of sunlight in to warm the Earth.
    (a) a cloud layer
    (b) an atmosphere
    (c) gravity
    (d) water

13. This layer keeps us "not too hot in the summer" and "not too cold in the winter." Scientists call this the ________ effect.
    (a) greenhouse effect
    (b) seasonal effect
    (c) ocean effect
    (d) lake effect

14. Certain gases in the atmosphere – water vapor, carbon dioxide, methane and nitrous oxide – help maintain the Earth's temperatures and climate. These are called: __________ .
    (a) ozone gases
    (b) solar gases
    (c) greenhouse gases
    (d) stomach gases

15. The solar energy that warms the Earth includes visible light, infrared and ______ coming from the sun.
    (a) gamma rays
    (b) ultraviolet radiation
    (c) microwaves
    (d) sunspots

16. The solar radiation that bounces off the Earth back toward the atmosphere is mostly ______ with a longer wavelength
    (a) gamma radiation
    (b) x-ray radiation
    (c) nuclear radiation
    (d) infrared radiation

17. The layer of the atmosphere closest to Earth is called the: __________ .
    (a) troposphere
    (b) stratosphere
    (c) exosphere
    (d) mesosphere

**18.** How are humans making greenhouse gases of our own?
(a) burning fossil fuels in our cars
(b) burning forests
(c) with large-scale agriculture
(d) all of these

**19.** Too many greenhouse gasses in the atmosphere may block heat from escaping into space and trap too much heat next to the Earth's surface causing: _____________.
(a) another ice age
(b) global warming
(c) earthquakes
(d) volcanic eruptions

**20.** Something that might happen because of global warming is: __________.
(a) melting polar ice caps
(b) more reflected sunlight off the ice pack
(c) lower sea levels
(d) a sale on bathing suits

**21.** Things you can do to help decrease global warming include:
(a) Keep your air conditioner on high.
(b) Turn off your lights when you're not using them.
(c) Keep your freezer door open.
(d) Eat more ice cream.

# Exercise -2

## Statement Based MCQ

**1.** Consider the following statements.
1. Recently the Uttarakhand High Court accorded the status of living human entities to the two most sacred rivers of India the Ganga and Yamuna.
2. In this context the court cited the example of the river Whanganui of Egypt.

**Select the correct answer from the following codes:**
(a) Only 2
(b) Only 1
(c) Both 1 and 2
(d) Neither 1 nor 2

**2.** Which of the following is/are correct about India's recently approved ratification of the tSecond Commitment Period of the Kyoto Protocol.
1. The protocol is related with carbon emission trading.
2. UNFCCC was negotiated in Rio de Janeiro in 1995
3. At present, there are 193 parties to the Protocol.

**Select the correct answer from the following codes:**
(a) Only 3
(b) Only 2 & 3
(c) Only 1
(d) None of the above

**3.** Which of the following is/are correct about the Indian Shad?
1. In January 2017 the West Bengal Govt. Gave legal protection to Hilsa Fish to stabilize its declining population.
2. Hilsa or the Indian Shad is the first fish variety in India to get legal protection.
3. It is the national fish of Pakistan.

**Select the correct answer from the following codes:**
(a) Only 1 & 2
(b) Only 3
(c) Only 2 & 3
(d) All of the above

**4.** India has recently launched Stage II of HCFC Phase Out Management Plan. In this context consider the following statements.
1. It aims to phase out use of Hydrochlorofluorocarbons (HCFCs), harmful ozone-depleting substances (ODS)
2. Under the Kyoto Protocol, the accelerated phase out of Hydrochlorofluorcarbons (HCFCs) is underway with a aim to complete phase out by 2030.
3. Montreal Protocol came into force in 1989 and has been ratified by 197 parties making it universally ratified protocol in UN history.

**Select the correct answer from the following codes:**
(a) Only 2 & 3
(b) Only 1
(c) Only 2
(d) Only 1 & 3

**5.** Which of the following is/are related to environment?
1. Ramsar Convention
2. GLOBE
3. UNFCC

**Select the correct answer from the following codes:**
(a) Only 1
(b) Only 3
(c) Only 1 and 3
(d) 1, 2 and 3

**6.** Recently Assam government has taken an initiative to develop Majuli as India's first carbon neutral district.
In this context consider the following statements.
1. Majuli is the biggest river island in the world.
2. Assam government has launched Sustainable Action for Climate Resilient Development in Majuli.
3. The fluvial riverine island is formed by the Manas river system and world's largest mid river delta system.

**Select the correct answer from the following codes:**
(a) Only 3
(b) Only 2 & 3
(c) Only 1 and 2
(d) All of the above

**7.** Recently the Southern Bench of the National Green Tribunal (NGT) suspended the Environmental Clearance (EC) granted to the India-based Neutrino Observatory (INO).
In this context consider the following statements:
1. The proposed underground laboratory will be studying the properties of the neutrino, which would be accompanied by research regarding black matter and double beta decay.
2. It would be modelled after the existing neutrino labs in Japan, Italy and Canada.

3. NGT suspended the EC because the INO project was just 4.5 km away from Mathikettan Shola National Park in Idukki district (Kerala) and one kilometre from Kerala-Tamil Nadu border.

**Select the correct answer from the following codes:**
(a) Only 1 & 3      (b) Only 3
(c) Only 2 & 3      (d) All of the above

8. Recently Wildlife Crime Control Bureau (WCCB)' is in news for fight against wild life crime.
In this context consider the following statements:
1. Operation Thunderbird is code-name of INTERPOL's multi-national and multi-species enforcement operation for wildlife protection.
2. Operation Save Kurma was species specific operation on turtles.
3. WCCB was established in June 2007 by amending the Wildlife (Protection) Act (WLPA), 1973, a special Act to protect the wildlife and fauna in the country.
Select the correct answer from the following codes:
(a) Only 1 & 2      (b) Only 1, 2 & 3
(c) Only 3      (d) None of the above

9. Recently Seemai Karuvelam (prosopis juliflora) trees are in news.
In this context consider the following statements:
1. The Madurai bench of the Madras High Court has ordered Tamil Nadu government to enact a law with prohibitory and penal clauses to eradicate Seemai Karuvelam.
2. Seemai Karuvelam tree species are native to West Africa. It was brought to Tamil Nadu in 1960s as medicinal plants.
3. It is an invasive species of tree harmful to the environment as it sucks lot of water ultimately affect the environment and agricultural activities.

**Select the correct answer from the following codes:**
(a) Only 3      (b) Only 2 & 3
(c) Only 1 & 3      (d) All of the above

10. Hope Island in Andhra Pradesh is a major concern.
In this context consider the following statements:
1. Olive Ridleys turtles are recognized as Vulnerable by the IUCN Red list.
2. In India, it is protected under the Wildlife (Protection) Act.
3. Hope Island in Andhra Pradesh has become graveyard for Olive Ridleys turtles

**Select the correct answer from the following codes:**
(a) Only 3      (b) Only 1
(c) All of the above      (d) None of the above

11. Consider the following statements regarding Ken-Betwa inter-linking of rivers (ILR) project.
1. The National Board for Wildlife (NBWL) has given its clearance for the Ken-Betwa inter-linking of rivers (ILR) project,
2. The project aims to transfer surplus water from the Ken River to the Betwa basin through concrete canal to irrigate India's worst drought-prone Bundelkhand region.
3. Nearly 8,650 hectares of forest land including part of Panna National Park in Madhya Pradesh will be submerged due to implementation of this project.
4. Nearly 8,650 hectares of forest land including part of Panna National Park in Uttar Pradesh will be submerged due to implementation of this project.

**Select the correct answer from the following codes:**
(a) Only 1, 2 & 4      (b) Only 3 & 4
(c) Only 1      (d) Only 2, 3 & 4

12. The centre has launched the first ever across-the-river survey in the Ganga to determine the population of aquatic life, especially that of the endangered Gangetic dolphin. Consider the following statements regarding the Gangetic dolphin:
1. The Ganges River dolphins are also known as "susu" and inhabits the river systems of Nepal, India and Bangladesh.
2. The species is found exclusively in lake habitat.
3. One of the main threats to the species is the loss of habitat due in large part to the creation of dams and irrigation projects.
**Which of the above statement(s) is/are correct?**
(a) Only 1 and 2      (b) Only 2 and 3
(c) Only 1 and 3      (d) Only 1, 2 and 3

13. As the smuggling networks strengthen, India continues to bear the disgrace of being the source of the illegal trade and export of tortoises and freshwater turtles (TFT). Consider the following statements in this regard:
1. 28 species of tortoises and freshwater turtles are found in India.
2. Turtles act as scavengers of cleaning up water bodies and generally are used as indicators of river health.
3. The National Mission for Clean Ganga envisages breeding and release of turtles to clean wetlands.
**Which of the following statements is true?**
(a) 1 and 3      (b) 2 and 3
(c) 1 and 2      (d) 1, 2 and 3

14. Recently, one of the affiliated organisations of Union Environment Ministry of India has revealed the state regarding level of pollution in Indian cities. Consider the following statements regarding this:
1. Nearly one third of Indian cities have breached annual pollution limits mandated by the Central Pollution Control Board (CPCB) between 2011 and 2015.
2. CPCB data show that 94 cities spanning states from Andhra Pradesh to Jammu and Kashmir and Assam to Gujarat were guilty of breaching the annual, particulate matter limit of 60 micro-gram per cubic metre.
3. The cities like Delhi, Mumbai and Pune measure PM 2.5 levels, most lack the sensors required to gauge the presence of these minute particles that are considered more toxic than the more commonly measured PM 10.
**Which of the following statement (s) is/are correct?**
(a) Only 1      (b) 1 and 2
(c) 2 and 3      (d) All of the above

**15.** Recently the first vertical garden of India has been setup at Bengaluru. In this context consider the following statements.
1. It will act as a sound proofing barrier and control pollution.
2. The first vertical gardens were setup in USA
3. The garden has an automatic drip irrigation system to water the plants on daily basis

**Which of the following statement(s) is/are correct?**
(a) Only 1 and 3      (b) Only 2
(c) Only 1 and 2      (d) All of the above

**16.** The National Green Tribunal has suspended the Environmental Clearance (EC) granted to the India-based Neutrino Observatory (INO). Consider the following statements regarding the Environment Clearance in India:
1. The guideline is that if any project falls within 5km from an inter-State boundary or within a notified national park or a sanctuary has to be considered a category 'A' project.
2. The Tribunal found that the Mathiketan Shola National Park was just about 4.9 km from the proposed project site making it a category 'A' project.
3. For category 'B' project, an Environmental Impact Assessment is necessary.

**Which of the above statements is correct?**
(a) 1 and 3      (b) 2 and 1
(c) 3 and 2      (d) 1, 2 and 3

**17.** A recent report states that West Bengal has the highest number of arsenic-affected people in the country. Consider the following statements regarding the arsenic level in drinking water in India.
1. The WHO's guideline for drinking water quality has given a permissible limit of arsenic in groundwater to be about 0.01mg per litre.
2. In India, the permissible limit of arsenic, in drinking water has been increased from .01mg per litre to .05mg per litre.

Which of the following statement(s) is/are correct?
(a) Only 1      (b) Only 2
(c) Both 1 and 2      (d) Neither 1 nor 2

**18.** With reference to the Agreement at the UNFCCC Meeting in Paris in 2015, which of the following statements is/are correct?
1. The Agreement was signed by all the member countries of the UN and it will go into effect in 2017.
2. The Agreement aims to limit the greenhouse gas emissions so that the rise in average global temperature by the end of this century does not exceed 2 °C or even 1.5 °C above pre-industrial levels.
3. Developed countries acknowledged their historical responsibility in global warming and committed to donate $ 1000 billion a year from 2020 to help developing countries to cope with climate change.

Select the correct answer using the code given below.
(a) 1 and 3 only      (b) 2 only
(c) 2 and 3 only      (d) 1, 2 and 3

**19.** With reference to 'Global Climate Change Alliance', which of the following statements is/are correct?

**[IAS Prelims 2017]**
1. It is an initiative of the European Union.
2. It provides technical and financial support to targeted developing countries to integrate climate change into their development policies and budgets.
3. It is coordinated by World Resources Institute (WRI) and World Business Council for Sustainable Development (WBCSD).

Select the correct answer using the code given below:
(a) 1 and 2 only      (b) 3 only
(c) 2 and 3 only      (d) 1, 2 and 3

**20.** Which of the following best describes/ describe the aim of 'Green India Mission' of the Government of India?

**[IAS Prelims 2016]**
1. Incorporating environmental benefits and costs into the Union and State Budgets thereby implementing the 'green accounting'
2. Launching the second green revolution to enhance agricultural output so as to ensure food security to one and all in the future
3. Restoring and enhancing forest cover and responding to climate change by a combination of adaptation and mitigation measures

Select the correct answer using the code given below.
(a) 1 only      (b) 2 and 3 only
(c) 3 only      (d) 1, 2 and 3

**21.** With reference to the Agreement at the UNFCCC Meeting in Paris in 2015, which of the following statements is/are correct? **[IAS Prelims 2016]**
1. The Agreement was signed by all the member countries of the UN and it will go into effect in 2017.
2. The Agreement aims to limit the greenhouse gas emissions so that the rise in average global temperature by the end of this century does not exceed 2 °C or even 1.5 °C above pre-industrial levels.
3. Developed countries acknowledged their historical responsibility in global warming and committed to donate $ 1000 billion a year from 2020 to help developing countries to cope with climate change.

Select the correct answer using the code given below.
**[IAS Prelims 2016]**
(a) 1 and 3 only      (b) 2 only
(c) 2 and 3 only      (d) 1, 2 and 3

**22.** Which of the following statements is/are correct?
Proper design and effective implementation of UN-REDD+ Programme can significantly contribute to
1. protection of biodiversity
2. resilience of forest ecosystems
3. poverty reduction

Select the correct answer using the code given below.

(a) 1 and 2 only   (b) 3 only

(c) 2 and 3 only   (d) 1, 2 and 3

23. Consider the following pairs : [2016-I]

| Terms sometimes seen in the news | Their origin |
| --- | --- |
| 1. Annex—I Countries | Cartagena Protocol |
| 2. Certified Emissions Reductions | Nagoya Protocol |
| 3. Clean Development Mechanism | Kyoto Protocol |

Which of the pairs given above is/are correctly matched?

(a) 1 and 2 only   (b) 2 and 3 only

(c) 3 only   (d) 1, 2 and 3

24. Which of the following statements regarding 'Green Climate Fund' is/are correct?   **[IAS Prelims 2015]**

1. It is intended to assist the developing countries in adaptation and mitigation practices to counter climate change.

2. It is founded under the aegis of UNEP, OECD, Asian Development Bank and World Bank.

Select the correct answer using the code given below.

(a) 1 only   (b) 2 only

(c) Both 1 and 2   (d) Neither 1 nor 2

25. With reference to 'Forest Carbon Partnership Facility', which of the following statements is/ are correct?

**[IAS Prelims 2015]**

1. It is a global partnership of governments, businesses, civil society and indigenous peoples.

2. It provides financial aid to universities, individual scientists and institutions involved in scientific forestry research to develop eco-friendly and climate adaptation technologies for sustainable forest management.

3. It assists the countries in their 'REDD+ (Reducing Emissions from Deforestation and Forest Degradation+)' efforts by providing them with financial and technical assistance.

Select the correct answer using the code given below.

(a) 1 only   (b) 2 and 3 only

(c) 1 and 3 only   (d) 1, 2 and 3

26. Which one of the following statements about the National Adaptation Fund for Climate Change is **not** correct?

**[CDS 2018-1]**

(a) The fund is meant to assist national and State level activities to meet the cost of adaptation measures.

(b) This scheme has been taken as a Central Sector Scheme.

(c) The Indian Council of Agricultural Research is the national implementing entity for the fund.

(d) The scheme has been in force since 2015-2016.

# Hints and Explanations

## EXERCISE-1

1. **(b)** The World Health Day is a global health awareness day celebrated every year on 7 April. Energy conservation day is celebrated every year by the people all over the India on 14th of December. World Food Day is celebrated every year around the world on 16 October in honour of the date of the founding of the Food and Agriculture Organization of the United Nations in 1945.

2. **(b)** France on January 24, 2017 issued its first "Green Bonds" with a record sale of worth seven billion euro thus leading a significant way towards establishment of a genuine market in renewable energy bonds. The proceeds from the bonds will be used by France to finance Projects to address climate change.

3. **(a)** National Physical Laboratory (NPL) has established an atmospheric monitoring station on the campus of Institute of Himalayan Bio-resource Technology (IHBT) at Palampur (H.P.) at an altitude of 1391m for generating the base date for atmospheric trace species & properties to serve as a reference for comparison of polluted atmosphere in India.

4. **(b)** 5. **(a)** 6. **(b)** 7. **(c)** 8. **(d)**
9. **(b)** Water vapour
10. **(a)** Checking ozone layer depletion
11. **(c)** both i) and ii)
12. **(b)** 13. **(a)** 14. **(c)** 15. **(b)** 16. **(d)** 17. **(a**
18. **(d)** 19. **(b)** 20. **(a)** 21. **(b)**

## EXERCISE-2

1. **(b)** The Uttarakhand High Court on 20 March 2017 accorded the status of living human entities to sacred rivers the Ganga and Yamuna. In this case the Court cited the example of Whanganui river in New Zealand. This river is the first in the world to be granted all the rights, duties, liabilities and legal status of a person. Therefore option (b) is the correct answer.

2. **(d)** The Second Commitment Period of the Kyoto Protocol is related with emission of Green House Gases (GHGs). The United Nations Framework Convention on Climate Change (UNFCCC) was negotiated at the Earth Summit in Rio de Janeiro in 1992. Presently there are 192 parties to the protocol because Canada withdrew from the protocol effective December 2012. Therefore option (d) is the correct answer.

3. **(a)** The Indian Shad or Hilsa fish is on the verge of extinction, therefore the West Bengal govt. In January 2017 gave a legal protection to it. It will become the first fish variety in India to get legal protection. It is the national fish of Bangladesh. Therefore, option (a) is correct while option (b) is wrong and (c) partially correct. Option (d) is wrong.

4. **(d)** Stage II of HCFCs Phase Out Management Plan (HPMP) for the 2017-23 period aims to phase out use of Hydrochlorofluorocarbons (HCFCs), harmful ozone-depleting substances (ODS) by switching over to non-ozone depleting and low global warming potential technologies. Under the Montreal Protocol, the accelerated phase out of Hydrochlorofluorcarbons (HCFCs) is underway with a aim to complete phase out by 2030, therefore option (c) is wrong. Option (a) and (b) are partially correct.

5. **(a)** Ramsar Convention is formally known as Convention on Wetlands of International Importance, especially as Waterfowl Habitat. It was signed on 2 February 1971 at Ramsar in Iran. That date is celebrated as World Wetland Day now. The theme of World Wetlands Day for 2017 is 'Wetlands for Disaster Risk Reduction'. This theme has been selected to raise awareness on the vital roles of healthy wetlands in reducing the impacts of extreme events on communities and in helping to build resilience. Other options are ruled out.

6. **(c)** Assam government has launched 'Sustainable Action for Climate Resilient Development in Majuli' (SACReD, Majuli) to make river island Majuli country's first ever Carbon Neutral district by 2020. The project - 'Sustainable Action for Climate Resilient Development in Majuli' has been initiated by Assam govt. It aims to combat climate change & reduce greenhouse gas emissions. Therefore statements I and II are correct. Option (a) is wrong because the fluvial riverine island is formed by the Brahmaputra river system. Option (b) is partially true. Option (d) is ruled out.

7. **(d)** In the context of the India-based Neutrino Observatory (INO) all of the above statements are correct.

8. **(a)** Statements I and II are correct. Option (b) is partially correct. WCCB is statutory multi-disciplinary body under the Union Ministry of Environment, Forests and Climate Change (MoEFCC) to combat organized wildlife crime in the country. It was established in June 2007 by amending the Wildlife (Protection) Act (WLPA), 1972, a special Act to protect the wildlife and fauna in the country. Statement III is not correct.

9. **(c)** Seemai Karuvelam tree species are native to West Africa. It was brought to Tamil Nadu in 1960s as fuelwood. Option (d) is ruled out and others are partially true.

10. (c) Hope Island in Andhra Pradesh has become graveyard for Olive Ridleys turtles after 54 carcasses of this species were spotted on the shores of island. All the options provide correct information.

11. (a) Panna National Park is situated in Madhya Pradesh. Therefore statement III is not correct.

12. (c) The Ganges River dolphin, or 'susu', inhabits the Ganges Brahmaputra-Meghna and Karnaphuli Sangu river systems of Nepal, India and Bangladesh. The species is found exclusively in freshwater habitat.

13. (d) 28 species of freshwater turtles and tortoises are also found in India. Turtles act as scavengers in cleaning up water bodies and generally being indicators of river health. Ironically, the National Mission for Clean Ganga envisages breeding and release of turtles to clean wetlands, even as poaching and trade continue across the Gangetic belt.

14. (d) According to the figures from the Union Environment Ministry-affiliated organisation the latest available and updated data sourced from 680 pollution-monitoring stations spread over 300 cities, measure levels of particulate matter (PM 10), nitrogen dioxide and sulphur dioxide. While cities such as Delhi are usually the worst performers with regard to pollution spikes in winter, the CPCB data show that 94 cities spanning states from Andhra Pradesh to Gujarat wee guilty of breaching the annual, particulate matter limit of 60 micro-grams per cubic metre.

15. (a) Vertical gardens control pollution and act as a sound proofing barrier. The Bengaluru vertical garden has an automatic drip irrigation system to water the plants on daily basis. But the first vertical gardens were setup in China not in USA. Therefore option (a) is the correct answer.

16. (b) Under the guidelines laid down by the Environmental Ministry, any project that falls within 5km from an inter-State boundary or within a notified national park or a sanctuary has to be considered a Category 'A' project that involves a number of processes before an EC is granted. In this case, the MoEF had called it a Category 'B' project, for which an Environmental Impact Assessment is not necessary. The Southern Bench of the National Green Tribunal has suspended the Environmental Clearance (EC) granted to the India-based Neutrino Observatory (INO) that was to come up in Theni.

17. (a) According to the WHO's guidelines for drinking water quality (2011), the permissible limit of Arsenic in groundwater is .01 mg per litre. However, in India the permissible limit in drinking water has recently been revised from .05 mg to .01mg per litre.

18. (b) (i) The agreement emphasized on urgent need to address the significant gap between the aggregate effect of Parties' mitigation pledges in terms of global annual emissions of greenhouse gases by 2020 and aggregate emission pathways consistent with holding the increase in the global average temperature to well below 2°C above preindustrial levels and pursuing efforts to limit the temperature increase to 1.5°C above preindustrial levels.
(ii) Paris Summit - not all nations have signed the agreement and there is no deadline to ratify it. hence, statement 1 is wrong. This eliminates a and b. And developed countries committed to give $100 billion by 2020. But, for future, there is no mention of giving $1,000 billion dollars. Therefore, third statement wrong. We are left with Answer (b) only.

19. (a) As per their organizations' "About us" page: EuropeAid (DG for International Cooperation and Development) drives and oversees the overall implementation of the GCCA. So third statement is wrong. By elimination we are left with "A".

20. (c) (i) The National Mission for a Green India was announced by the Prime Minister as one of the eight Missions under the National Action Plan on Climate Change (NAPCC). It recognizes that climate change phenomenon will seriously affect and alter the distribution, type and quality of natural resources of the country. GIM puts the "greening" in the context of climate change adaptation and mitigation, meant to enhance ecosystem services like carbon sequestration and storage (in forests and other ecosystems), hydrological services and biodiversity; along with provisioning services like fuel, fodder, small timber.
(ii) **Ref:** India Yearbook 2016 page 338: Environment ministry has launched National Mission for a Green India through a consultative process involving relevant stakeholders, aimed at both increasing the forest and tree cover by 5 million ha, as well as increasing the quality of the existing forest cover in another 5 million ha. Hence only statement 3 fits.

21. (b) (i) The agreement emphasized on urgent need to address the significant gap between the aggregate effect of Parties' mitigation pledges in terms of global annual emissions of greenhouse gases by 2020 and aggregate emission pathways consistent with holding the increase in the global average temperature to well below 2°C above preindustrial levels and pursuing efforts to limit the temperature increase to 1.5°C above preindustrial levels.
(ii) Paris Summit - not all nations have signed the agreement and there is no deadline to ratify it. hence, statement 1 is wrong. This eliminates a and b. And developed countries committed to give $100 billion by 2020. But, for future, there is no mention of giving $1,000 billion dollars. Therefore, third statement wrong. We are left with Answer (b) only.

22. (a) (i) Reducing emissions from deforestation and forest degradation (REDD) is a mechanism that has been under negotiation by the United Nations Framework Convention on Climate Change (UNFCCC) since

2005, with the objective of mitigating climate change through reducing net emissions of greenhouse gases through enhanced forest management in developing countries.

(ii) Under REDD+ Developing country will have to prove the 'result' they have fought deforestation without harming local communities or biological diversity. Only then, they'll get the Money. Therefore, 1 and 2 are correct.

Although REDD+ has galvanized significant support internationally, among both developed and developing countries, its implications for poverty alleviation at the local level remain unclear. hence 3rd statement is wrong. Therefore Answer (a).

23. (c) (i) The Kyoto Protocol separates countries into two groups. Annex I includes developed nations, while Non-Annex I refers to developing countries.

A CER is a certificate which is issued every time the United Nations prevents one tonne of $CO_2$ equivalent being emitted through carbon projects registered with the Clean Development Mechanism (CDM).

(ii) All three terms are associated with Kyoto Protocol. Therefore, answer "c" 3 only.

24. (a) The Green Climate Fund (GCF) is a fund within the framework of the UNFCCC founded as a mechanism to redistribute money from the developed to the developing world, in order to assist the developing countries in adaptation and mitigation practices to counter climate change. The Fund is governed by the GCF Board. The assets of the GCF will be administered by a trustee only for the purpose of, and in accordance with, the relevant decisions of the GCF Board. The World Bank was invited by the COP to serve as the interim trustee of the GCF, subject to a review three years after operation of the Fund.

25. (c) The Forest Carbon Partnership Facility is a global partnership of governments, businesses, civil society, and Indigenous Peoples focused on reducing emissions from deforestation and forest degradation, forest carbon stock conservation, the sustainable management of forests, and the enhancement of forest carbon stocks in developing countries (activities commonly referred to as REDD+).

26. (c) The National Adaptation Fund for Climate Change (NAFCC) is a Central Sector Scheme which was set up in the year 2015-16. The overall aim of NAFCC is to support concrete adaptation activities which mitigate the adverse effects of climate change. National Bank for Agriculture and Rural Development (NABARD) is the National Implementing Entity (NIE).

**6**

**Chapter**

# ENVIRONMENT MANAGEMENT

## Introduction

**Environmental management system (EMS)** refers to the management of an organization's environmental, programs in a comprehensive, systematic, planned and documented manner. It includes the organizational structure, planning and resources for developing, implementing and maintaining policy for *environmental protection*.

More formally, EMS is "a system and database which integrates procedures and processes for training of personnel, monitoring, summarizing, and reporting of specialized environmental performance information to internal and external stakeholders of a firm.

## ENVIRONRMENT MANAGEMENT SYSTEM

The most widely used standard on which an EMS is based is **International Organization for Standardization (ISO) 14001.** Alternatives include the EMAS.

An environmental management information system (EMIS) is an *information technology* solution for tracking *environmental data* for a company as part of their overall environmental management system.

### Brief history of environmental management systems

In 1992, BSI Group published the world's first environmental management systems standard, BS 7750. Prior to this, environmental management had been part of larger systems such as Responsible Care. BS 7750 supplied the template for the development of the ISO 14000 series in 1996, by the International Organization for Standardization, which has representation from committees all over the world (ISO) (Clements 1996, Brorson & Larsson, 1999). As of 2010, ISO 14001 is now used by at least 223149 organizations in 159 countries and economies.

### BSI Group

**BSI Group**, also known as the **British Standards Institution ( BSI)**, is the national standards body of the United Kingdom. BSI produces technical standards on a wide range of products and services, and also supplies certification and standards-related services to businesses.

BSI Group headquarters building in Gunnersbury, West London, featuring the BSI Group logo.

BSI Group was founded as the Engineering Standards Committee in London in 1901. It subsequently extended its standardization work and became the British Engineering Standards Association (BESI) in 1918, adopting the name British Standards Institution in 1931 after receiving a Royal Charter in 1929. In 1998 a revision of the Charter enabled the organization to diversify and acquire other businesses, and the trading name was changed to BSI Group.

The Group now operates in 182 countries. The core business remains standards and standards related services, although the majority of the Group's revenue comes from management systems assessment and certification work.

### ISO 14000 Standard

**ISO 14000** is a family of standards related to environmental management that exists to help organizations:

(a) minimize how their operations (processes, etc) negatively affect the environment (i.e. cause adverse changes to air, water, or land)

(b) comply with applicable laws, regulations, and other environmentally oriented requirements and (c) continually improve in the above.

The current version of ISO 14001 is ISO 14001:2015 which was published in September 2015.

ISO 14000 is similar to ISO 9000 quality management in that both pertain to the process of how a product is produced, rather than to the product itself. As with ISO 9001, certification is performed by third-party organizations rather than being awarded by ISO directly. The ISO 19011 and ISO 17021 audit standards apply when audits are being performed.

The ISO 14000 family includes most notably the ISO 14001 standard, which represents the core set of standards used by organizations for designing and implementing an effective Environmental Management System (EMS). Other standards included in this series are ISO 14004, which gives additional guidelines for a good EMS, and more specialized standards dealing with specific aspects of environmental management. The major objective of the ISO 14000 series of norms is "to promote more effective and efficient environmental management in organizations and to provide useful and usable tools that are cost-effective, system-based, and flexible, and reflect the best organizations and the best organizational practices available for gathering, interpreting, and communicating environmentally relevant information".

## ISO 14001 standard

ISO 14001 sets out the criteria for an Environmental Management System (EMS). It does not state requirements for environmental performance, but maps out a framework that a company or organization can follow to set up an effective EMS. It can be used by any organization that wants to improve resource efficiency, reduce waste, and drive down costs. Using ISO 14001 can provide assurance to company management and employees as well as external stakeholders that environmental impact is being measured and improved. ISO 14001 can also be integrated with other management functions and assists companies in meeting their environmental and economic goals.

ISO 14001, as with other ISO 14000 standards, is voluntary, with its main aim to assist companies in continually improving their environmental performance, while complying with any applicable legislation. Organizations are responsible for setting their own targets and performance measures, with the standard serving to assist them in meeting objectives and goals and in the subsequent monitoring and measurement of these.

The requirements of ISO 14001 are an integral part of the European Union's Eco-Management and Audit Scheme (EMAS).

---

**ECO-MANAGEMENT AND AUDIT SCHEME (EMAS)**

The **Eco-Management and Audit Scheme (EMAS)** is a voluntary environmental management instrument, which was developed in 1993 by the European Commission. It enables organizations to assess, manage and continuously improve their environmental performance. The scheme is globally applicable and open to all types of private and public organizations. In order to register with EMAS, organisations must meet the requirements of the EU-EMAS-Regulation. Currently, more than 4,600 organisations and more than 7,900 sites are EMAS registered.

---

## GOALS of EMS

The goals of EMS are to increase compliance and reduce waste.

- **Compliance** is the act of reaching and maintaining minimal legal standards. By not being compliant, companies may face fines, government intervention or may not be able to operate.

- **Waste reduction** goes beyond compliance to reduce environmental impact. The EMS helps to develop, implement, manage, coordinate and monitor environmental policies. Waste reduction begins at the design phase through pollution prevention and waste minimization. At the end of the life cycle, waste is reduced by recycling.

## FEATURES of EMS

An environmental management system:

- **Serves** as a tool, or process, to improve environmental performance and information mainly "design, pollution control and waste minimization, training, reporting to top management, and the setting of goals."

- **Provides** a systematic way of managing an organization's environmental affairs.

- Is the aspect of the organization's overall management structure that addresses immediate and long-term impacts of its products, services and processes on the environment. EMS assists with planning, controlling and monitoring policies in an organization.

- **Gives order** and consistency for organizations to address environmental concerns through the allocation of resources, assignment of responsibility and ongoing evaluation of practices, procedures and processes.

- **Creates** environmental buy-in from management and employees and assigns accountability and responsibility.

- **Sets** framework for training to achieve objectives and desired performance.

- **Helps** understand legislative requirements to better determine a product or service's impact, significance, priorities and objectives.

- **Focuses** on continual improvement of the system and a way to implement policies and objectives to meet a desired result. This also helps with reviewing and auditing the EMS to find future opportunities.

- **Encourages** contractors and suppliers to establish their own EMS.

## EMS Model

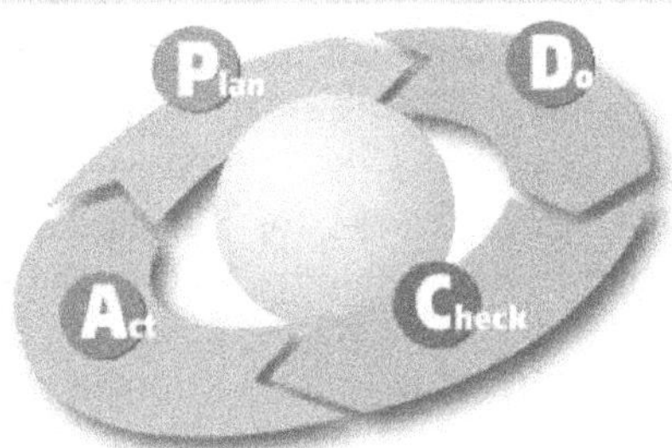


The PDCA Cycle

An EMS follows a **Plan-Do-Check-Act(PDCA),** Cycle. The diagram shows the process of first developing an environmental policy, planning the EMS, and then implementing it. The process also includes checking the system and acting on it. The model is continuous because an EMS is a process of continual improvement in which an organization is constantly reviewing and revising the system.

This is a model that can be used by a wide range of organizations -from manufacturing facilities to service industries to government agencies.

# Environment Management In India

Need of Environment Management in India

Environment Management systems are needed in India because:

1. India is the world's fourth largest (6.4%) and second fastest growing producer of greenhouse gases.
2. Delhi, Mumbai and Chennai are three of the world's ten most polluted cities.
3. Two-thirds of city dwellers lack sewerage; one-third lack portable, clean water.
4. India's urban population grows equivalent to another New York City every year.

# Trends in Environment in India

## Impact Assessment and Planning (IAP)

Assessing environmental and social impacts prior to setting up operations and obtaining environmental approval from the authorities is almost mandatory in most project categories. IAP assessment may be required for not only newly constructed facilities, but also for operations that will be undertaken in a current building.

## Environment Liability and Clean-up

Foreign invested has resulted in more current and historic environmental liabilities associated with property transactions in India.

## Sustainability and Regulatory Compliance

The increasing desire of Indian companies to meet world-class standards has led to establishing companies in India to take on sustainability initiatives.

## Climate Change

While India still lags the West in coming up with efficient regulation based on the development versus environment database, there is an increasing awareness in India that climate change need to be checked to control its effect on the environment.

# Objectives of Environment Management in India

## Conservation of Critical Environment Resources

Environment management becomes essential to conserve critical ecosystems and resources, and invaluable natural and made-made heritage, which are essential for life support, livelihoods, economic growth and human well being.

## Intra-generation Equity

To ensure equitable access to environmental resources and quality for all sections of society, and in particular, to support poor communities.

## Environmental Governance

To apply the principles of good governance with respect to transparency, rationality, accountability, and reduction in time and costs, to the management and regulation of use of environmental resources.

# Water Resource Management

## Groundwater

The stage of ground water development in India is 61%. The development of ground water in different areas has not been uniform. Intensive development of ground water in certain areas in the country has led to over-exploitation leading to decline in the level of ground water and sea water intrusion in coastal areas. Out of 5842 numbers of assessment administrative units, 802 units are 'over-exploited', 169 units are 'critical', 523 units are 'semi-critical', 4277 units are 'safe' and 71 units are 'saline'. Government of India, through the Department of Drinking Water and Sanitation, has taken significant steps to manage groundwater through the National Rural Drinking Water Programme (NRDWP).

o NRDWP provides grants for construction of rural water supply schemes with special attention on water-stressed and water quality affected areas, rainwater harvesting and groundwater recharge measures. It promotes conjunctive use of surface, groundwater and rooftop rainwater harvesting and actively supports convergence with other development programmes such as the MNREGS and Watershed Development Programmes. Support activities include setting up of State Water and Sanitation Missions and Water and Sanitation Support Organisations at State level, and community involvement in water quality monitoring.

o National Water Mission and the National Drinking Water and Sanitation Council prepare a convergent approach with the Ministries of Water Resources, Agriculture, Environment and Forests, Power, Industry and others. The Central Ground Water Authority is requested to regulate drilling of non-drinking water supply wells in over-exploited blocks. The Water Quality Assessment Authority, Central Pollution Control Board and the National River Conservation Directorate identify and take steps for suitable prevention and regulation of pollution of drinking water sources.

o Drip and sprinkler irrigation systems in water stressed areas are useful in conserving groundwater. Irrigation sprinklers are sprinklers used for irrigating agriculture, crops, vegetation, or for recreation, as a cooling system, or for the control of airborne dust, landscaping and golf courses. The sprinkler system irrigates the field and thus it is widely used in sandy areas as it checks the wastage of water through seepage and evaporation.

o Best groundwater management process include monitoring of ground water levels and rainfall, monitoring and regulating over-abstraction of ground water in over-exploited regions, water efficient agricultural practices, recycling and reuse of wastewater, water treatment by industry, and environmental water protection from industrial effluents, fertilizers, pesticides and untreated sewage. Stress need to be laid on the roles of Irrigation and Agriculture Departments in increasing efficiency of water use in agriculture.

o Rooftop Rain Water Harvesting is the technique through which rain water is captured from the roof catchments and stored in reservoirs. Harvested rain water can be stored in sub-surface ground water reservoir by adopting artificial recharge techniques to meet the household needs through storage in tanks. The Main Objective of rooftop rain water harvesting is to make water available for future use. Capturing and storing rain water for use is particularly important in dryland, hilly, urban and coastal areas.

o **Hariyali** is a watershed management project, launched by the Central Government, which aims at enabling the rural population to conserve water for drinking, irrigation, fisheries and afforestation as well as generate employment opportunities.

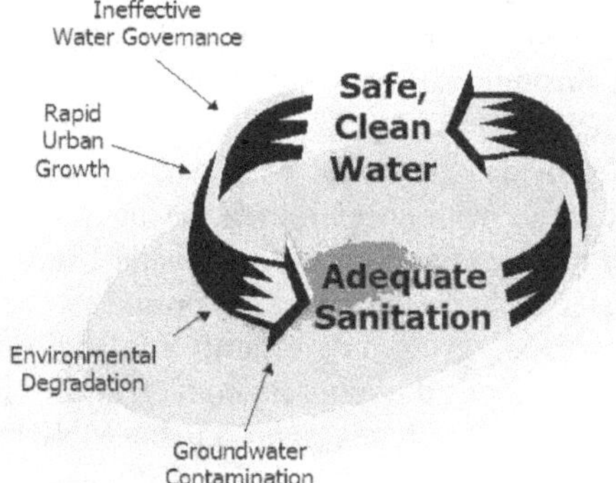


**Water Quality Management**

o Scientists at the Indian Institute of Technology-Madras (IIT-M) have developed Amrit, a low-cost arsenic filter using nano-filtration technology. This technology can be used for removing arsenic from drinking water.

o **ECO-India,** a three-year project, is co-funded by the European Commission's Seventh Framework Programme (FP7) and the Indian Department of Science and Technology (DST). It is focused on developing innovative and sustainable approaches for producing potable water at a community level. The first rural community deployment is set for West Bengal, India. The FP7 consortium will develop energy-efficient systems for advanced filtration and disinfection of drinking water supplies from surface-water ponds and groundwater tube wells with arsenic contamination, using Dryden Aqua and Trustwater technology. In addition, UFZ will lead the development of field-deployable arsenic sensors for screening tube-wells.

o Inland water quality-monitoring network is operated under a three-tier programme, Global Environment Monitoring System (GEMS), Monitoring of Indian National Aquatic Resources System (MINARS) and Yamuna Action Plan (YAP). Water samples are being analysed for 28 parameters consisting of 9 core parameters, 19 other physico-chemical and bacteriological parameters apart from the field observations. Biomonitoring is also carried out on specific locations. In view of limited resources, limited numbers of organic pollution related parameters are monitored for micro pollutants (toxic metals and POPs).

## Recycling Waste Water

Recycling the world's waste water, almost all of which goes untreated would ease global water shortages while protecting the environment. People have been using fresh water faster than nature can replace it, contributing in some regions to hunger, disease, conflict and migration. Two-thirds of humanity currently live in zones that experience water scarcity at least one month a year. Half of those people are in China and India. Besides reducing pollution at the source, policy initiatives must focus on removing contaminants from waste water flows, reusing water, and recovering useful by-products. The potential for reusing liquid waste can be understood by the fact that astronauts on the International Space Station drink recycled urine and use it to wash up. In Jordan and Israel, 90% and 50% of agricultural water, respectively, has been recovered for reuse.

Besides being recycled, waste water can also be a rich source of nutrients, minerals and energy. Harvesting phosphorus from urine supplied by urine-diverting toilets reduces waste water's nutrient load. More than a fifth of global phosphorus demand worldwide could be met by recycled human urine and feces. Waste can also be converted into fuel.

## Creating a More Resilient Environment To Climate Change

There is a need to create more resilient environment to adapt to climate change. A coalition of nations, river basin organizations, business and civil society can be made for more resilient to climate impacts. This concept was seen with the creation of the international Paris Pact on Water and Climate Change Adaptation to make water systems more resilient to climate impacts. The "Water Resilience Focus" event under the Lima to Paris Action Agenda on climate change also focused on other key partnerships and coalitions to make river basins, lakes, aquifers and deltas more resilient to climate change and reduce human interference with oceans.

Climate changes, along with unsustainable use of water, are causing widespread impacts on societies and economies, creating droughts, floods and warming which affect all water systems and trigger negative and often fatal impacts. This concept highlights individual commitments to implement adaptation plans, strengthening water monitoring and measurement systems in river basins and promoting financial sustainability and new investment in water systems management.

> The Delta Coalition includes 12 countries (Colombia, Egypt, Indonesia, Japan, South-Korea, Mozambique, Myanmar, Netherlands, Philippines, Vietnam, France and Bangladesh) to bring deltas to global policy discussions, build partnerships and focus on action, aiming to increase resilience for almost 250 million people in deltas in these 12 countries.

# Managing River Ganga

Ganga is an important Indian river which sustains a large pool of aquatic life. The degrading condition of Ganga is a major concern and needs an immediate action plan to save it from further ecological damage. Several steps have been taken by the government to ensure healthy environment of Ganga.

The National Green Tribunal has banned camping activity in the entire belt of **Kaudiyala to Rishikesh** on the banks of river Ganga in Uttarakhand. Rafting does not cause any serious pollution river or environment. NGT prohibits the use of any plastic items in the entire belt and restricts using mechanised riverbed mining in the Ganga till Haridwar.

Ganga project activities include ghat and crematoria construction/repair, river front beautification, installation and repair of sewage treatment plants (STPs). Ganga pollution can be controlled by treating the effluents coming from tanneries, sugar mills, distilleries and other industrial units in Uttar Pradesh's Kanpur.

# POLLUTION CONTROL

## Industrial pollution control

**1. Pollution charge**

Charge system will levy a fee or tax on the amount of pollution a firm or source generates. It is important for the firm to reduce emissions to the point, where its marginal abatement cost is equal to the tax rate. The charge system encourages the industries to reduce the pollutants further. The charges thus collected can form a fund for restoration of the environment. Another form of pollution charge is a deposit refund system, where consumers pay a surcharge when purchasing a potentially polluting product, and receive a refund on return of the product after useful life span at appropriate centers. The concept of extended producers' responsibility brought in to avoid accumulation of dangerous products in the environment.

**2. Tradable permits**

Under this system, firms that achieve the emission levels below their allotted level may sell the surplus permits. The firms which are required to spend more to attain the required degree of treatment/allotted levels, can purchase permits from others at lower costs and may be benefited.

**3. Government subsidy reduction**

Subsidies can provide incentive to address environmental problems. However, it has been reported that the subsidies encourage economically inefficient and environmentally unsound practices, and often leads to market distortions due to differences in the area. However, in the national interest, subsidies are important to sustain the expansion of production. In such cases, the subsidy may be comparable to the net social benefit.

**4. Eco-labeling**

Eco-labeling is the practice of supplying information on the environmental characteristics of a product or service to the general public. These labeling schemes can be grouped into three types.

**5. Wastewater treatment**

Segregation at source of pollutant generation is important. Preliminary treatment involves a number of unit processes to eliminate undesirable characteristics of wastewater. Processes include use of screen, grit chambers for removal of sand and large particles for grinding of coarse solids, pre-aeration for odour control and removal of oil.

**6. Emission Control**

The revised emission standards for thermal power plants were notified with respect to Particulate Matter (PM), Sulphur Dioxide (SO2), Nitrogen Oxide (NOx), Mercury (Hg) and water consumption on December 7, 2015, and shall come into force from December 6, 2017. The government had taken other steps to clean up the environment in areas adjoining thermal power plants. It included installation of continuous emission/effluent monitoring systems (CEMS), revised norms for fly ash utilisation, industry specific action plans for critically polluted areas where significant number of thermal power plants are located and development of green belt in surrounding areas.

**7. Effluent Treatment Plants**

Recently, the Supreme Court of India has ordered industries to set up Effluent Treatment Plants or (ETPs). These are used by leading companies in the pharmaceutical and chemical industry to purify water and remove any toxic and non toxic materials or chemicals from it. These plants are used by all companies for environment protection. An ETP is a plant where the treatment of industrial effluents and waste waters is done. The ETP plants are used widely in industrial sector, for example, pharmaceutical industry, to remove the effluents from the bulk drugs. During the manufacturing process of drugs, varied effluents and contaminants are produced. The effluent treatment plants are used in the removal of high amount of organics, debris, dirt, grit, pollution, toxic, non toxic materials, polymers etc. from drugs and other medicated stuff. The ETP plants use evaporation and drying methods, and other auxiliary techniques such as centrifuging, filtration, incineration for chemical processing and effluent treatment.

**8. Corporate Investments**

State-owned **Gujarat Alkalies and Chemicals Limited** has made an agreement with specialty chemicals maker Evonik Industries for setting up a multi-million hydrogen peroxide and propylene oxide project at Dahej in Gujarat. This project would be based on an innovative, environment-friendly HPPO technology. The world's first facility to manufacture carbon foam batteries will be set up at Bavla near Ahmedabad, Gujarat. **Firefly Energy India** is planning to build a plant to produce carbon foam batteries. State Bank of India has invested in the Carbon Disclosure Project, which is an organisation based in the United Kingdom which works with shareholders and corporations to disclose the greenhouse gas (GHG) emissions of major corporations .

**Corporate social responsibility** (CSR) represents the policies, practices and initiatives a company commits to in order to govern themselves with honesty and transparency and have a positive impact on social and environmental wellbeing. The Indian government has been trying to make it mandatory for companies to spend at least 2% of net profitability on CSR. A mutually time targeted programme is implemented under Corporate Responsibility for Environment Protection (CREP).

# Air Quality Management

## 1. Use of BS-IV vehicles

The Supreme Court ruled that health of citizens was more important than commercial interests of auto makers as it banned the sale and registration of Bharat Stage (BS)-III emission norm-compliant vehicles from 1 April, 2017 Bharat Stage or BS norms are standards for vehicular emissions. They lay down the permissible levels of pollutants that come out of the exhaust pipes of motor vehicles. The aim is to check air pollution and emissions that lead to global warming. India is set to enforce a new generation of vehicular pollution norms on 1 April, 2017 called BS IV. Only BS IV compliant vehicles can be manufactured, sold and registered, across the country after April 1. Centre for Science and Environment, estimates that the transition will lead to a significant decrease in PM emissions. Emissions can fall by as much as 80% from new trucks and by 50% from cars. Reductions in Hydrocarbon and NOx emissions from may come down by 41-80 % depending on the engine size. The difference between BS III and BS IV is that the latter are stricter and permit lower quantities of pollutants to be emitted by vehicles.

| Norms | CO(g/km) Carbon Monoxide | HC (Hydro carbons) + NOx Nitrogen Oxides (g/km) | RSPM (Respirable Suspended Particulate Matter) | Sulphur Content in Diesel |
|---|---|---|---|---|
| BS I | 2.72 | 0.97 | 0.14 | NA |
| BS II | 2.2 | 0.5 | 0.08 | 500 PPM |
| BS III | 2.3 | 0.35 (Combined) | 0.050 | 100 PPM |
| BS IV | 1.0 | 0.18 (Combined) | 0.025 | 50 PPM |

## 2. Ahmedabad's Air Action Plan

It has been developed using the suggestions and best practices prescribed by civic experts, medical practitioners and community leaders, both national and international (Mexico City, Beijing and Los Angeles). It is based on two strategies — a city-wide air quality monitoring system, called Air Quality Index (AQI), and a broad public information and education campaign called Air Information & Response (AIR) Plan. The Air Action Plan is modeled on the Heat Action Plan that was first implemented by Ahmedabad in 2013 and has now been scaled to 11 cities across India. Its aim was to protect communities from heat stress and longer, more intense heat waves that were becoming increasingly frequent due to climate change.

## 3. Roll-on Roll-Off (RORO) Service

This service was launched in the National Capital and included a multi-modal transportation model aimed at reducing Delhi's air pollution. The RO-RO have a direct impact on its air ambient quality and the capital would breathe clean air. According to plans, heavy commercial vehicles passing through Delhi will be loaded on flat railway wagons at railway terminals outside the capital and will get unloaded at the other end of the city. RO-RO service aims to reduce carbon emission and congestion on the roads of the NCR as about 66,000 diesel trucks pass through Delhi and its adjoining areas in a day.

## 4. Central Pollution Control Board

The government agency is implementing the Air (Prevention and Control of Pollution) Act 1981 to restore air quality. It is a statutory organisation under the Ministry of Environment, Forest and Climate Change (MoEF&CC). It was established in 1974 under the Water (Prevention and Control of pollution) Act, 1974. CPCB runs nation-wide programs of ambient air quality monitoring known as National Air Quality Monitoring Programme (NAMP). The network consists of 621 operating stations covering 262 cities/towns in 29 states and 5 Union Territories of the country. Under N.A.M.P., four air pollutants viz., Sulphur Dioxide (SO2), Oxides of Nitrogen as NO2, Suspended Particulate Matter (SPM) and Respirable Suspended Particulate Matter (RSPM/ PM10) have been identified for regular monitoring at all the locations. The monitoring of meteorological parameters such as wind speed and wind direction, relative humidity (RH) and temperature were also integrated with the monitoring of air quality.

## 5. Compressed Natural Gas (CNG) as Automobile Fuel

In Delhi and some other cities most of the public transport is running on CNG instead of diesel. CNG happens to be a very viable alternative to traditional fuels particularly for use in the automobile industry. Being low in pollutants, high in calorific value and heat yield, economical and available in abundance globally, CNG is the perfect alternative fuel for most automobiles. CNG is environment friendly as it reduces vehicular exhaust emissions significantly. Carbon Monoxide emissions are reduced to a maximum of 90% and Hydrocarbon emissions by 60% as compared to vehicles that use Petrol. Carbon Dioxide emissions, a cause for global warming, are also reduced significantly by 10%. There is the Closed Loop kit where the exhaust gases are inspected by the sensors and the volume of intake gas is tweaked accordingly to minimize pollution.

## 6. National Air Quality Index

A colour-coded national air-quality index has been used to monitor the air quality. The Ministery for Environment, Forests & Climate Change launched 'The National Air Quality Index' (AQI) to judge the air quality. The formulation of the index was a continuation of the initiatives under Swachh Bharat Mission. Air pollution has been a matter of environmental and health concerns, particularly in urban areas. Central Pollution Control Board along with State Pollution Control Boards has been operating National Air Monitoring Program (NAMP) covering 240 cities of the country. In addition, continuous monitoring systems that provide data on near real-time basis are also installed in a few cities.

## 7. Graded Response To Air Pollution

A graded response highlights the actions required to be taken as and when the concentration of pollutants, in this case particulate matter, reaches a certain level. At the current level of pollution lying between poor and moderate, the measures that are to be enforced under the plan include strict ban on garbage burning, closing brick kilns, mechanised sweeping of roads, enforcing ban on fire-crackers among others. If pollution increases to the next level, very poor, tougher measures are to be enforced including **hiking parking fees** by up to 4%, banning diesel generator sets and **increasing frequency of metro**. In this plan, **odd-even** car rationing scheme and **halt on construction** activities may be implemented across Delhi-NCR if air quality remains at the emergency level for 48-hours.

## 8. Cess on Diesel Vehicles

Cess on diesel vehicles will lead to the reduction in air pollution. The Environment Pollution (Prevention and Control) Authority (EPCA) for the National Capital Region (NCR) has recommended to levy a green cess of 20-22% on diesel vehicles. EPCA recommended a cess of 20% on the cost of vehicles with engines that are smaller than 1,500cc in size, and 22% on those over 1,500cc. The main reason behind EPCA's recommendation is to remove the existing incentive for buying diesel vehicles. Removing the fuel price differential, through the imposition of ECC (environment compensation charge) will be a step in removing the incentive for diesel vehicles. This is needed to reduce public health risk as diesel emissions are among the more harmful pollutants.

## 9. Hybrid and Electric Vehicles

Hybrid and electric vehicles are relatively much less polluting than the traditional petrol and diesel vehicles. The National Electric Mobility Mission Plan (NEMMP) aims to achieve national fuel security by promoting hybrid and electric vehicles in India. There is an ambitious target to achieve 6-7 million sales of hybrid and electric vehicles year on year from 2020 onwards. Government has launched Faster Adoption and Manufacturing of (Hybrid &) Electric Vehicles (**FAME India**) scheme under NEMMP. The aim of the Government through this scheme will be to allow hybrid and electric vehicles to become the first choice for the purchasers so that these vehicles can replace the conventional vehicles and thus reduce liquid fuel consumption in the country from the automobile sector.

## 10. Ethanol as a Fuel

Which is produced from sugarcane, maize, wheat, etc., can be mixed with gasoline to form different blends. As the ethanol molecule contains oxygen, it allows the engine to more completely combust the fuel, resulting in fewer emissions and thereby reducing the occurrence of environmental pollution. Since ethanol is produced from plants that harness the power of the sun, ethanol is also considered as renewable fuel. Ethanol Blended Petrol (EBP) programme was launched in January, 2003 which aimed to promote the use of alternative and environment friendly fuels and to reduce import dependency for energy requirements.

---

### AIR QUALITY MONITORING APP

The government of Rajasthan has introduced mobile application **RajVayu** for sharing information about air quality index of Jaipur, Udaipur and Jodhpur. The app was launched on the World Environment Day (5th June). With this, Rajasthan becomes first state in country to launch such app for sharing information about air quality index of cities.

**RajVayu app** gathers information based on the data collected by sophisticated air quality monitoring equipment and weather sensors. The app has been built by Rajasthan State Pollution Control Board (RSPCB) jointly with Indian Institute of Tropical Meteorology (IITM). It can share details about the air quality, such as levels of pollutants likes SOx, NOx, CO, Ozone particles and Particulate Matter (PM) with the city residents and tourists. It can also provide information about temperature, wind speed, humidity, weather forecast and advisories. This app is based on the System of Air Quality and Weather Forecasting Research (SAFAR-India) which is presently connected in Delhi, Mumbai and Pune. The services of this application would be expanded other cities in the state including in Ajmer, Alwar, Bhiwadi, Kota and Pali. Another application named 'Drishti' has been launched for monitoring of pollution levels in industrial regions.

## Noise Pollution

Noise pollution has major mental impact on living organism. Several initiatives have been taken to control noise pollution from various sources. The Union Ministry of Road Transport & Highways has made it mandatory for all automobile manufacturers to provide emission and noise pollution details for every vehicle they produce by April 2017. The ministry has amended Form 22 under the Central Motor Vehicles Act, 1989 through which manufacturers provide the initial certification of compliance of vehicles. It will include pollution standards, safety standards of component quality and road-worthiness certificate for all vehicles. The Union Ministry of Road Transport & Highways wants to award five star ratings to vehicles based on their emission and noise pollution standards.

**Amended Form 22:** It makes mandatory for all automobile manufacturers to provide emission and noise pollution details for every vehicle including makers of electric rickshaws and electric carts. It will include the engine number, chassis number and emission norm of the vehicle. It will apply to all vehicles including petrol, CNG, LPG, electric, diesel and hybrid. Automobile manufacturers need to specify the levels of each pollutant like carbon monoxide, hydro carbon, non-methane HC, NOx, HC+NOx, PM etc. for petrol and diesel vehicles. They will also have to specify the sound level for horn and pass-by noise values of all vehicles. Earlier, Form 22 only certified that the vehicle in question complied with the provisions of the Motor Vehicles Act, 1989.

## OIL DEGRADING BACTERIA

Scientists have found three new strains of oil-degrading bacteria in Kochi, Kerala. Earlier, laboratory tests of these new strains conducted were successful. The field trials will be conducted by the **Malabar Botanical Garden** and **Institute of Plant Sciences (MBGIPS),** Kozhikode and Bharat Petroleum Corporation Limited (BPCL). The study will allow the development of bioremediation agents to clean up petroleum pollutants from the environment.

Enzymes in oil-degrading bacteria (microorganisms) can degrade and utilise hydrocarbons as a source of carbon and energy. Scientists from successfully isolated key hydrocarbon-degrading enzyme produced by the bacteria. The three new strains isolated by MBGIPS include two species of Burkholderia and one species of Pseudomonas. These oil-degrading bacteria have been sequenced and submitted to the Genebank database on organisms.

## World Bank' Aid to Minimize Coal Use

The global development lenders such as World Bank and Asian Development Bank (ABD) should provide help countries including India to shift away from coal for energy purpose. The idea of funding was proposed by the World Coal Association to finance countries to help them to shift to more efficient technologies so that they can meet their COP21 commitments. Coal is needed to meet energy demands. Even if countries opt for renewable energy they are not going to do away with coal in overall energy mix. In absence of any funding, countries invest in inefficient sub-critical thermal plants, which have much higher CO2 and particulate matter (PM) emissions. The aid by global development lenders will help countries to adopt super critical and ultra-super critical (USC) plants technologies.

**Benefits of Aid:**

- Super critical and ultra-super critical (USC) plants technologies are capable of substantially reducing $CO_2$ emissions and virtually eliminate PM emissions.
- The aid will help countries in reducing their emissions from coal, rather than reducing coal itself and meet target provided in Intended Nationally Determined Contributions (INDCs).
- The target of Paris Agreement on Climate Change about reducing the emissions from coal power plants can be achieved.

## Forest Fire Mitigation

Parliamentary Standing Committee on Science and Technology released its report on forest fires which revealed that the frequency of forest fires across Central Indian forests and the Himalayan Pine forest have increased by 55% in 2016. Forest fires in India increased 125 percent in last two years (2015–2017). The States of Odisha, Chhattisgarh, and Madhya Pradesh accounted for 1/3rd of the forest fires. The Committee said that Chir pine needles, which are highly inflammable due to its high resin content, are main factor in occurring and spreading of forest fires. Incidents of fire in broad leaves forests were found to be minimal. The Committee also suggested that a national policy on managing forest fires should be prepared.

## Major Recommendations to Prevent Forest Fire

- Planting of broad tree leaves in forests, and after a period of five years, systematic replacement of chir pine trees in forests by broad leaves.
- Procurement of sweeping machines to clear roadsides of chir pine needles and dry leaves in vulnerable areas.
- Advocated large-scale incentives and programmes (including under the MGNREGA) to collect pines for use as fuel, and other incineration.
- A dedicated toll-free number for reporting incidents of forest fire in each state.
- Using corporate social responsibility funds for creating awareness campaigns on forest fires.
- Training on fire brigade officers of all states and equipping them with forest fire equipment so that in the event of forest fires they do not have to depend on outside agencies like NDRF.
- Creating ponds and other water harvesting structures within the forest to reduce river bank erosion and providing a handy tool for supply of water to douse forest fires.

## Waste Management

Around 62 million tonnes of waste is generated annually in the country at present, out of which 5.6 million tonnes is plastic waste, 0.17 million tonnes is biomedical waste, hazardous waste generation is 7.90 million tonnes per annum and 15 lakh tonne is e-waste. The responsibility of waste generators has been introduced to segregate waste into three categories – Wet, Dry and **Hazardous Waste**. The waste generator need to pay 'User Fee' to the waste collector and a 'Spot Fine' for littering and non-segregation. In case of hilly areas, land for construction of sanitary landfills in the hilly areas should be identified in the plain areas, within 25 kilometers. Waste processing facilities will have to be set up by all local bodies having 1 million or more population within two years.

**Some of the developments in the waste management sector in India are given below:**

o The source segregation of waste has been made compulsory to channelize the waste to wealth by recovery, reuse and recycle.

o No person is allowed to throw, burn, or bury the solid waste generated by him, on streets, open public spaces outside his premises, or in the drain, or water bodies.

o All hotels and restaurants need to segregate biodegradable waste and set up a system of collection or follow the system of collection set up by local body to ensure that such food waste is utilized for composting/biomethanation.

o Resident Welfare and market Associations, gated communities and institution with an area >5,000 sq. m are required to segregate waste at source- in to valuable dry waste like plastic, tin, glass, paper, etc. and handover recyclable material to either the authorized waste pickers or the authorized recyclers, or to the urban local body.

o The bio-degradable waste should be processed, treated and disposed through composting or bio-methanation within the premises as far as possible. The residual waste shall be given to the waste collectors or agency as directed by the local authority.

o New townships and Group Housing Societies have been made responsible to develop in-house waste handling, and processing arrangements for bio-degradable waste.

o The developers of Special Economic Zone, industrial estate, industrial park to leave at least 5% of the total area of the plot or minimum 5 plots/ sheds for recovery and recycling facility.

o All industrial facilities using fuel and located within 100 km from a solid waste based Refused derived fuel (RDF) plant shall make proper arrangements within six months from the date of notification of these rules to replace at least 5 % of their fuel requirement by RDF so produced.

o High calorific wastes to be used for co-processing in cement or thermal power plants.

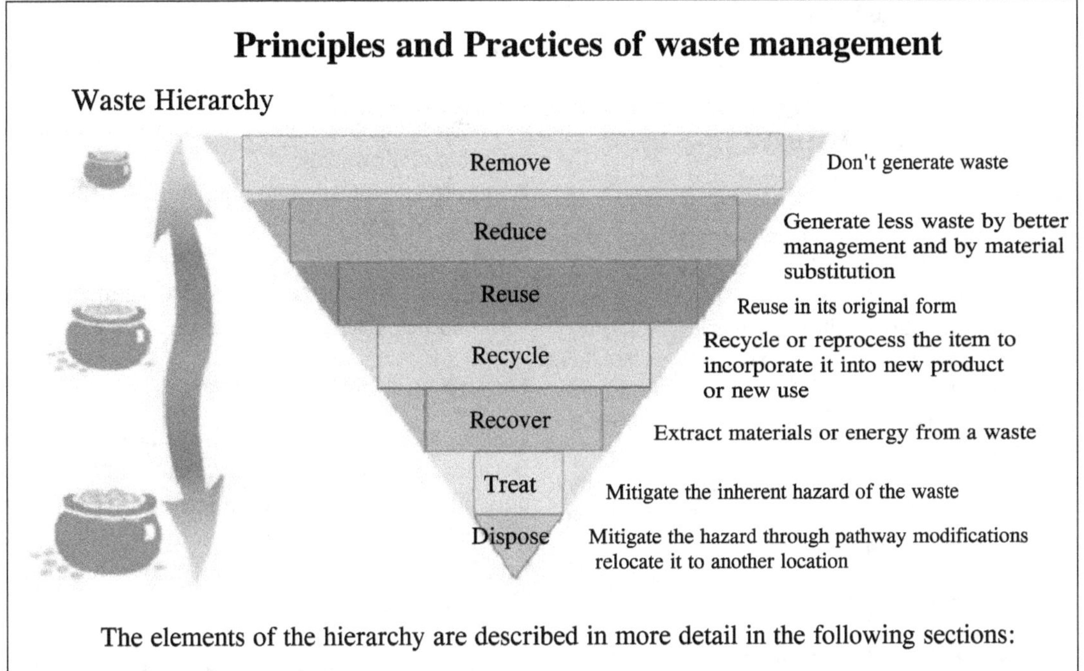



## National Solid Waste Association of India (NSWAI)

National Solid Waste Association of India (NSWAI) has been formed on 25th January 1996. It is also a member of the International Solid Waste Association (ISWA), and provides forum for exchange of information and expertise in the field of Solid Waste Management at the international level.

### The objectives of NSWAI are as follows:

- Inculcating solid waste management as a profession.
- Conduct research and development in solid waste management.
- Development of expertise in solid waste management
- Development of good solid waste management ideas.
- Development of standards in solid waste management.
- Improvement in law and its enforcement in the field of Solid Waste Management.
- Awareness and community involvement in Solid Waste Management.
- Professional recognition Nationally and Internationally and to get affiliation to the International Solid Waste Association.
- Development of a National Policy on Solid Waste Management In India.

## Soil Management

Soil plays a vital role in sustaining life by forming a growing medium for plants which is the primary source of energy and clean air. Vegetation cover prevents soil erosion, so more focus need be put on plantation of trees. Soil management can be achieved through the following ways:

o Efforts have been made to stabilize sand dunes in western Rajasthan by the Central Arid Zone Research Institute (CAZRI). The **Central Soil Conservation Board**, set up by the Government of India, has prepared a number of plans for soil conservation in different parts of the country. These plans are based on the climatic conditions, configuration of land and the social behavior of people. Even these plans are fragmental in nature. Integrated land use planning, therefore, seems to be the best technique for proper soil conservation.

o Organic farming is an alternative agricultural system which originated early in the 20th century in response to rapidly changing farming practices. Organic agriculture continues to be developed by various organic agriculture organizations today.

o Bio-fertilizer offers an economically attractive and ecologically sound means of reducing external inputs and improving the quality and quantity of internal sources. Bio-fertilizer is microorganism's culture capable of fixing atmospheric nitrogen when suitable crops are inoculated with them. The main inputs are microorganisms, which are capable of mobilizing nutritive elements from non-usable form to usable form through biological process. These are less expensive, eco-friendly and sustainable. The beneficial microorganisms in the soil that are greater significance to horticultural situations are biological nitrogen fixers, phosphate solubilisers and mycorrhizal fungi. Liquid bio-fertilizer is considered as an effective alternative to the lignite based bio-fertilizer.

o Many initiatives have been made to combat desertification and mitigate the effects of drought through national action programs that incorporate long-term strategies supported by international cooperation and partnership arrangements. United Nations Convention to Combat Desertification has proposed Science–Policy Interface (SPI) to facilitate a two-way science–policy dialogue and ensure the delivery of policy-relevant information, knowledge and advice on desertification/land degradation and drought (DLDD). The SPI is composed of 20 members and three observers, who are mostly scientific experts.

# Biodiversity Management

## Eco-Sensitive Zone

An Eco-Sensitive Zone (ESZ) has been proposed by the government in Sanjay Gandhi National Park in Mumbai. ESZ acts as a buffer for further protection around Protected Areas (PAs) such as National Parks and Wildlife sanctuaries. Activities around such areas are regulated and managed so as to protect the environment. ESZ is notified under Section 3 of the Environment (Protection) Act, 1986 by the Union Ministry of Environment and Forest. Many states have opposed ESZ because of presence of minerals and resources side by side. Local people in many areas are also opposed to ESZ for loss of livelihood due to restriction placed by it on various activities.

### ECO SENSITIVE ZONES

- The concept of ecologically sensitive areas is very much an Indian invention, rooted in attempts by civil society to use the Environmental Protection Agency (EPA) to promote sustainable development alongside protection of the natural heritage.
- The term 'Ecologically Fragile Area' was first used in 1991 for Dahanu Taluka in Maharashtra, followed by the declaration of other ESAs like Mahabaleshwar-Panchgani and Matheran.
- These are all initiatives of civil society organisations or are a consequence of a resolution of the Indian Board for Wildlife in 2002 to protect areas up to 10 kilometres from the boundaries of wildlife sanctuaries and national parks.
- Initially, there were no guidelines available on what areas may be considered ecologically sensitive, nor on working out an appropriate management regime. These issues were addressed in 2000 by the Pronab Sen Committee.
- The Sen Committee's foremost criterion for identification of ESA is endemism. Western Ghats harbours well over two thousand endemic species of flowering plants, fish, frogs, birds and mammals amongst the better known groups of organisms, and thousands more amongst less studied groups.
- Amongst themselves these span the entire Western Ghats and all conceivable habitats, including highly disturbed ones. The Western Ghats region also qualifies as an ESA under several other Sen Committee criteria.

- Under ESZ, commercial mining, polluting industries and large hydro-power projects are prohibited as per the ministry guidelines. At present the 29 ESZ notified by the Central government are spread across Haryana, Gujarat, Jharkhand, Karnataka, Sikkim, Goa, Maharasthra, Rajasthan, Gujarat and Uttarakhand.

**Guidelines on ESZ classify activities under three categories:**

**Prohibited:** Commercial mining, setting of saw mill, setting of industries causing pollution, establishment of major hydroelectric projects.

**Regulated:** Establishment of hotels and resorts, felling of trees, erection of electrical cables, drastic change of agricultural systems.

**Permitted:** Agriculture and horticulture practices by local communities, rain water harvesting, organic farming, etc.

## Drone to Monitor Tigers

Conservation drones are being used to monitor tiger reserves. Besides monitoring of tiger population in the reserves, the unmanned aircraft would collect and transmit visual data on animal movements, poaching activities and instances of forest fire from inaccessible forest terrains on a real-time basis. The drones could be used for the management of habitats and species.

The use of drones was suggested by the National Tiger Conservation Authority (NTCA) and the Wildlife Institute of India (WII), Dehradun. Drones were earlier used for conservation programmes in the forests of Assam and Madhya Pradesh. Drones were used in Panna Tiger Reserve.

In April 2013, the test flight of a small aircraft, Maja, was undertaken in Kaziranga Tiger Reserve. Later, in January 2014, three other drones were tested in Panna Tiger Reserve, where WII has initiated a long-term tiger reintroduction and monitoring project.

## Access and Benefit Sharing (ABS) Mechanism

Under this mechanism, a part of the profit earned from exploiting natural resources can be used for conserving natural resources. The National Biodiversity Authority proposed this mechanism for biodiversity conservation. The board had earlier issued notices to more than 1,100 manufacturers and traders of Ayurvedic drugs that are commercially utilising these bio resources. Many of the companies use these natural plants and products as ingredients in medicinal and other products. 95% of the ABS amount shall is transferred to the account of the Biodiversity Management Committee (BMC) of the respective region.

# Exercise -1

1. Select the correct sequence with reference to Environmental Management System ISO1401 :
   (a) Environmental policy → Implementation and operation → Checking and corrective action → Management review
   (b) Implementation and operation → Checking and corrective action → Management review → Environmental policy
   (c) Implementation and operation → Environmental policy → Checking and corrective action → Management review
   (d) Checking and corrective action → Management review → Implementation and operation → Environmental policy

2. Which of the following can be achieved through environment management?
   (a) Intra-generation Equity
   (b) Environmental Governance
   (c) Conservation of critical environment resources
   (d) all the above

3. Which of the following implemented the National Rural Drinking Water Programme?
   (a) Department of Drinking Water and Sanitation
   (b) Department of Drinking Water Supply
   (c) National Water Development Agency
   (d) None of the above.

4. Amrit, a low-cost arsenic filter using nano-filtration technology, has been developed by
   (a) Indian Institute of Technology-Madras
   (b) Indian Institute of Technology-Delhi
   (c) Indian Institute of Science-Bangalore
   (d) Indian Institute of Technology-Bombay

5. Which of the following activities has been banned in Ganga?
   (a) boating        (b) fishing
   (c) camping        (d) both (a) and (b)

6. Recently, which of the following states has proposed to introduce curriculum on water conservation?
   (a) Madhya Pradesh    (b) Rajasthan
   (c) Maharashtra       (d) Tamil Nadu

7. Thermal power plants in India have been warned for releasing which of the following pollutants?
   (a) Sulphur Dioxide   (b) Nitrogen Oxide
   (c) Mercury           (d) all the above

8. Which of the companies has made an agreement with specialty chemicals maker Evonik Industries for setting up an environmental-friendly project in Gujarat?
   (a) Gujarat Alkalies and Chemicals Limited
   (b) *Gujarat* Organics Limited
   (c) Bodal Chemicals Ltd.
   (d) BASF India Limited

9. Recent Supreme Court ruling banned which of the following type of vehicles?
   (a) BS-IV vehicles    (b) BS-III vehicles
   (c) diesel vehicles   (d) petrol vehicles

10. How much green cess has been proposed by the Environment Pollution (Prevention and Control) Authority (EPCA) for the National Capital Region (NCR) on diesel vehicles?
    (a) 20-22%    (b) 15-20%
    (c) 10-15%    (d) 20-25%

11. Which of the following apps has been launched for monitoring of pollution levels in industrial regions.
    (a) Drishti    (b) Watawaran
    (c) Shristi    (d) None of the above

12. The Delta Coalition is a collaborative delta policy of how many countries?
    (a) 14    (b) 20    (c) 17    (c) 12

13. Which of the following provides financial aid for reducing carbon emission?
    (a) World Bank         (b) United Nations
    (c) World Health Organization.
    (d) None

14. Which of the following contribute to soil management?
    (a) organic farming    (b) bio-fertilizer
    (c) intensive farming  (d) both (a) and (b)

15. Recently, the use of which of the following has been proposed to monitor tigers?
    (a) helicopters        (b) infrared camera
    (c) drones             (d) radio signal

16. Problem of solid waste can be reduced through
    (a) Timber use         (b) lesser pollution
    (c) population control  (d) recycling

17. Which of the following are natural filters which are used for treatment of sewage waste?
    (a) Sand               (b) Gravel
    (c) Plants             (d) All the above

18. What is the aim of 'Water4crops' project?
    (a) Use less water for crops
    (b) More irrigation facilities
    (c) Bio-treated wastewater reuse
    (d) Drip and Sprinkle Irrigation

19. Industrial pollution can be reduced through
    (a) eco-labeling       (b) Pollution charge
    (c) government subsidy (d) both (b) and (c)

20. Ganga pollution can be controlled through
    (a) sewage treatment   (b) rafting
    (c) camping            (c) dams

21. Inland water quality-monitoring network is operated under
    (a) Global Environment Monitoring System (GEMS)
    (b) Monitoring of Indian National Aquatic Resources System (MINARS)
    (c) Yamuna Action Plan (YAP)
    (d) all the above

22. Which of the following pollutants can be removed by
    (a) organic particles  (b) debris
    (c) grit               (d) all the above

23. What percent of total profitability need to be spent by companies in India towards environmental corporate social responsibility?
    (a) 5%    (b) 1%    (c) 3%    (d) 2%

24. Which of the following Indian banks has invested in the Carbon Disclosure Project?
    (a) State Bank of India    (b) HDFC Bank
    (c) Punjab National Bank   (d) Central Bank

25. Which of the following is a pollution monitoring app?
    (a) RajVayu             (b) KendraVayu
    (c) ShudhVayu           (d) both (b) and (c)

26. Amended Form 22 of pollution control applies to
    (a) CNG vehicles        (b) electric vehicles
    (c) diesel vehicles     (d) all the above

27. Which type of pollution can be controlled by super critical and ultra-super critical (USC) technologies?
    (a) water pollution     (b) $CO_2$ emission
    (c) radioactive emission (d) None

28. Which of the following plant is considered highly inflammable and responsible for forest fire?
    (a) Chir pine           (b) oak
    (c) fir                 (d) teak

# Exercise -2

1. Marine pollution is caused by
   1. Sewage
   2. Land runoff
   3. Oil spills
   4. Ocean mining
   Choose the correct code :
   (a) 1, 3, and 4 only     (b) 3 and 4 only
   (c) 1, 2, 3 and 4     (d) 4, 3, 2 only

2. Soil pollution is caused by :
   1. Industrial waste
   2. Agrochemicals
   3. Petrochemicals
   4. Detergents
   Choose the correct code :
   (a) 1 and 2 only     (b) 2, 3 and 4 only
   (c) 1, 2, 3 and 4     (d) 3 and 4 only

3. Read the following statements regarding the launch of Roll-on Roll-Off (RORO) Service.
   1. It was launched in Delhi region.
   2. It aims at controlling water pollution.
   3. It states that heavy commercial vehicles passing through Delhi will be loaded on flat railway wagons at railway terminals.
   Choose the correct option.
   (a) 1 and 2     (b) 2 and 3
   (c) 1, 2 and 3     (d) 1 and 3

4. Read the following statements regarding the Central Pollution Control Board.
   1. It is implementing the Air (Prevention and Control of Pollution) Act 1981 to restore air quality.
   2. It is a statutory organisation under the Ministry of Environment, Forest and Climate Change (MoEF&CC).
   3. It was established in 1974 under the Water (Prevention and Control of pollution) Act, 1974.
   Choose the correct option.
   (a) 1, 2 and 3     (b) 1 and 3
   (c) 2 and 3     (d) 1 and 3

5. Read the following statements regarding the National Air Quality Monitoring Programme (NAMP).
   1. Four air pollutants viz., Sulphur Dioxide ($SO_2$), Oxides of Nitrogen as $NO_2$, Suspended Particulate Matter (SPM) and Respirable Suspended Particulate Matter (RSPM/ PM10) have been identified.
   2. The monitoring of meteorological parameters such as wind speed and wind direction, relative humidity (RH) and temperature were also integrated with the monitoring of air quality.
   Choose the correct option.
   (a) only 1     (b) both 1 and 2
   (c) only 2     (d) None

6. Read the following statements regarding National Air Quality Index.
   1. It is a colour-coded national air-quality index.
   2. It was launched by the Minister for Environment, Forests & Climate Change.
   3. It was launched under the Swachh Bharat Mission.

Choose the correct option.
(a) 1 and 3     (b) 2 and 3
(c) 1, 2 and 3     (d) 1 and 2

7. Read the following statements regarding the Graded Response To Air Pollution.
   1. A graded response highlights the actions required to be taken as and when the concentration of pollutants reaches a certain level.
   2. The measures that are to be enforced under the plan include strict ban on garbage burning, closing brick kilns, mechanised and enforcing ban on fire-crackers.
   3. It has no provisions for odd-even car rationing scheme.
   Choose the correct option.
   (a) 1 and 2     (b) 2 and 3
   (c) 1 and 3     (d) 1, 2 and 3

8. Read the following statements regarding the National Electric Mobility Mission Plan.
   1. It aims at achieving national fuel security by promoting hybrid and electric vehicles.
   2. It promotes the use of conventional vehicles to reduce liquid fuel consumption.
   3. It targets at achieving 6-7 million sales of CNG vehicles by 2020.
   Choose the correct option.
   (a) 1 and 3     (b) 2 and 3
   (c) 1 and 2     (d) 1, 2 and 3

9. Read the following statements regarding using ethanol as fuel.
   1. Ethanol is can be produced from sugarcane, maize, and wheat
   2. Ethanol Blended Petrol (EBP) programme was launched in January 2009.
   3. Ethanol can be only be blended with diesel.
   Choose the correct option.
   (a) 1 and 3     (b) 2 and 3
   (c) 1 and 2     (d) only 1

10. Read the following statements regarding RajVayu app.
    1. It was launched in Madhya Pradesh.
    2. It shares information about air quality index.
    3. It was launched on the World Environment Day.
    Choose the correct option.
    (a) 1 and 2     (b) 2 and 3
    (c) 1, 2 and 3     (d) only 2

11. Read the following statements regarding amendment of Form 22 related to noise pollution.
    1. It was amended under the Central Motor Vehicles Act, 1990.
    2. It will include pollution standards, safety standards of component quality and road-worthiness certificate for all vehicles.
    3. The Union Ministry of Road Transport & Highways plans to introduce five star ratings to vehicles based on their emission and noise pollution standards.
    Choose the correct option.
    (a) 1, 2 and 3     (b) 2 and 3
    (c) 1 and 2     (d) 1 and 3

12. Read the following statements regarding the recent discovery of oil degrading bacteria.
    1. It cannot degrade hydrocarbons.
    2. It has been discovered in Kochi, Kerala.
    3. This bacteria does not have enzyme.
    Choose the correct option.
    (a) 1 and 2     (b) 2 and 3
    (c) 1, 2 and 3     (d) 1 and 3

13. Read the following statements regarding recycling of wastewater.
    1. 1t will increase water pollution.
    2. Recycled wastewater cannot be used in agriculture.
    3. It can also be a rich source of nutrients, minerals and energy.
    Choose the correct option.
    (a) only 3     (b) 1 and 2
    (c) 1 and 3     (d) 1, 2 and 3

14. Read the following statements regarding the World Bank's Climate Change Action Plan.
    1. It intends to control climate change by 2022.
    2. It helps developing countries to deliver their targets set in the national climate plans submitted for the historic climate agreement reached at COP21 in Paris in December 2015.
    3. It aims at integrating climate into urban planning through the Global Platform for Sustainable Cities.
    Choose the correct option.
    (a) 1 and 3     (b) 1 and 2
    (c) 2 and 3     (d) 1, 2 and 3

15. Read the following statements regarding suggestions for forest fire prevention.
    1. Planting narrow-leaf trees.
    2. Creating ponds and other water harvesting structures within the forest.
    3. Using corporate social responsibility funds for creating awareness campaigns on forest fires.
    Choose the correct option.
    (a) 1, 2 and 3     (b) 2 and 3
    (c) 1 and 2     (d) 1 and 3

16. Read the following statements regarding rules on waste management in India.
    1. Source segregation of waste has been made compulsory to channelize the waste.
    2. Special Economic Zone need to leave at least 10% of the total area for recovery and recycling facility.
    3. Bio-degradable waste should be processed, treated and disposed through composting or bio-methanation.
    Choose the correct option.
    (a) 1 and 2     (b) 2 and 3
    (c) 1, 2 and 3     (d) 1 and 3

17. Read the following statements regarding National Solid Waste Association of India.
    1. It is a member of the International Solid Waste Association (ISWA).
    2. It develops standards in solid waste management.
    3. It expertise in the field of Solid Waste Management at the national level.
    Choose the correct option.
    (a) 1 and 3     (b) 2 and 3
    (c) 1 and 2     (d) 1, 2 and 3

18. Read the following statements on United Nations Convention to Combat Desertification.
    1. It has proposed Science–Policy Interface (SPI) to facilitate a two-way science–policy dialogue and ensure the delivery of policy-relevant information.
    2. The SPI is composed of 25 members and three observers.
    Choose the correct option.
    (a) 1 and 2     (b) only 1
    (c) only 2     (d) None of the above

19. Read the following statements regarding an Eco-Sensitive Zone (ESZ).
    1. An ESZ has been proposed at Sanjay Gandhi National Park in Mumbai.
    2. ESZ acts as a buffer for further protection around Protected Areas (PAs) such as National Parks and Wildlife sanctuaries.
    3. ESZ is notified under Section 3 of the Environment (Management) Act, 1986 by the Union Ministry of Environment and Forest.
    Choose the correct option.
    (a) 1, 2 and 3     (b) 2 and 3
    (c) 1 and 2     (d) 1 and 3

20. Read the following statements regarding Access and Benefit Sharing (ABS) Mechanism.
    1. It is used for biodiversity conservation.
    2. It involves sharing a part of profit earned from natural resources.
    3. It involves paying tax to government for using natural resource.
    Choose the correct option.
    (a) 1 and 2     (b) 2 and 3
    (c) 1, 2 and 3     (d) 1 and 3

21. Which of the following activities is/are permitted in the Eco Sensitive Zones (ESZ)?
    1. Felling of trees
    2. Establishment of Hotels and Resorts
    3. Rain water harvesting
    Choose the correct alternative using the codes given below.
    (a) 1 and 2 only     (b) 3 only
    (c) 2 only     (d) 1, 2 and 3

22. Which of the following are correct
    1. India has only 2.4 percent of the land area, and accounts for 7-8 per cent of the recorded species of the world
    2. In terms of species richness, India ranks seventh in mammals, ninth in birds and fifth in reptiles.
    (a) 1     (b) 2
    (c) Both     (d) None

23. National Action Plan on Climate Change, 2008 (NAPCC) includes which of the following programmes:
    1. National solar mission.
    2. National mission for enhanced energy efficiency.
    3. National mission for sustainable habitat.

Choose the correct option.
(a)  1 and 2          (b)  2 and 3
(c)  all                 (d)  1 and 3

**24.** The use of biofertilizer helps in increasing the supply of primary nutrients to plants. Which of the following is/are examples of biofertilizers?
1.  Azotobacter
2.  Rhizobium
3.  Azospirillium
Choose the correct option.
(a) 1 and 2 only          (b) 1 and 3 only
(c) 2 and 3 only          (d) 1, 2 and 3

**25.** Read the following statements regarding ECO-India plan.
1.  It is a two-year project is co-funded by the European Commission's Seventh Framework Programme (FP7).
2.  It is focused on developing innovative and sustainable approaches for producing potable water at a community level.
3.  The first rural community deployment of the plan will be in West Bengal.
Choose the correct option.
(a)  only 1          (b)  1 and 3
(c)  2 and 3        (d)  only 2

**26.** Which of the following is incorrect.
1.  India is the world's sixth largest and second fastest growing producer of greenhouse gases.
2.  Delhi, Mumbai and Chennai are three of the world's least polluted cities.
3.  Two-thirds of city dwellers lack sewerage; one-third lack portable, clean water.
(a)  only 1          (b)  1 and 2
(c)  2 and 3        (d)  only 3

**27.** Which of the following are the key features of 'National Ganga River Basin Authority (NGRBA)'?

**(IAS Prelims 2016)**

1.  River basin is the unit of planning and management.
2.  It spearheads the river conservation efforts at the national level.
3.  One of the Chief Ministers of the States through which the Ganga flows becomes the Chairman of NGRBA on rotation basis.
Select the correct answer using the code given Below.
(a)  1 and 2 only          (b)  2 and 3 only
(c)  1 and 3 only          (d)  1, 2 and 3

# Hints and Explanations



1. (a)

2. (d) Environment management becomes important to conserve critical ecosystems and resources, and invaluable natural and made-made heritage, which are essential for life support, livelihoods, economic growth and human well being. To ensure equitable access to environmental resources and quality for all sections of society, and in particular to support poor communities. To apply the principles of good governance with respect to transparency, rationality, accountability, and reduction in time and costs, to the management and regulation of use of environmental resources.

3. (a) The Department of Drinking Water and Sanitation has taken launched the National Rural Drinking Water Programme (NRDWP). NRDWP provides grants for construction of rural water supply schemes with special attention on water-stressed and water quality affected areas, rainwater harvesting and groundwater recharge measures. It promotes conjunctive use of surface, groundwater and roof water rainwater harvesting and actively supports convergence with other development programmes such as the MNREGS. National Water Development Agency conducts surveys and investigations in respect of Peninsular Component of National Perspective for Water Resources Development.

4. (a) Scientists at the Indian Institute of Technology-Madras (IIT-M) have developed Amrit, a low-cost arsenic filter using nano-filtration technology. This technology can be used for removing arsenic from drinking water. Indian Institute of Technology-Delhi, Indian Institute of Science-Bangalore and Indian Institute of Technology-Bombay have not designed any such technology on purifying water.

5. (c) The National Green Tribunal has banned camping activity in the entire belt of Kaudiyala to Rishikesh on the banks of river Ganga in Uttarakhand. Rafting does not cause any serious pollution river or environment. NGT prohibits the use of any plastic items in the entire belt and restricts using mechanised riverbed mining in the Ganga till Haridwar.

6. (b) Rajasthan River Basin and Water Resources Planning Authority has planned to incorporate geo-tagging and advanced scientific techniques for water conservation works and aims to include water conservation lesson in school syllabus. New generation need to learn and understand importance of water conservation right from the beginning.

7. (d) Thermal power plants in India release Sulphur Dioxide, Nitrogen Oxide and Mercury as pollutants. These substances pollutes air and water causing health problems for humans and other organisms. Sulphur Dioxide cause acid rain which corrodes monuments and other buildings. Nitrogen Oxide is toxic to many organisms. Mercury when consumed causes disease called Minamata.

8. (a) State-owned Gujarat Alkalies and Chemicals Limited has made an agreement with specialty chemicals maker Evonik Industries for setting up a multi-million hydrogen peroxide and propylene oxide project at Dahej in Gujarat. This project would be based on an innovative, environment-friendly HPPO technology. *Gujarat* Organics Limited is quality ensuring Indian company in specialty chemical intermediate manufacturing for pharmaceuticals, foods and cosmetics. Bodal Chemicals Ltd. is a manufacturer of acid, direct and reactive dyestuffs and dye intermediates for textile, leather, plastics and papermaking applications.

9. (b) The Supreme Court ruled that health of citizens was more important than commercial interests of auto makers as it banned the sale and registration of Bharat Stage (BS)-III emission norm-compliant vehicles from April 1. Bharat Stage or BS norms are standards for vehicular emissions. They lay down the permissible levels of pollutants that come out of the exhaust pipes of motor vehicles. The aim is to check air pollution and emissions that lead to global warming. India is set to enforce a new generation of vehicular pollution norms on April 1 called BS IV. Only BS IV compliant vehicles can be manufactured.

10. (a) Cess on diesel vehicles will lead to the reduction in air pollution. The Environment Pollution (Prevention and Control) Authority (EPCA) for the National Capital Region (NCR) has recommended to levy a green cess of 20-22% on diesel vehicles. EPCA recommended a cess of 20% on the cost of vehicles with engines that are smaller than 1,500cc in size, and 22% on those over 1,500cc. The main reason behind EPCA's recommendation is to remove the existing incentive for buying diesel vehicles. Removing the fuel price differential, through the imposition of ECC

(environment compensation charge) will be a step in removing the incentive for diesel vehicles. This is needed to reduce public health risk as diesel emissions are among the more harmful pollutants.

11. (a) The government of Rajasthan has launched Drishti app for monitoring pollution levels in industrial regions. The app will help in monitoring air pollutants and assist in creating data on air pollution for future reference. There is no app by name Watawaran, Shristi and Shristi.

12. (d) The Delta Coalition includes 12 countries (Colombia, Egypt, Indonesia, Japan, South-Korea, Mozambique, Myanmar, Netherlands, Philippines, Vietnam, France and Bangladesh) to bring deltas to global policy discussions, build partnerships and focus on action, aiming to increase resilience for almost 250 million people in deltas in these 12 countries.

13. (a) The global development lenders such as World Bank and Asian Development Bank (ABD) provide help countries including India to shift away from coal for energy purpose. The idea of funding was proposed by the World Coal Association to finance countries to help them to shift to more efficient technologies so that they can meet their COP21 commitments. Coal is needed to meet energy demands. Even if countries opt for renewable energy they are not going to do away with coal in overall energy. United Nations provides strategic planning for controlling emission. World Health Organization is a UN agency which monitors world public health.

14. (d) Organic farming and bio-fertilizer increase soil fertility and help managing soil pollution. Organic farming involves crop and livestock production under limited use of pesticides, fertilizers, genetically modified organisms, antibiotics and growth hormones. Bio fertilizer is a substance which contains living microorganisms which, when applied to plant surfaces, colonize the rhizosphere or the interior of the plant and improves growth by increasing the supply or availability of primary nutrients to the host plant.

15. (c) Conservation drones are being used to monitor tiger reserves. Besides monitoring of tiger population in the reserves, the unmanned aircraft would collect and transmit visual data on animal movements, poaching activities and instances of forest fire from inaccessible forest terrains on a real-time basis. The drones could be used for the management of habitats and species.

16. (d) Problem of solid waste can be reduced through recycling. Recycling reduces the deposition of solid wastes in nature. Timber use will result in the reduction in the number of plants, leading to air pollution. Population control is not the effective measure to control solid waste disposal problem.

17. (d) India and the European Union collaborated to find a cost-effective technology for treatment of sewage waste for irrigation, especially in rural areas, using natural filters like sand and plants. The technology involves collecting the sewage waste before it reaches the water bodies and then treat it using natural filters like sand, gravel, pebbles and plants to remove the impurities. Under the project, many wetland plant species, such as Canna indica, lemon grass, napier, para grass, typha, water hyacinth, water lettuce and a weed species Agaratum conyzoides, have been identified for purifying the wastewater.

18. (c) The 'Water4crops' is one of the technology initiatives between India and European Union.
The project also proved that the construction of wetland reduces the amount of pollutants, chemical oxygen demand (COD) in wastewater by 30-92 per cent.

19. (d) Charge system will levy a fee or tax on the amount of pollution a firm or source generates. It is important for the firm to reduce emissions. Subsidies can provide incentive to address environmental problems. However, it has been reported that the subsidies encourage economically inefficient and environmentally unsound practices. Eco-labeling is the practice of supplying information on the environmental characteristics of a product or service to the general public.

20. (a) Ganga pollution can be controlled through the treatment sewage before releasing them into the Ganga. Rafting and camping increase water pollution and causes land degradation along Ganga. Construction of dams pose a threat to the dolphin population.

21. (d) **Inland water quality-monitoring network** is operated under a three-tier programme, Global Environment Monitoring System (GEMS), Monitoring of Indian National Aquatic Resources System (MINARS) and Yamuna Action Plan (YAP). Water samples are being analysed for 28 parameters consisting of 9 core parameters, 19 other physico-chemical and bacteriological parameters apart from the field observations. Biomonitoring is also carried out on specific locations. In view of limited resources, limited numbers of organic pollution related parameters are monitored for micro pollutants (toxic metals and POPs).

22. (d) The effluent treatment plants are used in the removal of high amount of organics, debris, dirt, grit, pollution, toxic, non toxic materials, polymers etc. from drugs and other medicated stuff. The ETP plants use evaporation and drying methods, and other

auxiliary techniques such as centrifuging, filtration, incineration for chemical processing and effluent treatment.

23. (d) Corporate social responsibility (CSR) represents the policies, practices and initiatives a company commits to in order to govern themselves with honesty and transparency and have a positive impact on social and environmental wellbeing. The Indian government has been trying to make it mandatory for companies to spend at least 2 percent of net profitability on CSR.

24. (a) State Bank of India has invested in the Carbon Disclosure Project, which is an organisation based in the United Kingdom which works with shareholders and corporations to disclose the greenhouse gas (GHG) emissions of major corporations.

25. (a) The government of Rajasthan has introduced mobile application RajVayu for sharing information about air quality index. The app was launched on the World Environment Day (5th June). With this, Rajasthan becomes first state in country to launch such app for sharing information about air quality index of cities. There is no app by name KendraVayu and ShudhVayu.

26. (d) Amended Form 22 makes it mandatory for all automobile manufacturers to provide emission and noise pollution details for every vehicle including makers of electric rickshaws and electric carts. It will apply to all vehicles including petrol, CNG, LPG, electric, diesel and hybrid. Automobile manufacturers need to specify the levels of each pollutant like carbon monoxide, hydro carbon, non-methane HC, NOx, HC+NOx, PM etc. for petrol and diesel vehicles.

27. (b) Super critical and ultra-super critical (USC) technologies are capable of substantially reducing $CO_2$ emissions and virtually eliminate PM emissions. It requires less coal per megawatt-hour, leading to lower emissions (including carbon dioxide), higher efficiency and lower fuel costs per megawatt. These technologies are not used in nuclear power stations.

28. (a) Chir pine needles, which are highly inflammable due to its high resin content, are main factor in occurring and spreading of forest fires. Incidents of fire in broad leaves forests were found to be minimal. Oak , fir and teak are comparatively less inflammable.

## EXERCISE-2

1. (c)

2. (c)

3. (d) This service was launched in the National Capital and included a multi-modal transportation model aimed at reducing Delhi's air pollution. The RO-RO have a direct impact on its air ambient quality and the capital would breathe clean air. According to plans, heavy commercial vehicles passing through Delhi will be loaded on flat railway wagons at railway terminals outside the capital and will get unloaded at the other end of the city. RO-RO service aims to reduce carbon emission and congestion on the roads of the NCR as about 66,000 diesel trucks pass through Delhi and its adjoining areas in a day.

4. (a) The government agency is implementing the Air (Prevention and Control of Pollution) Act 1981 to restore air quality. It is a statutory organisation under the Ministry of Environment, Forest and Climate Change (MoEF&CC). It was established in 1974 under the Water (Prevention and Control of pollution) Act, 1974. CPCB runs nation-wide programs of ambient air quality monitoring known as National Air Quality Monitoring Programme (NAMP). The network consists of 621 operating stations covering 262 cities/towns in 29 states and 5 Union Territories of the country.

5. (b) NAMP has identified four air pollutants, Sulphur Dioxide ($SO_2$), Oxides of Nitrogen as $NO_2$, Suspended Particulate Matter (SPM) and Respirable Suspended Particulate Matter (RSPM/ PM10, for regular monitoring at all the locations. The monitoring of meteorological parameters such as wind speed and wind direction, relative humidity (RH) and temperature were also integrated with the monitoring of air quality. These parameters affects the presence of air pollutants in the environment.

6. (c) It is a colour-coded national air-quality index has been used to monitor the air quality. The Minister for Environment, Forests & Climate Change launched 'The National Air Quality Index' (AQI) to judge the air quality. The formulation of the index was a continuation of the initiatives under Swachh Bharat Mission. Air pollution has been a matter of environmental and health concerns, particularly in urban areas. Central Pollution Control Board along with State Pollution Control Boards has been operating National Air Monitoring Program (NAMP) covering 240 cities of the country. In addition, continuous monitoring systems that provide data on near real-time basis are also installed in a few cities.

7. (d) Graded Response To Air Pollution: A graded response highlights the actions required to be taken as and when the concentration of pollutants, in this case particulate matter, reaches a certain level. At the current level of pollution lying between poor and moderate, the measures that are to be enforced under the plan include strict ban on garbage burning, closing brick

kilns, mechanised sweeping of roads, enforcing ban on fire-crackers among others. In this plan, odd-even car rationing scheme and halt on construction activities may be implemented across Delhi-NCR.

8. (c) National Electric Mobility Mission Plan (NEMMP) aims to achieve national fuel security by promoting hybrid and electric vehicles in India. There is an ambitious target to achieve 6-7 million sales of hybrid and electric vehicles year on year from 2020 onwards. Government has launched Faster Adoption and Manufacturing of (Hybrid &) Electric Vehicles (FAME India) scheme under NEMMP. The aim of the Government through this scheme will be to allow hybrid and electric vehicles to become the first choice for the purchasers so that these vehicles can replace the conventional vehicles and thus reduce liquid fuel consumption in the country from the automobile sector.

9. (d) Ethanol can be used as automobile fuel which is produced from sugarcane, maize, wheat, etc., It can be mixed with gasoline to form different blends. As the ethanol molecule contains oxygen, it allows the engine to more completely combust the fuel, resulting in fewer emissions and thereby reducing the occurrence of environmental pollution. Since ethanol is produced from plants that harness the power of the sun, ethanol is also considered as renewable fuel. Ethanol Blended Petrol (EBP) programme was launched in January, 2003 which aimed to promote the use of alternative and environment friendly fuels and to reduce import dependency for energy requirements.

10. (c) The government of Rajasthan has introduced mobile application RajVayu for sharing information about air quality index of Jaipur, Udaipur and Jodhpur. The app was launched on the World Environment Day (5th June). RajVayu app gathers information based on the data collected by sophisticated air quality monitoring equipment and weather sensors. This app is based on the System of Air Quality and Weather Forecasting Research (SAFAR-India) which is presently connected in Delhi, Mumbai and Pune. The services of this application would be expanded other cities in the state including in Ajmer, Alwar, Bhiwadi, Kota and Pali.

11. (b) The Union Ministry of Road Transport & Highways has made it mandatory for all automobile manufacturers to provide emission and noise pollution details for every vehicle they produce by April 2017. The ministry has amended Form 22 under the Central Motor Vehicles Act, 1989 through which manufactures provide the initial certification of compliance of vehicles. It will include pollution standards, safety standards of component quality and road-worthiness certificate for all vehicles. The Union Ministry of Road Transport & Highways in wants to award five star ratings to vehicles based on their emission and noise pollution standards.

12. (a) Scientists have found three new strains of oil-degrading bacteria in Kochi, Kerala. Earlier, laboratory tests of these new strains conducted were successful. The field trials will be conducted by the Malabar Botanical Garden and Institute of Plant Sciences (MBGIPS), Kozhikode and Bharat Petroleum Corporation Limited (BPCL). The study will allow the development of bioremediation agents to clean up petroleum pollutants from the environment. Enzymes in oil-degrading bacteria (microorganisms) can degrade and utilise hydrocarbons as a source of carbon and energy. Scientists from successfully isolated key hydrocarbon-degrading enzyme produced by the bacteria. The three new strains isolated by MBGIPS include two species of Burkholderia and one species of Pseudomonas.

13. (a) Recycling of wastewater after treatment reduces water pollution and help in the conservation of water. Besides reducing pollution at the source, policy initiatives must focus on removing contaminants from waste water flows, reusing water, and recovering useful by-products. The potential for reusing liquid waste can be understood by the fact that astronauts on the International Space Station drink recycled urine and use it to wash up. In Jordan and Israel, 90% and 50% of agricultural water, respectively, has been recovered for reuse.

14. (c) The World Bank's Climate Change Action Plan aims at tackling climate change over the next five years i.e. by 2020. It seeks to help developing countries to deliver their targets set in the national climate plans submitted for the historic climate agreement reached at COP21 in Paris in December 2015. The Climate Change Action Plan is designed to help countries meet their Paris COP 21 pledges and manage increasing climate impacts.

15. (b) Forest fire can be prevented by planting of broad tree leaves in forests, and after a period of five years, systematic replacement of chir pine trees in forests by broad leaves. Forest fires results mainly due to drying up of forest area. Planting of broad-leaf plats

can prevent forest fires as they provide more shade. Narrow-leaf trees provide less area under shade and allow more sunlight to enter the forest area leading to drying up of the region.

16. (d) Around 62 million tonnes of waste is generated annually in the country at present, out of which 5.6 million tonnes is plastic waste. The government has made rules on waste management which mention that it is mandatory to segregate waste to channelize the waste. Special Economic Zone need to leave at least 5% of the total area for recovery and recycling facility. Bio-degradable waste should be processed, treated and disposed through composting or bio-methanation. *Composting* is the process of recycling decomposed organic materials into a rich soil known as *compost*. Biomethanation is a process by which organic material is converted to biogas under anaerobic conditions with the help of microorganisms.

17. (c) National Solid Waste Association of India (NSWAI) has been formed on 25th January 1996. It is also a member of the International Solid Waste Association (ISWA), and provides forum for exchange of information and expertise in the field of Solid Waste Management at the international level. The objectives of NSWAI include development of standards in solid waste management, development of expertise in solid waste management, conduct research on solid waste management.

18. (b) United Nations Convention to Combat Desertification has proposed Science–Policy Interface (SPI) to facilitate a two-way science–policy dialogue and ensure the delivery of policy-relevant information, knowledge and advice on desertification/land degradation and drought (DLDD). The SPI is composed of 20 members and three observers, who are mostly scientific experts.

19. (c) An Eco-Sensitive Zone (ESZ) has been proposed by the government in Sanjay Gandhi National Park in Mumbai. ESZ acts as a buffer for further protection around Protected Areas (PAs) such as National Parks and Wildlife sanctuaries. Activities around such areas are regulated and managed so as to protect the environment. ESZ is notified under Section 3 of the Environment (Protection) Act, 1986 by the Union Ministry of Environment and Forest. Many states have opposed ESZ because of presence of minerals and resources side by side.

20. (a) In this mechanism, a part of the profit earned from exploiting natural resources can be used for conserving natural resources. The National Biodiversity Authority proposed this mechanism for biodiversity conservation. The board had earlier issued notices to more than 1,100 manufacturers and traders of Ayurvedic drugs that are commercially utilising these bio resources. Many of the companies use these natural plants and products as ingredients in medicinal and other products. 95% of the ABS amount shall is transferred to the account of the biodiversity management committee (BMC) of the respective region.

21. (b) ESZ acts as a buffer for further protection around Protected Areas (PAs). Several activities are prohibited in ESZ such as Commercial mining, setting of saw mill, setting of industries causing pollution, and establishment of major hydroelectric projects. Establishment of hotels and resorts, felling of trees, erection of electrical cables, and drastic change of agricultural systems, are regulated. Activities such as agriculture and horticulture practices by local communities, rain water harvesting, organic farming etc., are permitted.

22. (c) India, a mega diversity country with only 2.4 percent of the land area, accounts for 7-8 per cent of the recorded species of the world In terms of species richness. India ranks seventh in mammals, ninth in birds and fifth in reptiles. It hosts 3 biodiversity hotspots: the Western Ghats, the Himalayas and the Indo-Burma region. These hotspots have numerous endemic species.

23. (c) National Solar Mission aims to promote the development and use of solar energy for power generation, with the ultimate objective of making solar competitive with fossil-based energy options. It highlights National Mission for Enhanced Energy Efficiency plan. It recommends mandating specific energy consumption decreases in large energy-consuming industries, with a system for companies to trade energy-saving certificates. It also focuses on National Mission on Sustainable Habitat to promote energy efficiency as a core component of urban planning by extending the existing Energy Conservation Building Code.

24. (d) Rhizobium is used for leguminous crops. Azotobacter can be used with crops like wheat, maize, mustard, cotton, potato and other vegetable crops. Azospirillum inoculations are recommended mainly for sorghum, millets, maize, sugarcane and wheat. Bio-fertilizers add nutrients through the natural processes of nitrogen fixation, solubilizing phosphorus, and stimulating plant growth through the synthesis of growth-promoting substances.

25. (c) ECO-India is a three-year project is co-funded by the European Commission's Seventh Framework Programme (FP7) and the Indian Department of Science and Technology (DST). It is focused on developing innovative and sustainable approaches for producing potable water at a community level. The first rural community deployment is set for West Bengal, India.

26. (a) India is the world's sixth largest and second fastest growing producer of greenhouse gases. According to Biennial Update Report, India's total green house gas (GHG) emissions in 2010 was 2.136 billion tonnes Carbon dioxide equivalent. Delhi, Mumbai and Chennai are three of the world's most polluted cities. Two-thirds of city dwellers lack sewerage; one-third lack portable, clean water.

27. (a) (i) National Ganga River Basin Authority (NGRBA) is a financing, planning, implementing, monitoring and coordinating authority for the Ganges River, functioning under the water resource ministry of India. The mission of the organisation is to spearhead the river conservation efforts at the national level.

(ii) In 2014, UPSC asked similar question, where one of the statement was- "PM is chairman of NGRBA". That statement was right as per India Yearbook 2014. Therefore, here statement 3 is wrong, CM can't by the chairman of NGRBA. By elimination, we reach answer (a).

# 7 Chapter

# SUSTAINABLE DEVELOPMENT

## Introduction

Sustainable development aims at meeting the basic needs of all people in general and the poor majority in particular- their employment, food, energy, water, housing, etc., by ensuring the growth of agriculture, manufactures, power and services with due consideration for environmental concerns.

Over the past two decades, economic growth has lifted more than 660 million people out of poverty and has raised the income levels of millions more, but too often it has come at the expense of the environment and poor communities.

Through a variety of market, policy, and institutional failures, Earth's natural capital has been used in ways that are economically inefficient and wasteful, without sufficient reckoning of the true costs of resource depletion. The burning of fossil fuels supported rapid growth for decades but set up dangerous consequences, with climate change today threatening to roll back decades of development progress. At the same time, growth patterns have left hundreds of millions of people behind: 1.2 billion still lack access to electricity, 870 million are malnourished, and 780 million are still without access to clean, safe drinking water.

Sustainable development recognizes that growth must be both inclusive and environmentally sound to reduce poverty and build shared prosperity for today's population and to continue to meet the needs of future generations. It is efficient with resources and carefully planned to deliver both immediate and long-term benefits for people, planet, and prosperity.

**The three pillars of sustainable development** – economic growth, environmental stewardship, and social inclusion – carry across all sectors of development, from cities facing rapid urbanization to agriculture, infrastructure, energy development and use, water availability, and transportation. Cities are embracing low-carbon growth and public transportation. Farmers are picking up the practices of climate-smart agriculture. Countries are recognizing the value of their natural resources, and industries are realizing how much they can save through energy and supply chain efficiency.

## CONCEPT OF SUSTAINABLE DEVELOPMENT

The term was used by the **Brundtland Commission** which coined what has become the most often-quoted definition of sustainable development as development that "meets the needs of the present without compromising the ability of future generations to meet their own needs."

Sustainable development implies economic growth together with the protection of environmental quality, each reinforcing the other. It is maintaining a delicate balance between the human need to improve lifestyles and preserving **natural and cultural ecosystems.** The field of sustainable development can be conceptually broken into three constituent parts: **environmental sustainability, economic sustainability** and **socio-political sustainability**. The essence of this form of development is a stable relationship between human activities and the natural world, which does not diminish the prospects for future generations to enjoy a quality of life at least as good as our own.

**Participatory democracy** is a prerequisite for achieving sustainable development.

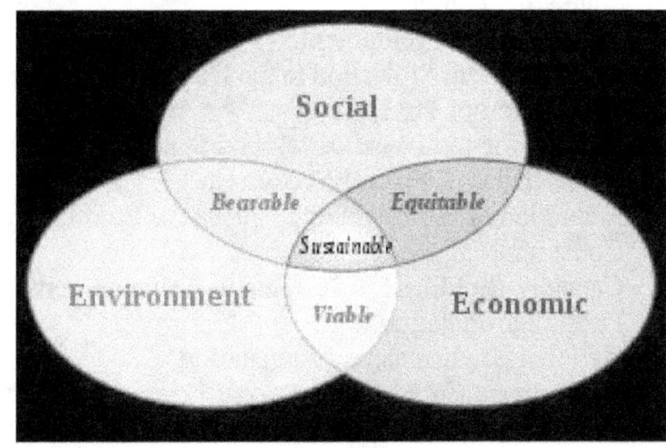



*Scheme of sustainable development: at the confluence of three constituent parts.*

The linkage between environment and development was globally recognized in 1980, when the **International Union for the Conservation of Nature** published the **World Conservation Strategy** and used the term "sustainable development".

This term has been used as a unifying theme in presenting environmental and social concerns about worrisome trends towards accelerated environmental degradation and social polarization in the 1970s and 1980s.

The concept came into general usage after the **Brundtland Commission Report** (1987), formally called the **Report of World Commission on Environment and Development (WCED)**. WCED was set up by the United Nations General Assembly. Thus, the term 'sustainable development' was widely adopted by mainstream development agencies following the publication in 1987 of **"Our Common Future"** by the World Commission on Environment and Development (WCED), chaired by the then prime minister of Norway, **Gro Harlem Brundtland**.

The Brundtland Report coined the most often cited phrase to describe the principle of sustainable development as… development that meets the needs of the present without compromising the ability of future generations to meet their own needs.

**It contains within it two key concepts:**

- The concept of *needs*, in particular the essential needs of the world's poor to whom overriding priority should be given and;
- The idea of *limitations* imposed by the state of technology and social organisations to meet their own needs.

# Rio Declaration

**The Rio Declaration (1992)** consisted of 27 principles intended to guide future sustainable development around the world.

It emphasised the links between environment and development and 176 nations agreed on the following five agreements:

- The Rio Declaration
- The Biodiversity Convention
- The Framework Convention on Climate Change
- The Agreement of Forest Principles
- Agenda 21

## 27 Principles

- The role of humans.
- State sovereignty.
- The Right to development.
- Environmental Protection in the Development Process.
- Eradication of Poverty.
- Priority for the Least Developed State.
- Cooperation to Protect Ecosystem.
- Reduction of Unsustainable Patterns of Production and Consumption.
- Capacity Building for Sustainable Development.
- Public Participation.
- National Environmental Legislation.
- Supportive and Open International Economic System.
- Compensation for Victims of Pollution and other Environmental Damage.
- State Cooperation to Prevent Environmental Dumping.
- Precautionary Principle.
- Internalization of Environmental Costs.
- Environmental Impact Assessments.
- Notification of Natural Disaster.
- Prior and Timely Notification.

- Women have a Vital Role.
- Youth Mobilization.
- Indigenous Peoples have a Vital Role.
- People under Oppression.
- Warfare.
- Peace, Development and Environmental Protection.
- Resolution of Environmental Disputes.
- Cooperation between State and People.

Some Scholars have regarded the Rio Declaration as **Third Generation Human Rights**.

## Convention on Biological Diversity

Convention on Biological Diversity is a legally binding document, which came as an outcome of **Earth Summit** in Rio de Janeiro on 5 June 1992 and entered into force on 29 December 1993. It is commonly known as **"Biodiversity Convention"**.

### Objectives

Conservation of biological diversity (or biodiversity); Sustainable use of its components; and Fair and equitable sharing of benefits arising from genetic resources.

The idea is to develop national strategies for the conservation and sustainable use of biological diversity.

### Parties

198 countries / territories including India are parties to the CBD. The United States has signed but not ratified the convention. The CBD has 23 preamble paragraphs and 42 articles. The preamble paragraphs interalia recognize and reaffirm the following:

- Intrinsic value of biodiversity.
- Biodiversity conservation as common concern of humankind.
- Sovereign rights of States over their biological resources.
- Responsibility of States to conserve and sustainable use their biodiversity.
- Precautionary approach towards biodiversity conservation.
- Vital role of local communities and women in conservation, and sustainable use of biodiversity.
- Need for provision of new and additional financial resources and access to technologies to developing countries to address biodiversity loss.
- Economic and social development and poverty eradication are the first and overriding priorities of developing countries.

By 2009, US, Iraq, Somalia and Andorra had to sign and ratify the CBD. With Iraq's accession to the CBD in July 2009, the US, Somalia and Andorra are now the only remaining countries that have not signed / ratified the CBD. US has ratified the UNFCCC and UNCCD (United Nations Convention to Combat Desertification), but did not ratify the CBD. The main concerns of United States are the CBD provisions, which call for **technology transfer** to developing countries. US thinks that it could threaten US intellectual property interests. Further, there is another reason that the obligations for financial aid under the CBD are vague. Strangely, the other developed countries have not shared these concerns.

## The Agreement of Forest Principles

The **Rio Forest Principles** is the informal name given to the Non-Legally Binding Authoritative Statement of Principles for a Global Consensus on the Management, Conservation and Sustainable Development of All Types of Forests (1992), a document produced at the United Nations Conference on Environment and Development (UNCED), informally known as the Earth Summit. It is a non-legally binding document that makes several recommendations for conservation and sustainable development forestry.

Of these **Biodiversity Convention** and **Framework Convention on Climate Change** were signed at Rio, although negotiated earlier. Action towards concluding a **convention on Desertification** was also taken. The most significant achievement of action was for sustainable development at local, national and global levels.

The World Summit on Sustainable Development, or Earth Summit took place in Johannesburg, South Africa from August 26 to September 4, 2002 to discuss sustainable issues.

The United Nations 2005 World Summit, **Rio10** outcome document refers to economic development, social development and environmental protection as the "interdependent and mutually reinforcing pillars" of sustainable development.

The United Nations Conference on Sustainable Development (UNCSD), also known as **Rio 2012, Rio+20 or Earth Summit 2012** was the third international conference on sustainable development aimed at reconciling the economic and environmental goals of the global community. Hosted by Brazil in Rio de Janeiro from 13 to 22 June 2012, Rio+20 was a 20-year follow-up to the 1992 Earth Summit / United Nations Conference on Environment and Development (UNCED) held in the same city, and the 10th anniversary of the 2002 World Summit on Sustainable Development (WSSD) in Johannesburg.

However, the modern concept of sustainable development is derived mostly from the 1987 Brundtland Report; it is also rooted in earlier ideas about sustainable forest management and twentieth century environmental concerns. As the concept developed, it has shifted to focus more on economic development, social development and environmental protection for future generations. It has been suggested that the term 'sustainability' should be viewed as humanity's target goal of human-ecosystem equilibrium '*homeostasis*', while 'sustainable development' refers to the **holistic approach** and temporal processes that lead us to the end point of sustainability.

## UN Framework Convention on Climate Change

The United Nations Framework Convention on Climate Change (UNFCCC) is an international environmental treaty negotiated at the Earth Summit in Rio de Janeiro from 3 to 14 June 1992, then entered into force on 21 March 1994. The UNFCCC objective is to "stabilize greenhouse gas concentrations in the atmosphere at a level that would prevent dangerous anthropogenic interference with the climate system".The main challenges to sustainable development which are global in character include poverty and exclusion, unemployment, climate change, conflict and humanitarian aid, building peaceful and inclusive societies, building strong institutions of governance, and supporting the rule of law. The Open Working Group of the United Nations, while acknowledging the United Nations Framework Convention on Climate Change, has proposed the 17 aims for its Sustainable Development Goals (SDGs) accompanied by some specific targets .

# Building Blocks of Sustainability

### Agenda 21

**Agenda 21**, an action plan of the United Nations (UN) related to sustainable development, clearly identified information, integration and participation as key building blocks to help countries achieve development that recognizes these interdependent pillars - economic development, environmental development, social development and cultural development.

Agenda 21 emphasizes that broad public participation in decision-making is a fundamental prerequisite for achieving sustainable development.

---

### AGENDA 21

Agenda 21 is the outcome of the 1992 Earth Summit. It is the "Voluntary" action plan of the United Nations (UN) related to sustainable development. This 40 point document was a comprehensive blueprint of action to be taken globally, nationally and locally by organizations of the UN, governments, and major groups in every area in which humans directly affect the environment. For implementation of these points a Commission on Sustainable Development was established as a high level forum on sustainable development. Agenda 21 was adopted by the UNCED (United Nations Conference on Sustainable Development) in June 1992. It recognised that humanity was at a defining moment—it could either continue with the present policies which deepen economic divisions within and among countries, which increase poverty, hunger, sickness and illiteracy worldwide and which continue to deteriorate the ecosystems on which the Earth depends: OR we could change course and bring about a better and sustainable future for all through better management of the ecosystem.

Agenda 21 supported the liberalisation of trade and removal of distortions in international trade. It calls for increased investment in developing countries and better management of financial resources. It calls for combating poverty through policies in respect of population, health care and education, the rights of women and disadvantaged people. It emphasises the need to provide improved shelter, energy efficient technology, human resource development, protecting the atmosphere, combating deforestation and advocates sustainable agriculture and use of biotechnology.

The United Nations Division for Sustainable Development acts as the secretariat to the Commission and works 'within the context of' Agenda 21.

## Rio+5

The Rio+5 was the special session of the UN General Assembly organized in 1997 for appraisal of five years of progress on the implementation of Agenda 21.

## LA21

**Local Agenda 21** is a local-government-led, community-wide, and participatory effort to establish a comprehensive action strategy for environmental protection, economic prosperity and community well-being in the local jurisdiction or area. This requires the integration of planning and action across economic, social and environmental spheres. Key elements are full community participation, assessment of current conditions, target setting for achieving specific goals, monitoring and reporting.

## Major Challenges of Sustainable Development

There are many   challenges to sustainable development like **persistent poverty; globalisation and socioeconomic transitions; sustainable development and climate change; human security, violence and conflict.**

The world has made real progress in reducing poverty in the last 20 years. There is, however, far more to do in ensuring that the benefits of growth are distributed equitably, particularly in fast-growing middle income countries (MICs). There are also big risks, including shocks in the world economy, potentially significant challenges of civil conflict and fragility, long-term resource scarcities and climate change. Policy needs to engage with change, focusing especially on the supra-national level to deliver global public goods. The most significant contemporary challenge is how to address collective action problems in an increasingly multi-polar world.

### Challenge 1: Persistent poverty

Twenty years ago extreme poverty was the norm in many regions. In Asia and Sub-Saharan Africa more than half of the population lived on less than $1.25 in 1990 (Melamed, 2012). Between a quarter and half of all children in the two regions were underweight, and in Africa only half of all children were in school.

### Challenge 2: Globalisation and socio-economic transitions

Globalisation may be understood as the widening, deepening and speeding up of worldwide interconnectedness in all aspects of social, cultural, political and economic life – a phenomenon that has accelerated in the past 50 years . All regions have become more globalised by most measures of economic interconnectedness. Exports, inward flows and stocks of foreign direct investment (FDI) and remittances all grew in value and in their percentage of GDP between 1970 and 2010 (World Bank, 2011). But the peak was in 2008, with a considerable contraction afterwards as a result of the global financial crisis.

### Challenge 3: Sustainable development and climate change

When modelling the impacts of the latest trends in $CO_2$ emissions, projections show that global average temperatures will increase by about 3.5°C by 2100 (Climate Action Tracker, 2012;

IEA, 2011). This is well above the 2°C of warming considered by many to be the threshold for triggering dangerous, runaway climate change (UK Met Office, 2010). Even with rapid decarbonisation and a green growth revolution, most climate scientists now consider 2°C to be unobtainable, though this remains a target for political negotiations. Such rapid warming has fundamental implications for development and economic activity.

Though climate-change poses a variety of challenges, important of them include: agriculture and food security; water stress and water insecurity; rising sea levels; and biodiversity and human health; which have immense relevance from the perspective of developing countries in general and India in particular.

There are many ways to pursue sustainable developments strategies that contribute to mitigation of climate change. A few examples are presented below:

- Adoption of cost-effective energy efficient technologies to electricity generation, transmission distribution and end-use can reduce costs and local pollution in addition to reduction of greenhouse gas emission.
- Shift to renewable, which are cost effective, can enhance sustainable energy supply; can reduce local pollution and greenhouse gas emissions.
- Adoption of forest conservation, reforestation, afforestation and sustainable forest management practices can contribute to conservation of biodiversity, watershed protection rural employment generation, increased incomes to forest dwellers and carbon sink enhancement.

**Challenge 4: Human security, violence and conflict**

Over the past decade the threat of inter-state conflict has reached historically low levels, suggesting that this is an era of unprecedented peace and security. But this is only a partial picture. Security issues are very high on the development agenda, particularly civil conflict, terrorism, trans-national criminal networks, and some forms of social violence (e.g. urban gangs).

## Challenges Tension Between Developing and Developed Countries

**"The Future We Want"** has faced sharp criticism and been viewed as a disappointment by a variety of groups that see it as "vague and weak" because of the results caused by the lack of cooperation and consensus between the developed and developing nations. For example, environmental and antipoverty advocates have criticized **Rio+20** for lacking the detail and ambition required to address challenges of sustainable development and poverty eradication. Additionally, the European Union Environment Commissioner, **Janez Potocnik**, stressed that Rio+20 "did not lead to all the results the European Union hoped for." Unfortunately, the tension between developing and developed countries resulted in Rio+20 producing a one-sided outcome document favouring developing countries.

The views of developed countries were notably absent in the outcomes encompassed in "The Future We Want." This marked a change from previous international environmental agreements like the Rio Declaration and Agenda 21 that respected the views of both groups. The one-sided nature of

Rio+20 undermined advancing sustainable development on a global scale, which resulted in it being a failure overall. Efforts on the international level will continue to fail until the leadership in all countries makes the conscious choice to cooperate with each other. Without the necessary political will, little more will be done internationally to advance sustainable development.

Methods of sustainable development for developed and developing countries differ. If very rapid population growth, poverty, gender inequality and inadequate systems of education and medicine are typical for developing countries, developed countries mostly face such problems as excessive consumption of natural resources and environmental pollution. However, both the developed and the developing countries except for those devastated by war or natural disasters are developing according to the pattern of natural evolution and their economies as well as welfare are growing, although at different paces. But in reality the developed countries don't agree to follow the mitigation as required in the name of economic slowdown. They argue if all majors will be followed it is very difficult to fulfill the basic needs of people. They follow a double standard and blame the developing countries. On the other hand they impose different sanctions. But in reality the developing countries are badly affected but they are committed to follow the goals.

There is a sharp tension between developing and developed countries, due to their divergent viewpoints on how to approach sustainable development. These remarkably different perspectives have led to the tension between the two groups as they struggle to define and implement sustainable development.

Leadership in developing countries is primarily concerned with upward mobility, sovereignty, the costs of sustainable development, and the causes of environmental degradation. Developing countries approach sustainable development from the viewpoint of a need within their countries for socioeconomic upward mobility. The underlying problem of poverty must be addressed for sustainable development to become practicable for developing countries.

## Sustainable Development Goals (SDGs)

With the expiry of the Millenium Development Goals (MDGs) which guided global development till 2015, the International community negotiated sustainable Development Goals (SDGs) for the period 2016-30.

The Sustainable Development Goals (SDGs) are a new, universal set of goals, targets and indicators that UN member states will be expected to use to frame their agendas and political policies over the next 15 years. The Sustainable Development Goals (SDGs), are officially known as *Transforming our world: the 2030 Agenda for Sustainable Development*. There are 17 Sustainable Development Goals, associated 169 targets and 304 indicators.

This included the following goals:

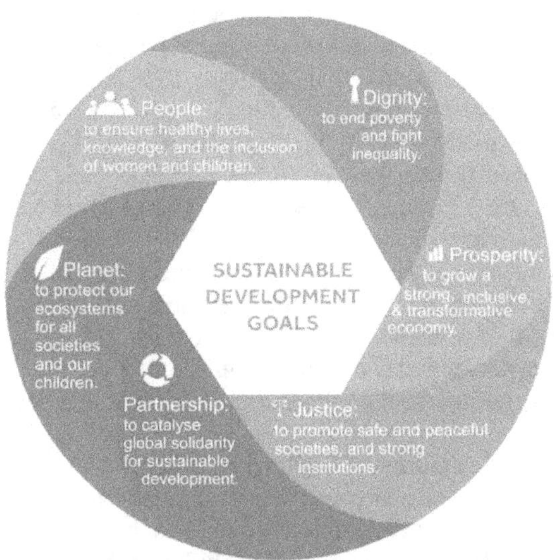


1. End poverty in all its forms everywhere.
2. End hunger, achieve food security and improved nutrition and promote **sustainable agriculture.**
3. Ensure healthy lives and promote well-being for all at all ages.
4. Ensure inclusive and equitable quality education and promote lifelong learning opportunities for all.
5. Achieve gender equality and empower all women and girls.
6. Ensure availability and sustainable management of water and sanitation for all.
7. Ensure access to affordable, reliable, sustainable and modern energy for all.
8. Promote sustained, inclusive and sustainable economic growth, full and productive employment and decent work for all.
9. Build resilient infrastructure, promote inclusive and sustainable industrialization and foster innovation.
10. Reduce inequality within and among countries.
11. Make cities and human settlements inclusive, safe, resilient and sustainable.
12. Ensure sustainable consumption and production patterns.
13. Take urgent action to combat climate change and its impacts
14. Conserve and sustainably use the oceans, seas and marine resources for sustainable development.
15. Protect, restore and promote sustainable use of terrestrial ecosystems, sustainably manage forests, combat desertification, and halt and reverse land degradation and halt biodiversity loss.
16. Promote peaceful and inclusive societies for sustainable development, provide access to justice for all and build effective, accountable and inclusive institutions at all levels.
17. Strengthen the means of implementation and revitalize the global partnership for sustainable development.

## The Sustainable Development Goals Report 2018

The Sustainable Development Goals Report 2018 found that conflict and climate change were major contributing factors leading to growing numbers of people facing hunger and forced displacement, as well as curtailing progress towards universal access to basic water and sanitation services.

For the first time in more than a decade, there are now approximately 38 million more hungry people in the world, rising from 777 million in 2015 to 815 million in 2016. According to the report, conflict is now one of the main drivers of food insecurity in 18 countries. In 2017, the world experienced the costliest North Atlantic hurricane season on record, driving the global economic losses attributed to the disasters to over $300 billion.

At the same time, the Report found that more people are leading better lives than they were just a decade ago. The proportion of the world's workers living with their families on less than 1.90 per person a day declined significantly over the past two decades, falling from 26.9 per cent in 2000 to 9.2 per cent in 2017.

The under-five mortality rate dropped by almost 50 per cent and in the least developed countries, the proportion of population with access to electricity has more than doubled between 2000 and 2016. However, in 2015, 2.3 billion people still lacked even a basic level of sanitation service and 892 million people continued to practice open defecation. In 2016, there were 216 million cases of malaria compared to 210 million cases in 2013 and close to 4 billion people were left without social protection in 2016.

The SDG Report presents an overview of progress toward achieving the Goals, which were unanimously adopted by countries in 2015 the global community moves forward to achieve the SDGs and address existing challenges, reliable, timely, accessible and disaggregated data is critically needed. This requires technology and innovation, increased resources and political commitment to build strong data and statistical systems in all countries.

## Other findings of the Report include:

- Rates of child marriage have continued to decline around the world. In Southern Asia, a girl's risk of marrying in childhood has dropped by over 40 per cent between 2000 and 2017
- Nine out of 10 people living in cities breathe polluted air.
- In 2016, the absolute number of people living without electricity dropped below the symbolic threshold of one billion.
- Land degradation threatens the livelihoods of over one billion people.

# SUSTAINABLE DEVELOPMENT IN INDIA

India presented its strategies for sustainable development in the World Summit on Sustainable Development (WSSD), Johannesburg, South Africa which was held from 26 August - 4 September 2002. Empowering People for Sustainable Development (EPSD) the document introduces the essential framework for sustainable development in India. The framework included democratic continuity, devolution of power, independent judiciary, civil control over the armed forces, independent media, transparency and people's participation.

**The four objectives of EPSD were:** combating poverty, empowering people using core competence in science and technology and setting environmental standards.

# International Renewable Energy Agency (IRENA)

IRENA has 150 member nations with Headquarters in Abu Dhabi.

The International Renewable Energy Agency (IRENA) is an intergovernmental organisation that supports countries in their transition to a sustainable energy future, and serves as the principal platform for international cooperation, a centre of excellence, and a repository of policy, technology, resource and financial knowledge on renewable energy.

IRENA promotes the widespread adoption and sustainable use of all forms of renewable energy, including bioenergy, geothermal, hydropower, ocean, solar and wind energy in the pursuit of sustainable development, energy access, energy security and low-carbon economic growth and prosperity.

## National Action Plan for Climate Change (NAPCC)

India launched an ambitious NAPCC in June 2008 which seeks to chart out a responsible plan to combat climate change through a policy of sustainable development.

The following are the main principles of NAPCC:

- Protecting the poor through an inclusive and sustainable development strategy, sensitive to climate change;
- Achieving national growth and poverty alleviation objectives while ensuring ecological sustainability;
- Efficient and cost effective strategies for end-use-demand side management;
- Extensive and accelerated deployment of appropriate technologies for adaption and mitigation;
- New and innovative market, regulatory, and voluntary mechanisms for sustainable development and
- Effective implementation through unique linkages with civil society, local governments and public-private partnerships.

The **National Action Plan on Climate Change** identifies measures that promote our development objectives while yielding co-benefits for addressing climate change effectively.

It outlines a number of steps to simultaneously advance India's development and climate change-related objectives of adaptation and mitigation.

*It has set up eight national missions for India's sustainable development.*

### 1. National Solar Mission

Also known as **Jawaharlal Nehru National Solar Mission** was approved by Government of India on 11 January 2010. The Solar Mission was initiated with an aim to achieve long term Energy and Ecology security which was planned to implement in three stages to install the capacity of 20,000 MW by the end of the 13th Five Year Plan in 2022.

The three stages are as follows:

*Stage-I:* 2010-2013 target 1,000-2,000 MW.

*Stage-II:* 2013-2017 target 4,000-10,000 MW.

Stage-III: 2017-2022 target 20,000 MW.

Custom and excise duty for several input raw materials for manufacturing of solar power devices is exempted by the government to reduce the cost of solar power.

## INTERNATIONAL SOLAR ALLIANCE - 1

International Solar Alliance (ISA) is launched at the CoP21 Climate Conference in Paris on 30th November as a special platform for mutual cooperation among 121 solar resource rich countries lying fully or partially between Tropic of Cancer and Tropic of Capricorn.

The alliance is dedicated to address special energy needs of ISA member countries.

International Agency for Solar Policy and Application (IASPA) will be the formal name of International Solar Alliance. The ISA secretariat will be set up in National Institute of Solar Energy, Gurgaon.

### 2. National Mission for Enhanced Energy Efficiency

Current initiatives are expected to yield savings of 10,000 MW. Building on the Energy Conservation Act 2001, the plan recommends mandating specific energy consumption decreases in large energy-consuming industries, with a system for companies to trade energy-savings certificates; energy incentives; including reduced taxes on energy-efficient appliances, and financing for public-private partnerships to reduce energy consumption through demand-side management programmes in the municipal buildings and agricultural sectors.

### 3. National Mission on Sustainable Habitat

To promote energy efficiency as a core component of urban planning, the plan calls for; extending the existing energy conservation building code; a greater emphasis on urban waste management and recycling; including power production from waste; strengthening the enforcement of automotive fuel economy standards and using pricing measures to encourage the purchase of efficient vehicles; and incentives for the use of public transport.

### 4. National Water Mission

With water scarcity projected to worsen as a result of climate change, the plan sets a goal of a 20% improvement in water use efficiency through pricing and other measures.

### 5. National Mission for Sustaining the Himalayan Ecosystem

The plan aims to conserve biodiversity, forest cover, and other ecological values in the Himalayan region, where glaciers that are a major source of India's water supply are projected to recede as a result of global warming.

### 6. National Mission for a "Green India"

Goals include the afforestation of 6 million hectares of degraded forest lands and expanding forest cover from 23% to 33% of India's territory.

### 7. National Mission for Sustainable Agriculture

The plan aims to support climate adaption in agriculture through the development of climate-resilient crops, expansion of weather insurance mechanisms, and agricultural practices.

### 8. National Mission on Strategic Knowledge for Climate Change

To gain a better understanding of climate science, impacts and challenges, the plan envisions a new Climate Science Research Fund, improved climate modelling, and increased international collaboration. It also encourages private sector initiatives to develop adaption and mitigation technologies through venture capital fund.

## Strategies for Sustainable Development

### Use of Non-conventional Sources of Energy

India is hugely dependent on thermal and hydro power plants to meet its power needs. Both of these have adverse environmental impacts. Thermal power plants emit large quantities of carbon dioxide which is a green house gas. It also produces fly ash which, if not used properly, can cause pollution of water bodies, land and other components of the environment. Hydroelectric projects inundate forests and interfere with the natural flow of water in catchment areas and the river basins. Wind power and solar rays are good examples of conventional but cleaner and greener energy sources but are not yet been explored on a large scale due to lack of technological devices.

### LPG, Gobar Gas in Rural Areas

Households in rural areas generally use wood, dung cake or other biomass as fuel. This practice has several adverse implications like deforestation, reduction in green cover, wastage of cattle dung and air pollution. To rectify the situation, subsidised LPG is being provided. In addition, gobar gas plants are being provided through easy loans and subsidy. As far as liquefied petroleum gas (LPG) is concerned, it is a clean fuel — it reduces household pollution to a large extent. Also, energy wastage is minimised.

### CNG in Urban Areas:

In Delhi, the use of Compressed Natural Gas (CNG) as fuel in public transport system has significantly lowered air pollution and the air has become cleaner in the last few years.

### Wind Power:

In areas where speed of wind is usually high, wind mills can provide electricity without any adverse impact on the environment. Wind turbines move with the wind and electricity is generated. No doubt, the initial cost is high. But the benefits are such that the high cost gets easily absorbed.

### Solar Power through Photovoltaic Cells

India is naturally endowed with a large quantity of solar energy in the form of sunlight. We use it in different ways. Plants use solar energy to perform photosynthesis. Now, with the help of **photovoltaic cells,** solar energy can be converted into electricity. These cells use special kind of materials to capture solar energy and then convert the energy into electricity. This technology is extremely useful for remote areas and for places where supply of power through grid or power lines is either not possible or proves very costly. This technique is also totally free from pollution.

### Mini-hydel Plants

Mini-hydel plants use the energy streams to move small turbines. The turbines generate electricity which can be used locally. Such power plants are more or less environment-friendly as they do not change the land use pattern in areas where they are located; they generate enough power to meet local demands. This means that they can also do away with the need for large scale transmission towers and cables and avoid transmission loss.

### Traditional Knowledge and Practices

Traditionally, Indian people have been close to their environment. They have been more a component of the environment and not its controller. If we look back at our agriculture system, healthcare system, housing, transport, etc. we find that all practices have been environment friendly. Only recently have we drifted away from the traditional systems and caused large scale damage to the environment and also our rural heritage. Now, it is time to go back. One apt example is in healthcare. India is very much privileged to have about 15,000 species of plants which have medicinal properties. About 8,000 of these are in regular use in various systems of treatment including the folk tradition. With the sudden onslaught of the western system of treatment, we were ignoring our traditional systems such as Ayurveda, Unani, Tibetan and folk systems. Not only are these are environment friendly, they are relatively free from side effects and do not involve large-scale industrial and chemical processing.

### Biocomposting

Large tracts of productive land have been adversely affected, water bodies including ground water system have suffered due to chemical contamination and demand for irrigation has been going up year after year due to chemical fertilisers. Farmers, in large numbers all over the country, have again started using compost made from organic wastes of different types. Indirectly, the civic authorities are benefited too as they have to dispose reduced quantity of waste.

### Biopest Control

With the advent of **green revolution**, the entire country entered into a frenzy to use more and more chemical pesticides for higher yield. Soon, the adverse impacts began to show; food products were contaminated, soil, water bodies and even ground water were polluted with pesticides. Even milk, meat and fishes were found to be contaminated. To meet this challenge, efforts are on to bring in better methods of pest control. One such step is the use of pesticides based on plant products. Neem trees are proving to be quite useful.

## Budgetary Provisions

The country has been taking laudable and decisive steps in facilitating a low carbon economy with ambitious targets - renewable energy deployment of 175 GW installed capacity by 2022, development of 100 smart cities for its citizens, and implementation of a **Zero Defect Zero Effect** (ZED) approach in manufacturing. Such initiatives have the potential to not only drive economic growth but also improve quality of life. In this direction:

- Programme for sustainable management of ground water resources is allocated with ₹6,000 crore
- **Rashtriya Gram Swaraj Abhiyan** is allocated Rs. 655 crore. The scheme will help Panchayat Raj Institutions deliver Sustainable Development Goals.

India is also ramping up efforts to mobilise the finance needed to promote sustainable development, the most notable one, through a special budgetary provision of a coal cess, under the nation clean energy fund.

### National Clean Energy Fund.

Having raised ₹25,000 crore successfully since FY11, about one third of the fund is estimated to have been used to promote renewable energy and water resource management.

### Response to climate change

Climate change with its indelible impact on the financial system, has emerged as a priority in budget provisions, and needs an integrated response that can make India's economic growth more resilient through timely policy interventions and market reforms.

### Increase Budget Allocations to Key Sectors

The increased budget to the **Swachch Bharat Abhlyan** ($ 530 million or ₹3500 crore is expected to have a manifold impact on bringing down costs attributed to lack of sanitation. Similar opportunities exist in various sectors, which would serve the dual purpose of future-proofing the economy while mainstreaming sustainable practices:

- Increased funding towards sustainable agriculture could help adoption of newer technologies and climate resilient practices thus multiplying productivity;
- Increased budget for watershed management and ground water replenishment would contribute to water security;
- Allocating part of highway project costs to avenue plantations would increase India's carbon sink; and
- Channelising funds towards adoption of cleaner technologies (energy conservation, increased use of renewable energy and rainwater harvesting) in public infrastructure would mitigate climate related costs and increase resilience

*Align climate and development goals to financial systems*

The Department of Expenditure under the Ministry of Finance could identify climate and development related schemes, policies, initiatives and institutions to track the allocated budget with emphasis on outputs, deliverables, and impact assessment. In essence, this would evaluate the implementation progress of the Sustainable Development Goals (SDG) and the NDCs through robust and comparable data, while also putting SDG and NDC related budget allocations in perspective with other expenditure. This would also enable India Inc. to better align its own strategic and financial allocations to these goals.

*Incentivise states for effective implementation*

The third and perhaps the most important intervention could be to incentivise states based on effective implementation of climate and development related policies and projects. This would not only result in a healthy competition amongst states, but would also highlight the better performing states to potential investors, for channelising the 'patient capital' available globally.

*Deepen the green bond market*

One of the existing financial mechanisms driving the global economy's transition to a greener future is **Green bonds**. Since the first green bond in 2007, the market has grown exponentially, peaking in 2016, with cumulative issuances pegged at over $ 180 billion globally. A growing number of corporates and financial institutions have been able to attract foreign investments using green bonds, demonstrating how innovations in emerging markets have the potential to capture global attention.

The Securities and Exchange Board of India (SEBI), recognising green bonds as a key tool towards financing the nation's climate and development targets, has issued official guidelines for Indian green bond issuers, placing India amongst a select set of pioneering countries which has developed national level guidelines.

With the Indian Government's emphasis on municipal bonds to augment financing to urban local bodies, green municipal bonds have the potential to not only attract both domestic and global capital, but also bolster transparency and accountability in the civil bodies.

# Exercise -1

1. By the year 2022, India's target of producing power from wind energy is
   - (a) 50 GW
   - (b) 60 GW
   - (c) 75 GW
   - (d) 120 GW

2. The theme 'Transforming our world : 2030 Agenda' pertains to :
   - (a) Protection of ozone layer
   - (b) Climate change - Action plans
   - (c) Sustainable development goals
   - (d) Millennium development goals

3. Ratio of energy transfer at different trophic levels in the food chain is called :
   - (a) Metabolic efficiency
   - (b) Ecological efficiency
   - (c) Energy flow rate
   - (d) Food chain complexity

4. Green house effect is warming due to
   - (a) infra-red rays reaching earth
   - (b) moisture layer in atmosphere
   - (c) increase in temperature due to increase in carbon dioxide concentration of atmosphere
   - (d) ozone layer of atmosphere.

5. Sustainable Development Goals and targets are to be achieved by:
   - (a) 2020
   - (b) 2025
   - (c) 2030
   - (d) 2050

6. "A Million Voices: The World We Want" is report by:
   - (a) WHO
   - (b) IUCN
   - (c) UNISEF
   - (d) UN

7. Which among the following is not a target under sustainable development goals?
   - (a) Zero poverty
   - (b) Quality education
   - (c) Combat HIV/AIDS, Malaria and Other Diseases
   - (d) Decent work and economic growth

8. Sustainable Development implies:
   - (a) Sustained Development in real GDP
   - (b) Long lasting development without negatively impacting the environment
   - (c) Full exploitation of natural resources
   - (d) Reduction in unemployment and poverty

9. The objective of the Green energy Corridor is to:
   - (a) Create special industrial zones which will be powered by renewable energy.
   - (b) Fund geothermal based energy projects.
   - (c) Facilitate the flow of renewable energy into the national power grid.
   - (d) none of the above.

10. The 12th Five year plan aims at:
    - (a) Greening 5 million ha under Green India Mission.
    - (b) Integrated Ecotourism District Plans covering 10% of all potential Protected Areas (PAs) by 2017.
    - (c) Cleaning all the critically polluted rivers by 2020 and 80% by 2017.
    - (d) All of the above

11. National Mission for a Green India' under National Action Plan on Climate Change (NAPCC) is replacing:
    - (a) National Mission on Combating Desertification
    - (b) National Afforestation Programme
    - (c) Forest Conservation programme
    - (d) Joint Forest Management programme

12. The 'Neeranchal' initiative is for:
    - (a) Giving impetus to watershed development in the country
    - (b) Providing safe and clean drinking water
    - (c) Providing water for industries
    - (d) Popularizing drip and sprinkle irrigation

13. Which committee has been constituted to assess ground situation at Cauvery basin?
    - (a) M N Rao Committee
    - (b) KK Paul Committee
    - (c) GS Jha Committee
    - (d) SK Jha Committee

14. What is the theme of 2016 International Day for Disaster Reduction?
    - (a) My City is Getting Ready!
    - (b) Live to Tell
    - (c) Living with Disability and Disaster
    - (d) Resilience is for Life

15. Which of the following adjustments would be made to any increase in GDP in order to derive an 'Index of Sustainable Economic Welfare' (ISEW)?
    - (a) Subtract the monetary value of non-defensive public expenditures
    - (b) Subtract the monetary value of personal consumption
    - (c) Subtract the monetary value of capital formation
    - (d) Subtract the costs of environmental degradation

16. Which of the following is NOT a characteristic of the "emissions trading" policy instrument?
    - (a) It involves a mechanism whereby the permits available are initially distributed to producers who are potential emitters of a given pollutant
    - (b) The price mechanism for tradable emissions permits helps to allocate the restricted supply of permits to those who most value them
    - (c) All producers are required to be equally efficient in reducing emissions of the pollutant
    - (d) The right to pollute can be transferred between different parties at a price determined by the market in tradeable emissions permits

17. Which one of the following characteristics is widely regarded as being an important aspect of sustainable development?
    (a) Inter-generational equity
    (b) Increasing consumption expenditure
    (c) Intra-generational inequity
    (d) Increased levels of saving

18. Why is transport one of the most intractable factors in considering the global environmental problem?
    (a) Our transport capabilities worldwide have not expanded fast enough for us to cope with the consequences of global warming
    (b) Transport demand grows faster than possible technological improvements can reduce the output of greenhouse gases and the depletion of nonrenewable fossil fuel reserves
    (c) Reducing the growth of the transport sector will hold back economic growth, and hence reduce the resources we have available to deal with the global environmental problem
    (d) World oil refinery capacity has failed to expand in line with the demand for internal combustion fuels

19. What do we mean when we say "think globally, act locally" in relation to environmental problems?
    (a) Global environmental problems are essentially issues which need to be solved by international negotiations, and in the interim individuals must take care to protect themselves from any adverse consequences produced for them by these problems
    (b) Environmental problems have to be thought about at a global level in order to get an accurate idea of the total problem facing us, but these problems are essentially produced by our activities as individuals and firms at a local level, and it is at this level that we must focus our responses
    (c) Extensive research and thinking has been carried out by global level research organizations about the causes of environmental problems, which have produced possible strategies and actions which can be applied at a local level

    (d) While these problems, as we experience them in relation to sustainability issues, are produced by processes operating at a global level, we all have a role to play in our local context in making individual and collective responses, as communities and companies, which will help ameliorate the effects of these problems

20. Focusing on reducing carbon production to reduce carbon dioxide emissions is argued to be the wrong variable to focus on because:
    (a) It is impossible to achieve
    (b) The focus should be on carbon consumption
    (c) It has nothing to do with carbon dioxide emissions
    (d) The focus should be on carbon elimination

21. We have had twenty years of international conferences on what to do about the global environmental crisis, and some commentators say absolutely nothing has been achieved. This shows that:
    (a) There is a complete lack of international commitment to positive action
    (b) It is very difficult to devise appropriate policies
    (c) The environmental crisis is only one of the issues that nations negotiate about, and agreement on environmental issues has to be compatible with agreements on other issues, such as trade
    (d) There is no agreement on the environmental issues facing the global community

22. What is Rio+20 Conference, often mentioned in the news?　　　　　　　　　　　**[IAS Prelimes 2015]**
    (a) It is the United Nations Conference on Sustainable Development
    (b) It is a Ministerial Meeting of the World Trade Organization
    (c) It is a Conference of the Inter-governmental Panel on Climate Change
    (d) It is a Conference of the Member Countries of the Convention on Biological Diversity

# Exercise -2

1. Which of the following are the 17 new Sustainable Development Goals?
   1. Conserve and sustainably use the oceans, seas and marine resources
   2. Reduce inequality within and among countries
   3. Take urgent action to combat climate change and its impacts

   (a) 1, 3
   (b) 2, 3
   (c) 1, 2
   (d) All of the above

2. What is not true about "The Earth Summit in Rio de Janeiro 1992"?
   1. The first global environment conference, the UN sought to help Governments rethink economic development and find ways to halt the destruction of irreplaceable natural resources and pollution of the planet.
   2. The first global environment conference, the UN sought to help Governments rethink political development and find ways to halt the destruction of irreplaceable natural resources and pollution of the planet.
   3. The second global environmental conference, the UN sought to help Governments rethink environmental development and find ways to halt the destruction of irreplaceable natural resources and pollution of the planet.

   **Code:**
   (a) Only 1
   (b) Only 2
   (c) 1, 2, and 3
   (d) All are incorrect

3. Which of the following are correct regarding Sustainable development goals?
   1. They were accepted by the governments in COP 21
   2. There are total 17 goals present under SDG
   3. SDG talks about inequality within country only and nothing about in between the countries.

   **Codes:**
   (a) 1, 2
   (b) 2, 3
   (c) 2 only
   (d) All

4. Which of the following statement(s) is /are correct?
   1. The 8 Millennium Development Goals will be replaced by 17 Sustainable Development Goals.
   2. These 17 SDGs will be adopted by Member States at the Sustainable Development Summit in September 2015.

   **Codes:**
   (a) Only 1
   (b) Only 2
   (c) Both 1 and 2
   (d) None of the above

5. Consider the following statements about the Pradhan Mantri Surakshit Matritva Abhiyan (PMSMA):
   1. The programme aims to reduce maternal and infant mortality rates through safe pregnancies and safe deliveries
   2. The programme provides comprehensive and quality antenatal care to pregnant women on the 9th of every month in government hospitals
   3. The programme also involves the doctors from the private sector to provide free services

   Which of the above statements are correct?
   **Code:**
   (a) 1 & 2 Only
   (b) 2 & 3 Only
   (c) 1 & 3 Only
   (d) 1, 2 & 3

6. Consider the following statement(s) related to Rio+20, 1992
   1. Securing renewed political commitment for inclusive development
   2. Assessing the progress and implementation gaps in meeting previous commitments
   3. Addressing new and emerging challenges

   What is/are not the objectives of Rio+20, 1992 Conference?
   **Code:**
   (a) Only 1
   (b) Only 2
   (c) Only 1 & 2
   (d) 1, 2, 3

7. Which of the followings are the aims of the Basel Convention?
   1. The reduction of hazardous waste generation and the promotion of environmentally sound management of hazardous wastes, wherever the place of disposal;
   2. The restriction of trans-boundary movements of hazardous wastes except where it is perceived to be in accordance with the principles of environmentally sound management.
   3. A regulatory system applying to cases where trans-boundary movements are permissible

   **Codes:**
   (a) Only 1 & 2
   (b) Only 1 & 3
   (c) Only 2 & 3
   (d) All of the above

8. The United Nations General Assembly (UNGA) has declared the year 2017 as the International Year of Sustainable Tourism Development. In this context consider the following statements:
   1. The declaration recalls to advance the universal 2030 Agenda
   2. Tourism falls under three targets of the SDGs, i. e., Goals—8, 12 and 14
   3. UNTO is the United Nations Specialized Agency for Tourism

   What is/are correct?
   **Codes:**
   (a) Only 3
   (b) Only 1 & 3
   (c) Only 2
   (d) Only 1 & 2

9. In the context of recently concluded sixth edition of Asia Pacific Ministerial Conference on Housing and Urban Development (APMCHUD), New Delhi, consider the following statements;
   1. Urban Agenda was adopted at the UN Conference on Housing and Sustainable Urban Development, known as "Habitat 3" conference

2. APMCHUD is an intergovernmental mechanism for collaboration and cooperation in the field of housing and development among East Asia countries.
3. It adopted Delhi Declaration and implementation plan for aligning urban development strategies of member countries with New Urban Agenda adopted at Quito, Eucador.
4. Asia Pacific Region accounts for 60% of the world population and 55% of global urban population. Find the correct answer from the given code.

**Code:**
(a) Only 1, 2 & 4　　(b) Only 1, 2 & 3
(c) Only 1, 3 & 4　　(d) All of the above

10. India has achieved the poverty reduction target, however, progress is uneven. In this context consider the following statements.
1. In order to meet the 2015 target, the PHCR level has to be 23.9%.
2. India developed its position due to economic growth including in agriculture as well as increased social spending on interventions such as MGNREGA and the National Rural Health Mission (NRHM).
3. By 2030, eradicate extreme poverty for all people everywhere, currently measured as people living on less than $1.25 a day
4. A cut by the union government in the social sector schemes will not be a challenge to achieve goal 1.
Which of the following statement(s) is/are correct?

**Code:**
(a) Only 3 & 4　　(b) Only 1, 2 & 3
(c) Only 1 & 3　　(d) All of the above

11. Consider the following statements
1. The sustainable development goals were first proposed in 1972 by a global think tank called the 'Club of Rome'
2. The sustainable Development Goals have to be achieved by 2030.
Which of the statements given above is/are correct?
(a) 1 only　　(b) 2 only
(c) Both 1 and 2　　(d) Neither 1 nor 2

12. Which of the following best describes/describe the aim of 'Green India Mission' of the Government of India
1. Incorporating environmental benefits and costs into the Union and State Budgets there by implementing the 'green accounting'
2. Launching the second green revolution to enhance agricultural output so as to ensure food security to one and all in the future
3. Restoring and enhancing forest cover responding to climate change by a combination of adaptation and mitigation measures
Select the correct answer using the code given below:
(a) Only 1　　(b) Only 2 and 3
(c) Only 3　　(d) Only 1, 2 and 3

13. Which of the following statements regarding 'Green Climate Fund' is/are correct?
1. It is intended to assist the developing countries in adaptation and mitigation practices to counter climate change.

2. It is founded under the aegis of UNEP, OECD, Asian Development Bank and World Bank.
Select the correct answer using the code given below:
(a) 1 only　　(b) 2 only
(c) Both 1 and 2　　(d) Neither 1 nor 2

14. The 'Kudumba shree' Programme is:
1. A woman oriented community based poverty eradication programme.
2. A programme to encourage savings among poor women.
3. A programme to provide monetary assistance to the women to meet the cost of delivery.
Which of the above statement(s) is/are correct?
(a) Only 1 and 2　　(b) Only 3
(c) Only 1　　(d) 1, 2 and 3

15. With reference to the International Union for Conservation of Nature and Natural Resources (IUCN) and the Convention on International Trade in Endangered Species of Wild Fauna and Flora (CITES), which of the following statements is/are correct?
1. IUCN is an organ of the United Nations and CITES is an international agreement between governments.
2. IUCN runs thousands of field projects around the world to better manage natural environments.
3. CITES is legally binding on the States that have joined it, but this Convention does not take the place of national laws.
Select the correct answer using the code given below.

**Code:**
(a) Only 1　　(b) Only 2 and 3
(c) Only 1 and 3　　(d) 1, 2 and 3

16. Which of the following is incorrect about organic farming:-
1. It uses biological pest control techniques
2. It saves water
3. It can immediately meet the goals of food security
4. It uses fertilizers
Select the correct answers using the choices given below:
(a) 2 only　　(b) 1 & 2 only
(c) 2 & 3 only　　(d) 2 & 4 only

17. Consider the following statements:
1. The Sustainable Development Goals were first proposed in 1972 by a global think tank called the 'Club of Rome'.
2. The Sustainable Development Goals have to be achieved by 2030.
Which of the statements given above is/are correct?
(a) 1 only　　(b) 2 only
(c) Both 1 and 2　　(d) Neither 1 nor 2

18. With reference to 'Agenda 21', sometimes seen in the news, consider the following statements:
**[IAS Prelimes 2016]**
1. It is a global action plan for sustainable development
2. It originated in the World Summit on Sustainable Development held in Johannesburg in 2002.
Which of the statements given above is/are correct?
(a) 1 only　　(b) 2 only
(c) Both 1 and 2　　(d) Neither 1 nor 2

# Hints and Explanations



1. (b)  2. (c)  3. (b)  4. (c)

5. (c) According to 'Transforming our world Agenda' countries will have the opportunity to adopt a set of global goals to end poverty, protect the planet, and ensure prosperity for all as part of a new sustainable development agenda. Each goal has specific targets to be achieved over the next 15 years i.e. 2030.

6. (d) The voices of more than 1 million people all over the world were gathered to produce a United Nations report that reflects their priorities concerning development issues, which will help Member States shape the post-2015 sustainability agenda.

7. (c) Combat HIV/AIDS, Malaria and Other Diseases is not a target of sustainable development while others are.

8. (b) Brutland Commission in our Common Future, also known as the Brutland Report defined sustainable development as—development that meets the needs of the present without compromising the ability of future generations to meet their own needs. Option (a) and (d) are partially true while option (c) is negative to the concept.

9. (c) Facilitates the flow of renewable energy into the national power grid. The aim of the 'green energy corridor' project is to facilitate the flow of renewable energy into the national grid. The 'green energy corridor' is aimed at synchronizing electricity produced from renewable sources, such as solar and wind, with conventional power stations in the grid.

10. (d)      11. (b)

12. (a) It will bring about institutional changes in watershed and rainfed agricultural management practices in India.

13. (c) The Union Ministry for Water Resources, River Development and Ganga Rejuvenation has constituted a high-level technical team to visit the river Cauvery basin area in Karnataka and Tamil Nadu to assess the ground situation. GS Jha, the Chairman of Central Water Commission (CWC), will head the Cauvery supervisory committee.

14. (b) The International Day for Disaster Reduction (IDDR) is observed annually on 13 October across the world encourage citizens and governments to take part in building more disaster resilient communities and nations. The day seeks to spread awareness about reining the risks of disasters around the world and also reduce exposure of people and communities to disasters. "Live to Tell: Raising Awareness, Reducing Mortality" is the theme for 2016. The 2016 edition of IDDR marks the launch of the new Sendai Framework for Disaster Risk Reduction by United Nations Office for Disaster Risk Reduction (UNISDR). UNISDR's campaign for the day is Sendai Seven that seeks to create a wave of awareness about actions taken to reduce mortality around the world.

15. (d) An increase in GDP is conventionally used as a measure of how much better off we are getting. But it includes expenditures on things which are actually related to how much worse off we are getting (such as expenditures on goods to protect ourselves from assault with increasing crime levels e.g. guns), and does not include things such as the costs of the destruction of our natural environment, which everyone would value as part of their overall level of economic welfare. This is included in a measure such as ISEW. So increasing GDP can be consistent with declining ISEW.

16. (c) The point here is that typically firms will be unequally efficient in reducing emissions, and the trading mechanism will over time create a situation where the least environmentally efficient firms will have to buy permits to cover their excess emissions, and this will give them an incentive to move to less polluting production methods.

17. (a) Fairness or equity within and between generations are two key ideas of the notion of sustainable development, so inter-generational equity was the one to select here. The other alternatives are either irrelevant or inimical to the achievement of sustainable development (increased saving might be indirectly relevant, depending on what the saving was used for.)

18. (b) The first and fourth alternatives are clearly ruled out which do not have anything to do with environmental problems, except to make them worse. The second alternative is clearly correct, but the third has just enough of a grain of truth to lead the unwary astray. In fact, this argument is actually put forward in some circles, and relates back to some very involved arguments about the relationship between transport and economic development. Apart from the issue of the immediacy of our global environmental problem, vis-a-vis the long term nature of potential gains in economic growth from transport investment, a basic problem for those who support this argument is that research over many years has failed to demonstrate that transport investment reliably produces the economic growth effects claimed for it.

19. (d) While these problems, as we experience them in relation to sustainability issues, are produced by processes operating at a global level, we all have a role to play in our local context in making individual and collective responses, as communities and companies, which will help ameliorate the effects of these problems.

20. (b) In a situation where many countries such as UK after many years have made little progress towards achieving their Kyoto emissions reduction targets, critics are starting to point out that the situation would be much worse if these countries had not managed to get reduce their carbon production by exporting it to countries like China, by de facto exporting jobs.

But the effect is illusionary, because we still import back from countries such as China the goods which we might have produced ourselves. Of course, the reason for exporting the jobs in the first place is to take advantage of low cost production locations. But if we keep consuming as we did before, at a global level nothing is achieved. We need to focus on carbon consumption. Hence 'The focus should be on carbon consumption' is the correct answer; 'It is impossible to achieve' is not true, as carbon production can be reduced at an aggregate level; 'It has nothing to do with carbon dioxide emissions' is simply wrong, as it is very much to do with carbon dioxide emissions; while 'The focus should be on carbon elimination' is merely a red herring; it does not mean anything.

21. (c) It would be very difficult to argue that nations generally are not committed to positive action in this area, so 'There is a complete lack of international commitment to positive action' is not correct. But of course, 'commitment' is a difficult word, as the outcomes of a conference are not simple yes/no statements, but complex agreements where individual nations, or blocks of nations, have priorities which others find difficult to accede to. Equally, there is no denying that it can be difficult to devise appropriate policies, but there is no doubt that over the years there has been evident progress, so 'It is very difficult to devise appropriate policies' is not correct. Of course, the big problem in reaching international agreement on climate issues is that not only are the issues to be resolved within these conferences highly complex, but the conferences do not take place in isolation from international discussions and debates on other issues, and environmental issues might for a group of nations be a bargaining counter from which concessions on some other entirely unrelated issue can be secured. So 'The environmental crisis is only one of the issues that nations negotiate about, and agreement on environmental issues has to be compatible with agreements on other issues, such as trade' is the correct answer here.

22. (a) The United Nations Conference on Environment and Development (UNCED), also known as the Rio Summit or Earth Summit. It was a major United Nations conference held in Rio de Janeiro from 3 to 14 June 1992. In 2012, the United Nations Conference on Sustainable Development was also held in Rio, and is also commonly called Rio+20 or Rio Earth Summit 2012.

### EXERCISE - 2

1. (d) The goals are to be achieved in 15 years i.e. till 2030. The goals are –
   1. Build resilient infrastructure, promote inclusive and sustainable industrialization and foster innovation
   2. Reduce inequality within and among countries
   3. Ensure sustainable consumption and production patterns
   4. Take urgent action to combat climate change and its impacts
   5. Conserve and sustainably use the oceans, seas and marine resources for sustainable development
   6. Protect, restore and promote sustainable use of terrestrial ecosystems, sustainably manage forests, combat desertification, and halt and reverse land degradation and halt biodiversity loss
   7. Promote peaceful and inclusive societies for sustainable development, provide access to justice for all and build effective, accountable and inclusive institutions at all levels
   8. Strengthen the means of implementation and revitalize the global partnership for sustainable development

2. (a) From 3-14 June 1992, Rio de Janeiro hosted the United Nations Conference on Environment and Development (UNCED). The focus of this conference was the state of the global environment and the relationship between economics, science and the environment in a political context. The conference concluded with the Earth Summit, at which leaders of 105 nations gathered to demonstrate their commitment to sustainable development. In 1972, Stockholm, Sweden, hosted the first United Nations Conference on the Human Environment, which was attended by 113 delegates and two heads of state. Therefore option (a) is correct in the given context.

3. (c)    4. (c)

5. (d) Pradhan Mantri Surakshit Matritva Abhiyan (PMSMA) is a national social movement which shall engage the doctors from the private sector and other stakeholders to deliver free services at government hospitals on 9th of every month. The programme is poised to work towards achieving the Sustainable Development Goals (SDGs) in maternal and child healthcare. The programme aims to reduce the Infant Mortality Rate (IMR), Maternal Maternity Rate (MMR).

6. (a)    7. (d)

8. (d) The World Tourism Organization (UNWTO), the United Nations Specialized Agency for Tourism, has been mandated to facilitate the organization and implementation of the International Year, in collaboration with governments, relevant organizations of the United Nations system, international and regional organizations and other relevant stakeholders. The United Nations General Assembly (UNGA) has declared the year 2017 as the International Year of Sustainable Tourism for Development. Tourism is under three targets of the SDGs: They are (i) Goal 8: Promote sustained, inclusive and sustainable economic growth, full and productive employment and decent work for all. (ii) Goal 12: Sustainable Consumption and Production and (iii) Goal 14: Conserve and sustainably use the oceans, seas and marine resources for sustainable development.

9. (c) APMCHUD is an intergovernmental mechanism for collaboration and cooperation in the field of hous-

ing and development among Asia Pacific countries. Therefore statement II is wrong. Other statements are correct.

10. **(b)** A cut by the union government in the social sector schemes will not be a challenge to achieve goal 1 is wrong because social schemes are meant for poverty eradication. Other statements are correct.

11. **(b)** At the United Nations Sustainable Development Summit on 25 September 2015, world leaders adopted the 2030 Agenda for Sustainable Development, which includes a set of 17 Sustainable Development Goals (SDGs) to end poverty, fight inequality and injustice, and tackle climate change by 2030. The history of the SDGs can be traced to 1972 when governments met under the auspices of the United Nations Human and Environment Conference. The 'Club of Rome' is a global think tank that deals with a range of international political issues.

12. **(c)** The National Mission for Green India (GIM) is one of the eight Missions outlined under the National Action Plan on Climate Change (NAPCC). It aims at protecting; restoring and enhancing India's diminishing forest cover and responding to climate change by a combination of adaptation and mitigation measures. It envisages a holistic view of greening and focuses on multiple ecosystem services, especially, biodiversity, water, biomass, preserving mangroves, wetlands, critical habitats etc. along with carbon sequestration as a co-benefit. This mission has adopted an integrated cross-sectoral approach as it will be implemented on both public as well as private lands with a key role of the local communities in planning, decision making, implementation and monitoring.

13. **(a)** The Green Climate Fund (GCF) is a fund within the framework of the UNFCCC founded as a mechanism to redistribute money from the developed to the developing world, in order to assist the developing countries in adaptation and mitigation practices to counter climate change. The Green Climate Fund was designated as an operating entity of the financial mechanism of the UNFCCC, in accordance with Article 11 of the Convention. Arrangements will be concluded between the Conference of the Parties (COP) and the Fund to ensure that it is accountable to, and functions under the guidance of, the COP. The Fund is governed and supervised by a Board that will have full responsibility for funding decisions and that receives the guidance of the COP.

14. **(a)**

15. **(b)** IUCN is a voluntary organization, not an agency of United Nations.. Some facts about IUCN: Founded in 1948 as the world's first global environmental organization ; Today the largest professional global conservation network ; A leading authority on the environment and sustainable development ; More than 1,200 member organizations including 200 government and 900 non-government organizations ; A neutral forum for governments, NGOs, scientists, business and local communities to find practical solutions to conservation and development challenges; Thousands of field projects and activities around the world

16. **(c)**

17. **(b)** At the United Nations Sustainable Development Summit on 25 September 2015, world leaders adopted the 2030 Agenda for Sustainable Development, which includes a set of 17 Sustainable Development Goals (SDGs) to end poverty, fight inequality and injustice, and tackle climate change by 2030. The history of the SDGs can be traced to 1972 when governments met under the auspices of the United Nations Human and Environment Conference. The 'Club of Rome' is a global think tank that deals with a range of international political issues.

18. **(a)** Agenda 21 is a non-binding, voluntarily implemented action plan of the United Nations with regards to sustainable development. It is a product of the Earth Summit held in Rio de Janeiro, Brazil, in 1992. Therefore, only first statement right.

# 8 Chapter

# CONVENTIONS, POLICIES, REPORTS & TERMS

## ENVIRONMENTAL SUMMITS/ CONVENTIONS

### Ramsar Convention, 1971

This convention is adopted for the protection of wetlands. It recognises ecological functions and the economic, cultural, scientific and recreational values of wetlands. Under this, the state parties should designate at least one national wetland of international importance. Parties should assess the impact of any change of use of wetlands, should establish wetland as natural reserves, manage and make wisely use of the migratory stocks of waterfowl (bird) etc.

## The 1972 United Nations Conference on Human Environment

The Conference was organised by the United Nations General Assembly in Stockholm from 5 to 16 June, 1972. It provided a general framework for the preservation and conservation of human environment. It provided common principles to inspire and guide people of the world in the preservation and enhancement of the human environment.

Conservation of environment remained a dominant theme in the conference. Trends underway before the Stockholm Conference relating to marine pollution, transboundary air and water pollution, and protection of wild and marine endangered species were reinforced. The issue of relationship between development and environmental degradation was only peripherally addressed in the Conference.

The Conference adopted three non-binding instruments:

1. A resolution on institutional and financial arrangement;
2. A declaration containing 26 principles; and
3. An action plan containing 109 recommendations

## World Heritage Convention, 1972

It highlights the universal value of the cultural and natural heritage. It advocates the international support for maintenance of the **World Heritage sites**. A state party has an obligation to identify, protect, conserve and transmit to future generations the unique cultural and natural Heritage of that country. Those sites that are nominated by the states will be enlisted on the World Heritage list.



The coveted title of a world heritage site is granted by United Nations Educational, Scientific and Cultural Organisation (UNESCO). To qualify for the status, a site must possess the following attributes: It should represent a masterpiece of human creative genius, exhibit an important interchange of human values over a span of time, be an outstanding example of type of traditional human settlement or land-use, especially when it has become vulnerable under the impact of irreversible change. Some of the **World Heritage sites in** the **South Asian region** include the Archaeological Ruins of Mohenjodaro and Taxila in Pakistan, Historic Mosque City of Bagerhat, Ruins of Buddhist Vihara at Paharpur, Sagarmatha National Park, Royal Chitwan National Park, Lumbini (birthplace of Buddha), Ruined city of Anuradhapura, monumental remains of Polonnaruwa and Galle, the Golden Temple of Dambulla in SriLanka.

## World Heritage sites in India

### Cultural (29)

- Agra Fort (1983)
- Ajanta Caves (1983)
- Archaeological Site of Nalanda Mahavihara at Nalanda, Bihar (2016)
- Buddhist Monuments at Sanchi (1989)
- Champaner-Pavagadh Archaeological Park (2004)
- Chhatrapati Shivaji Terminus (formerly Victoria Terminus) (2004)
- Churches and Convents of Goa (1986)
- Elephanta Caves (1987)
- Ellora Caves (1983)
- Fatehpur Sikri (1986)
- Great Living Chola Temples (1987,2004)
- Group of Monuments at Hampi (1986)
- Group of Monuments at Mahabalipuram (1984)
- Group of Monuments at Pattadakal (1987)

- Hill Forts of Rajasthan (2013)
- Historic City of Ahmadabad (2017)
- Humayun's Tomb, Delhi (1993)
- Khajuraho Group of Monuments (1986)
- Mahabodhi Temple Complex at Bodh Gaya (2002)
- Mountain Railways of India (1999,2005,2008)
- Qutb Minar and its Monuments, Delhi (1993)
- Rani-ki-Vav (the Queen's Stepwell) at Patan, Gujarat (2014)
- Red Fort Complex (2007)
- Rock Shelters of Bhimbetka (2003)
- Sun Temple, Konarak (1984)
- Taj Mahal (1983)
- The Architectural Work of Le Corbusier, an Outstanding Contribution to the Modern Movement (2016)
- The Jantar Mantar, Jaipur (2010)
- Victorian Gothic and Art Deco Ensembles of Mumbai (2018)

**Natural (7)**

- Great Himalayan National Park Conservation Area (2014)
- Kaziranga National Park (1985)
- Keoladeo National Park (1985)
- Manas Wildlife Sanctuary (1985)
- Nanda Devi and Valley of Flowers National Parks (1988,2005)
- Sundarbans National Park (1987)
- Western Ghats (2012)

**Mixed (1)**

- Khangchendzonga National Park (2016)

## London Dumping Convention, 1972

This Convention is designed to control the dumping of wastes in the sea. It requires the states to limit the dumping of such substances as radioactive material, biological and chemical warfare agents, persistent plastics, heavy metals and toxic organics. In 1993, bans on the ocean disposal of low level radioactive material and industrial wastes were adopted. A protocol was added in 1996. Under this, seven more substances were listed. These substances can be dumped only after getting permission.

## Marpol Convention, 1973/78

This Convention is aimed at preventing or reducing the discharges (international or accidental) from ships into seas. It greatly limits the amount of oil spill and ship generated waste which can be discharged into the sea. There is a complete ban against dumping in areas designated as special areas, for example, in the Caribbean Sea and Gulf of Mexico.

## CITES, 1973 (Convention on International Trade in Endangered Species)

Under this convention, parties should identify species that are, or may be threatened by trade. They should also identify those species that may be threatened unless the trade is regulated. The former should be listed in Appendix I and the latter in Appendix-II. Commercial trade is forbidden for species listed in Appendix-I, for example, dolphins and whales. While not banned, the trade is strictly regulated in respect of species listed in Appendix-II.

| ENDANGERED SPECIES |
|---|

According to the **World Wildlife Fund**, by the year 2025, one fifth of the existing species could be extinct. Following are some of the endangered species:

***Sumatran Tiger.*** This is listed as critically endangered with the total population estimated at just 400 to 500. The world lost more than 90% of its tiger population in the 20th century and there are fewer than 5,000 alive in the wild, mainly in India, China, Siberia and Indonesia. Three of eight tiger sub-species are extinct: the Bali tiger, the Caspian tiger and the Javan tiger.

***Sumatran oran-utang.*** With the forest habitats being cut down or burnt, these species are estimated at 4,000 to 6,000. In 1997, forest fires throughout Indonesia saw many oran-utangs flee into the hands of captors and hunters, although some were relocated to reserves. The species could be extinct by 2010, in case they are not protected.

***Northern White Rhino.*** There are thought to be fewer than 25 northern white rhinos, all in Garamba National Park, Africa, and they are one of the world's 12 most endangered species. The decline has been attributed to poaching by rebel troops in Congo.

***Snow leopard.*** The existing number is estimated to be fewer than 2,500 as the species is declining in China, Russia and Pakistan and is on the verge of extinction in Mongolia. The illegal trade in the bones and body parts for traditional medicines threatens its survival.

***Mountain Guerilla.*** Only 650 are said to be alive in the Virunga range of volcanic mountains on the borders of Congo, Rwanda and Uganda.

***Giant Panda.*** According to a survey, China's giant panda population is estimated at 160. The Chinese Government established 10 panda reserves, protecting about 45% of the panda habitat.

## Law of the Sea Convention, 1982 (Parts V & XII)

It seeks to protect and preserve the marine environment. It directs the states to take measures to prevent, reduce and control the marine pollution, protect fragile ecosystems, monitor risk/effects of marine pollution etc. A state should not cause damage to the other states by pollution. It should notify other states where marine environment is in imminent danger. In the **EEZ (Exclusive Economic Zone)**, there should not be over exploration of living resources by the coastal state.

## Vienna Convention on the Protection of the Ozone Layer, 1985 & Montreal Protocol, 1987

Ozone is a protective layer of the atmosphere. It shields the earth from the Sun's harmful radiation. We all know that CFCs (Chlorofluorocarbons) deplete ozone. The Vienna Convention, 1985 followed by 1987 Montreal Protocol aims at phasing out the production and consumption of ozone depleting substances. The **Montreal Protocol** sets firm targets for the states for phasing out the CFCs. But it has permitted the developing states to delay their compliance of the protocol. It has also provided for the transfer of necessary technology to the developing states. The convention also restricts the trading of ozone depleting substances.

## Basel Convention (On the control of Trans-boundary Movements of Hazardous Wastes), 1989

Hazardous wastes cause severe damage. Most often these Hazardous Wastes (hereafter referred as to HW) are exported by the developed states to the developing states. Therefore, this convention has special significance to them. This convention seeks to minimise the level of HW from its source of generation. No export is allowed to the countries which prohibit the HW unless consent is given by them. There should also be no export if there is a reason to believe that these wastes will not be managed by the importer in an environment friendly and sound manner. The availability of disposal facilities in the importing state should be ensured by the exporting state before exporting the HW. State parties should develop and prescribe guidelines for environmentally sound management of HW.

# Climate Change Convention, 1992

Long term fluctuations in temperature and other aspects are known as climate change. Global warming is a major environment problem shaking the entire world. It is caused due to the GHG (Green House Gas) emissions. According to the United Nations, climate change is "change of climate that is attributed to human activity that alters the composition of the global atmosphere and which is in addition to natural climate variability observed over comparable time periods ". This convention aims to stabilise the GHG emissions. The convention lays down general commitments applicable to all (annexed as well as non-annexed) state parties. These are to limit GHG emissions, gather relevant information, develop plans to mitigate and adapt to climate change, and cooperate in research and development.

Under the convention, state parties fall into two categories, Annexed and NonAnnexed states. Annexed states are sub-divided into Annex - I (consisting of industrial states, OECD states and economies in transition) and Annex-II states (consisting only of OECD States). Annex-I states have specific commitments to bring down their GHG emission to 1990 level. The Annex-II states also have to bring down the GHG emissions but their baseline limit is not 1990. The baseline can be voluntarily fixed by them. In 1997, Kyoto Protocol was attached to the convention to supplement it. By this, the specific and legally binding targets are fixed for the industrialised states to cut at least 5% from 1990 level. The target period is from 2008 to 2012. The Protocol also suggested the mechanisms for the fulfilment of targets.

## Biodiversity Convention, 1992

It is the first global treaty which adopted a comprehensive ecosystems approach. Biodiversity is very essential for ensuring sustainable development. Initially the North wanted to declare biodiversity as the Common Heritage of Mankind. But the South refused because it wanted to retain the sovereign supremacy over its biodiversity. The convention outlined 3 objectives:

(1) Conservation of biodiversity.
(2) Sustainable use of the components of biodiversity and
(3) Fair and equitable sharing of the benefits of using biodiversity.

Under the convention, the states have obligations to develop national programmes for conserving and sustainably using the biodiversity, prepare inventories of bio - resources, take ex-situ & in situ conservation measures, establish a system of protected areas etc; it should be noted that the South is very rich in its biodiversity. Therefore, it has high stakes in this convention.

The Cartagena Protocol is an attachment to biodiversity convention. It is based on the precautionary principle. The benefits and dangers of biotechnology are not fully known. Therefore according to this Protocol, adequate measures of protection must be taken in matters of transfer, handling and use of living modified organisms.

## UN Convention on Desertification, 1994

States are directed to give priority to combat desertification and mitigate the effects of drought. They have to prepare and implement the national programmes in this regard. The CCD, as it is popularly called, endorses and employs a 'bottom-up' approach to international environmental cooperation. Its activities are related to the control and alleviation of desertification and the effects are to be closely linked to the needs and participation of local land users.

The Parties to the Convention have to make the prevention of desertification a priority in national policies and must promote awareness of desertification among their citizens.

## Stockholm Convention

Stockholm Convention on Persistent Organic Pollutants is an international environmental treaty, signed in 2001 and effective from May 2004, that aims to eliminate or restrict the production and use of persistent organic pollutants.

# Marrakech Climate Change Conference - November 2016

- The twenty-second session of the **Conference of the Parties** (COP 22), the twelfth session of the Conference of the Parties serving as the meeting of the Parties to the Kyoto Protocol (CMP 12), and the first session of the Conference of the Parties serving as the meeting of the Parties to the Paris Agreement (CMA 1) were held in **Bab Ighli**, Marrakech, Morocco from 7 November to 18 November 2016.

- The Conference successfully demonstrated to the world that the implementation of the Paris Agreement is underway and the constructive spirit of multilateral cooperation on climate change continues.

# United Nations Climate Change Conference

- The United Nations Framework Convention on Climate Change (**UNFCCC**) has come into the existence on 21 March 1994. Till date, it has near-universal membership.

The **197 countries** that have ratified the Convention are called **Parties to the Convention**.

- The UNFCCC is a "**Rio Convention**", one of three adopted at the "**Rio Earth Summit**" in 1992. Its sister Rio Conventions are the UN Convention on Biological Diversity and the Convention to Combat Desertification. The three are intrinsically linked. It is in this context that the Joint Liaison Group was set up to boost cooperation among the three conventions, with the ultimate aim of developing synergies in their activities on issues of mutual concern. It now also incorporates the **Ramsar Convention** on Wetlands.

- Preventing "dangerous" human interference with the climate system is the ultimate aim of the UNFCCC.

## List of United Nations Climate Change Conferences known as Conferences of Parties (COP)

| UN Climate Change Conference | Date and Place | Agenda | Decision/Resolution |
|---|---|---|---|
| COP 1 | From 28 March to 7 April 1995 in Berlin, Germany | • It voiced concerns about the adequacy of countries' abilities to meet commitments under the Body for Scientific and Technological Advice (SBSTA) and the Subsidiary Body for Implementation (SBI). | • COP 1 agreed on "Activities Implemented Jointly", first joint measures in international climate action. |
| COP 2 | July 1996 in Geneva, Switzerland | • Its ministerial declaration was noted (but not adopted) on 18 July 1996. | • Accepted the scientific findings on climate change preffered by the IPCC in its second assessment (1995).<br>• Rejected uniform "harmonized policies" in favor of flexibility.<br>• Called for "legally binding mid-term targets". |
| COP 3 (also known as **Kyoto Protocol**) | December 1997 in Kyoto, Japan | • The greenhouse gas emissions reduction obligation. | • It adopted the Kyoto Protocol and outlined the greenhouse gas emissions reduction obligation for Annex I countries.<br>• Kyoto mechanisms such as emissions trading, clean development mechanism and joint implementation.<br>• Annex B countries agreed to legally binding reductions in greenhouse gas emissions of an average of 6 to 8% below 1990 levels between the years 2008–2012.<br>• The United States would be required to reduce its total emissions on an average of 7% below 1990 levels. |
| COP 4 | November 1998 in Buenos Aires | • The unresolved issues in Kyoto would be finalized at this meeting. | • The parties adopted a 2-year "Plan of Action" to advance efforts and to devise mechanisms for implementing the Kyoto Protocol, to be completed by 2000.<br>• Argentina and Kazakhstan expressed their commitment to take on the greenhouse gas emissions reduction obligation, the first two non-Annex countries to do so. |
| COP 5 | From 25 October to 5 November 1999, in Bonn, Germany | • Only a primary a technical meeting | • No major conclusion. |
| COP 6 | From 13 November to 25 November 2000, in The Hague, Netherlands. | • High-level negotiation over the major political issues.<br>• The United States' proposal to allow credit for carbon "sinks" in forests and agricultural lands.<br>• How developing countries could obtain financial assistance to deal with adverse effects of climate change and meet their obligations to plan for measuring and possibly reducing greenhouse gas emissions. | • Disagreements over consequences for non-compliance by countries that did not meet their emission reduction targets.<br>• Compromises agreed between the United States and some EU countries.<br>• Rejected the compromise positions.<br>• The talks in The Hague collapsed.<br>• Jan Pronk, the President of COP 6, suspended COP-6 without agreement while it was later announced that the COP 6 meetings (termed "COP 6 bis") would be resumed in Bonn, Germany, in the second half of July. |

| | | | |
|---|---|---|---|
| COP 6<br><br>Negotiation resumed) | From 17 July to 27 July 2001, in Bonn, Germany | • Flexible mechanism<br>• Joint implementation<br>• Clean Development Mechanism<br>• Carbon sinks<br>• Compliance<br>• Financing | • It was agreed that credit would be granted for broad activities that absorb carbon from the atmosphere or store it, including forest and cropland management, and re-vegation, with no over-all cap on the amount of credit that a country could claim for sinks activities.<br>• A cap of 13 million tons could be credited to Japan (which represents about 4% of its base-year emissions).<br>• For cropland management, countries could receive credit only for carbon sequestration increases above 1990 levels.<br>• Inclusion of broad outlines of consequences for failing to meet emissions targets that would include a requirement to "make up" shortfalls at 1.3 tons to 1, suspension of the right to sell credits for surplus emissions reductions, and a required compliance action plan for those not meeting their targets. |
| COP 7 | From 29 October to 10 November 2001 in Marrakech, Morocco | • To work on the Buenos Aires Plan of Action.<br>• Finalising most of the operational details.<br>• Setting the stage for nations to ratify the Kyoto Protocol. | • Operational rules for international emissions trading among parties to the Protocol and for the CDM and joint implementation;<br>• A compliance regime that outlined consequences for failure to meet emissions targets but deferred to the parties to the Protocol, once it came into force, the decision on whether those consequences would be legally binding;<br>• Accounting procedures for the flexibility mechanisms;<br>• A decision to consider at COP 8 how to achieve a review of the adequacy of commitments that might lead to discussions on future commitments by developing countries. |
| COP 8 | From 23 October to 1 November 2002 in New Delhi | • Agenda mostly of second-order and technical issues | • Adopted the Delhi Ministerial Declaration on Climate Change and Sustainable Development.<br>• Adopted rules of procedure for the executive board of the Clean Development Mechanism (CDM).<br>• Completed work on the reporting required of developed countries to assess their compliance under the Kyoto Protocol.<br>• Adopted guidance to the Global Environment Facility (GEF) for managing two new funds established at COP-7 to assist developing countries.<br>• Adopted new guidelines for national communications to be submitted by developing countries. |
| COP 9 | From 1 December to 12 December 2003 in Milan, Italy | • Agricultural biodiversity<br>• Global Strategy for Plant Conservation<br>• Invasive Alien Species<br>• Forest Diversity<br>• Incentive Measures<br>• Ecosystem Approach | • The parties agreed to use the Adaptation Fund established at COP7 in 2001 primarily in supporting developing countries better adapt to climate change.<br>• The fund would also be used for capacity-building through technology transfer.<br>• The parties also agreed to review the first national reports submitted by 110 non-Annex I countries. |
| COP 10 | From 9 December to 17 December 2004 in Buenos Aires, Argentina | • Organizational matters.<br>• Consideration of reports.<br>• Access and benefit sharing.<br>• Strategic issues for evaluating progress and supporting implementation.<br>• Issues for in-depth consideration<br>• Other substantive issues arising from decisions of the conference of the parties.<br>• Administrative and budgetary matters. | • Buenos Aires programme of work on adaptation and response measures.<br>• Capacity-building for developing countries (non-Annex I Parties).<br>• Capacity-building for countries with economies in transition.<br>• Work of the Least Developed Countries Expert Group.<br>• Implementation of the global observing system for climate.<br>• Development and transfer of technologies.<br>• Status of, and ways to enhance, implementation of the New Delhi work programme on Article 6 of the Convention. |

| COP 11 | From 28 November and 9 December 2005, in Montreal, Quebec, Canada | • Capacity building.<br>• Development and transfer of technologies.<br>• The adverse effects of climate change on developing and least developed countries.<br>• The several financial and budget-related issues including guidelines to the global environment facility (gef). | • Expression of gratitude to the Government of Canada and the people of the city of Montreal. |
|---|---|---|---|
| COP 12 | From 6 November to 17 November 2006 in Nairobi, Kenya | • It was designed to mitigate climate change and help countries adapt to the effects. | • Expression of gratitude to the Government of Kenya and the people of the city of Nairobi. |
| COP 13 | From 3 December 17 December 2007, at Nusa Dua, in Bali, Indonesia | • Adaptation Fund.<br>• Further guidance relating to the clean development mechanism.<br>• Guidance on the implementation of Article 6 of the Kyoto Protocol.<br>• Scope and content of the second review of the Kyoto Protocol pursuant to its Article 9.<br>• Compliance under the Kyoto Protocol.<br>• Good practice guidance for land use, land-use change and forestry activities under Article 3, paragraphs 3 and 4, of the Kyoto Protocol. | • Agreement on a timeline and structured negotiation on the post-2012 framework (the end of the first commitment period of the Kyoto Protocol) was achieved with the adoption of the Bali Action Plan.<br>• The Ad Hoc Working Group on Long-term Cooperative Action under the Convention (AWG-LCA) was established as a new subsidiary body to conduct the negotiations aimed at urgently enhancing the implementation of the Convention up to and beyond 2012. |
| COP 14 | From 1 December to 12 December 2008 in Poznań, Poland | • Election of the President of the Conference at its fourteenth session.<br>• Adoption of the rules of procedure.<br>• Adoption of the agenda.<br>• Election of officers other than the President.<br>• Admission of organizations as observers.<br>• Review of implementation of commitment and of other provisions the Convention. | • Delegates agreed on principles for the financing of a fund to help the poorest nations cope with the effects of climate change and they approved a mechanism to incorporate forest protection into the efforts of the international community to combat climate change.<br>• Expression of gratitude to the Government of the Republic of Poland and the people of the city of Poznan. |
| COP 15 | From 7 December to 18 December 2009 in in Copenhagen, Denmark | • Financial mechanism of the Convention.<br>• National communications.<br>• Capacity-building under the Convention.<br>• Development and transfer of technologies.<br>• Reducing emissions from deforestation in developing countries: approaches to stimulate action. | • Outcome of the work of the Ad Hoc Working Group on Long-term Cooperative Action under the Convention.<br>• Copenhagen Accord.<br>• Amendment to Annex I to the Convention.<br>• Methodological guidance for activities relating to reducing emissions from deforestation.<br>• Work of the Consultative Group of Experts on National Communications from Parties not included in Annex I to the Convention.<br>• Expression of gratitude to the Government of the Kingdom of Denmark and the people of the city of Copenhagen. |

| | | | |
|---|---|---|---|
| COP 16 | From 28 November to 10 December 2010 in Cancún, Mexico | • Financial mechanism of the Convention.<br>• National communications.<br>• Development and transfer of technologies.<br>• Capacity-building under the Convention.<br>• Implementation of Article 4, paragraphs 8 and 9, of the Convention.<br>• Article 6 of the Convention. | • Parties agreed to: commit to a maximum temperature rise of 2 degrees Celsius above pre-industrial levels; make fully operational by 2012 a technology mechanism to boost the development and spread of new climate-friendly technologies; establish a Green Climate Fund to provide financing for action in developing countries via thematic funding windows.<br>• They also agreed on a new Cancun Adaptation Framework, which included setting up an Adaptation Committee to promote strong, cohesive action on adaptation. |
| COP 17 | From 28 November to 9 December 2011 in Durban, South Africa | • Financial mechanism of the Convention.<br>• National communications.<br>• Development and transfer of technologies.<br>• Equitable access to sustainable development.<br>• Unilateral trade measures.<br>• Accelerated access to critical mitigation and adaptation technologies and related intellectual property rights. | • Adoption of the report of the Conference of the Parties on its seventeenthsession. |
| COP 18 | From 26 November to 7 December 2012 in Doha, Qatar | • Article 17 of the Convention contains procedures for the adoption of protocols to the Convention.<br>• In accordance with Article 17, Parties have submitted six proposals.<br>• Five proposals were submitted in 2009 and were communicated to Parties and signatories to the Convention by 6 June 2009 and, for information, to the Depositary on 25 June 2009. | • The Doha Amendment to the Kyoto Protocol (to be accepted before entering into force) featuring a second commitment period running from 2012 until 2020 limited in scope to 15% of the global carbon dioxide emissions due to the lack of commitments of Japan, Russia, Belarus, Ukraine, New Zealand (nor the United States and Canada, who are not parties to the Protocol in that period) and due to the fact that developing countries like China (the world's largest emitter), India and Brazil are not subject to emissions reductions under the Kyoto Protocol.<br>• Language on loss and damage, formalized for the first time in the conference documents.<br>• Russia, Belarus and Ukraine objected at the end of the session. |
| COP 19 | From 11 to 23 November 2013 in Warsaw, Poland | • Further advancing the Durban Platform.<br>• Long-term climate finance.<br>• Warsaw international mechanism for loss and damage associated with climate.<br>• Report of the Green Climate Fund to the Conference of the Parties and guidance to the Green Climate Fund.<br>• Arrangements between the Conference of the Parties and the Green Climate Fund.<br>• Report of the Global Environment Facility to the Conference of the Parties and guidance to the Global Environment Facility. | • A draft report on the work of the session will be prepared for adoption by the COP at the end of the session.<br>• The COP will be invited to adopt the draft report and authorize the Rapporteur to complete the report after the session under the guidance of the President and with the assistance of the secretariat.<br>• Expression of gratitude to the Government of the Republic of Poland and the people of the city of Warsaw. |

| | | | |
|---|---|---|---|
| COP 20 | From 1 December to 12 December 2014 in Lima, Peru | • Gender and climate change.<br>• Other matters referred to the Conference of the Parties by the subsidiary bodies.<br>• Capacity-building under the Convention.<br>• Warsaw International Mechanism for Loss and Damage associated with Climate Change Impacts. | • Lima Call for Climate Action.<br>• Warsaw International Mechanism for Loss and Damage associated.<br>• Report of the Global Environment Facility to the Conference of the Parties.<br>• Further guidance to the Least Developed Countries Fund.<br>• Methodologies for the reporting of financial information by Parties included. |
| COP 21 | From 30 November to 12 December 2015 in Paris, France | • Placing emphasis on concepts like climate justice and sustainable lifestyles, the Paris Agreement for the first time brings together all nations for a common cause under the UNFCCC.<br>• One of the main focuses of the agreement is to hold the increase in the global average temperature to well below 2°C above pre- industrial level and on driving efforts to limit it even further to 1.5°C. | • Negotiations resulted in the adoption of the Paris Agreement on 12 December, governing climate change reduction measures from 2020.<br>• The adoption of this agreement ended the work of the Durban platform, established during COP17.<br>• The agreement will enter into force (and thus become fully effective) on November 4, 2016. On October 4, 2016 the threshold for adoption was reached with over 55 countries representing at least 55% of the world's greenhouse gas emissions ratifying the Agreement. |
| COP 22 | From 7 November to 18 November 2016 in Marrakech, in the North-African country of Morocco | • A focal issue of COP 22 is that of water scarcity, water cleanliness, and water-related sustainability, a major problem in the developing world, including many African states.<br>• Prior to the event a special initiative on water was preside by Charafat Afailal, Morocco's Minister in Charge of Water and Aziz Mekouar, COP 22 Ambassador for Multilateral Negotiations. | • Preparations for the entry into force of the Paris Agreement and the first session of the Conference of the Parties serving as the meeting of the Parties to the Paris Agreement.<br>• Paris Committee on Capacity-building.<br>• Warsaw International Mechanism for Loss and Damage associated with Climate Change Impacts.<br>• The Paris Agreement has been adopted and brought into force, but work needs to be done to put flesh onto its basic structure.<br>• Report of the Green Climate Fund to the Conference of the Parties and guidance to the Green Climate Fund.<br>• Outcome of the first round of the international assessment and review process (2014 – 2015). |
| COP 23 | COP 23 is expected to be held from 6 November to 17 November 2017 in Bonn, Germany | • In this conference, the main topics of dispute were related to financial support mitigation action discrimination and loss and damage.<br>• The question was raised in the Bone Conference that the developed countries who have occupied a large portion of the available carbon space will help the poor and developing countries.<br>• What actions have been taken so far by the rich countries to reduce greenhouse gas emissions and should not the use of coal be limited? | • Consensus on coal phase-out is agreed on a phased manner.<br>• It was decided to set up green-buildings and expedite eco-mobility.<br>• It is decided to identify gender related factors while working towards addressing issues.<br>• It was decided to give importance to local people's opinion in climate talks.<br>• Decision to discuss the issue of greenhouse gas emissions through agricultural operations.<br>• An important progress in the conference was in the form of 'Talanoa Dialogue'. |

## The Kyoto Protocol (1997) in Japan

The Kyoto Protocol to the United Nations Framework Convention on Climate Change (UNFCCC) sets binding obligations on industrialised countries to reduce emissions of greenhouse gases. The UNFCCC is an international environmental treaty with the goal of achieving the "stabilisation of greenhouse gas concentrations in the atmosphere at a level that would prevent dangerous anthropogenic interference with the climate system." The Protocol was adopted on 11 December 1997 in Kyoto, Japan, and entered into force on 16 February 2005. As of September 2011, 191 states have signed and ratified the protocol. The United States signed but did not ratify the Protocol and Canada withdrew from it in 2011. Other United Nations member states which did not ratify the protocol are Afghanistan, Andorra and South Sudan.

## World Bank's Environmental Agenda

Although the environment is not an explicit part of the World Bank's agenda, it has taken aboard environmental concerns over the last few years. Not only has the Bank spent a lot of money on the environment and brought aboard over 300 specialists, but also it has put together broad environmental objectives. These **objectives** are:

1. addressing potentially adverse environmental impacts of World Bank financed activities,
2. assisting member countries promote environmental protection,
3. helping member countries to set and implement sound environmental programmes, and
4. promoting global environmental participation through the Global Environment Facility (GEF)

**National Biodiversity Congress (NBC) 2017** The National Biodiversity Congress (NBC) 2017 was held in Thiruvananthapuram, capital of Kerala. The event is hosted by the Kerala State Biodiversity Board. It aims to identify practical, evidence-based case studies at the regional level to support the plan of action.

The focal theme of 2017 NBC was "Mainstreaming Biodiversity for Sustainable Development".

# Environmental Laws & Acts

## Environmental Laws of India

In the Constitution of India it is clearly stated that it is the duty of the state to 'protect and improve the environment and to safeguard the forests and wildlife of the country'. It imposes a duty on every citizen 'to protect and improve the natural environment including forests, lakes, rivers, and wildlife'. Reference to the environment has also been made in the Directive Principles of State Policy as well as the Fundamental Rights. The Department of Environment was established in India in 1980 to ensure a healthy environment for the country. This later became the Ministry of Environment and Forests in 1985.

The constitutional provisions are backed by a number of laws – acts, rules, and notifications. The EPA (Environment Protection Act), 1986 came into force soon after the Bhopal Gas Tragedy and is considered an umbrella legislation as it fills many gaps in the existing laws. Thereafter a large number of laws came into existence as the problems began arising, for example, Handling and Management of Hazardous Waste Rules in 1989.

## General Laws & ACIS.

**The Environment (Protection) Act (1986)**
It authorizes the central government to protect and improve environmental quality, control and reduce pollution from all sources, and prohibit or restrict the setting and /or operation of any industrial facility on environmental grounds.

**The Environment (Protection) Rules (1986)**
These lay down procedures for setting standards of emission or discharge of environmental pollutants.

**The objective of Hazardous Waste (Management and Handling) Rules (1989)** is to control the generation, collection, treatment, import, storage, and handling of hazardous waste.

**The Manufacture, Storage, and Import of Hazardous Rules (1989)** define the terms used in this context, and sets up an authority to inspect, once a year, the industrial activity connected with hazardous chemicals and isolated storage facilities.

**The Manufacture, Use, Import, Export, and Storage of hazardous Micro-organisms/ Genetically Engineered Organisms or Cells Rules (1989)** were introduced with a view to protect the environment, nature, and health, in connection with the application of gene technology and microorganisms.

**The Public Liability Insurance Act and Rules and Amendment, (1992)** was drawn up to provide for public liability insurance for the purpose of providing immediate relief to the persons affected by accident while handling any hazardous substance.

**The National Environmental Tribunal Act (1995)** has been created to award compensation for damages to persons, property, and the environment arising from any activity involving hazardous substances.

**The National Environment Appellate Authority Act (1997)** - has been created to hear appeals with respect to restrictions of areas in which classes of industries etc. are carried out or prescribed subject to certain safeguards under the EPA.

**The Biomedical waste (Management and Handling) Rules (1998)** is a legal binding on the health care institutions to streamline the process of proper handling of hospital waste such as segregation, disposal, collection, and treatment.

**The Environment (Siting for Industrial Projects) Rules, (1999)** lay down detailed provisions relating to areas to be avoided for siting of industries, precautionary measures to be taken for site selecting as also the aspects of environmental protection which should have been incorporated during the implementation of the industrial development projects.

**The Municipal Solid Wastes (Management and Handling) Rules, (2000)** apply to every municipal authority responsible for the collection, segregation, storage, transportation, processing, and disposal of municipal solid wastes.

**The Ozone Depleting Substances (Regulation and Control) Rules (2000)** have been laid down for the regulation of production and consumption of ozone depleting substances.

**The Batteries (Management and Handling) Rules, (2001)** - rules shall apply to every manufacturer, importer, re-conditioner, assembler, dealer, auctioneer, consumer, and bulk consumer involved in the manufacture, processing, sale, purchase, and use of batteries or components so as to regulate and ensure the environmentally safe disposal of used batteries.

**The Noise Pollution (Regulation and Control) (Amendment) Rules (2002)** lay down such terms and conditions as are necessary to reduce noise pollution, permit use of loud speakers or public address systems during night hours (between 10:00 p.m. to 12:00 midnight) on or during any cultural or religious festive occasion

**The Biological Diversity Act (2002)** is an act to provide for the conservation of biological diversity, sustainable use of its components, and fair and equitable sharing of the benefits arising out of the use of biological resources and knowledge associated with it

# Forest and Wildlife

**The Indian Forest Act and Amendment, (1984)** is one of the many surviving colonial statutes. It was enacted to 'consolidate the law related to forest, the transit of forest produce, and the duty leviable on timber and other forest produce'.

**The Wildlife Protection Act, Rules 1973 and Amendment 1991** provides for the protection of birds and animals and for all matters that are connected to it whether it be their habitat or the waterhole or the forests that sustain them.

**The Forest (Conservation) Act and Rules, (1981)** provides for the protection of and the conservation of the forests.

## Water

**The Easement Act (1882)** allows private rights to use a resource that is, groundwater, by viewing it as an attachment to the land. It also states that all surface water belongs to the state and is a state property.

**The Indian Fisheries Act (1897)** establishes two sets of penal offences whereby the government can sue any person who uses dynamite or other explosive substance in any way (whether coastal or inland) with intent to catch or destroy any fish or poisonous fish in order to kill.

**The River Boards Act (1956)** enables the states to enroll the central government in setting up an Advisory River Board to resolve issues in inter-state cooperation.

**The Merchant Shipping Act (1970)** aims to deal with waste arising from ships along the coastal areas within a specified radius.

**The Water (Prevention and Control of Pollution) Act (1974)** establishes an institutional structure for preventing and abating water pollution. It establishes standards for water quality and effluent. Polluting industries must seek permission to discharge waste into effluent bodies. The CPCB (Central Pollution Control Board) was constituted under this act.

**The Water (Prevention and Control of Pollution) Cess Act (1977)** provides for the levy and collection of cess or fees on water consuming industries and local authorities.

**The Water (Prevention and Control of Pollution) Cess Rules (1978)** contains the standard definitions and indicate the kind of and location of meters that every consumer of water is required to affix.

**The Coastal Regulation Zone Notification (1991)** puts regulations on various activities, including construction, are regulated. It gives some protection to the backwaters and estuaries.

## Air

**The Factories Act (1948) and Amendment in 1987** was the first to express concern for the working environment of the workers. The amendment of 1987 has sharpened its environmental focus and expanded its application to hazardous processes.

**The Air (Prevention and Control of Pollution) (1981) Act** provides for the control and abatement of air pollution. It entrusts the power of enforcing this act to the CPCB .

**The Air (Prevention and Control of Pollution) Rules (1982)** defines the procedures of the meetings of the Boards and the powers entrusted to them.

**The Atomic Energy Act (1982)** deals with the radioactive waste.

**The Air (Prevention and Control of Pollution) Amendment Act (1987)** empowers the central and state pollution control boards to meet with grave emergencies of air pollution.

**The Motor Vehicles Act (1988)** states that all hazardous waste is to be properly packaged, labelled, and transported.

## Environmental Protection Act 1986

In the wake of the Bhopal Tragedy, the Government of India enacted the Environment Protection Act of 1986 under Article 253 of the Constitution. Passed in March 1986, it came into force on 19 November 1986. The purpose of the Act is to implement the decisions of the United Nations Conference on the Human Environments they relate to the protection and improvement of the human environment and the prevention of hazards to human beings, other living creatures, plants and property. The Act is an "umbrella" legislation designed to provide a framework for central government coordination of the activities of various central and state authorities established under previous laws, such as the Water Act and the Air Act.

**National Adaptation Programme of Action (NAPA):** A National Adaptation Programme of Action (NAPA) is a type of plan submitted to the United Nations Framework Convention on Climate Change (UNFCCC) by Least Developed Countries, to describe the country's perception of its most "urgent and immediate needs to adapt to climate change".

## Wild Life Protection Act (1972) National Parks, Sanctuaries and other Protected Areas

The Wildlife Protection Act 1972 is the first umbrella act to protect plants as well as animals. It was last amended in 2006 to give statutory status to Project Tiger. The act extends to the whole of India, except the State of Jammu and Kashmir which has its own wildlife act. It defines five types of protected areas viz. National Parks, Wildlife Sanctuaries, Community Reserves, Conservation Reserves and Tiger Reserves. The act has six schedules with varying degrees of protection to different kinds of animals and plants.

## Wild Life Sanctuary

A wildlife sanctuary is defined by State Government via a notification. There is no need to pass a legislation (act) by the state assembly to declare a wildlife sanctuary. Fixation and alternation of boundary can be done by state legislature via resolution. No need to pass an act for alternation of boundaries. No alternation of boundaries in wildlife sanctuaries can be done without approval of the NBWL (National Board of Wildlife) Limited human activities are permitted in the sanctuary.

## National Parks

Similar to the Wildlife Sanctuaries, a National Park is defined by state government via notification. The state government can fix and alter boundaries of the National Parks with prior consultation and approval with National Board of Wildlife. There is no need to pass an act for alternation of boundaries of National Parks. No human activities are permitted in a National Park.

## Conservation Reserves and Community Reserves

These areas provide a greater role and opportunity for local communities, stakeholders and civil society to protect many areas of conservation value that cannot be designated under strict categories such as wildlife sanctuaries or national parks.

## Schedules of the Wild Life Protection Act

There are six schedules in wildlife protection act with varying degrees of protection. Out of the six schedules, Schedule I and part II of Schedule II provide absolute protection and offences under these are prescribed the highest penalties. The penalties for Schedule III and Schedule IV are less and these animals are protected. Schedule V includes the animals which may be hunted. Such animals include Common crow, Fruit bats, Mice & Rats only. Schedule VI contains the plants, which are prohibited from cultivation and planting. These plants are as follows:

- Beddomes' cycad (Cycas beddomei)
- Blue Vanda (Vanda soerulec)
- Kuth (Saussurea lappa)
- Ladies slipper orchids (Paphiopedilum spp.)
- Pitcher plant (Nepenthes khasiana)
- Red Vanda (Rananthera inschootiana)

Whose permission is needed to hunt a man-eater? India does not have a robust scientific or policy mechanism to minimise tiger human conflicts. A Standard Operating Procedure was released by the National Tiger Conservation Authority a few years back to deal with emergency arising due to straying of tigers to human settlements. The guidelines prohibit killing the tiger unless it has been declared a maneater. Only the chief wildlife warden of a state can permit hunting of man-eaters.

## Air (Prevention and Control of Pollution) Act, 1981

The Parliament enacted the Air (Prevention and Control of Pollution) Act, 1981 to arrest the deterioration in the air quality.

The notable points from this act are as follows:

- The Act makes provisions for the establishing of Central Pollution Control Board (CPCB) at the apex level and State Pollution Control Boards at the state level.
- The CPCB advises the Central Government on any matter concerning the improvement of the quality of the air and prevention, control and abatement of air pollution. It also helps to plan and cause to be executed a nation-wide programme for the prevention, control and abatement of air pollution. It provides technical assistance to and guidance to the State Pollution Control Board. It also lays down the down standards for the quality of air.
- The SPCBs plan a comprehensive programme for prevention, control and abatement of air pollution and to secure the execution thereof. They also advise the State Government on any matter concerning prevention, control and abatement of air pollution.
- The "air pollutant" means any solid, liquid or gaseous substance (including noise) present in the atmosphere in such concentration as may be or tend to be injurious to human beings or other living creatures or plants or property or environment.

  This act provides that the State Government may, after consultation with the State Board, by notification declare any area or areas within the State as air pollution control areas. The state government is also powered to make any alternations in the area pollution control areas such as merging the areas. If the state government, after consultation with the State Board, is of opinion that the use of any fuel or burning of any non-fuel material other than an approved fuel, in any air pollution control area or part thereof, may cause or is likely to cause air pollution, it may, by notification, prohibit the use of such fuel in such area.

- The further provisions of the act say that no person shall, without the previous consent of the State Board, establish or operate any industrial plant in an air pollution control area. Every person to whom consent has been granted by the State Board, shall comply with the conditions and norms prescribed by the board such as prevention and control of the air pollution. Failure to do so brings penalty including jail term of at least 1.5 years.

## The Water (Prevention and Control of Pollution) Act - 1974, amended in 1988

This was enacted to provide for the prevention and control of water pollution, and for the maintaining or restoring of wholesome of water in the country. The Central and State Pollution Control Boards have been constituted under section 3 and 4 of the Act respectively. The Act was amended in 1978 and 1988 to clarify certain ambiguities and to vest more powers in Pollution Control Board.

## Prevention of Cruelty to Animals Act

The PCA Act, 1960 is enacted to prevent the infliction of unnecessary pain and suffering on animals. PCA Act deals with captive and domestic animals. Chapter IV of the act deals with the regulation of experimentation. Chapter V requires mandatory registration of performing animals. It has also established Animal Welfare Board of India as a statutory body providing advice to the Union Government on matters relating to the promotion of animal welfare and animal welfare laws. The important functions of the board include: Recognition of animal welfare organizations providing financial assistance to recognised animal welfare organizations (AWOs). The board prescribes changes to animal welfare laws and rules. It works to raise awareness among the public. As per PCA Act Section 3 and Section 11(1)(m), it is an offence against a person who incites any animal to fight with a view to provide entertainment. Section 22 of the PCA Act, 1960 deals with restrictions on exhibition and training of performing animals.

The MoEFCC wants to amend the key section 22 of the PCA Act, 1960. It proposes to add a new sub-section to section 22. Since, the subject matter of the issue falls under the concurrent list (entry 17), the Union Government can bring changes to the PCA Act, 1960. The following changes will be made:

The amendment to section 22 will allow exhibition of performing animals at events in a manner prescribed by the religion or practiced traditionally as a part of the culture.

This will indirectly allow events like Jallikattu of Tamil Nadu, bullock cart races in Maharashtra, Karnataka, Punjab, Haryana, Kerala, Gujarat etc.

The events will be allowed to happen with the prior approval of the concerned district authorities and shall be monitored by the state animal welfare boards. The welfare boards have to make sure that unnecessary pain and suffering is not inflicted or caused to the animal during the course of the event. The amendment also seeks to increase the fine for infliction of unnecessary pain or suffering on animals to make it more deterrent.

### National Wildlife Action Plan for 2017-2031

In the first week of February 2016, the Ministry of Environment, Forests and Climate Change (MOEFCC) had come up with a draft third National Wildlife Action Plan for 2017-2031. This plan was drafted by a 12 member committee chaired by JC Kala, a former secretary to the ministry. The draft contains detailed recommendations to be followed in the protected areas. Once approved, this plan will replace the second National Wildlife Action Plan (2002-2016). The first and second National Wildlife Action Plans were adopted in 1983 and 2002 respectively.

#### *Salient Features*

The key areas of focus of this plan is 17, which includes integration of climate change into wildlife planning, conservation of coastal and marine ecosystem, mitigation of human-wildlife conflict, focus on wildlife health among others.

### Wildlife Conservation

The draft plan places special emphasis on rehabilitation of threatened species along with conserving their habitats like inland aquatic, coastal and marine ecosystems.

### Protection of Protected Areas

Protection of protected areas includes ban on certain activities, regulation on tourism and law enforcement.

Ban on certain activities:

- Mining and big irrigation projects would not be permitted in protected areas and wildlife corridors.
- The plan asks the environment ministry to work with Ministry of Steel to bar mining activities in Protected Areas and wildlife corridors.
- Further, it wants proper rehabilitation of degraded and abandoned mining areas.
- It has classified sand mining as a highly destructive activity in which many stakeholders are involved including politicians.
- It wants Ministry of water resources to opt for minor irrigation projects instead of big irrigation projects in the protected areas.
- It has favoured the use of water harvesting units like ponds, check dams, wells etc.

### Tourism

While the plan encourages tourism in wild life areas, it wants restrictions to be placed on the number of tourists and vehicles entering inside a protected area. It provides for the strict monitoring and regulation of the tourism activities. In case of any conflict between tourism and conservation interests of Protected Areas, the plan categorically favours the conservation interests of Protected Areas. It wants to add emphasis on tourism facilities which are sustainable, eco-friendly, clean and wholesome and moderately priced rather than lavish five star facilities.

**Law enforcement:** The draft calls for setting up of new regional forensic laboratories, a special Tiger protection force, special courts to deal with wildlife crimes such as poaching and smuggling. It has observed that the investigation of wildlife crime still lags behind despite the establishment of the National Wildlife Crime Control Bureau and has called for the capacity building of frontline guards and officers responsible for investigating wildlife crimes.

#### *Neglect of Wildlife living outside of the forests*

In this draft, wildlife living outside the forest areas has been neglected. Wolves, great Indian bustards, hyenas, leopards, tigers, elephants among others are known to live outside of the forests. The draft is silent about the management of these populations.

### Regulation of technology

The forest department makes use of drones and camera traps to monitor the protected areas. The draft has ignored the ethical and social consequences of the use of such technologies and has not come up with any framework for self regulation regarding the usage of such technological instruments. The fact that the use of drones and camera traps may violate the privacy of the local people living in protected areas is completely ignored.

### Issue of feral dogs and cats

The draft plan is the first national policy which acknowledges the damages caused by the feral dogs and cats in the wildlife habitats. It simply states that the issue must be managed. Apart from that the draft is silent about the suggestive measures which need to be taken to address the issue.

### Invasion of exotic species

The draft plan wants a national policy to check invasion of exotic species by 2018. But before drafting, it wants a complete inventory and mapping of species and area. Critics argue that preventing invasion of exotic species needs more attention and such efforts should begin immediately. The draft plan instead wants to do mapping first, which seems to be an excuse to delay implementation.

### Duration of plan

It is viewed that implementing the same plan for conservation for 14 long years will make it ineffective. The plan period must be kept shorter to absorb the contemporary realities and scientific advances.

# ENVIRONMENTAL POLICIES

## National Environment Policy 2006

National Environment Policy 2006 is a response to India's national commitment to a clean environment, mandated in the Constitution in Articles 48 A and 51 A (g), (DPSP) strengthened by judicial interpretation of Article 21. It is recognized that the maintenance of the healthy environment is not the responsibility of the state alone. It is the responsibility of every citizen and thus a spirit of partnership is to be realized through the environment management of the country. Here is the summary of the National Environment Policy 2006:

### Key Environment Challenges

The key environmental challenges that India faces are related to the nexus of environmental degradation with poverty in its many dimensions, and economic growth. Challenges are intrinsically connected with the state of environmental resources, such as land, water, air, and their flora and fauna.

### Drivers of Degradation

Proximate drivers of environmental degradation are population growth, inappropriate technology and consumption choices, and poverty, leading to changes in relations between people and ecosystems, and development activities such as intensive agriculture, polluting industry, and unplanned urbanization. Other drivers of degradation are the lack of clarity or enforcement of rights of access and use of environmental resources, policies which provide disincentives for environmental conservation (and which may have origins in the fiscal regime), market failures (which may be linked to shortcomings in the regulatory regimes), and governance constraints.

### Impact on Health

Poor environmental quality has adversely affected human health. Environmental factors are estimated as being responsible in some cases for nearly 20% of the burden of disease in India, and a number of environment-health factors are closely linked with dimensions of poverty (e.g. malnutrition, lack of access to clean energy and water). Interventions such as reducing indoor air pollution, protecting sources of safe drinking water, protecting soil from contamination, improved sanitation measures, and better public health governance, offer tremendous opportunities in reducing the incidence of a number of critical health problems.

### Objectives of the Policy

- Conservation of Critical Environmental Resources.
- Intra-generational Equity.
- Livelihood Security for the Poor Inter-generational Equity.
- Integration of Environmental Concerns in Economic and Social Development.
- Efficiency in Environmental Resource.
- Use Environmental Governance.
- Enhancement of Resources for Environmental Conservation

### Principles of National Environment Policy 2006

The Policy evolved from the recognition that only such development is sustainable, which respects ecological constraints, and the imperatives of justice. The Objectives stated above are to be realized through various strategic interventions by different public authorities at Central, State, and Local Government levels. They would also be the basis of diverse partnerships. The principles followed in the policy are:

- Human Beings are at the Centre of Sustainable Development Concerns.
- Right to development must be fulfilled so as to equitably meet developmental and environmental needs of present and future generations.
- In order to achieve sustainable development, environmental protection shall constitute an integral part of the development process and cannot be considered in isolation from it.
- Where there are credible threats of serious or irreversible damage to key environmental resources, lack of full scientific certainty shall not be used as a reason for postponing cost-effective measures to prevent environmental degradation.
- In various public actions for environmental conservation, economic efficiency would be sought to be realized.

Impacts of acts of production and consumption of one party may be visited on third parties who do not have a direct economic nexus with the original act. Such impacts are termed "externalities". The National Environment Policy promotes the internalization of environmental costs, including through the use of incentives based policy instruments, taking into account the approach that the polluter should, in principle, bear the cost of pollution, with due regard to the public interest, and without distorting international trade and investment.

### Legal Liabilities in the Policy

The environmental redressal mechanism based on doctrines of criminal liability, have not proved sufficiently effective, and need to be supplemented. The policy adopts the civil liability for environmental damage that would deter environmentally harmful actions, and compensate the victims of environmental damage. The alternatives to Civil Liability may also apply viz. Fault Based Liability and Strict Liability. In Fault Based Liability a party is held liable if it breaches a preexisting legal duty, for example, an environmental standard. Strict liability imposes an obligation to compensate the victim for harm resulting from actions or failure to take action, which may not necessarily constitute a breach of any law or duty of care.

### The Doctrine of Public Trust

As per this doctrine, the State is not an absolute owner, but a trustee of all natural resources, which are by nature meant for public use and enjoyment, subject to reasonable conditions, necessary to protect the legitimate interest of a large number of people, or for matters of strategic national interest.

### Legislative Reforms

A judicious mix of civil and criminal processes and sanctions will be employed in the legal regime for enforcement, through a review of the existing legislation. The policy calls for identification of the emerging areas for new legislation, due to better scientific understanding, economic and social development, and development of multilateral environmental regimes, in line with the National Environment Policy. It also calls for review the body of existing legislation in order to develop synergies among relevant statutes and regulations.

### Environment Impact Assessment

The policy focuses on encouraging the regulatory authorities, Central and State, to institutionalize regional and cumulative environmental impact assessments (R/CEIAs) to ensure that environmental concerns are identified and addressed at the planning stage itself.

### Environmentally Sensitive Zones (ESZs)

The Environmentally Sensitive Zones are the areas with identified environmental resources having "Incomparable Values" which require special attention for their conservation. In order to conserve and enhance these resources, without impeding legitimate socio-economic development of these areas, the National Environment policy aims to identify and give legal status to Environmentally Sensitive Zones in the country having environmental entities with "Incomparable values" requiring special conservation efforts. The policy also envisages formulating area development plans for these zones on a scientific basis, with adequate participation by the local communities.

### Desert Habitats

The arid and semi-arid region of India covers 127.3 mha (38.8%) of India's geographical area and spreads over 10 states. The Indian desert fauna is extremely rich in species diversity of mammals and winter migratory birds. However the pressures of a rapidly increasing population on the natural resource base necessitate adoption of innovative and integrated measures for conservation of desert ecosystems. The policy aims at measures such as intensive water and moisture conservation through practices based on traditional and science based knowledge, and relying on traditional infrastructure.

### Panchayats & Women Participation

The policy aims at working towards giving the legal recognition of the traditional entitlements of forest dependent communities taking into consideration the provisions of the (PESA). This would remedy a serious historical injustice, secure their livelihoods, reduce possibilities of conflict with the forest departments, and provide long-term incentives to these communities to conserve the forests.

### Integrated Development of Wildlife Habitats

This is an umbrella programme for three main schemes to protect the wildlife of the country viz. Project Tiger, Project Elephant and Integrated development of wildlife Habitats. These schemes are implemented as Centrally Sponsored Schemes. Conservation of Natural Resources and Eco-systems This programme aims to conserve the natural resources and eco-system in areas like, corals, mangroves, Bio-spheres, wetland and lakes.

### Wild Life

The policy aims to expand the Protected Area (PA) network of the country, including Conservation and Community Reserves, to give fair representation to all bio-geographic zones of the country. In doing so, develop norms for delineation of PAs in terms of the Objectives and Principles of the National Environment Policy, in particular, participation of local communities, concerned public agencies, and other stakeholders, who have a direct and tangible stake in protection and conservation of wildlife, to harmonize ecological and physical features with needs of socio-economic development.

### Wetlands

The Ramsar Convention defines wetlands as, 'areas of marsh, fen, peat land or water, whether natural or artificial, permanent or temporary, with water that is static or flowing, fresh, brackish or salt, including areas of marine water the depth of which at low tide does not exceed six meters', thereby giving a wide scope to the term. Wetlands are under threat from drainage and conversion for agriculture and human settlements, besides pollution. The policy aims at setting up a legally enforceable regulatory mechanism for identified valuable wetlands, to prevent their degradation and enhance their conservation. Develop a national inventory of such wetlands.

### Coastal Regulation Zone (CRZ)

The policy aims to revisit the Coastal Regulation Zone (CRZ) notifications to make the approach to coastal environmental regulation more holistic, and thereby ensure protection to coastal ecological systems, coastal waters, and the vulnerability of some coastal areas to extreme natural events and potential sea level rise. In pursuance with the Policy CRZ Notification 2011 was released recently.

### National Coastal Zone Management Programme

Ministry is implementing a reengineered Coastal Regulation Zone (CRZ) Notification 2011 to ensure livelihood security to fishing and other local community to conserve and protect coastal stretches and to promote development based on scientific principles.

Another **Notification on island Protection Zone** is also being implemented for similar purposes for the island of Andaman & Nicobar and the Lakshadweep. Ministry is also implementing a World Bank Assisted Integrated Coastal Zone Management Project.

### National Mission for a Green India

With objective to increase the forest cover and also protect the existing forest land, the Ministry has two plan schemes namely, Green India Mission: National Afforestation Programme and Intensification of Forest Management.

## Green India Mission

The National Mission for a Green India or Green India Mission (GIM) is one of the eight missions India's action plans to address the challenge of climate change. It was launched in February 2014 for protecting; restoring and enhancing India's diminishing forest cover and responding to climate change by a combination of adaptation and mitigation measures.

The mission recognises the influence forests on environmental amelioration through climate change mitigation, water security, food security, biodiversity conservation and livelihood security of forest living as well as dependent communities.

### Objectives of National Mission for A Green India

1. To protect, restore and enhance India's falling forest cover.
2. To respond to climate change through a combination of adaptation as well as mitigation measures.
3. To increased forest-based livelihood incomes.
4. To enhance annual Carbon sequestration by 50 to 60 million tonnes in the year 2020.

### Goals of the National Mission for A Green India

1. Improvement in quality of forest cover and ecosystem services of forests /non-forests, including moderately dense, open forests, degraded grassland and wetlands (5 m ha).

2. Eco-restoration/afforestation of scrub, shifting cultivation areas, cold deserts, mangroves, ravines and abandoned mining areas (1.8 m ha).
3. Improvement in forest and tree cover in urban/peri-urban lands (0.20 m ha).
4. Improvement in forest and tree cover on marginal agricultural lands/fallows and other non-forest lands under agroforestry /social forestry (3 m ha).
5. Management of public forest/ non-forests areas (taken up under the Mission) by the community institutions
6. Adoption of improved fuelwood-use efficiency and alternative energy devices by project-area households.
7. Diversification of forest-based livelihoods of about 3 million households living in and around forests.

## Issues and challenges

### Inadequate budget allocation

- B.E. of ₹ 45.01 Crore for FY 2016-17 - grossly insufficient.
- Committed liability for 2016-17 is ₹ 97.87 Crore.
- Additional allocation of ₹ 628.51 Cr is required for FY.
- Average requirement of the fund- around ₹ 1800 Crore/pa.

### National River Conservation Programme

NRCP covers polluted stretches of 39 rivers in 190 towns in 20 States at a sanctioned cost of ₹7,639 crore. The main objective of NRCP is to improve water quality of polluted stretches of rivers to acceptable standards by preventing pollution load reaching the rivers by undertaking various pollution abatement works.

### National Green Tribunal

The National Green Tribunal has been established on 18.10.2010 under the National Green Tribunal Act 2010 for effective and expeditious disposal of cases relating to environmental protection and conservation of forests and other natural resources including enforcement of any legal right relating to environment and giving relief and compensation for damages to persons and property and for matters connected therewith or incidental thereto. It is a specialized body equipped with the necessary expertise to handle environmental disputes involving multi-disciplinary issues. The Tribunal shall not be bound by the procedure laid down under the Code of Civil Procedure, 1908, but shall be guided by principles of natural justice.

The Tribunal's dedicated jurisdiction in environmental matters shall provide speedy environmental justice and help reduce the burden of litigation in the higher courts. The Tribunal is mandated to make and endeavour for disposal of applications or appeals finally within 6 months of filing of the same. Initially, the NGT is proposed to be set up at five places of sittings and will follow circuit procedure for making itself more accessible. New Delhi is the Principal

Place of Sitting of the Tribunal and Bhopal, Pune, Kolkata and Chennai shall be the other four place of sitting of the Tribunal.

## Environmental Policy in India

- Wildlife (Protection) Act, 1972
- Water (Prevention and Control of Pollution) Act, 1974
- Forest (Conservation) Act, 1980
- Air (Prevention and Control of Pollution) Act, 1981
- Environment (Protection) Act, 1986
- Hazardous Wastes (Management and Handling) Rules, 1989
- Public Liability Insurance Act, 1991
- Environmental Impact Assessment Notification, 1994
- National Environment Tribunals Act, 1995
- National Environment Appellate Authority Act, 1997
- Biological Diversity Act, 2002
- Environmental Impact Assessment Notification, 2006 (supersession of 1994 Notification)
- National Green Tribunal Act, 2010
- **Glossary**

# TSR Subramanian Committee Reports

In August 2014, the NDA Government had set up a high-level committee to review the six environment laws in India and recommend specific amendments to bring them in line with current requirements. The Committee was headed by the former cabinet secretary TSR Subramanian. The six laws under review were:

- Indian Forest Act 1927
- Wild Life (Protection) Act 1972
- Water (Prevention and Control of Pollution) Act 1974
- Air (Prevention and Control of Pollution) Act 1981
- Forest Conservation Act 1980
- Environment (Protection) Act 1986.

# Initiatives

## R20 Regions of Climate Action

R20 Regions of Climate Action is a non-profit environmental organization. It was founded in 2010 by Arnold Schwarzenegger and other global leaders in cooperation with the United Nations. Its mission is to help sub-national governments to implement low-carbon and climate-resilient projects, as well as to share best practices in renewable energy and energy efficiency, in order to build a green economy.

# IMPORTANT TERMS

***Adaptive radiation:*** Evolutionary diversification of a generalized ancestral form with production of a number of adaptively specialized forms. Closely related species look very different, as a result of having adapted to widely different ecological niches.

***Agroforestry:*** An ecologically based farming system, that, through the integration of trees in farms, increases social, environmental and economic benefits to land users.

***Allen's Rule:*** Warm-blooded animals (endotherms) from colder climates usually have shorter limbs than do endotherms from warmer climates.

***Anthropogenic climate change:*** Climate change with the presumption of human influence, usually warming.

***Alpha diversity:*** In ecology, alpha diversity ($\alpha$-diversity) is the mean species diversity in sites or habitats at a local scale. The term was introduced by R. H. Whittaker together with the terms beta diversity ($\beta$-diversity) and gamma diversity ($\gamma$-diversity).

***Allee effect:*** Concept in population ecology that describes the positive relation between the size of a given population and its growth.

**Basel Convention:** The Basel Convention on the Control of Transboundary Movements of Hazardous Wastes and their Disposal is an international agreement for restricting the transfer of hazardous waste from one country to the other.

**Bonn Convention:** Bonn Convention is the international Convention on the Conservation of Migratory Species of Wild Animals.

**Brundtland Commission:** Brundtland Commission is the World Commission on Environment and Development which published a report entitled Our Common Future in 1987, formally promoted the concept of sustainable development and urged all nations to focus on sustainable development.

***Bagasse:*** The fibrous residue of sugar cane milling used as a fuel to produce steam in sugar mills.

***Beta diversity:*** ($\beta$-diversity or true beta diversity) is the ratio between regional and local species diversity.

***Bluewater:*** Collectible water from rainfall; the water that falls on roofs and hard surfaces usually flowing into rivers and the sea and recharging the ground water. In nature the global average proportion of total rainfall that is blue water is about 40%

***Biodiversity Hotspot:*** A biodiversity hotspot is an area with unusual concentration of species, many of which are endemic. It is marked by serious threat to its biodiversity by humans. The concept was given in 1988 by Norman Myers.

**CITES:** CITES or the Convention on International Trade in Endangered Species of Wild Fauna and Flora is an international treaty for the protection of endangered plants and animals.

***Carbon diet:*** A carbon diet refers to reducing the impact on climate change by reducing greenhouse gas principally $CO_2$ production.

***Car pooling:*** Giving people lifts to help reduce emissions and traffic.

***Carbon budget***: A measure of carbon inputs and outputs for a particular activity.

***Carbon credit***: A market-driven way of reducing the impact of greenhouse gas emissions; it allows an agent to benefit financially from an emission reduction. There are two forms of carbon credit, those that are part of national and international trade and those that are purchased by individuals. Internationally, to achieve Kyoto Protocol objectives, 'caps' (limits) on participating country's emissions are established. To meet these limits countries, in turn, set 'caps' (allowances or credits: 1 convertible and transferable credit = 1 metric tonne of CO2 emissions) for operators. Operators that meet the agreed 'caps' can then sell unused credits to operators who exceed 'caps'. Operators can then choose the most cost-effective way of reducing emissions. Individual carbon credits would operate in a similar way cf. carbon offset.

*Carbon footprint*: A measure of the carbon emissions that are emitted over the full life cycle of a product or service and usually expressed as grams of CO2-e.

*Carbon taxes*: A surcharge on fossil fuels that aims to reduce carbon dioxide emissions.

*Clean Development Mechanism (CDM):* The Clean Development Mechanism (CDM) is one of the Flexible Mechanisms defined in the Kyoto Protocol (IPCC, 2007) that provides for emissions reduction projects which generate Certified Emission Reduction units (CERs) which may be traded in emissions trading schemes.

*Debt-for-Nature Swap*: A financial transaction in which a portion of a developing nation's foreign debt is forgiven in exchange for local investments in conservation measures.

*Detritivore* (detritus feeder): Animals and plants that consume detritus (decomposing organic material), and in doing so contribute to decomposition and the recycling of nutrients.

*Dobson unit*: Dobson is the most common unit for measuring ozone concentration. One Dobson unit is the number of molecules of ozone that would be required to create a layer of pure ozone 0.01 millimetres thick at a temperature of 0 degree Celsius and pressure of 1 atmosphere.

*Ecological niche*: The habitat of a species or population within its ecosystem.

*Ecological succession:* The more-or-less predictable and orderly changes in the composition or structure of an ecological community with time.

*Ecological sustainability:* The capacity of ecosystems to maintain their essential processes and function and to retain their biological diversity without impoverishment.

*El Niño:* A warm water current which periodically flows southwards along the coast of Ecuador and Peru in South America, replacing the usually cold northwards flowing current; occurs once every five to seven years, usually during the Christmas season (the name refers to the Christ child); the opposite phase of an El Niño is called a La Niña.

*Extinction event:* (Mass extinction, extinction-level event, ELE) - a sharp decrease in the number of species in a relatively short period of time.

**Environmental Offsetting:** Ensuring full compensation for impact on the environment due to economic development is known as environmental offsetting.

*Food miles:* Food miles is a term which refers to the distance food is transported from the time of its production until it reaches the consumer. Food miles are one factor used when assessing the environmental impact of food, including the impact on global warming.

*Footprint:* (Ecological Footprint) in a very general environmental sense a "footprint" is a measure of environmental impact. However, this is usually expressed as an area of productive land (the footprint) needed to counteract the impact.

*Green Star*: Green Star is a voluntary sustainability rating system for buildings in Australia. It was launched in 2003 by the Green Building Council of Australia. The Green Star rating system assesses the sustainability of projects at all stages of the built environment lifecycle.

*Gamma diversity*: ($\gamma$-diversity) is the total species diversity in a landscape.

*k-selected species:* A species that forms a group of strong competitors in a crowded environment and that has fewer but stronger offspring.

*Kyoto Protocol, Kyoto agreement:* An international agreement signed in Japan in 1997, attached to the UN Framework Convention on Climate Change. Under the agreement, which has been in force in Ireland since 2005, industrialised countries promised to reduce their combined greenhouse gas emissions to at least 5% below 1990 levels over the period 2008-2012. See also UN Framework Convention on Climate Change.

*Kerbside collection*: Collection of household recyclable materials (separated or co-mingled) that are left at the kerbside for collection by local council services.

*Keystone species*: A species that has a disproportionate effect on its environment relative to its abundance, affecting many other organisms in an ecosystem and help in determine the types and numbers of various others species in a community.

**Montreal Protocol:** Montreal Protocol on Substances that Deplete the Ozone Layer is a protocol to the international Vienna Convention for the Protection of the Ozone Layer by phasing out production of numerous substances that are responsible for ozone depletion.

*Montreaux Record:* It is a voluntary mechanism to highlight specific wetland of international importance under the Ramsar convention, but which are facing immediate challenges. In particular, the Montreux Record is a register of listed Ramsar sites where changes in ecological character have occurred, are occurring, or are likely to occur as a result of technological developments, pollution or other human interference.

*Pantanal:* The world's largest wetland is the Pantanal, which covers 200,000 square kilometres (during the wet season) through Brazil, Paraguay and Bolivia, although 80% of it is in Brazil. It is a land of flooded grasslands, savannas and tropical forests.

*Rain shadow*: Arid or semi-arid climatical conditions of an area due to its position leeward of a mountain range.

*Rainwater harvesting:* Collecting rainwater either in storages or the soil mostly close to where it falls; the attempt to increase rainwater productivity by storing it in pondages, wetlands etc., and helping to avoid the need for infrastructure to bring water from elsewhere. Practiced on a large scale upstream this reduces available water downstream.

**Ramsar Convention:** Ramsar Convention or the Convention on Wetlands of International Importance is an international Convention for the conservation and sustainable utilization of wetlands around the world.

**Rio+20:** The United Nations Conference on Sustainable Development which took place in 2012 at Rio de Janeiro, Brazil is known as Rio+20 because it is the third in the series of UN Conferences on Sustainable Development and took place exactly 20 years after the first such conference was hosted in 1992 in Rio de Janeiro itself.

*Soil conditioner:* Any composted or non-composted material of organic origin that is produced or distributed for adding to soils, it includes ‹soil amendment›, ‹soil additive›, ‹soil improver› and similar materials, but excludes polymers that do

not biodegrade, such as plastics, rubbers, and coatings.

*Source-sink dynamics*: A theoretical model used by ecologists to describe how variation in habitat quality may affect the population growth or decline of organisms.

*Sustainable consumption*: Sustainable resource use - a change to society's historical patterns of consumption and behaviour that enables consumers to satisfy their needs with better performing products or services that use fewer resources, cause less pollution and contribute to social progress worldwide.

**Stockholm Convention:** Stockholm Convention on Persistent Organic Pollutants is an international Convention which aims to eliminate or restrict the production and use of persistent organic pollutants (POPs).

*Whitegoods*: Household electrical appliances like refrigerators, washing machines, clothes dryers, and dishwashers.

**Wetlands:** Any water body such as lakes, rivers, aquifers, swamps, marshes, wet grasslands, peatlands, oases, estuaries, deltas, coastal areas, coral reefs and all human-made sites such as fish ponds, rice paddies, reservoirs and salt pans are known as wetlands.

*Zero emissions:* An engine, motor or other energy source that does not produce any gas or release any harmful gases directly into the environment.

# Exercise -1

1. Protection and improvement of environment and safeguarding of forest and wildlife is emphasized in constitution of India under the Article
   - (a) 48 A
   - (b) 21
   - (c) 47
   - (d) 46

2. Environmental Relief Fund was established under the provisions of
   - (a) The Environment (Protection) Act, 1986
   - (b) The Indian Wild Life (Protection) Act, 1972
   - (c) The Public Liability Insurance Act, 1991
   - (d) The Forest (Conservation) Act, 1980

3. According to Convention on International Trade in Endangered species (CITES) COP 17, which one of the following is transferred from CITES Appendix II to Appendix I by January 2017.
   - (a) Gorilla
   - (b) Pangolin
   - (c) Tapir
   - (d) Mongoose

4. The climate meet COP-22 was held in which country ?
   - (a) Morocco
   - (b) South Africa
   - (c) Malaysia
   - (d) Indonesia

5. Articles 21, 48-A and 51-A(g), which aim to protect and improve the environment and safe guard forests and wildlife, incorporate which of the following principles of environmental law ?
   - (a) Polluter pays principle
   - (b) Precautionary principle
   - (c) Principle of strict liability
   - (d) Moral duty of the state

6. Which is the correct classification of forests under the Indian Forest Act, 1927 ?
   - (a) Grasslands, tropical forests, wetlands
   - (b) Protected forest, reserved forest, village forest
   - (c) Wildlife sanctuary, national parks, biosphere reserve
   - (d) Private forest, social forest, town forest

7. A Ramsar site not able to perform its ecological functions comes under :
   - (a) Montreal protocol
   - (b) Montreux record
   - (c) Montreal record
   - (d) Montreaux protocol

8. For the scientific research or investigations, the chief wildlife warden may grant the permission to public to enter a sanctuary under the section :
   - (a) 35 of The wildlife (Protection) Act 1972
   - (b) 28 of The Wildlife (Protection) Act 1972
   - (c) 72 of The Indian Forest Act 1922
   - (d) 73 of The Indian Forest Act 1927

9. The Access and Benefit Sharing (ABS) Protocol adopted by COP-10 at Nagoya is regarding the fair and equitable sharing of benefits arising from the use of:
   - (a) The genetic resources of the earth.
   - (b) Exclusive Economic Zones (EEZs)
   - (c) Marine and coastal areas significant for 'eco-tourism'.
   - (d) Technology transfer mechanisms for Clean Energy Development.

10. The 'Montreaux Record' is a register of:
    - (a) Invasive Alien Species and their ecological hazards outside their native environment.
    - (b) Wetland sites under the threat of anthropogenic activities.
    - (c) Endangered species of tropical and sub-tropical fauna.
    - (d) Coastal cities under direct threat of consequences of global warming.

11. What is carbon credit?
    - (a) It is the difference between the carbon emission allowed and actually emitted carbon
    - (b) It is the loan amount by IMF for reducing pollution
    - (c) It is the loan given to poor people for buying Modern Stoves
    - (d) All of the above

12. Which among the following multilateral convention seeks to protect the human health and environment from Persistent Organic Pollutants (POPs)?
    - (a) Bonn Convention
    - (b) Stockholm Convention
    - (c) Rotterdam Convention
    - (d) Basel Convention

13. Which of the following state governments has launched Shyama Prasad Mukherjee Jan Van Vikas Scheme for the development of villages around tiger reserves?
    - (a) Gujarat
    - (b) Maharashtra
    - (c) Madhya Pradesh
    - (d) Rajasthan

14. The NTCA has recently declared which two national parks as tiger reserves?
    - (a) Kudremukh and Rajaji
    - (b) Ratapani and Sunabeda
    - (c) Guru Ghasidas and Rajaji
    - (d) Rajaji and Sunabeda

15. Which one of the following committee was constituted to review environmental laws in the country?
    - (a) Subramanian Committee
    - (b) Kasturi Rangan Committee
    - (c) Madhav Nair Committee
    - (d) Ullas Karanth Committee

16. In context of environment, the term "dirty dozen" refers to
    - (a) 12 most harmful greenhouse gases
    - (b) 12 ozone depleting substances
    - (c) 12 persistent organic pollutants
    - (d) none of the above

17. The United Nations Frame work Convention on Climate Change (UNFCCC) is an international treaty drawn at:

(a) United Nations Conference on the Human Environment, Stockholm, 1972

(b) UN Conference on Environment and Development, Rio de Janerio, 1992

(c) World Summit on Sustainable Development, Johannesburg, 2002

(d) UN Climate change conference, Copenhagen, 2009

**18.** Which among the following multilateral environment agreements (MEAs) is not correctly paired with the respective issue it deals with?

(a) Montreal Protocol of 1987 – Ozone Depleting Substances

(b) Bonn Convention of 1979 – The conservation of Migratory Species

(c) Basel Convention of 1989 – Regulation of transboundary movement,transit, handling and use of Living Modified Organisms.

(d) Rotterdam Convention of 1998 – Consensual International Trade in certain Hazardous Chemicals and Pesticides.

**19.** The declaration reached at the 16th Conference of the Parties to the UN Framework Convention on Climate Change (UNFCCC) in December 2010 is also called the:

(a) Cancun Agreement

(b) Rio Declaration

(c) Kyoto Protocol

(d) Treaty on Nuclear Disarmament

**20.** 'Gadgil Committee Report' and 'Kasturirangan Committee Report', sometimes seen in the news, are related to:

(a) constitutional reforms

(b) Ganga Action Plan

(c) Linking of rivers

(d) Protection of Western Ghats

**21.** Environmental Impact Assessment (EIA) is mandatory under which one of the following India legislations:

(a) Indian Forest Act

(b) Air (Prevention and Control of Pollution) Act

(c) Wildlife Protection Act

(d) Environment (Protection) Act

**22.** United Nation's Convention to Combat Desertification (UNCCD) defines 'desertification' as:

(a) Spread and expansion of deserts

(b) Deserts encroaching arable lands rendering them useless

(c) Land degradation in dry lands resulting from various factors

(d) None of the above

**23.** The 'Hyderabad pledge' of COP-11 is regarding:

(a) Commitment to reduce subsidies

(b) Financial Commitment to Wetland conservation

(c) Commitment to reduce emissions

(d) Financial commitment to achieve Aichi targets

**24.** Which of the following addresses traditional knowledge associated with genetic resources considering the rights of the indigenous and local communities?

(a) Hyderabad Pledge of COP - 11

(b) Nagoya - Kuala Lumpur Supplementary Protocol

(c) Nagoya Protocol

(d) All of the above

**25.** Which among the following awards has been recently instituted by the Government of India for individuals or communities from rural areas that have shown extraordinary courage and dedication in protecting Wildlife?

(a) Indira Gandhi Paryavaran Puraskar

(b) Medini Puruskar Yojana

(c) Amrita Devi Bishnoi Award

(d) Pitambar Pant National Award

**26.** 'Net metering' is sometimes seen in the news in the context of promoting the     **[IAS Prelims 2016]**

(a) production and use of solar energy by the households/consumers

(b) use of piped natural gas in the kitchens of households

(c) installation of CNG kits in motor-cars

(d) installation of water meters in urban households

**27.** 'Gadgil Committee Report' and 'Kasturirangan Committee Report', sometimes seen in the news, are related to     **[IAS Prelims 2016]**

(a) constitutional reforms

(b) Ganga Action Plan

(c) linking of rivers

(d) protection of Western Ghats

**28.** In India, if a species of tortoise is declared protected under Schedule I of the Wildlife (Protection) Act, 1972, what does it imply?     **[IAS Prelims 2017]**

(a) It enjoys the same level of protection as the tiger.

(b) It no longer exists in the wild, a few individuals are under captive protection; and now it is impossible to prevent its extinction.

(c) It is endemic to a particular region of India.

(d) Both (b) and (c) stated above are correct in this context.

# Exercise -2

1. The main objectives of the Wildlife (Protection) Act, 1972 are
   1. Restricting hunting, killing or overexploitation of species.
   2. Protection of wildlife, preservation of natural habitats and environment.
   3. Recognizing the right of people to a healthy environment.
   Choose the correct answer :
   (a) and 2 only
   (b) 2 and 3 only
   (c) 1 and 3 only
   (d) 1, 2 and 3

2. Match the List-I and List-II. Identify the correct answer from the code given below :

   | List-I (Acts) | List-II (Year) |
   | --- | --- |
   | 1. Environmental Protection Act | (i) 1991 |
   | 2. Air (Prevention and Control of Pollution) Act | (ii) 1977 |
   | 3. Water (Prevention and Control of Pollution) Act | (iii) 1981 |
   | 4. Public Liability Insurance Act | (iv) 1986 |

   **Code :**

   |     | (a) | (b) | (c) | (d) |
   | --- | --- | --- | --- | --- |
   | (a) | (i) | (ii) | (iii) | (iv) |
   | (b) | (ii) | (iii) | (iv) | (i) |
   | (c) | (iii) | (iv) | (i) | (ii) |
   | (d) | (iv) | (iii) | (ii) | (i) |

3. The National Air Quality Monitoring Programme (NAMP) run by Central Pollution Control Board, monitors which of the following pollutants at all locations?
   1. Carbon dioxide
   2. Sulphur dioxide
   3. Oxides of nitrogen
   4. Suspended particulate matter
   Select the correct answer using the codes given below:
   Codes:
   (a) 1, 2 and 3 only
   (b) 1 ,3 and 4 only
   (c) 2 ,3 and 4 only
   (d) 1 ,2, and 4 only

4. Which of these pairs are correctly matched ?
   1. Minamata convention: mercury
   2. Stockholm convention: persistant organic pollutants
   3. Basel convention: lead
   Select the correct answer using the codes given below.
   Codes:
   (a) 1 and 2 only
   (b) 1 and 3 only
   (c) 2 and 3 only
   (d) 1,2 and 3

5. Consider the following statements:
   1. No human activity is allowed inside tiger reserves.
   2. Tourism is allowed in national parks.
   Which of the statements given above is/are correct?
   Codes:
   (a) 1 only
   (b) 2 only
   (c) Both 1 and 2
   (d) Neither 1 nor 2

6. The Wildlife Protection Act, 1972 provides for various categories of protected areas. These include:
   1. National parks
   2. Wildlife sanctuaries
   3. Biosphere reserve
   4. Tiger reserves
   Select the correct answer using the codes given below.
   Codes:
   (a) 1 and 2 only
   (b) 1 and 3 only
   (c) 2 and 3 only
   (d) 1, 2 and 4 only

7. Which of the following are correct
   1. Alpha diversity (within-community diversity) refers to the rate of replacement of species along a gradient of habitats or communities.
   2. Gamma diversity (overall) refers to the diversity of the habitats over the total landscape or geographical area.
   Select the correct answer using the codes given below.
   Codes:
   (a) Only 1
   (b) Only 2
   (c) Both 1& 2
   (d) Neither 1 nor 2

8. Over 140 countries have agreed on the first international treaty that aims to reduce the emission and release of mercury into the air, water and land. Treaty is named as the Minamata convention. Which of the following is correct with regard to this treaty:
   1. The convention prohibits primary mining of mercury.
   2. The use of mercury in products like CFL, batteries, soaps, cosmetics and medical appliances must be phased out by 2020.
   3. Treaty keeps exception for the products like vaccines' preservatives and products related to religious faith.
   Codes:
   (a) 1 only
   (b) 1, 2 & 3
   (c) 3 only
   (d) 1 & 2 only

9. Forest Rights Act recognizes the rights of forest dwellers over forestland and forest resources such as minor forest produce they have traditionally been extracting and using. Which of the following statements is/are correct with regard to this Act.
   1. Forest dwellers can transport minor forest produce by any appropriate means of transport.
   2. A committee set up by Gram Sabha issues transit passes for transporting minor forest produce.
   Codes:
   (a) 1 only
   (b) 2 only
   (c) Both 1& 2
   (d) Neither 1 & 2

10. The Union Ministry of Environment & Forest has introduced a new scheme called the 'Emissions Trading Scheme' which of the following statements is/are correct with regard to this scheme:
    1. This is a market-based scheme to reduce air pollution.
    2. It has been implemented only in 3 states till now.
    3. The scheme allows the Pollution control boards to set a cap on the level of pollution permitted in an industrial area, and then allows the industries to self regulate to ensure that pollution does not exceed this cap.

4.  This scheme is the first of its kind in the world.
Codes:
(a)  1, 2, 3 & 4          (b)  1 & 3 only
(c)  2 & 3 only           (d)  1, 2 & 3

**11.** Which of the following statements is/are correct about Dark Matter:
1.  Dark matter does not interact with any electromagnetic radiation.
2.  Dark matter interacts with ordinary matter through gravity only.
3.  The force between dark matter and ordinary matter is repulsive.
Codes:
(a)  1 only.              (b)  1 & 2 only.
(c)  2 & 3 only.          (d)  1, 2 & 3.

**12.** The National Green Tribunal Act, 2010 was enacted in consonance with which of the following provisions of the constitution of India?
1.  Right to Healthy Environment, construed as a part of Right to Life under Article 21.
2.  Provision of grants for raising the level of administration in the scheduled Areas for the welfare of Scheduled Tribes under Article 275 (10
3.  Powers and functions of Gram Sabha as mentioned under Article 243 (A)
Select the correct answer using the codes given below:
Codes:
(a)  Only 1              (b)  Only 2 & 3
(c)  Only 1 & 3          (d)  1, 2 & 3

**13.** Consider the following pairs of Conventions and their Objectives:
1.  Minamata Convention: Against toxic mercury and mercury compounds.
2.  Cartagena Protocol: Safe transfer, handling and use of living modified organisms resulting from modern biotechnology.
3.  Water Convention: To protect and manage the transboundary surface waters and groundwaters.
4.  Espoo Convention: To prevent, reduce and control significant adverse transboundary environmental impact from proposed activities.
Which of the above pairs are correctly matched?
Codes:
(a)  2 and 3 only        (b)  1, 2 and 3 only
(c)  2 and 4 only        (d)  1, 2, 3 and 4

**14.** Consider the following questions.
1.  The Government of India was the first country in South Asia to join IUCN as a stage member in 1969.
2.  It is also the first and the only country in the region to host the General Assembly of IUCN in 1969.
Codes:
(a)  Only I             (b)  Only II
(c)  Neither I nor II    (d)  Both I and II

**15.** Consider the following statements:
1.  The International Plant Protection Convention (IPCC) is a multilateral treaty to protect plant resources from deforestation arising out of industrialization.
2.  The treaty is overseen by International Union for Conservation of Nature.

Which of the statements given above is/are correct?
(a)  Only 1             (b)  Only 2
(c)  Only 1 and 2       (d)  Neither 1 nor 2

**16.** Consider the following statements
1.  CBIT is an outcome of the UNFCCC's Paris agreement in 2015 and expected to address the issue of transparency
2.  It will help developing countries monitor and report the progress on their climate actions
3.  WTO has been requested to act as the trustee for the fund, who was also a trustee in the initial hand holding of GEF
Which of the statements given above is/are correct?
Codes:
(a)  Only 2 &3          (b)  Only 1
(c)  Only 1 & 2         (d)  Only 3

**17.** Consider the following statements:
1.  Brundtland Commission was a commission established by the United Nations in 1983 as World Commission on Environment and Development (WCED).
2.  Gro Harlem Brundtland was the former Prime Minister of Japan and was chosen due to her strong background in the sciences and public health.
3.  Brundtland Report is formally called as Our Common Future: Report of the World Commission on Environment and Development 1987.
Which of the statements given above is/are correct?
Codes:
(a)  Only 1 & 3         (b)  Only 3
(c)  Only 3 & 2         (d)  All of the above

**18.** What is/are the importance of the 'United Nations Convention to Combat Desertification'?
1.  It aims to promote effective action through innovative national programs and supportive inter-national partnerships.
2.  It has a special/particular focus on South Asia and North Africa regions, and its Secretariat facilitates the allocation of major portion of financial resources to these regions.
3.  It is committed to bottom-up approach, encouraging the participation of local people in combating the desertification.
Select the correct answer using the code given below.
(a)  1 only             (b)  2 and 3 only
(c)  1 and 3 only       (d)  1, 2 and 3

**19.** Consider the following statements with respect to 'Convention on International Trade in Endangered Species of Wild Fauna and Flora (CITES)',
1.  **The focus of the convention is to completely control the trade of wild species.**
2.  It was formed in 1973 and regulates the international trade in over 35,000 wild species of plants and animals.
Which of the above statement/s is/are correct?
Select the correct code:
(a)  Only 1             (b)  Only 2
(c)  Both 1&2           (d)  Neither 1 nor 2

**20.** Consider the following statements:
1. IUCN classify protected areas according to their management objectives.
2. National parks of India are in the category IUCN 1.

Which of the statements given above is/are correct?

Codes:
(a) 1 only 　　　　 (b) 2 only
(c) Both 1 and 2 　 (d) Neither 1 nor 2

**21.** Which of the following wastes have been regulated by the Basel Convention on Control of Transboundary Movements of Hazardous Wastes and their Disposal?
1. PCBs, used lead acid batteries, etc.
2. Biomedical and Healthcare wastes
3. Incinerator Ash
4. Used oils
5. Household waste

Which of the statements given above is/are correct?

Codes:
(a) Only 2, 3 and 5 　 (b) Only 1, 2, 3 and 4
(c) Only 1, 2 and 4 　 (d) All of the above

**22.** Match the following summits with their locations.
1. COP 11 - Copenhagen
2. COP 18 - Lima
3. COP 20 - Doha
4. COP 19 - Warsaw

Which of the statements given above is/are correct?

Codes:
(a) Only 1, 2 and 4 　 (b) Only 1, 2 and 3
(c) All of the above 　 (d) None of the above

**23.** Which of the following are missions under the Nation Action Plan on Climate Change?
1. National Mission for Sustainable Agriculture
2. National Mission for Sustainable Development
3. National Mission on Sustainable Habitat
4. National Water Mission
5. National Mission for Enhanced Energy Efficiency

Which of the statements given above is/are correct?

Codes:
(a) Only 1 and 2 　　 (b) Only 1, 2, 3 and 5
(c) Only 1, 3, 4 and 5 (d) All of the above

**24.** The Montreal Protocol on Substances that Deplete the Ozone Layer aims to control the production and use of:
1. Dichloromethane
2. CFCs
3. HFCs

Select the correct answer using the codes given below.

Codes:
(a) 1 and 2 only 　 (b) 2 only
(c) 2 and 3 only 　 (d) 1,2 and 3

**25.** Consider the following statement and state which of the following is/are true?
1. Montreal Protocol deal with ozone layer depletion and Kyoto Protocol deals with global warming and greenhouse gas emission.
2. Montreal Protocol has banned the emission of hydrofluorocarbons (HFCs).

Select the correct answer using the codes given below.

Codes:
(a) Only 1 　　 (b) Only 2
(c) Both 1 & 2 　 (d) Neither 1 or 2

**26.** Consider the following statements:
1. The CBD is the first comprehensive global agreement addressing to all aspects related to biodiversity.
2. COP 10 was held from 18 to 29 October 2010 at the Nagoya Conference centre, in Nagoya, Aichi Prefecture, Japan.

Select the correct answer using the codes given below.
(a) Only 1 　　 (b) Only 2
(c) Both 1& 2 　 (d) None of the above

**27.** Consider the following statements.
1. In 1972 the United Nations held the first international conference on human environment in Stockholm.
2. The agenda was prepared by Rene Dubos and other experts.

Select the correct answer using the codes given below.

Codes:
(a) Only 1 　　 (b) Only 2
(c) Both 1& 2 　 (d) None of the above

**28.** Consider the following statements:
1. 2011—COP was held in South Africa
2. It was COP's 17th meet and MOP's 8th meet.

Which of the statements given above is/are correct?
(a) Only 1 　　 (b) Only 2
(c) Both 1 & 2 　 (d) None of the above

**29.** With reference to the International Union for Conservation of Nature and Natural Resources (IUCN) and the Convention on International Trade in Endangered Species of Wild Fauna and Flora (CITES), which of the following statements is/are correct?
1. IUCN is an organ of the United Nations and CITES is an international agreement between governments
2. IUCN runs thousands of field projects around the world to better manage natural environments.
3. CITES is legally binding on the States that have joined it, but this Convention does not take the place of national laws.

Select the correct answer using the code given below.

Codes:
(a) 1 only 　　 (b) 2 and 3 only
(c) 1 and 3 only (d) 1, 2 and 3

**30.** Which of the following International Conventions (India being a signatory) have a bearing on conservation of wildlife in India?
1. International Whaling Commission (IWC)
2. Convention on International Trade in Endangered Species of wild fauna and flora (**CITES**)
3. United Nations Educational, Scientific and Cultural Organization-World Heritage Convention (UNESCO-WHC)
4. Convention on Migratory Species (CMS)
5. International Union for Conservation of Nature and Natural Resources (**IUCN**)

Choose the correct answer using the codes below:

Codes:
(a) 1, 2 and 3 only 　 (b) 3, 4 and 5 only
(c) 2 only 　　　　　 (d) All of the above

**31.** Which of the following statements regarding 'Green Climate Fund' is/are correct?
1. It is intended to assist the developing countries in adaptation and mitigation practices to counter climate change.
2. It is founded under the aegis of UNEP, OECD, Asian Development Bank and World Bank
Select the correct answer using the code given below.
Codes:
(a) 1 only     (b) 2 only
(c) Both 1 and 2     (d) Neither 1 nor 2

**32.** Consider the following about Green Climate Fund (GCF).
1. It was established under United Nations Environment Programme (UNEP).
2. It is aimed at achieving the goal set out by United Nations Framework Convention on Climate Change (UNFCCC).
3. It is a mechanism to redistribute money from the developed to the developing world. Choose the correct answer using the codes below.
Codes:
(a) 1 and 2 only     (b) 2 and 3 only
(c) 1 and 3 only     (d) All of the above

**33.** In the context of Amendment to Montreal Protocol, 2017, consider the following statements.
1. 170 countries have reached a historic deal to phase out Hydrofluorocarbons (HFCs) after years of protracted and at times seemingly intractable negotiations in Kigali, Rwanda accepted an amendment to the Montreal Protocol
2. Developing countries must reduce HFCs use by 10% by 2019 from 2011-2013 levels, and 85% by 2036.
3. A third group of developing countries, including India, Pakistan and Arab Gulf states, must begin the process in 2028 and reduce emissions by 10% by 2032 from 2024-2026 levels, and then by 85% by 2047
Choose the correct answer using the codes below.
(a) Only 2 & 3     (b) Only 2
(c) Only 1 & 3     (d) All of the above

**34.** The term 'Intended Nationally Determined Contributions' is sometimes seen in the news in the context of
**[IAS Prelims 2016]**
(a) pledges made by the European countries to rehabilitate refugees from the war-affected Middle East
(b) plan of action outlined by the countries of the world to combat climate change
(c) capital contributed by the member countries in the establishment of Asian Infrastructure Investment Bank
(d) plan of action outlined by the countries of the world regarding Sustainable Development Goals

**35.** What is/are the importance/importance of the 'United Nations Convention to Combat Desertification'?
**[IAS Prelims 2016]**
1. It aims to promote effective action through innovative national programs and supportive inter-national partnerships.
2. It has a special/particular focus on South Asia and North Africa regions, and its Secretariat facilitates the allocation of major portion of financial resources to these regions.
3. It is committed to bottom-up approach, encouraging the participation of local people in combating the desertification.
Select the correct answer using the code given below.
(a) 1 only     (b) 2 and 3 only
(c) 1 and 3 only     (d) 1, 2 and 3

**36.** Consider the following pairs:     **[IAS Prelims 2016]**

| Terms sometimes seen in the news | Their origin |
| --- | --- |
| 1. Annex-I Countries | Cartagena Protocol |
| 2. Certified Emissions Reductions | Nagoya Protocol |
| 3. Clean Development Mechanism | Kyoto Protocol |

Which of the pairs given above is/are correctly matched?
(a) 1 and 2 only     (b) 2 and 3 only
(c) 3 only     (d) 1, 2 and 3

**37.** With reference to 'dugong', a mammal found in India, which of the following statements is/are correct?
**[IAS Prelims 2015]**
1. It is a herbivorous marine animal.
2. It is found along the entire coast of India.
3. It is given legal protection under Schedule I of the Wildlife (Protection) Act, 1972.
Select the correct answer using the code given below.
(a) 1 and 2     (b) 2 only
(c) 1 and 3     (d) 3 only

**38.** Which of the following best describes/ describe the aim of 'Green India Mission' of the Government of India?
**[IAS Prelims 2016]**
1. Incorporating environmental benefits and costs into the Union and State Budgets thereby implementing the 'green accounting'
2. Launching the second green revolution to enhance agricultural output so as to ensure food security to one and all in the future
3. Restoring and enhancing forest cover and responding to climate change by a combination of adaptation and mitigation measures
Select the correct answer using the code given below.
(a) 1 only     (b) 2 and 3 only
(c) 3 only     (d) 1, 2 and 3

**39.** According to the Wildlife (Protection) Act, 1972, which of the following animals cannot be hunted by any person except under some provisions provided by law?
**[IAS Prelims 2017]**
1. Gharial     2. Indian wild ass
3. Wild buffalo
Select the correct answer using the code given below:
(a) 1 only     (b) 2 and 3 only
(c) 1 and 3 only     (d) 1, 2 and 3

# Hints and Explanations

**EXERCISE-1**

1. (a)   2. (c)   3. (b)   4. (a)   5. (b)   6. (b)

7. (b)   8. (b)

9. (a) The Nagoya Protocol on Access to Genetic Resources and the Fair and Equitable Sharing of Benefits Arising from their Utilization to the Convention on Biological Diversity is an international agreement which aims at sharing the benefits arising from the utilization of genetic resources in a fair and equitable way. It entered into force on 12 October 2014, 90 days after the date of deposit of the fiftieth instrument of ratification.

10. (b) The Montreux Record is a register of wetland sites on the List of Wetlands of International Importance where changes in ecological character have occurred, are occurring, or are likely to occur as a result of technological developments, pollution or other human interference. It is maintained as part of the Ramsar List.

11. (a) Carbon credit shows that country or any entity emit the carbon below the limit prescribed by the government, hence country or entity can sell it in Exchange where carbon are treated.

12. (b) The Stockholm Convention on Persistent Organic Pollutants is a global treaty to protect human health and the environment from chemicals that remain intact in the environment for long periods, become widely distributed geographically, accumulate in the fatty tissue of humans and wildlife, and have harmful impacts on human health or on the environment. In response to this global problem, the Stockholm Convention, which was adopted in 2001 and entered into force in 2004, requires its parties to take measures to eliminate or reduce the release of POPs into the environment. As set out in Article 1, the objective of the Stockholm Convention is to protect human health and the environment from persistent organic pollutants.

13. (b) Maharashtra Cabinet has approved Shyama Prasad Mukherjee Jan Van Vikas Scheme for development of villages around tiger reserves. Aim of this scheme is comprehensive development of villages in and around the buffer zones of tiger reserves.

14. (a) The NTCA has accorded final approval to Kudremukh National Park in Karnataka and Rajaji National Park in Uttarkhand for being declared as tiger reserves by respective states.

15. (a) T S R Subramanian Committee was constituted to review environmental laws in India. The committee has submitted its recommendations to the government recently.

16. (c) 12 persistent organic pollutants. These were the 12 initial compounds that were listed under the Stockholm convention.

17. (b) In 1992, countries joined an international treaty, the United Nations Framework Convention on Climate Change, as a framework for international cooperation to combat climate change by limiting average global temperature increases and the resulting climate change, and coping with impacts that were, by then, inevitable

18. (c) The Basel Convention on the Control of Transboundary Movements of Hazardous Wastes and Their Disposal, usually known simply as the Basel Convention, is an international treaty that was designed to reduce the movements of hazardous waste between nations, and specifically to prevent transfer of hazardous waste from developed to less developed countries (LDCs). It does not, however, address the movement of radioactive waste.

19. (a) The 2010 United Nations Climate Change Conference was held in Cancún, Mexico, from 29 November to 10 December 2010. The conference is officially referred to as the 16th session of the Conference of the Parties (COP 16) to the United Nations Framework Convention on Climate Change (UNFCCC) and the 6th session of the Conference of the Parties serving as the meeting of the Parties (CMP 6) to the Kyoto Protocol. Earth Summit 1992 was the United Nations Conference on Environment and Development (UNCED), commonly known as the Rio Summit, Rio Conference. The Kyoto Protocol is a protocol (update) to the United Nations Framework Convention on Climate Change. It was initially adopted on 11 December 1997 in Kyoto, Japan. The international efforts to promote nuclear non-proliferation started after the World War II. At that time, there was only nuclear arsenal of the world in United States. A Baruch Plan was proposed in US in 1946 which recommended the verifiable dismantlement and destruction of the U.S. nuclear arsenal.

20. (d) They are associated with Western Ghat conservation plan.

21. (d) Under Environment (Protection) Act 1986, EIA is now mandatory for 29 categories of developmental activities which involve investment of more than Rs 50 Crores.

22. (c) UNCCD is one of the Rio conventions that focusses on desertification, land degradation and drought (DLDD). Dry lands include arid, semiarid and dry sub humid regions. It does not connote spread of deserts.

23. (b) US$50 million during India's two - year COP presidency, focused on enhancing India's human and technical resources to attain the CBD's objectives, and for promoting capacity building in developing countries. It established the foundation for the mobilization of resources to achieve the Aichi targets.

24. (c) It addresses traditional knowledge associated with genetic resources with provisions on access, benefit - sharing and compliance. It also addresses genetic grant access to them.

25. (c) (i) The Kyoto Protocol separates countries into two groups. Annex I includes developed nations, while Non-Annex I refers to developing countries.
A CER is a certificate which is issued every time the United Nations prevents one tonne of CO2 equivalent being emitted through carbon projects registered with the Clean Development Mechanism (CDM).
(ii) All three terms are associated with Kyoto Protocol. Therefore, answer "c" 3 only.

26. (a) (i) A Net metering is a billing mechanism that credits solar energy system owners for the electricity they add to the grid. Net metering allows residential and commercial customers who generate their own electricity from solar power to feed electricity they do not use back into the grid.
(ii) Under Net-metering system, Customer installs a solar or windpower plant on his premise, gets it grid-connected with the electricity distribution company (DISCOM) Hence (a) is the apt choice.

27. (d) (i) The Gadgil Commission was an environmental research commission appointed by the Ministry of Environment and Forests of India. The Commission submitted the report to the Government of India on 31 August 2011. The Kasturirangan Committee Report has sought to balance the two concerns of development and environment protection, by watering down the environmental regulation regime proposed by the Western Ghats Ecology Experts Panel's Gadgil report in 2012.
(ii) They're associated with Western Ghat conservation plan.

28. (a) Tiger is given as Schedule I animal. So "A" is correct.

### EXERCISE-2

1. (d)
2. (d)
3. (c) 2 ,3 and 4 only. The objectives of the N.A.M.P. are to determine status and trends of ambient air quality; to ascertain whether the prescribed ambient air quality standards are violated. Under N.A.M.P., four air pollutants viz ., Sulphur Dioxide ($SO_2$), Oxides of Nitrogen as NO2, Suspended Particulate Matter (SPM) and Respirable Suspended Particulate Matter (RSPM / PM10) have been identified for regular monitoring at all the locations.

4. (a) 1 and 2 only. The Basel Convention is for the Control of Transboundary Movements of Hazardous Wastes and Their Disposal. It was designed to reduce the movements of hazardous waste between nations, and specifically to prevent transfer of hazardous waste from developed to less developed countries (LDCs). It does not, however, address the movement of radioactive waste. The Minamata Convention on Mercury is an international treaty designed to protect human health and the environment from anthropogenic emissions and releases of mercury and mercury compounds. Stockholm Convention on Persistent Organic Pollutants is an international environmental treaty that aims to eliminate or restrict the production and use of persistent organic pollutants (POPs).

5. (b) 2 only. The second statement is a simple fact, which you must know. A tiger reserve has two zones – core and buffer. In the buffer zone, human activity is allowed.

6. (d) Biosphere reserves are created by merely a notification and they DO NOT require legislation. National parks, wildlife sanctuaries, tiger reserves, community reserves, conservation reserves are backed up by the Wildlife Protection Act, 1972.

7. (c) The terms alpha, beta, and gamma diversity were all introduced by R. H. Whittaker to describe the spatial component of biodiversity. Alpha diversity is just the diversity of each site (local species pool). Beta diversity represents the differences in species composition among sites. Gamma diversity is the diversity of the entire landscape (regional species pool).

8. (b) The Minamata convention provides controls and reductions across a range of products, processes and industries where mercury is used, released or emitted. Major highlights of the Minamata Convention on Mercury include a ban on new mercury mines, the phase-out of existing ones, control measures on air emissions, and the international regulation of the informal sector for artisanal and small-scale gold mining. Use of mercury in coal-fired power plants, small and artisanal gold mines and cement production has to be reduced. Countries with small and artisanal gold mines will have to devise

strategies to reduce the use of mercury in gold production in three years. The use of mercury in products like batteries, CFLs, soaps, cosmetics and medical appliances like thermometer will be phased out by 2020.

9. (c) The Union ministry of tribal affairs has notified the amended rules for the implementation of the Forest Rights Act (FRA) of 2006. Accordingly, Forest dwellers can transport minor forest produce by any appropriate means of transport. Transit passes for transporting minor forest produce will be issued by a committee constituted by the gram sabha. The committee constituted under the gram sabha will prepare conservation and management plan for community forest resources after forest dwellers' rights on such resources are recognized.

10. (d) Ministry of Environment has decided to try out pilot projects of emission trading schemes in the states of Tamil Nadu, Maharashtra and Gujarat. The pilot systems for the three included states will cover 1,000 industries. Emissions trading or cap-and-trade is a market-based approach used to control pollution by providing economic incentives for achieving reductions in the emissions of pollutants. There are active trading programs in several air pollutants.

11. (b) The name refers to the fact that it does not emit or interact with electromagnetic radiation, such as light, and is thus invisible to the entire electromagnetic spectrum. The most widely accepted hypothesis on the form for dark matter is that it is composed of weakly interacting massive particles (WIMPs) that interact only through gravity and the weak force. Dark matter was first detected as a result of strong unexplained attractive effects on orbits of stars. It has since been used to account for gravitational concentrations of ordinary matter that resulted in stars and galaxies. This is again an attractive and not a repulsive effect.

12. (a) The National Green Tribunal Act, 2010 embraces the objective that the right to healthy environment has been construed as a part of the right to life under Article 21 of the constitution in the judicial pronouncement in India.

13. (d) 1. Minamata Convention: to protect the human health and the environment from anthropogenic emissions and releases of mercury and mercury compounds. 2. Cartagena Protocol: To ensure an adequate level of protection in the field of the safe transfer, handling and use of living modified organisms resulting from modern biotechnology that may have adverse effects on the conservation and sustainable use of biological diversity, taking also into account risks to human health, and specifically focusing on transboundary movements. 3. Water Convention: To protect

and ecologically sound manage the transboundary surface waters and groundwaters. To prevent, control and reduce water pollution from point and non-point sources. 4. Espoo Convention: To prevent, reduce and control significant adverse transboundary environmental impact from proposed activities. Also called EIA convention.

14. (d) The establishment of the IUCN India National Committee (INC) - a first of its kind committee in the region - consisting of IUCN's Indian members and Chaired by the Secretary, Ministry of Environment, Forests and Climate Change (MoEF&CC), Government of India (GoI) marked the beginning of the close association between IUCN and GoI to coordinate on environmental issues. India became a State Member of IUCN in 1969, through the Ministry of Environment, Forest and Climate Change (MoEFCC).

15. (d) The International Plant Protection Convention (IPCC) is a multilateral treaty for international cooperation and aims to protect plant resources from harmful pests which may be introduced through international trade. The convention created a governing body consisting of each party, known as the commission of phytosanitary measures which oversees the implementation of the convention.

16. (c) Capacity-Building Initiative for Transparency (CBIT) Fund is an outcome of the UNFCCC's Paris agreement in 2015. It will help developing countries monitor and report the progress on their climate actions. World Bank has been requested to act as the trustee for the fund, who was also a trustee in the initial hand holding of GEF. Therefore option (d) is wrong and option (c) is correct.

17. (a) Formally known as the World Commission on Environment and Development (WCED), the mission of Brundtland Commission is to unite countries to pursue sustainable development together. The Chairperson of the Commission, Gro Harlem Brundtland, was appointed by Javier Pérez de Cuéllar, former Secretary General of the United Nations, in December 1983. To rally countries to work and pursue sustainable development together, the UN decided to establish the Brundtland Commission. Gro Harlem Brundtland was the former Prime Minister of Norway and was chosen due to her strong background in the sciences and public health. The Brundtland Commission officially dissolved in December 1987 after releasing Our Common Future, also known as the Brundtland Report, in October 1987. Statement 2 is wrong.

18. (c) 2nd statement wrong because, the implementation of the UNCCD is geared around five regional implementation annexes: Annex 1 for Africa, Annex 2 for Asia, Annex 3 for Latin America and

the Caribbean, Annex 4 for Northern Mediterranean and Annex 5 for Central and Eastern Europe. Third statement is right. Therefore, answer is option (c).

19. (b) The Convention on International Trade in Endangered Species of Wild Fauna and Flora (CITES) is an international regulatory treaty between 182 member states. It was formed in 1973 and regulates the international trade in over 35,000 wild species of plants and animals.

The focus of the convention is not solely on the protection of species. It also promotes controlled trade that is not detrimental to the sustainability of wild species. It has become the best-known conservation convention in the world.

20. (a) IUCN protected area management categories classify protected areas according to their management objectives. The National parks of India are in the category IUCN 2. National Park Category II protected areas are large natural or near natural areas set aside to protect large-scale ecological processes, along with the complement of species and ecosystems characteristic of the area, which also provide a foundation for environmentally and culturally compatible, spiritual, scientific, educational, recreational, and visitor opportunities.

21. (d) It includes household wastes and incinerator ash (residue that comes from incinerating household waste) under other wastes.

22. (d) These United Nations Climate Change Conferences are yearly conferences held in the framework of the United Nations Framework Convention on Climate Change (UNFCCC). They serve as the formal meeting of the UNFCCC Parties (Conferences of the Parties) (COP) to assess progress in dealing with climate change. Year 2005: COP 11 / CMP 1, Montreal, Canada; Year 2009: COP 15 / CMP 5, Copenhagen, Denmark; Year 2012: COP 18 / CMP 8, Doha, Qatar; Year 2013: COP 19 / CMP 9, Warsaw, Poland; Year 2014: COP 20 / CMP 10, Lima, Peru; Year 2015: COP 21 / CMP 11, Paris, France.

23. (c) There are Eight National Missions - National Solar Mission, National Mission for Enhanced Energy Efficiency, National Mission on Sustainable Habitat, National Water Mission, National Mission for Sustaining the Himalayan Ecosystem, National Mission for a "Green India", National Mission for Sustainable Agriculture, and National Mission on Strategic Knowledge for Climate Change.

24. (b) Montreal protocol aims to phase out several groups of halogenated hydrocarbons that have been shown to play a role in ozone depletion. All of these ozone depleting substances contain either chlorine or bromine (substances containing only fluorine do not harm the ozone layer). These include CFCs and HCFCs. HFCs replaced CFCs and HCFCs. HFCs pose no harm to the ozone layer because, unlike CFCs and HCFCs, they do not contain chlorine. The Montreal Protocol therefore does not address HFCs. But HFCs cause global warming. Dichloromethane is a new entry among gases that depletes ozone layer, but at present it has not been included under Montreal Protocol.

25. (b) The Montreal Protocol on Substances that Deplete the Ozone Layer (a protocol to the Vienna Convention for the Protection of the Ozone Layer) is an international treaty designed to protect the ozone layer by phasing out the production of numerous substances that are responsible for ozone depletion. It was agreed on 26 August 1987, and entered into force on 26 August 1989, followed by a first meeting in Helsinki, May 1989. Produced mostly in developed countries, hydrofluorocarbons (HFCs) replaced CFCs and HCFCs. HFCs pose no harm to the ozone layer because, unlike CFCs and HCFCs, they do not contain chlorine.

26. (c) The CBD, one of the two agreements adopted during the Earth Summit held in Rio de Janeiro in 1992, is the first comprehensive global agreement which addresses all aspects relating to biodiversity. The Convention, while reaffirming sovereign rights of nations over their biological resources, establishes three main goals: (i) conservation of biological diversity, (ii) sustainable use of its components and (iii) fair and equitable sharing of benefits arising out of the use of genetic resources. The tenth meeting of the Conference of the Parties (COP 10) was held in Nagoya, Aichi Prefecture, Japan, from 18 to 29 October 2010. COP 10 included a high-level ministerial segment organized by the host country in consultation with the Secretariat and the Bureau. The highlevel segment took place from 27 to 29 October 2010.

27. (c) Both the statements are correct.

28. (a) The 2011 United Nations Climate Change Conference (COP17) was held in Durban, South Africa, from 28 November to 11 December 2011 to establish a new treaty to limit carbon emissions. The conference was officially referred to as the 17th session of the Conference of the Parties (COP 17) to the United Nations Framework Convention on Climate Change (UNFCCC) and the 7th session of the Conference of the Parties serving as the meeting of the Parties (CMP 7) to the Kyoto Protocol.

29. (b) Statement 1 is not correct.

30. (d) India is a party to five major international conventions related to Wild Life conservation, viz., Convention on International Trade in Endangered Species of wild fauna and flora (CITES), International Union for Conservation of Nature and Natural Resources (IUCN), International Whaling Commission (IWC), United Nations Educational, Scientific and Cultural Organization-World Heritage Committee (UNESCO-WHC) and the Convention on Migratory Species (CMS).

31. (a) The Green Climate Fund (GCF) is a fund within the framework of the UNFCCC founded as a mechanism to assist developing countries in adaptation and mitigation practices to counter climate change.

32. (b) The Green Climate Fund (GCF) is a fund within the framework of the UNFCCC founded as a mechanism to redistribute money from the developed to the developing world, in order to assist the developing countries in adaptation and mitigation practices to counter climate change. The GCF is based in the new Songdo district of Incheon, South Korea. It is governed by a Board of 24 members and initially supported by an Interim Secretariat.

33. (c) Statement 2 is wrong it should be Developed countries.

34. (b) (i) Countries across the globe committed to create a new international climate agreement by the conclusion of the U.N. Framework Convention on Climate Change (UNFCCC) Conference of the Parties (COP21) in Paris in December 2015.
(ii) INDC are associated with UNFCCC-Climate change. Hence b) is the apt choice.

35. (c) (i) United Nations Convention to Combat Desertification (UNCCD) aims to promote effective action through innovative national programmes and supportive international partnerships. UNCCD is committed to a bottom-up approach, encouraging the participation of local people in combating desertification.
(ii) As per of the convention, Statement 3 is right. But UNCCCD focuses on Africa, Asia, Latin America and the Caribbean, Northern Mediterranean and Central and Eastern Europe. Hence statement 2 is wrong. Therefore, answer (c).

36. (c) This award is given for significant contribution in the field of wildlife protection, which is recognised as having shown exemplary courage or having done exemplary work for the protection of wildlife. A cash award of Rupees One lakh is presented to individuals/institutions involved in wildlife protection.

37. (c) The dugong is a medium-sized marine mammal. Dugong is listed under schedule 1 of India Wildlife Protection Act, 1972. In 2008, a MoU was signed between the Ministry of Environment and Forests and the Government of India, in order to conserve dugongs. In fact the highest level of legal protection is accorded to dugongs in India.

38. **(c)** (i) The National Mission for a Green India was announced by the Prime Minister as one of the eight Missions under the National Action Plan on Climate Change (NAPCC). It recognizes that climate change phenomenon will seriously affect and alter the distribution, type and quality of natural resources of the country. GIM puts the "greening" in the context of climate change adaptation and mitigation, meant to enhance ecosystem services like carbon sequestration and storage (in forests and other ecosystems), hydrological services and biodiversity; along with provisioning services like fuel, fodder, small timber.
(ii) **Ref:** *India Yearbook 2016 page 338: Environment ministry has launched National Mission for a Green India through a consultative process involving relevant stakeholders, aimed at both increasing the forest and tree cover by 5 million ha, as well as increasing the quality of the existing forest cover in another 5 million ha. Hence only statement 3 fits.*

39. (d) The schedule 5 vermin- crow, fruitbat, mice and rat can be killed. Since the animals given in above MCQ are outside that list hence answer is "D".

# CURRENT ECOLOGICAL DEVELOPMENTS

**9 Chapter**


## Introduction

There have been several ecological developments in India and around the world. The ecological changes have profound impact on the flora and fauna of terrestrial and aquatic environments. Ecological balance is necessary for achieving sustainable environment. In this chapter, we will discuss the current ecological developments in India and around the world.

Ecological balance is a theory which highlights that natural conditions, including numbers of various animal and plant species, remain stable on their own through variations over time. The theory, also known as balance of nature, also holds that natural equilibrium can be changed significantly by new species entering an ecosystem, the disappearance of some species, man-made changes to the environment or natural disasters.


Ecological Imbalance in India is governed by the following factors:

(a) Conservation of Land and Soil

(b) Forest density

(c) Utilization of water resources

(d) Mining Practices

(e) Level of Industrial and Atmospheric Pollution.

## COASTAL ECOLOGY

### Blue Economy

Blue Economy refers to the integration of ocean economy development with the idea of social inclusion, environmental sustainability and innovative, dynamic business models. It is an approach wherein renewable and organic inputs are fed into sustainably designed systems to promote "blue growth". Such "blue growth" has solved the problems of resource scarcity and waste disposal, while ensuring sustainable development that enhances human welfare in an holistic manner. Blue Economy has also led to creating a healthy ocean environment, supporting higher productivity.

The concept of Blue Economy is introduced by entrepreneur **Gunter Pauli.** Bilateral and multilateral work, involving the environment, energy, defense and food production can be achieved with Blue Economy. The newly set up **Blue Economy Strategic Thought Forum India**, under the guidance of the **National Maritime Foundation**, has focuses on multiple ways in which the blue economy will influence human activities.

The central principle of the blue economy is the idea of integrating nutrients and energy the way ecosystems do. Cascading energy and nutrients leads to sustainability by reducing or eliminating inputs, such as energy, and eliminating waste.

### Coastal Area Conservation

The coastal environment is facing a number of pressures, arising out of the needs of people, and the multiple uses that coastal and marine areas can be put to. Coastal area in India has seen major developmental changes in recent years as given below:

- There have been major changes in land-use along the coast after the implementation of **Coastal Regulation Zone** (CRZ) Rules, particularly in Karnataka, Goa and Kerala. The rule proposes to remove the ban on reclamation of land in coastal areas for commercial or tourism activities even in ecologically-sensitive areas.

  Under the Environmental Protection Act 1986, notification was released in 1991 for regulation of activities in the coastal area by Ministry of Environment and Forests. These notification known as Coastal Regulation Zone Notification defined the Coastal Regulation Zone or CRZ as coastal land up to 500m from the High Tide Line and a range of 100m along banks of creeks, estuaries, backwaters and rivers subject to tidal fluctuations is CRZ. According to Coastal Regulation Zone notifications, it is divided into 4 zones given below:

1. **CRZ I** – It includes the ecologically sensitive areas, essential in maintaining ecosystem of the coast. These lie between the HTL and LTL. Only exploration of natural gas and extraction of salt is permitted.

2. **CRZ II** – It form up to the shoreline of the coast. Authorized structures are not allowed to be constructed in this zone.

3. **CRZ III** – This form rural and urban localities. Only certain activities relating to agriculture and public utilities allowed here.

4. **CRZ IV** – This includes the aquatic area up to the territorial limit (12 nautical miles). Fishing and allied activities permitted in this zone. Solid waste can be let off in this zone.

- Agenda 21 has resulted in better living standards of the coastal population, ensuring reduction in the degradation of coastal area due to pollution, marine erosion, loss of resources and habitat destruction. **Agenda 21** requires new approaches to marine and coastal area management and development, at the national, sub-regional, regional and global levels.

**The following areas are highlighted under agenda 21:**

1. Integrating management and sustainable development of coastal areas, including exclusive economic zones.
2. Protection of marine environment.
3. Sustainable use and conservation of marine living resources of the high seas.
4. Sustainable use of marine living resources under national jurisdiction.
5. Addressing critical uncertainties for the management of the marine environment and climate change.
6. Strengthening international, including regional, cooperation and coordination.
7. Sustainable development of small islands.

- Gahirmatha beach (Odisha) where mass nesting of the endangered Olive Ridley turtle takes place was given marine sanctuary status in 1997.
- India has been identified as one of the 27 countries most vulnerable to the impacts of global warming related accelerated sea level rise (UNEP, 1989), which threatens coastal habitat due to human influence.

### Coastal Ocean Monitoring and Prediction System

Extensive monitoring of marine pollution along the coastal waters was initiated at 76 locations and it has been shown that the disposal of untreated sewage from towns, cities and villages cause decrease of dissolved oxygen and increase of nitrate and pathogenic bacteria in the sea close to the shore. The data collected revealed that pollution problems are confined up to 1 km in the sea except at Mumbai where the pollution problem prevails up to 3 km in the sea. Model to predict the movement of oil during oil spills has been developed for the coasts of Mumbai and Chennai. Works to develop similar models for the coasts of Goa, Kerala and Visakhapatnam have been undertaken.

# MARINE ECOLOGY

## Fishing

Ecological and environmental parameters play a primary role in the formation of fish biomass. Periodic changes in such natural phenomena as ocean currents, water temperature and oxygen layers affect the ecological and environmental balance. Ecological imbalances due to fishing in India are given below:

(a) Ecological damage caused by inshore mechanized fishing in state like Kerala, Goa, Tamil Nadu, Orissa.
(b) Indo-Norwegian Project leading to the development of mechanized fishing.
(c) Maharashtra and Tamil Nadu fully exploiting their maximum sustainable yield (MSY).
(d) Adverse impact on marine ecology due to introduction of exotic fish such as Brown Trout, Loch Leven Trout, Rainbow Trout.

### Harmful Algal Blooms

A number of harmful algal blooms have been found in various coastal waters of India such as Noctiluca bloom in Kochi, Noctiluca bloom in Goa, bloom of Gonyaulax in Manglore. Efforts are underway to monitor the spatial and temporal variations of blooms using Ocean Colour Monitor sensors available on board both Indian and foreign satellites.

### Island Development Activities

Ornamental fish culture was established in 2009 at Kavaratti to commercialize in the Agatti Island of Lakshadweep. Other activities such as live-bait culture, pearl culture, biodiversity studies, etc. of Lakshadweep have been taken up.

**Ecosystem Modelling:** Under the programme on Ecosystem modelling, hydrodynamic modelling of Chilika and Kochi backwaters have been initiated. Field investigations for ecosystem modelling for Sundarbans have been started. Water quality criteria for copper, cadmium and mercury have been determined and are referred to the Central Pollution Control Board. Over 20 training programmes on hazard mapping, satellite oceanography, and marine pollution have been conducted.

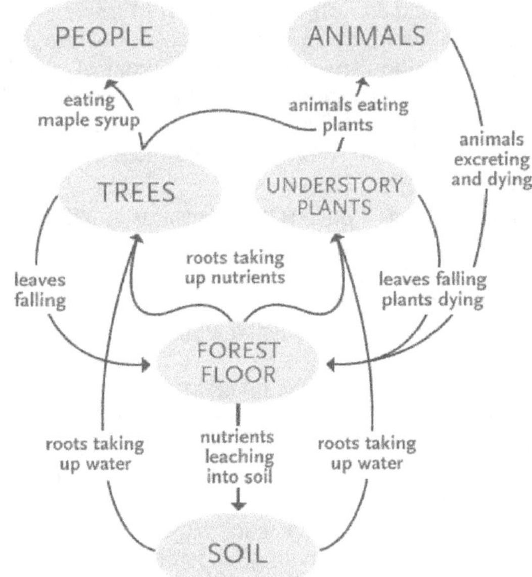


**Fig:** Ecological model showing the dependence of organisms on each other.

### Project Green Ports

Ministry of Shipping has started 'Project Green Ports' to make major ports across India cleaner and greener. It will have two verticals – one is 'Green Ports Initiatives' related to environmental issues and second is 'Swachh Bharat

Abhiyaan'. Under 'Green Ports Initiatives', 12 initiatives will be implemented. Some of the initiatives focus on acquiring equipment required for monitoring environmental pollution, acquiring dust suppression system, setting up of waste water treatment plants, developing projects for producing renewable energy, completion of shortfalls of Oil Spill Response (OSR) facilities, prohibition of disposal of almost all kind of garbage at sea, improving the quality of harbour wastes etc. Under Swachh Bharat Abhiyaan initiative, few activities are identified promoting cleanliness at the port premises.

> **Extinction of Dolphins from Ganges River:** This vast area of Ganga has been altered by the construction of more than 50 dams and other irrigation-related projects, with severe consequences for the river dolphins. The population of the Ganges River Dolphin has declined to less than 1,800 from 6,000 in 1982 due to construction of dams and water pollution caused by pesticides, fertilizers, and industrial effluents.

## Ganga Cleaning Campaign

Ganga is India's largest river basin. It occupies 26% of the country's landmass and supports 43% of its population. In 1986, the government of India launched the **Ganga Action Plan (GAP)**. In August 2009, GAP was re-launched with a reconstituted National Ganga River Basin Authority. The objectives of the authority was to improve the water quality of the river to acceptable standards (defined as bathing water quality standards) by preventing pollutants reaching it by intercepting the sewage and treating it before discharge into the river. Recent initiatives such as '**River Development**' and '**Ganga Rejuvenation**' by the Minister of Water Resources, and the establishment of the National Mission for Clean Ganga, show a commitment to address some of the concerns with special attention given to pollution control. Under the **Namami Gange Programme**, Central Pollution Control Board (CPCB) has identified 1,000 polluting industries that need to treat industrial effluents before releasing them into the river.

### Clean Ganga Fund

The **Clean Ganga Fund** (CGF) ensures funding of the following Ganga cleaning activities:

1. Control of non-point pollution from agricultural runoff, human defecation, cattle wallowing, etc.
2. Setting up of waste treatment and disposal plants along the river around the cities.
3. Conservation of the biotic diversity of the river.
4. Community based activities to reduce polluting human interface with the river.
5. Development of public amenities including activities such as Ghat redevelopment.
6. Research and Development projects and innovative projects for new technology and processes for cleaning the river.
7. Independent oversight through intensive monitoring and real time reporting.

# WETLAND ECOLOGY

A wetland is an area of land whose soil has high water content. Wetlands include swamps, marshes and bogs, among others. The water found in wetlands can be saltwater, fresh water, shallow water or brackish water. These accounts for 18.4%

of India's total geographical area. Wetlands are one of the most productive eco-system, comparable to tropical evergreen forests in the biosphere and play a significant role in the ecological sustainability of a region.

## Montreux Record

It is a register of wetland sites on the List of Wetlands of International Importance where changes in ecological character have occurred, are occurring, or are likely to occur as a result of technological developments, pollution or other human interference. It is maintained as part of the Ramsar List.

## Wetlands International

It is a global organisation that is responsible for sustaining and restoring wetlands and their resources for people and biodiversity. It is an independent, not-for-profit, global organisation, supported by government and NGO membership from around the world.

### Some wetlands of international importance

- The Ramsar List is the world's largest network of protected areas.
- There are over 2,200 Ramsar Sites around the world. They cover over 2.1 million square kilometres, an area larger than Mexico.
- The world's first Site was the Cobourg Peninsula in Australia, designated in 1974.
- The world's largest Sites are Ngiri-Tumba-Maindombe in the Democratic Republic of Congo and Queen Maud Gulf in Canada; these Sites each cover over 60,000 square kilometres.
- The countries with the most Ramsar Sites are the United Kingdom with 170 and Mexico with 142.
- Bolivia has the largest area with 148,000 km2 under Ramsar protection

## Functions of Wetlands

- Nutrients recycling
- Water purification
- Floods mitigation
- Maintenance of stream flow
- Ground Water recharging
- Provide drinking water, fish, fodder, fuel, etc
- Control rate of runoff in urban areas
- Buffer shorelines against erosion
- Comprise an important resource for sustainable tourism, recreation and cultural heritage
- Stabilization of local climate
- Source of livelihood to local people
- Genetic reservoir for various species of plants (especially rice)
- Supporting specific diversity
- Habitat to aquatic flora and fauna, as well as numerous species of birds, including migratory species.
- Filtration of sediments and nutrients from surface water

## Development in Wetland Ecology

Recent developments in the wetland ecology are given below:
- 115 wetlands in India have been identified by the government, which require urgent conservation and management interventions. The government prioritizes conservation of wetlands in the country so as to prevent their further degradation and ensuring their wise use for the benefit of local communities and overall conservation of biodiversity.

- The list of Ramsar sites in India are one of the most threatened of all ecosystems and has an international importance. Largest Wetland of India includes Vembanad lake, Chilika lake, Kolleru lake and Loktak Lake. These Wetlands are home to many species of water birds as well as the animals.
- Remote Sensing and Geographic Information System (GIS) tools have been used in flood zonation mapping, in monitoring irrigation and cropping patterns, water quality analysis and modelling, change analyses and in mapping of surface water bodies and wetlands.
- Normalized Difference Vegetation Index (NDVI) is used for separation of water bodies, as the wetland areas fall in lower NDVI zone.
- Salt-resistant varieties of rice have been discovered that will allow growing rice in saline wetland areas.

## National Wetland Conservation Programme (NWCP)

Government of India opertionalized National Wetland Conservation Programme (NWCP) in closed collaboration with concerned State Government during the year 1985/86. Under the programme 115 wetlands have been identified till now by the Ministry which requires urgent conservation and management initiatives.

### Aim of the Scheme

Conservation and wise use of wetlands in the country so as to prevent their further degradation.

### Objectives of the Scheme

The scheme was initiated with the following objectives:-
- to lay down policy guidelines for conservation and management of wetlands in the country;
- to undertake intensive conservation measures in priority wetlands;
- to monitor implementation of the programme; and
- to prepare an inventory of indian wetlands.

## Conservation of wetlands

Several steps have been taken to prevent wetland degradation as given below:
- Separation of wetlands using latest technology, proper enforcement of laws and stringent punishments for violators.
- Prevention of unsustainable aquaculture and cultivation of shellfish.
- Treating industrial effluents and water from farm lands before discharging into wetlands.
- Using wetlands on a sustainable basis by giving enough time for natural regeneration. Artificial regeneration for quick recovery.
- Applying afforestation, weed control, preventing invasive species is the key to wetland conservation.
- Implement preventive measures to stop the introduction of exotic invasive species like water hyacinth.
- Soil conservation measures and afforestation. Preventing grazing in peripherals of wetlands.
- Wildlife conservation, sustainable tourism, eco-tourism and sensitizing local populace.
- Eutrophication abatement by processing nutrient rich discharge into the water body.
- Involving local population in the conservation of wetlands.

## RAMSAR CONVENTION ON WETLAND

The Convention on Wetlands, signed in Ramsar, Iran, in 1971, is an intergovernmental treaty which provides the framework for national action and international cooperation for the conservation and wise use of wetlands and their resources. There are presently 158 Contracting Parties to the Convention, with 1758 wetland sites, totaling 161 million hectares, designated for inclusion in the Ramsar List of Wetlands of International Importance. Ramsar Convention is the only global environment treaty dealing with a particular ecosystem. The Ramsar Convention on Wetlands was developed as a means to call international attention to the rate at which wetland habitats were disappearing, in part due to a lack of understanding of their important functions, values, goods and services. Governments that join the Convention are expressing their willingness to make a commitment to helping to reverse that history of wetland loss and degradation.

In addition, many wetlands are international systems lying across the boundaries of two or more countries, or are part of river basins that include more than one country. The health of these and other wetlands is dependent upon the quality and quantity of the transboundary water supply from rivers, streams, lakes, or underground aquifers. This requires framework for international discussion and cooperation toward mutual benefits.

## ECOSYSTEM AT PERIL

Encroachments, siltation in the canals and fish-ponds and drop in the quantity of sewage the wetlands received have impacted the ecology of East Kolkata Wetlands

### How the System Works

Through an integrated canal network, partly-natural partly-manmade, the sewage reaches the fishponds, where wastewater gets treated by algae-bacteria symbiosis in a span of 21-28 days. Simultaneously, fishes grow profusely without requiring any food supplement. The treated water is then released in Kultigang, near the Sunderbans ecosystem, through a network of canals. Low cost pisciculture in the wetlands is the reason Kolkata gets fishes for cheap.

| **How it is threatened** | **What is being done** |
|---|---|
| Siltation of fish-ponds and canals have affected the basic hydrological functioning, while decrease in sewage quantity is affecting the livelihood of the people preserving it. | Remsar senior advisor Law Young has recommended a thorough review of population increase, loss of area due to encroachment, socio-economic study of the fishing community, review of the map drawn in 1985 and clear demarcation of its boundaries. |

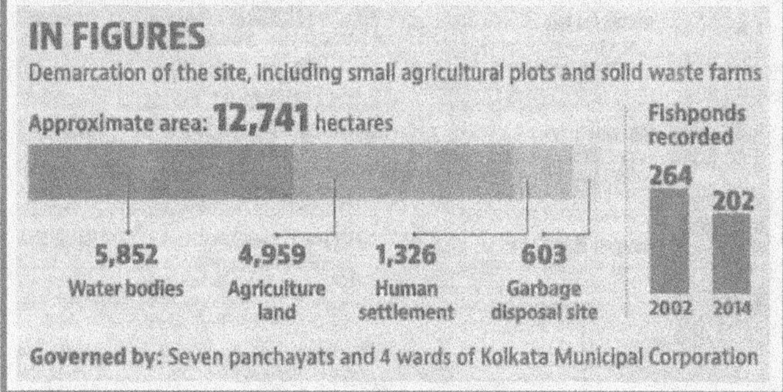



# HIMALAYAN ECOLOGY

The ecology of the Himalayas changes with climate, rainfall, altitude, and soils. The climate ranges from tropical at the base of the mountains to permanent ice and snow at the highest elevations. Recent ecological developments in the Himalayan region are given below:

- Climate change in the Indian Himalayan region is monitored by National Mission for Sustaining the Himalayan Ecosystem (NMSHE). The mission was launched under the National Action Plan on Climate Change (NAPCC) with a budget outlay of Rs. 550 crore during the XII Five Year Plan period.
- **Indian Himalayas Climate Adaptation Programme (IHCAP)** has generated knowledge of climate change impacts on natural resources, ecosystem services, and the communities depending on them, contributing to policy and practice for enhanced adaptation.
- The 3097 MW Etalin hydropower project has been deferred in Arunachal Pradesh as the hydropower project would affect biodiversity hotspots.
- Several plant species have been grown in the Himalayas, including Himalayan Blue Poppy, Creeping Cotoneaster, Deodar Cedar.

**Current steps to protect Himalayan ecosystem also include:** (a) balancing glaciers and associated hydrological cycles; (b) predicting and managing natural hazards; (c) biodiversity conservation and protection; (d) wildlife conservation and protection; (e) regulating science to help governance issues related to sustenance of the Himalayan ecosystem; (f) assisting in restoration and rehabilitation process of Uttarakhand.

# WESTERN GHAT ECOLOGY

Western Ghats is a mountain range that runs parallel to the western coast of the Indian peninsula. It is a **UNESCO World Heritage Site** and is one of the eight **"hottest hot-spots"** of biological diversity in the world. The Western Ghats are home to thousands of animal species including at least 325 globally threatened species.

## Madhav Gadgil Committe Report on Western Ghats

Gadgil Commission is named after its chairman Madhav Gadgil. The Commission was formally known as Western Ghats Ecology Expert Panel (WGEEP). The Commission submitted the report to the Government of India on 31 August 2011. The Gadgil Report highlights:

1. The Western Ghats Ecology Expert Panel (WGEEP) designated the entire hill range as an Ecologically Sensitive Area (ESA).
2. The panel, in its report, has classified the 142 taluks in the Western Ghats boundary into Ecologically Sensitive Zones (ESZ).
3. ESZ-1 zone was given high priority and almost all developmental activities (mining, thermal power plants etc) were restricted in it.
4. Gadgil report recommended that no new dams based on large-scale storage should be constructed in Ecologicall Sensitive Zone 1. Since both the Athirappilly of Kerala and Gundia of Karnataka hydel project sites fall in Ecologically Sensitive Zone 1, these projects should not be accorded environmental clearance.
5. Gadgil Committee report reveals that the present system of governance of the environment should be changed. It asked for bottom to top approach (right from Gram sabhas) rather than a top to bottom approach. It also asked for decentralization and more powers to local authorities.
6. The Commission recommended constitution of a Western Ghats Ecology Authority (WGEA), as a statutory authority under the Ministry of Environment and Forests.

# URBAN ECOLOGY

- **Eco-friendly Construction**

  Building rating systems are a popular tool to bring momentum in achieving energy efficiency and sustainability in buildings. India has currently two rating systems namely, LEED and GRIHA. The Leadership in Energy and Environmental Design (LEED) Green Building Rating System gives ratings of platinum, gold, silver, or "certified", based on green building attributes. The Indian Ministry of New and Renewable Energy have adopted a national rating system- GRIHA, which was developed by The Energy and Resources Institute (TERI).

- **Eco-cities**

  In India, the concept of Eco cities was introduced in 2000 and starting 2001 six medium and small Eco-cities were planned by the Ministry of Environment and Forest (MoEF) in association with Central Pollution Control Board (CPCB) and with technical assistance from German technical cooperation (GTZ). The focus of the project is pollution control, improvement of environmental quality, protection of environmental resources like rivers and lakes, improving sanitary conditions, improving the needed infrastructure and creating aesthetic environs in the chosen towns. The cities included **Tirupathi, Vrindavan, Kottayam, Ujjain, Puri and Thanjavur.**

- ## Smart Cities

  The Government of India has planned to develop 'Smart Cities' with an aim to maintain balance in urban ecology. Urban expansion has degraded and destroyed natural habitats across most Indian cities and small towns, transforming urban forests, lakes, and wetlands into polluted areas, and converting them into vast expanses of concrete construction. Smart Cities will ensure that urban development do not lead to negative ecological impact on the environment.

- ## BS-IV vehicles

  Automobile Emission Control: Recent Supreme Court ruling has asserted that auto manufacturers cannot sell BS-III vehicles from April 1, 2017 when BS -IV compliance comes into force. BS -IV vehicles are relatively less polluting than BS-III vehicles. National Green Tribunal (NGT) has proposed ban diesel vehicles that are at least 10 years old from plying in the national capital region (NCR) centred on Delhi. Vehicular pollution can be controlled if the exhaust outlets of all motor vehicles are installed on the top instead of near the base. BS-IV trucks are 80% cleaner than BS-III.

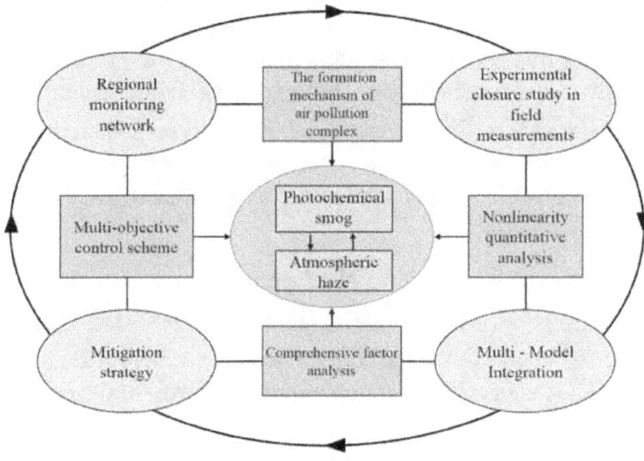


  **Fig:** A cyclic model to control air pollution.

- ## Green Airports

  Cochin International Airport is the first green airport where 46,000 solar panels are installed. Vadodara's Harni Airport in Gujarat, is India's second green airport after Kochi. This new facility has rainwater harvesting systems and energy-saving cooling mechanisms that was designed and built by the Airports Authority of India (AAI).

- ## Bio-toilets

  The proposed bio-toilets in Indian railway is ecologically more efficient than conventional system of direct discharge toilets that leads to public health issues and environmental hazards.

- The Ministry of Environment, Forest and Climate Change adopted new environment standard for Gensets running on LPG, natural gas (NG), diesel with LPG/NG and petrol with LPG/NG.

- **Kolkata** will be the first to use biogas in buses. Biogas is a eco-friendly and cheap fuel and can be used as an alternative to fossil fuels in some segments. The Government of West Bengal has also assured that if a commercial vehicle switches over to biogas, it will be exempted from the ceiling and will not be banned after 15 years.

> Majuli, the world's biggest river island, is going to become India's first carbon neutral district. It is also now a biodiversity heritage site. It is formed by Brahmaputra river, in Assam. It is also first island district of the country.

**Ecological Developments of the Mining Industry**

The ecological impact of mining is monitored by National Conservation Strategy and Policy Statement on Environment and Development. Recent developments in the mining ecology are given below:

- Revision of National Mineral Policy to ensure that ecological balance is maintained while mining.

- Mining companies follow environment-friendly practices such as using appropriate technology, efficient use of energy, preservation of biological diversity.

- The government has finally notified nearly 57,000 square km area in the Western Ghats region as ecologically sensitive area (ESA) where all kinds of mining activities, large constructions, thermal power plants and highly polluting industries would no longer be allowed. The 56,825 square km of land is spread over six states of Gujarat, Maharashtra, Goa, Karnataka, Kerala and Tamil Nadu.

## Forest Ecology

In 2002, India set up a National Forest Commission to review and assess India's policy and law, its effect on India's forests. Indian forests are home to a wide variety of animal and plant species which are vital to maintaining ecological balance. Indian forests have seen a lot of changes in recent as given below:

- **Chipko Movement** stated in 1973 **for** forest conservation.

- There is a drop in **jhum cultivation**, which included burning of forest to make area available for farming.

- India has added over 4 million hectares of forest cover, a 7% increase, between 1990 and 2010.

- **Afforestation** and **reforestation** of 6 million hectares of degraded forest land covered under the National Mission with participation of Joint Forest Management Committees (JFMCs) would result in adding another 18 mt of carbon by 2020.

- There has been an increase in forest/tree cover to the extent of 5 million hectares and improve quality of forest/tree cover on another 5 mha of forest/non-forest lands, with the help of National Mission for Green India (GIM).

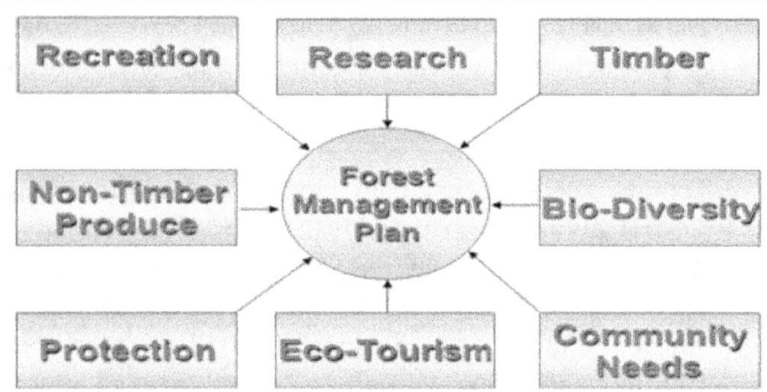


## Forest Carbon Partnership Facility

It is a global partnership of governments, businesses, civil society, and indigenous peoples focused on reducing emissions from deforestation and forest degradation, forest carbon stock conservation, the sustainable management of forests, and the enhancement of forest carbon stocks in developing countries (activities commonly referred to as REDD+).

### ISFR 2017: KEY FINDINGS

- Forest and Tree Cover of the country has increased by 8,021 sq km (1%) as compared to assessment of 2015. The very dense forest has increased by 1.36% as compared to last assessment This is very heartening as VDF absorbs maximum carbon dioxide from the atmosphere.

- The increasing trend of forest and tree cover is largely due to the various national policies aimed at conservation and sustainable management of our forests like Green India Mission, National Agro-Forestry policy (NAP), REDD plus policy, Joint Forest Management (JFM), National Afforestation Programme and funds under Compensatory Afforestation to States.

- Successful agro-forestry practices, better conservation of forests, improvement of scrub areas to forest areas, increase in mangrove cover, conservation and protection activities have also led to increase in the forest and tree cover.

- Green Highways (plantations & Maintenance) Policy to develop 1,40,000 km long tree line with plantation along with both sides of national highways will go a long way in enhancing the forest & tree cover.

- Top 5 states where maximum forest cover has increased are Andhra Pradesh (2,141 sq kms), Karnataka (1,101 sq kms), Kerala (1,043 sq kms), Odisha (885 sq kms) and Telangana (565 sq kms).

- Top 5 states where forest cover has decreased are Mizoram (531 sq km), Nagaland (450 sq km), Arunachal Pradesh (190 sq km), Tripura (164 sq km) and Meghalaya (116 sq km). It is important to mention here that these states are in the North Eastern region of the country where the total forest cover is very high i.e. more than 70% in each state.

- The main reasons for the decrease are - shifting cultivation, other biotic pressures, rotational felling, diversion of forest lands for developmental activities, submergence of forest cover, agriculture expansion and natural disasters.

### Water bodies inside forests have increased over a decade

- Forests play a vital role in water conservation and improve the water regime in the area.

- State Forest Departments besides plantation and protection also undertake steps to improve water conservation through different interventions such as building Check dams, vegetation barriers, percolation ponds, contour trenches etc. under various Central & State Government schemes

- As per the latest assessment, water bodies inside forest cover have increased by 2,647 sq kms during the last decade.

- Maharashtra (432 sq kms), Gujarat (428 sq kms), Madhya Pradesh (389 sq kms) are top three states showing increase in water bodies within forest areas. Overall, almost all the states have shown a positive change in water bodies.

### Mangrove cover of the country has shown a positive change

- As per ISFR 2017, mangrove forests have increased by 181 sq kms. Maharashtra (82 sq kms), Andhra Pradesh (37 sq kms) and Gujarat (33 sq kms) are the top three gainers in terms of mangrove cover. 7 out of the 12 mangrove states have shown an increase in mangrove cover and none of them show any negative change.

- Mangrove eco-systems are rich in biodiversity and provide a number of ecological services. They also play a major role in protecting coastal areas from erosion, tidal storms and tsunamis.

### Striving towards achieving NDC goal

- India is striving towards achieving its NDC goal of creating additional carbon sink of 2.5 to 3.0 billion tonnes of $CO_2$ equivalent through additional forest and tree cover by 2030.

- As per present assessment total carbon stock in forest is estimated to be 7,082 million tonnes. There is an increase of 38 million tonnes in the carbon stock of country as compared to the last assessment.

## CLEAN ENERGY

Continuous efforts have been made in India and around the globe to promote clean energy that create a balance in ecology. Some developments in the clean energy sector are given below:

- Renewable electricity targets India have been upscaled to grow from just under 43 GW in April 2016 to 175 GW by the year 2022, including 100 GW from solar power, 60 GW from wind power, 10 GW from bio power and 5 GW from small hydro power.

- The Government aims at achieving 40% cumulative electric power capacity from non fossil fuel sources by 2030.

- Several solar cities have come up in the Urban Sector for promoting solar water heating systems in homes, hotels, hospitals and industry; deployment of SPV systems/devices in urban areas for demonstration and awareness creation; establishment of 'Akshya Urja Shops', design of Solar Buildings and promoting urban and industrial waste/biomass to energy projects.

- Rooftop solar market in India has grown at the rate of 90%. As of March 31, 2016, the total installed capacity of rooftop solar energy is 740 MW.

- Ethanol has been increasingly used as a fuel for automobiles and regulations provide for the mandatory blending of 5% of ethanol with petrol (to be increased to 10%). The Government also plans to free the movement of ethanol across the country and eliminate local taxes thereby increasing its usage.

## International Solar Alliance

It is an alliance of more than 120 countries, most of them being sunshine countries, which come either completely or partly between the Tropic of Cancer and the Tropic of Capricorn. The alliance's primary objective is efficient exploitation of solar energy to reduce dependence on fossil fuels. The launching of such an alliance in Paris shows the efforts of the global communities to mitigate climate change and to switch to a low-carbon growth path. India has pledged a target of installing 100GW by 2022 and reduction in emission intensity by 33–35% by 2030 to let solar energy reach to the most unconnected villages and communities and also towards creating a clean planet. India's pledge to the Paris Summit offered to bring 40% of its electricity generation capacity from non-fossil sources (renewable, large hydro, and nuclear) by 2030.

## Energy consumption and efficiency

Bureau of Energy Efficiency (BEE) is an Indian government agency of, under the Ministry of Power created in March 2002 under the provisions of the nation's 2001 Energy Conservation Act. The agency's aim is to develop programmes which will increase the conservation and efficient use of energy in India. The government has proposed to make it mandatory for certain appliances in India to have ratings by the BEE starting in January 2010.

## Unnat Jyoti by Affordable LEDs for All (UJALA)

It was launched on 1 May 2015, replacing the **"Bachat Lamp Yojana"**. The scheme reduced their electricity consumption by 55 billion (US$820 million). The scheme was announced as **"Domestic Efficient Lighting Programme (DELP)"** which focused on the use of bulbs in place of incandescent bulbs, tube lights and CFL bulbs as they efficient, long lasting and economical in their life cycle duration.

The Bureau of Energy Efficiency (BEE) has introduced a new star rating methodology called **Indian Seasonal Energy Efficiency Ratio (ISEER)** for air conditioners. This provides rating methodology factors in variance in higher temperature in India and rates air conditioners accordingly. Consumers can now purchase air conditioners with higher efficiency leading to lower electricity bills. Ratings based on ISEER have been introduced on a voluntary basis for Variable Speed (Inverter) Air Conditioners since June 2015 and proposed to be merged with fixed speed air conditioners in the mandatory regime from January 2018.

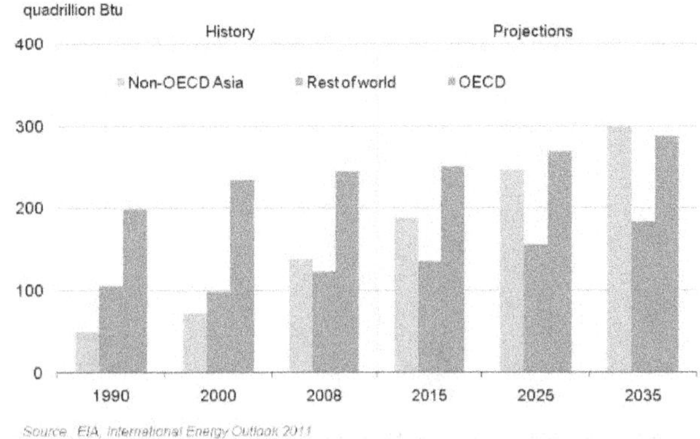


Figure 1. China and India account for about half of the world increase in energy use

Source: EIA, International Energy Outlook 2011

> **Scientists in Juelich, Germany**, have developed the world's largest artificial sun, called **Synlight**, for using it to develop climate-friendly fuels. The Synlight consists of 149 spotlights all together resembling a gigantic honeycomb. The lights, which are xenon short-arc lamps that's usually found in cinemas, simulate natural sunlight during a season that doesn't get much sunlight.

# LAND USE AND SOIL ECOLOGY

Land-use change has important implications for sustainable livelihood of local communities. Several initiatives has resulted in the change in the land use and soil ecology. These are as follows:

- Geographic information system (GIS)-based landscape ecological planning for Western Ghats of India.

- Vetiver grass (*Vetiveria zizanioides*) is widely grown of soil and moisture conservation.

- To check wind erosion, planting of trees in the opposite direction of the wind has been taken into consideration.

> Wind Erosion: It is a serious environmental problem attracting the attention of many across the globe. It is a common phenomenon occuring mostly in flat, bare areas; dry, sandy soils; or anywhere the soil is loose, dry, and finely granulated.

- Increasing use of **cover crops**, such as rye and **wheat**, to reduce soil erosion, limit nitrogen leaching, suppress weeds and increase soil organic matter.

- **Terrace cultivation** is being encouraged in many places in India to prevent soil erosion. This is a method of growing crops on sides of hills or mountains by planting on graduated terraces built into the slope.

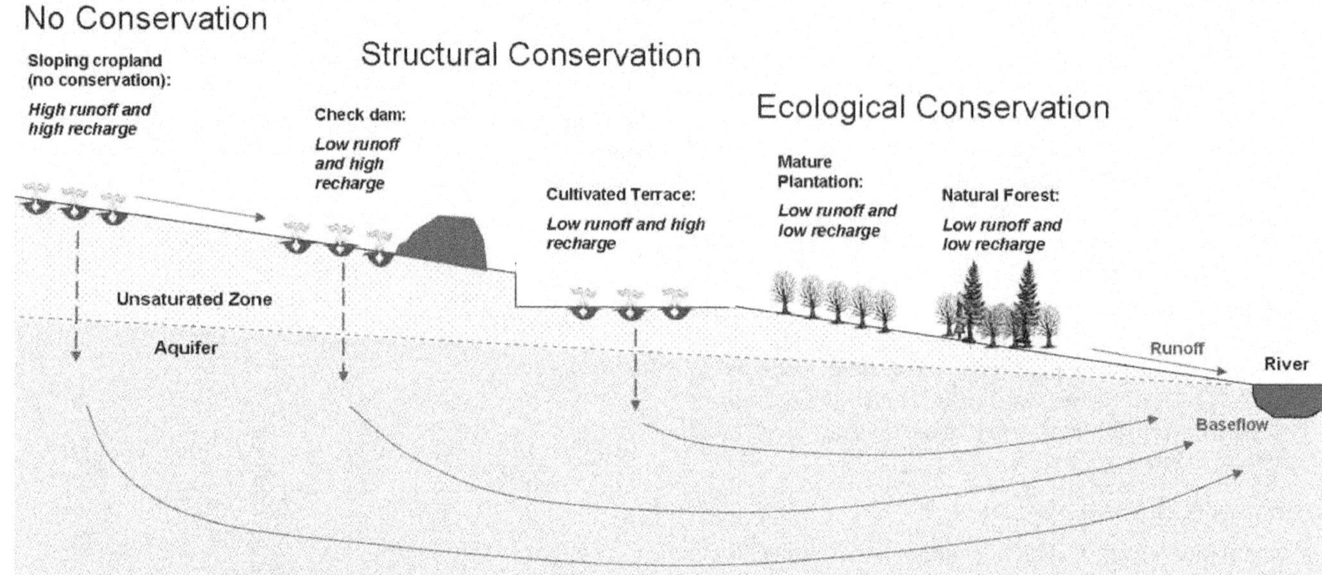


## Preventing Desertification

Efforts have been made to prevent desertification in India by being a party to the United Nations Convention to Combat Desertification (UNCCD). Rajasthan accounts for the most desertified land, followed by Gujarat, Maharashtra and Jammu and Kashmir and Orissa and Andhra Pradesh.

Following steps have been taken to prevent desertification:

1. **Fixation of soil** is done through the use of shelter belts, woodlots and windbreaks. Windbreaks are made from trees and bushes and are used to reduce soil erosion and evapotranspiration. Some soils due to lack of water can become consolidated rather than porous. Some techniques such as tillage are then used to still allow the planting of crops.

2. Contour trenching involves the digging deep trenches in the soil. The trenches are made parallel to the height lines of the landscape, preventing the water from flowing within the trenches and causing erosion. Stone walls are placed around the trenches to prevent the trenches from closing up again. The method was invented by Peter Westerveld.

3. Enriching of the soil and restoration of its fertility is often done by plants. Of these, leguminous plants which extract nitrogen from the air and fix it in the soil, and food crops/trees as grains, barley, beans and dates are the most important. Sand fences can also be used to control drifting of soil and sand erosion.

4. Different types of desert reclamation methodologies are used. An example for this is the salt-flats in the Rub' al Khali desert in Saudi-Arabia. These salt-flats are one of the most promising desert areas for seawater agriculture and could be revitalized without the use of freshwater or much energy.

5. Farmer-managed natural regeneration (FMNR) is another technique that has produced successful results for desert reclamation. This simple and low-cost method has enabled farmers to regenerate some 30,000 square kilometers in Niger. The process involves enabling native sprouting tree growth through selective pruning of shrub shoots. The residue from pruned trees can be used to provide mulching for fields thus increasing soil water retention and reducing evaporation.

> ➤ Every year, under the **'Operation Guerrilla Green'** movement, a month-long ecologically important campaign/festival is held by Gond and Korku communities/ tribes in Madhya Pradesh, where they plant saplings of fruit-bearing trees on government, forest, private or panchayat land.
>
> ➤ Agronomical trial on paddy and wheat crops with **Neem coated urea** as source of Nitrogen has produced higher yield at research and farm level. Looking into the importance of Neem Coated urea and its acceptance by the farmers, Ministry of Agriculture included the Neem coated urea in Fertiliser Control Order (FCO).

## Drip Irrigation

Drip irrigation is a type of irrigation that saves water and fertilizer by allowing water to drip slowly to the roots of many different plants, either onto the soil surface or directly onto the root zone, through a network of valves, pipes, tubing, and emitters. It is achieved through narrow tubes that deliver water directly to the base of the plant. It preferred over surface irrigation for various reasons, often including concern about minimizing evaporation.

**Advantages of Drip Irrigation:**

1. Fertilizer and nutrient loss is minimized due to reduced leaching.

2. Recycled and portable water can be used.

3. Soil erosion is lessened.

4. Weed growth is minimized.

# ECOTOURISM

In the recent year, it has been found that there is a growing trend towards travel to eco tourism destinations like National Parks and Wildlife Sanctuaries. Ecotourism deals with interaction with biotic components of the natural environments. Ecotourism focuses on socially responsible travel, personal growth, and environmental sustainability. Ecotourism involves travel to destinations where flora, fauna, and cultural heritage are the primary attractions. Ecotourism is intended to offer tourists insight into the impact of human beings on the environment.

The Indian Union Ministry of Environment and Forest (MoEF) is forming new guidelines for responsible tourism in the country's 733 different wildlife sanctuaries and national parks which include alpine and flower valleys, bird habitats, and marine, reptile and coastal parks.

## Features

**Ecotourism have the following characteristics**
1. Low-impact visitor behaviour.
2. Sensitivity towards local cultures and biodiversity.
3. Support for local conservation efforts.
4. Sustainable benefits to local communities.
5. Local participation in decision-making.
6. Educational components for both the traveler and local communities.

## Goals of Ecotourism

1. Eco-tourism focuses on local cultures, wilderness adventures and volunteering.
2. Personal growth and learning new ways to live on our vulnerable.
3. On cultural artifacts from the locality.
4. Travel to destinations where the flora, fauna, and cultural heritage are the primary attractions.

# WASTE DISPOSAL

- **Tirunelveli** is first to achieve 100% segregation of waste at source across households and establishments. It involved securing undertakings from each household to segregate biodegradable and non-biodegradable waste, campaigns though TV and local radio channels targeting housewives and roping in religious leaders and NGOs.

- Coimbatore has planned to have a 50 metric ton bio gas plant that will generate electricity using food waste collected from hotels and restaurants.

- Delhi has adopted scientific waste management plan which involves collection of waste from streets by auto tippers to fix compactor transfer station (FCTS) from where the waste, after compressing, is taken to the waste to energy plant.

- A new colour code is implemented in hospitals of Visakhapatnam, for disposal of biomedical waste. Under this plan, blue cardboard bins are introduced to dispose certain kinds of hospital waste such as cytotoxins and broken glass.

## THE WASTE HIERARCHY

# Exercise -1

1. Which of the following state where mass nesting of the endangered Olive Ridley turtle takes place was given marine sanctuary status?
   - (a) West Bengal
   - (b) Odisha
   - (c) Tamil Nadu
   - (d) Kerala

2. Inshore mechanized fishing leading to ecological damage has been observed in
   - (a) Kerala
   - (b) Goa
   - (c) Tamil Nadu
   - (d) All the above

3. Which of the following project is related to mechanized fishing ?
   - (a) Indo-Norwegian Project
   - (b) Indo-Chinese Project
   - (c) Indio-Sri Lankan Project
   - (d) Indo-Tibetan Project

4. Which state(s) has/have fully exploited maximum sustainable yield?
   - (a) Maharashtra
   - (b) Tamil Nadu
   - (c) Both (a) and (b)
   - (d) None of the above

5. Which of the following species of exotic fish have affected marine ecology ?
   - (a) Brown Trout
   - (b) Loch Leven Trout
   - (c) Rainbow Trout
   - (d) All the above

6. Algale blooms can be monitored by using
   - (a) Ocean Colour Monitor sensors
   - (b) Pressure censors
   - (c) Temperature sensors
   - (d) Both (b) and (c)

7. Which of the following includes ecosystem modelling?
   - (a) Hydrodynamic modelling of Chilika Lake
   - (b) Hydrodynamic modelling of Dal Lake
   - (c) Agronomic modelling of Chilika Lake
   - (d) Both (a) and (b)

8. Which of the following forms the part of Project Green Ports?
   - (a) Green Ports Initiatives
   - (b) Swachh Bharat Abhiyaan
   - (c) Ujwal Bharat
   - (d) Both (a) and (b)

9. A new colour code is implemented in hospitals of Visakhapatnam to
   - (a) for disposal of
   - (b) for producing biogas
   - (c) for the treatment of cancer
   - (d) to mark energy consumption

10. Recently, attempts have been made to produce electricity from
    - (a) wood
    - (b) food waste
    - (c) coal
    - (d) radioactive material

11. Which of the following is correct about World Wide Fund for Nature's (WWF) 2014 Living Planet Report.
    - (a) Wildlife population have declined by 52 percent
    - (b) Wildlife populations have increased by 1 percent
    - (c) Wildlife populations have shown no change.
    - (d) Population of Tigers has increased

12. The event Kanha-Pench Walk 2016 was held to conserve
    - (a) Tigers
    - (b) Lions
    - (c) Elephants
    - (d) Deer

13. Which of the following animals' behavior was studied by Dudhwa Tiger Reserve and National Trust for Nature Conservation (NTNC) with the help of a monitoring technique.
    - (a) Tiger
    - (b) Lion
    - (c) Greater One-Horned Rhinoceros
    - (d) Elephants

14. Which of the following components was recently introduced in the scheme 'Integrated Development of Wildlife Habitats'?
    - (a) Recovery of Endangered Species
    - (b) Conservation of lions
    - (c) Recovery of tigers
    - (d) Recovery of Elephants

15. Movement of lions, tigers, elephants, olive ridley turtles and other wild animals can be monitored with the help of
    - (a) Radio collars
    - (b) Global Positioning System
    - (c) Satellite uplink facilities
    - (d) All the above

16. Which of the following tribes organize a month-long ecological campaign/festival?
    - (a) Gond
    - (b) Korku
    - (c) Bhail
    - (d) Both (a) and (b)

17. 'Operation Guerrilla Green' movement was held in which of following states?
    - (a) Uttar Pradesh
    - (b) Madhya Pradesh
    - (c) Rajasthan
    - (d) Odisha

18. World's largest artificial sun is called
    - (a) Sunlight
    - (b) Sonlight
    - (c) ArtSun
    - (d) Sunlit

19. Which of the following rating methodology has been introduced by the Bureau of Energy Efficiency (BEE) for air conditioners?
    - (a) Indian Seasonal Energy Efficiency Ratio
    - (b) Indian Energy Efficiency Ratio
    - (c) House Energy Rating Ratio
    - (d) None of the above

20. Which of the following is true for Inverter Air Conditioners?
    (a) They can operate on inverters
    (b) They consume less energy
    (c) Their rating is based on Indian Seasonal Energy Efficiency Ratio
    (d) Both (b) and (c)

21. Ocean Colour Monitor sensors are used to monitor
    (a) fish movement       (b) algal blooms
    (c) oil spills          (d) both a and b

22. Which of the following resulted in the reduction of the number of dolphins from Ganga.
    (a) Construction of dams
    (b) water pollution
    (c) industrial effluents
    (d) all the above

23. Which of the following is correct about BS -III vehicles in India?
    (a) BS -III vehicles have been banned in India.
    (b) Manufactures of BS -III vehicles will have to pay more tax for BS -III vehicles.
    (c) BS-IV trucks are 80 per cent cleaner than BS-III.
    (d) both a and c

24. Which of the following help in preventing desertification?
    (a) United Nations Convention to Combat Desertification
    (b) Indian Convention to Combat Desertification
    (c) World Convention to Combat Desertification
    (d) United Nations Convention on Preventing Desertification

# Exercise -2

1. Consider the following four statements about wetland ecosystems :
   1. They are the transitional zones between terrestrial and aquatic ecosystems.
   2. They are highly productive.
   3. They are the source of greenhouse gases.
   4. They normally occur in the floodplain of rivers.

   Choose the correct answer :
   (a) 1 and 2 only     (b) 1, 2 and 3 only
   (c) 2, 3 and 4 only     (d) 1, 2, 3 and 4

2. Read the following statements regarding the Economics of Ecosystems and Biodiversity (TEEB)?
   1. It is a study by environmental economist Pavan Sukhdev.
   2. It is an international initiative that focuses on global economic benefits of wildlife.
   3. Its objective is to highlight the growing cost of biodiversity loss and ecosystem degradation.

   Choose the correct option.
   (a) 1 and 2     (b) 2 and 3
   (c) 1, 2 and 3     (d) 1 and 3

3. Read the following statements regarding Tiger Repository.
   1. The Wildlife Institute of India (WII) has India's first repository on tigers, under its new Tiger Cell.
   2. The repository consists of huge database on tiger conservation and population estimation which has been prepared with collaborated effort with the National Tiger Conservation Authority (NTCA).
   3. India's first tiger cell was set up at Forest Research Institute.

   Choose the correct action.
   (a) 1 and 2     (b) 2 and 3
   (c) 1 and 3     (d) 1, 2 and 3

4. Read the following statements regarding Operation Thunder Bird.
   1. Wildlife Crime Control Bureau (WCCB) has launched the programme.
   2. It aims at preventing hunting of endangered birds.
   3. It is code-name of International Criminal Police Organization.

   Choose the correct option.
   (a) 2 and 3     (b) 1 and 2
   (c) 1 and 3     (d) 1, 2 and 3

5. Read the following statements about Project Tiger.
   1. It was launched in April 1973.
   2. It aimed at ensuring a viable population of Bengal tigers in their natural habitats and also to protect them from extinction.
   3. It was launched under the Wildlife Conservation Act.

   Choose the correct option.
   (a) 2 and 3     (b) 1 and 3
   (c) 1 and 2     (d) 1, 2 and 3

6. Read the following statements regarding Blue Economy.
   1. It refers to the integration of ocean economy development with the idea of social inclusion and environmental sustainability.
   2. It uses renewable and organic inputs to feed into sustainably designed systems.
   3. It does not help reduce waste disposal.

   Choose the correct option.
   (a) 1, 2, and 3     (b) 2 and 3
   (c) 1 and 3     (d) 1 and 2

7. Read the following statements regarding coastal conservation in India.
   1. Coastal Regulation Zone (CRZ) Rules proposes to remove the ban on reclamation of land in coastal areas for commercial or tourism activities even in ecologically-sensitive areas.
   2. Agenda 21 focuses on reduction in fishing activities.

   Choose the correct option.
   (a) 1 only     (b) 2 only
   (c) both 1 and 2     (d) none of the above

8. Read the following statements regarding Coastal Ocean Monitoring and Prediction System.
   1. It predicts the level of dissolved oxygen and nitrate in the sea close to the shore.
   2. The movement of oil during oil spills has been studied with the help of the system.
   3. The coats of Goa, Kerala and Visakhapatnam have used the system.

   Choose the correct option.
   (a) 1, 2 and 3     (b) 1 and 3
   (c) 2 and 3     (d) 1 and 2

9. Read the following statements regarding Project Green Ports.
   1. It was a part of Swachh Bharat Abhiyaan.
   2. It aims at acquiring dust suppression system.
   3. It bans fishing activities along coast.

   Choose the correct option.
   (a) only 1     (b) 1 and 2
   (c) 2 and 3     (d) 1, 2 and 3

10. Read the following statements regarding Indian marine ecology.
    1. Ecological damage is caused by inshore mechanized fishing in state like Kerala, Goa, Tamil Nadu, Orissa.

2. Indo-Norwegian Project is related to installing solar plants along the coast.
3. Marine ecology is affected by exotic fish.
   Choose the correct option.
   (a) 1 and 3          (b) 2 and 3
   (c) 1, 2 and 3       (d) Only 3

11. Read the following statements regarding Ecosystem Modelling.
    1. It has been used for hydrodynamic modelling of Chilika and Kochi backwaters.
    2. Water quality criteria for copper, cadmium and mercury have been determined.
    3. It focuses on 20 training programmes on hazard mapping, satellite oceanography, and marine pollution.
    Choose the correct option.
    (a) 1 and 2          (b) 2 and 3
    (c) 1, 2 and 3       (d) only 1

12. Which of the following is not correct regarding Ganga Action Plan.
    1. It was launched by the National Ganga River Basin Authority.
    2. It aimed at beatification of Ganga.
    3. It focused on rehabilitation of soft-shelled turtles.
    Choose the correct option.
    (a) only 1           (b) 1 and 2
    (c) 2 and 3          (d) only 2

13. With reference to a conservation organization called Wetlands International', which of the following statements is/are correct?
    1. It is an intergovernmental organization formed by the countries which are signatories to Ramsar Convention.
    2. It works at the field level to develop and mobilize knowledge, and use the practical experience to advocate for better policies.
    Select the correct answer using the code given below.
    (a) Neither 1 nor 2   (b) only 1
    (c) both 1 and 2      (d) 2 only

14. Read the following statements regarding Montreux Record.
    1. It is a register of wetland sites where changes in ecological character have occurred, are occurring, or are likely to occur as a result of technological developments.
    2. It is maintained as part of the Ramsar List.
    Choose the correct option.
    (a) Neither 1 nor 2   (b) only 1
    (c) both 1 and 2      (d) 2 only

15. Read the following statements regarding Indian wetlands.
    1. Largest wetland of India includes Vembanad lake, Chilika lake, Kolleru lake and Loktak Lake.
    2. Remote Sensing and Geographic Information System (GIS) tools have been used in flood zonation mapping in wetlands.

3. Normalized Difference Vegetation Index (NDVI) is used for separation of wetland areas.
   Choose the correct option.
   (a) 1, 2 and 3       (b) 2 and 3
   (c) only 2           (d) 1 and 3

16. Read the following statements regarding Indian Himalayan ecology.
    1. Climate change in the Indian Himalayan region is monitored by National Mission for Sustaining the Himalayan Ecosystem (NMSHE).
    2. Indian Himalayas Climate Adaptation Programme (IHCAP) aims to study climate change impacts on natural resources.
    3. Himalayan plants include Blue Poppy, Creeping Cotoneaster, **and** Deodar Cedar.
    Choose the correct option.
    (a) only 3           (b) 1, 2 and 3
    (c) 1 and 3          (d) only 1

17. Read the following statements regarding Madhav Gadgil Committe Report on Western Ghat.
    1. The Western Ghats Ecology Expert Panel (WGEEP) designates the Western Ghat as an Ecologically Sensitive Area (ESA).
    2. Gadgil report recommended that permission need to be sought for dam construction in Ecological Sensitive Zone 1.
    3. The constitution of a Western Ghats Ecology Authority (WGEA) was recommended as a statutory authority under the Ministry of Environment and Forests.
    Choose the correct option.
    (a) 2 and 3          (b) 1 and 3
    (c) 1 and 2          (d) 1, 2 and 3

18. Read the following statements regarding Eco-cities in India.
    1. Six medium and small Eco-cities were planned by the Ministry of Environment and Forest (MoEF) in association with Central Pollution Control Board (CPCB).
    2. The focus of the project was pollution control and improvement of environmental quality.
    3. One of the proposed eco-cities is Chennai.
    Choose the correct option.
    (a) 1 and 2          (b) 1 and 3
    (c) 2 and 3          (d) 1, 2 and 3

19. Read the following statements regarding forest conservation.
    1. National Forest Commission was set up in 2002 to review and assess India's policy and law on forest
    2. Chipko Movement stated in 1975 for forest conservation.
    3. Jhum cultivation helped in forest conservation.

Choose the correct option.
  (a)  only 1       (b)  1 and 2
  (c)  2 and 3      (d)  1 and 3

20. Read the following statements regarding Forest Carbon Partnership Facility.
  1.  It is an Indian organisation which focuses on reducing emissions.
  2.  It aims at enhancing forest carbon stocks in developed countries.
  Choose the correct option.
  (a)  1 only        (b)  2 only
  (c)  1 and 2      (d)  None of the above

21. Read the following statements regarding Indian Forest Survey 2013.
  1.  Main reasons for declined forest cover include abiotic pressure.
  2.  Odisha has highest density of forest.
  3.  Shortening of Jhum cycle causes forest loss.
  Choose the correct option.
  (a)  1 and 2      (b)  2 and 3
  (c)  1, 2 and 3    (d)  only 3

22. Read the following statements regarding International Solar Alliance.
  1.  It is an alliance of more than 120 countries.
  2.  Its objective is efficient exploitation of solar energy to reduce dependence on fossil fuels.
  3.  India has set a target of installing 100GW by 2022 with the help of the alliance.
  Choose the correct option.
  (a)  1, 2 and 3    (b)  2 and 3
  (c)  1 and 3      (d)  only 1

23. Read the following statements regarding soil conservation.
  1.  Vetiver grass is mainly grown to prevent soil and moisture conservation.
  2.  Planting of trees in the same direction of the wind prevents soil erosion.
  3.  Increasing use of cover crops reduce soil erosion.
  Choose the correct option.
  (a)  1 and 3      (b)  1 and 2
  (c)  2 and 3      (d)  1, 2 and 3

24. Read the following statements regarding Operation Thunder Bird programme.
  1.  It was initiated by the Wildlife Crime Control Bureau (WCCB).
  2.  It aim at preventing wild birds.
  3.  It had convened Operation Save Kurma, a species specific operation on turtles.
  Choose the correct option.
  (a)  1 and 2      (b)  1 and 3
  (c)  2 and 3      (d)  1, 2 and 3

25. Which of the following statements is/are correct?
  1.  India is a member of South Asia Wildlife Enforcement Network (SAWEN).
  2.  It aims at combating wildlife crime by strengthening its ties with the member countries.
  (a)  only 1        (b)  1 and 2
  (c)  only 2       (d)  None

26. Consider the following statements:
  1.  The International Solar Alliance was launched at the United Nations Climate Change Conference in 2015.
  2.  The Alliance includes all the member countries of the United Nations.
  Which of the statements given above is/are correct?
  (a)  1 only        (b)  2 only
  (c)  Both 1 and 2   (d)  Neither 1 nor 2

# Hints and Explanations

### EXERCISE-1

1. **(b)** Gahirmatha beach (Odisha) were mass nesting of the endangered Olive Ridley turtle takes place was given marine sanctuary status in 1997. All the species of sea turtles in the coastal water or Odisha are listed as "vulnerable" in the IUCN Red Data Book. The sea turtles are protected under the 'Migratory Species Convention' and CITES (Convention of International Trade on Wildlife Flora and Fauna).

2. **(d)** Inshore mechanized fishing leading to ecological damage has been observed in Kerala Goa, Tamil Nadu and Kerala. Indian subcontinent is covered on three sides by the marine sea coast and has contributed for the major fish catches of India. The development of the marine fisheries has undergone a transformation from traditional fishing method to mechanized fishing all along the coast during the last four decades. Inshore fishing has led to land degradation and loss of fish species at alarming rate.

3. **(a)** Indio-Norwegian Project was first established in Neendakara, Kerala in 1953, and the aim was modernisation of fisheries of Kerala, as well as focus on health, sanitation and water supply. The project was moved to Ernakulam in 1961, now focusing on fisheries only. Norway gave technical and financial assistance to India.

4. **(c)** Maharashtra and Tamil Nadu have exploited maximum sustainable yield. Maximum sustainable yield or MSY is the largest yield that can be taken from a species' stock over an indefinite period. Focusing on, the concept or MSY aims to maintain the population size at the point of maximum growth rate by harvesting the individual that would normally be added to the population. The government in Maharashtra has framed several policies to exploit their population and resources to achieve Maximum sustainable yield.

5. **(d)** Introduction of Brown Trout, Loch Leven Trout and Rainbow Trout have a negative impact on marine ecology. The genetic impact of introduction of exotic fishes on native fishes can be seen in the form of ecological, biological and genetic effect of introduction. Alteration/extinction of gene pools results with crossbreeding or hybridization and backcrossing of the species.

6. **(d)**

7. **(a)** The Chilika Lagoon a Ramsar Site of international importance and the largest brackish water lagoon in Indian sub-continent is one of the richest repositories of aquatic biodiversity and a source of fishery, sustaining the livelihood and nutritional need of about 0.2 million local fisherfolk. Hydrodynamic modelling of Chilika characterizes the ecosystem of a region suitable for flora and fauna. Dal Lake shows less biodiversity in comparison of Chilika Lake.

8. **(d)**

9. **(a)** A new colour code is implemented in hospitals of Visakhapatnam, for disposal of Under this plan, blue cardboard bins are introduced to dispose certain kinds of hospital waste such as cytotoxins and broken glass.

10. **(b)** Coimbatore has planned to have 50 metric ton that will generate electricity using food collected from hotels and restaurants. This initiative will help in recycling the waste in a productive manner.

11. **(a)** World Wide Fund for Nature's (WWF) 2014 Living Plant Report has revealed that wildlife populations of vertebrate species such as mammals, birds, reptiles, amphibians, and fish, have declined by 52 percent over the last 40 years. The population of tigers has also increased. The decline in wildlife population is due to ecological changes.

12. **(a)** The third Kanha-Pench Walk 2016 came ended in Khatiya village on the buffer of the Kanha Tiger Reserve in Madhya Pradesh. The event is jointly organized by WWF-India and the Madhya Pradesh Forest Department to build awareness on the importance of conserving the Kanha-Pench corridor which connects two major tiger source populations in Central India.

13. **(c)** Along with the Dudhwa Tiger Reserve staff, WWF-India launched a robust monitoring technique with the help of the National Trust for Nature Conservation (NTNC) to study the behaviour of Greater One-Horned Rhinoceros.

14. **(a)** The centrally Sponsored Scheme 'Integrated Development of Wildlife Habitats' has been changed by including a new component namely 'Recovery of Endangered Species' and 16 species have been identified for recovery including Snow Leopard, Bustard (including Floricans), Dolphin, Hangul, Nilgiri Tahr, Marine Turtles, Dugong, Edible Nest Swiftlet, Asian Wild Buffalo, Nicobar Megapode.

15. **(d)** Radio collars with Very High Frequency, Global Positioning System and Satellite uplink facilities, are used by research institutions including Wildlife

Institute of India (WII), Dehradun, State Forest Departments and the National Tiger Conservation Authority (NTCA) to monitor the movement of lions, tigers, elephants, olive ridley turtles, and other wild animals to study their movements and their use pattern of the habitat.

16. (d) Every year, under the 'Operation Guerrilla Green' movement, a month-long ecologically important campaign/festival is held by Gond and Korku communities/ tribes in Madhya Pradesh, where they plant saplings of fruit-bearing trees on government, forest, private or panchayat land. Bhil tribe does not observe any such ecological festival.

17. (b) The 'Operation Guerrilla Green' movement, a month-long ecological important campaign/festival is held by Gond and Korku communities/ tribes in Madhya Pradesh, where they plant saplings of fruit-bearing trees on government, forest, private or panchayat land.

18. (a) Scientists in Juelich, Germany, have developed the world's largest artificial sun called Sunlight, for using it to develop climate-friendly fuels. The Sunlight consists of 149 spotlights all together resembling a gigantic honeycomb. The lights, which are xenon short-arc lamps that's usually found in cinemas, simulate natural sunlight during a season that doesn't get much sunlight.

19. (a) The Bureau of Energy Efficiency (BEE) has introduced a new star rating methodology called Indian Seasonal Energy Efficiency Ratio (ISEER) for air conditioners. This evolved rating methodology factors in variance in higher temperature in India and rates air conditioners accordingly. Consumers can now purchase air conditioners with higher efficiency leading to lower electricity bills. Consumers can now purchase air conditioners with higher efficiency leading to lower electricity bills. Indian Energy Efficiency Ratio and House Energy Rating Ratio have not been developed by Bureau of Energy Efficiency (BEE).

20. (d) Ratings based on ISEER have been introduced on a voluntary basis for Variable Speed (Inverter) Air Conditioners since June 2015 and proposed to be merged with fixed speed air conditioners in the mandatory regime from January 2018. They consume less energy as their compressor speed can be automatically controlled according to room temperature. They cannot operate on inverters as their electricity consumption is more than supplied by inverters.

21. (b) A number of harmful algal blooms have been found in various coastal waters of India such as Noctiluca bloom in Kochi, Noctiluca bloom in Goa, bloom of Gonyaulax in Manglore. Efforts are underway to monitor the spatial and temporal variations of blooms using Ocean Colour Monitor sensors available on board both Indian and foreign satellites.

22. (d) Ganga has been altered by the construction of more than 50 dams and other irrigation-related projects, with severe consequences for the river dolphins. The population of the Ganges River Dolphin has declined to less than 1,800 from 6,000 in 1982 due to construction of dams and water pollution caused by pesticides, fertilizers, and industrial effluents.

23. (d) Automobile Emission Control: Recent Supreme Court ruling has asserted that auto manufacturers cannot sell BS-III vehicles from April 1, when BS-IV compliance comes into force. BS-IV vehicles are relatively less polluting than BS-III vehicles. National Green Tribunal (NGT) has proposed ban diesel vehicles that are at least 10 years old from plying in the national capital region (NCR) centred on Delhi. Vehicular pollution can be controlled if the exhaust outlets of all motor vehicles are installed on the top instead of near the base. BS-IV trucks are 80 per cent cleaner than BS-III.

24. (a) The United Nations Convention to Combat Desertification is a Convention to combat desertification and mitigate the effects of drought through national action programs that incorporate long-term strategies supported by international cooperation and partnership arrangements. It is the only internationally legally binding framework organised to address the problem of desertification.

## EXERCISE-2

1. (d)

2. (d) TEEB is a study by environmental economist Pavan Sukhdev. It is an international initiative that focuses on global economic benefits of biodiversity. Its objective is to highlight the growing cost of biodiversity loss and ecosystem degradation and to draw together expertise from the fields of science, economics and policy to allow practical actions.

3. (a) The Wildlife Institute of India (WII) has India's first repository on tigers, under its new Tiger Cell. The repository consists of huge database on tiger conservation and population estimation which has been prepared with collaborated effort with the National Tiger Conservation Authority (NTCA). India's first tiger cell was set up at Wildlife Institute of India in Dehradun, India.

4. (c) Wildlife Crime Control Bureau (WCCB) has the programme from January 30 to February 19, 2017 to end poaching of India's wildlife animals. It also had convened Operation Save Kurma, a species specific operation on turtles between 15 December 2016 and 30 January 2017. It is code-name of INTERPOL's (International Criminal Police Organization) multi-

national and multi-species enforcement operation for wildlife protection.

5. (d) It was launched in April 1973 under the Wildlife Conservation Act to address the problem of shrinking tiger population in India. It aimed at ensuring a viable population of Bengal tigers in their natural habitats and also to protect them from extinction, and preserving areas of biological importance as a natural heritage.

6. (c) Blue Economy involves the integration of ocean economy development with the idea of social inclusion, environmental sustainability and innovative, dynamic business models. It is a approach wherein renewable and organic inputs are fed into sustainably designed systems to promote "blue growth". It helps in waste disposal, while ensuring sustainable development that enhances human welfare in a holistic manner.

7. (a) There have been major changes in land-use along the coast after the implementation of Coastal Regulation Zone (CRZ) Rules. The rule proposes to remove the ban on reclamation of land in coastal areas for commercial or tourism activities even in ecologically-sensitive areas. Agenda 21 has resulted in better living standards of the coastal population, ensuring reduction in the degradation of coastal area due to pollution, marine erosion, loss of resources and habitat destruction.

8. (a) With the help of the Coastal Ocean Monitoring and Prediction System, extensive monitoring of marine pollution along the coastal waters was initiated at 76 locations and it has been shown that the disposal of untreated sewage from towns, cities and villages cause decrease of dissolved oxygen and increase of nitrate and pathogenic bacteria in the sea close to the shore. Model to predict the movement of oil during oil spills has been developed for the coasts of Mumbai and Chennai. Works to develop similar models for the coasts of Goa, Kerala and Visakhapatnam have been undertaken.

9. (b) The project will have two verticals, one is 'Green Ports Initiatives' related to environmental issues and second is 'Swachh Bharat Abhiyaan'. It aims at preparation and monitoring plan, acquiring equipments required for monitoring environmental pollution, acquiring dust suppression system, setting up of sewage/waste water treatment plants/garbage disposal plant, setting up projects for energy generation from renewable energy sources.

10. (a) Ecological damage caused by inshore mechanized fishing in state like Kerala, Goa, Tamil Nadu, Orissa. Indo-Norwegian Project is leading to the development of mechanized fishing. Adverse impact on marine ecology is due to the introduction of exotic fish such as Brown Trout, Loch Leven Trout, Rainbow Trout.

11. (c) Under the programme on Ecosystem modelling, hydrodynamic modelling of Chilika and Kochi backwaters have been started. Water quality criteria for copper, cadmium and mercury have been studied and are referred to the Central Pollution Control Board. Over 20 training programmes on hazard mapping, satellite oceanography, and marine pollution have been conducted. Ecosystem models have applications in a wide variety of fields, such as natural resource management, ecotoxicology and environmental health.

12. (d) Ganga occupies 26 per cent of the country's landmass and supports 43 per cent of its population. In 1986, the government of India launched the Ganga Action Plan (GAP). In August 2009, GAP was re-launched with a reconstituted National Ganga River Basin Authority. The objectives of the authority was to improve the water quality of the river to acceptable standards by preventing pollutants reaching it by intercepting the sewage and treating it before discharge into the river. It also aimed at rehabilitation of soft-shelled turtles.

13. (d) It is a global organisation that is responsible for sustaining and restoring wetlands and their resources for people and biodiversity. It is an independent, not-for-profit, global organisation, supported by government and NGO membership from around the world. Wetlands International's work includes research and community-based field projects to advocacy and engagement with governments and international policy fora and conventions.

14. (c) It is a register of wetland sites on the List of Wetlands of International Importance where changes in ecological character have occurred or are likely to occur as a result of technological developments, pollution or other human interference. It is maintained as part of the Ramsar List. Ramsar sites in India comprises Indian wetlands that are of international importance under the Ramsar Convention.

15. (a) 115 wetlands in India have been identified by the government which require urgent conservation and management interventions. The list of Ramsar sites in India are one of the most threatened of all ecosystems and has an international importance. Largest Wetland of India includes Vembanad lake, Chilika lake, Kolleru lake and Loktak Lake. Remote Sensing and Geographic Information System (GIS) tools have been used in flood zonation mapping, in monitoring irrigation and cropping patterns.

16. (b) Climate change in the Indian Himalayan region is monitored by National Mission for Sustaining the Himalayan Ecosystem (NMSHE). **Indian**

**Himalayas Climate Adaptation Programme (IHCAP)** has generate knowledge of climate change impacts on natural resources, ecosystem services, and the communities depending on them, contributing to policy and practice for enhanced adaptation. Several plant species have been grown in the Himalayas, including Himalayan Blue Poppy, Creeping Cotoneaster, Deodar Cedar.

17. (c) The Western Ghats Ecology Expert Panel (WGEEP) decided to designated the entire hill range as an Ecologically Sensitive Area (ESA) as the region had many endangered species of organisms. Gadgil report recommended that no new dams based on large-scale storage be should be constructed in Ecological Sensitive Zone 1. The commission recommended constitution of a Western Ghats Ecology Authority (WGEA), as a statutory authority under the Ministry of Environment and Forests.

18. (a) In India, the concept of Eco cities was introduced in 2000 and starting 2001 six medium and small Eco-cities were planned by the Ministry of Environment and Forest (MoEF) in association with Central Pollution Control Board (CPCB) and with technical assistance from German technical cooperation (GTZ). The focus of the project is pollution control, improvement of environmental quality, protection of environmental resources like rivers and lakes, improving sanitary conditions, improving the needed infrastructure and creating aesthetic environs in the chosen towns. The cities included Tirupathi, Vrindavan, Kottayam, Ujjain, Puri and Thanjavur.

19. (a) In 2002, India set up a National Forest Commission to review and assess India's policy and law, its effect on India's forests. Indian forests are home to a wide variety of animal and plant species which are vital to maintaining ecological balance. Chipko Movement stated in 1973 for forest conservation and was based on the Gandhian philosophy of peaceful resistance to achieve the goals. There is a drop in jhum cultivation, which included burning of forest to make area available for farming.

20. (d) It is a global partnership of governments, businesses, civil society, and indigenous people focused on reducing emissions from deforestation and forest degradation, forest carbon stock conservation, the sustainable management of forests, and the enhancement of forest carbon stocks in developing countries (activities commonly referred to as REDD+).

21. (d) Forest Survey 2013 highlights that the raking of states based on forest density is given as Madhya Pradesh (First), Arunachal Pradesh (second), Chhattisgarh (third), Maharashtra (fourth) and Odisha (fifth). Main reasons for declined forest cover include biotic pressure, shortening of Jhum cycle, open caste mining and earthquake-induced landslides.

22. (a) International Solar Alliance is a group of more than 120 countries, most of them being sunshine countries, which come either completely or partly between the Tropic of Cancer and the Tropic of Capricorn. The alliance's primary objective is efficient exploitation of solar energy to reduce dependence on fossil fuels. The launching of such an alliance in Paris shows the efforts of the global communities to mitigate climate change and to switch to a low-carbon growth path. India has pledged a target of installing 100GW by 2022.

23. (a) Vetiver grass (Vetiveria zizanioides) is widely grown to prevent soil and moisture conservation. It binds the soil properly. To check wind erosion, planting of trees in the opposite direction of the wind has been taken into consideration. Planting of trees in the opposite direction of the wind reduces the intensity of wind and hence prevents soil erosion. Increasing use of cover crops, such as rye and wheat, have been practiced to reduce soil erosion.

24. (b) Wildlife Crime Control Bureau (WCCB) has initiated the programme from January 30 to February 19, 2017 to end poaching of India's wildlife animals. It also had convened Operation Save Kurma, a species specific operation on turtles between 15 December 2016 and 30 January 2017. It is code-name of INTERPOL's (International Criminal Police Organization) multi-national and multi-species enforcement operation for wildlife protection.

25. (b) India is a member of South Asia Wildlife Enforcement Network (SAWEN). It aims at combating wildlife crime by strengthening its ties with the member countries for controlling the trans-boundary wildlife crimes through coordination, communication, collaboration, cooperation and capacity building in the region.

26. (a) (i) The COP-21 Climate Conference was held in Paris, France from 30 November to 12 December 2015. During this conference, India and France have launched the International Solar Alliance (ISA). International Solar Alliance includes an alliance of 121 countries located between Tropic of Cancer and Tropic of Capricorn.
(ii) While ISA was launched on Sidelines of Paris Summit, therefore first statement right but it includes only the 121 countries between Capricorn and Cancer receiving sunlight for 300 days or more. Hence 2nd statement wrong.

www.ingramcontent.com/pod-product-compliance
Lightning Source LLC
La Vergne TN
LVHW060503070726
842759LV00029BA/882